Macroeconomic Patterns and Stories

Edward E. Leamer

Macroeconomic Patterns and Stories

 Springer

Dr. Edward E. Leamer
University of California
UCLA
Anderson School of Management
Global Economics & Management Area
110 Westwood Plaza
Los Angeles CA 90095-1481
edward.leamer@anderson.ucla.edu

ISBN 978-3-540-46388-7   e-ISBN 978-3-540-46389-4

Library of Congress Control Number: 2008933370

Cover design: WMX Design GmbH, Heidelberg, Germany

Printed on acid-free paper

9 8 7 6 5 4 3 2 1

springer.com

Preface

The story of this book began with my difficult transition from teaching international economics and econometrics in Economics Ph.D. programs at Harvard and UCLA to teaching in the MBA programs at the Anderson School at UCLA. On the basis of 20 years of apparent teaching success in Ph.D. education, I arrived at the Anderson School in 1990 with a self-image as a star teacher, but I was greeted with highly disturbing mediocre teaching evaluations. Faced with a data set that was inconsistent with my view of reality, I did what analysts usually do – I formulated a theory why the data were misleading.

Here is how I thought about it. Two aspects of the course – content and amusement – drive numerical course evaluations. If you rank courses by the average of the content score and the amusement score, then the component that can be measured most accurately will determine the ranking. Do you understand why? It is what averaging does: it eliminates the noise. Suppose, for example, that a student cannot tell anything about the content, and the content score is simply a random number, varying from student to student. Those random numbers will average out across students to about the same number for each course. As the average course content score is about the same for every course, it is the amusement score that will drive the rankings. Thus the difference between my success in economics and my failure in the business school reflected the differences in the student populations – the Ph.D. students could detect content differences across courses, while the business school students did not have a clue. Gosh, those thoughts made me feel better. But it did not last long. I cannot imagine a more distressing way to spend one's life than to be an unappreciated teacher except for being a despised teacher. It was a very tough mountain to climb, but after nine times teaching the course, and improving, I was awarded the Executive MBA teaching award in 2001 and 2002. How satisfying was that!

I am not writing an autobiography here, so why bother with this information? Because, first it introduces the central idea of the book: patterns and stories (the teaching evaluation data and the story I told myself). Second, it reveals the bad news and the good news. The bad news is that I am not a macroeconomist and thus cannot claim an expert's knowledge of the theory of the field. The good news is that

I am not a macroeconomist, and I do not carry the heavy intellectual baggage that most macroeconomists lug around.

The fields in which I have made academic contributions are first econometric methodology and then the analysis of international microeconomics data. When I moved to the Anderson School of Management at UCLA in 1990, I fished around for something to teach that would make me happy and the students too. That is a rare double combination of desires. I decided that I would teach the students how to turn numbers into knowledge, using macroeconomic data as the case.

After teaching the lessons of macro data for ten years, I was ready when the Dean called to ask me to be the Director of the UCLA Anderson Forecast, which is one of the most long-lived and prominent macroeconomics forecasts, included in the Wall Street Journal panel of forecasters, the Livingston Survey and the Blue Chip Forecasts. But, it should be admitted, forecasting the economy is an enterprise held in low repute among academic economists. I see it differently. Making a quarterly forecast, telling the story that lies behind it, and discovering when you are right and when you are wrong is a powerful way to learn what is important and what is not. I think I have learned a lot, and I have tried to pack the lessons into this book. Whether that is useful or not is for you to judge.

In the midst of this teaching and forecasting, I heard on NPR that "humans are pattern-seeking story-telling animals," which sums up with great rhetorical accuracy what economists do. I am going to show you some patterns, and then tell causal stories about them.

Causal stories are the right way of saying it. We should be very wary of drawing causal conclusions from the nonexperimental macroeconomic data we will be exploring. I know more than most that correlations are in the data but causation is in the mind of the observer. I know that temporal orderings (first the lighting of the match, and then the fire) do not by themselves reveal causality (weather forecasts, which come first, do not "cause" the weather), even though Clive Granger has christened the *post hoc ergo propter hoc* fallacy with the name "Granger Causality." I know it is impossible to find a scientifically validated causal chain connecting monetary policy with housing with the economy overall. But that will not stop me, as it has not stopped other economists from drawing firm causal conclusions mostly from a war-chest of thought experiments conducted strictly in their heads. In contrast to most, I am going to go to great lengths to collect the basic facts about the US economy, and use those facts to influence my opinions.

That said, I offer the surprising patterns that I see and the interesting stories that come to mind. I think you will be amazed by the patterns and amused by the stories.

Pedagogical Goals

There are two pedagogical goals of this book. One goal is to describe the most important features of the macroeconomy in a readable, organized, and informative way.

The other goal is to demonstrate how people can learn from numbers, by seeking patterns and telling stories.

Both of these goals are or should be part of the core teaching mission of every MBA program because of the following:

1. MBAs need to talk the talk: Most managers at the highest levels of business firms are conversant in the lore of the business cycle – how much growth in sales is likely, where interest rates are going, what will happen to the housing market, etc. If we expect our MBAs to rise to the highest levels of management, they will need to have well-formed opinions based on real evidence about the nature of the business cycle. If we get them interested, and give them the tools to decode the countless articles in the business press about the latest macroeconomic data, we should be able to capture their interest, and set them off on a life-long learning journey.

If we decide not to teach macroeconomics, the next most important skill is golf.

2. MBAs need ways of finding insights: A personal computer and the Internet provide managers access to virtually unlimited textual and numerical data. That enormous data set is completely worthless unless it is transformed into knowledge through some form of filtering. Ability to transform the Internet data first into knowledge and then into insights should be one of the core skills that MBA training provides. A study of macroeconomic data and the business cycle is a great way of making this point. Students who begin a 10-week course with virtually no knowledge of macroeconomics, self-conscious and unsure, by the end of a course of pattern-seeking and story-telling become self-confident "experts," capable of making their own discoveries and confident enough to see the flaws in the opinions of others that they read in the *Wall Street Journal*, the *New York Times* and the *Financial Times*.

Features

Chapters cover the behavior of every major US macroeconomic variable including GDP, employment, unemployment, inflation, interest rates, and exchange rates. After explaining what these variables are and how they are measured, attention turns to understanding the recessions: what are their symptoms, how frequently do they occur, which businesses suffer and which prosper in recessions, and what helps to predict the next one? Then comes discussion of longer-term issues, including savings and investment, the Federal deficit and the external deficit, and housing as an asset to support us in our retirements.

I show what the US business cycle is like: It is not a business cycle at all. It is really a consumer cycle in the sense that the first expenditure component to turn down prior to a recession is usually consumer spending on homes, then consumer durables, and only when the recession is fully upon us does business spending on equipment and software weaken, and last are the longest lived business assets: factories and office building. Not always, but eight times out of ten.

This and thousands of other facts can be found in this book, delivered in what I hope to be a provocative and entertaining style.

There is little traditional macroeconomic theory in this book, though there are several "stories" about unemployment and the business cycle. The traditional macro theory is great for economics majors but it leaves no lasting impression on most other students and not much even on economics majors. (How many readers of the *Wall Street Journal* can remember the IS-LM model they studied in college? How many of the journalists who write those articles have even the slightest awareness of the IS-LM model or any other macro model?) I rely much more heavily on the data to help students form their own point of view. I try to bring the reader along with me on this journey to understanding. Because visual displays are much more memorable than any table of numbers, the argument is highly graphical and uses a minimum amount of numerical statistical analysis.

Exercises

Updated images, review exercises, and homeworks can be found on the Internet at:

http://www.anderson.ucla.edu/faculty/edward.leamer/

The homeworks parallel the book.

- What is GDP?
- How do the four key macro variables behave? (growth, interest rates, inflation and unemployment)
- Is your job at risk in recessions?
- What helps to predict an oncoming recession?
- What can cure a recession?
- Is there a housing bubble?
- How can the US external deficit be closed?
- Is the US on a new productivity trend?

UCLA Anderson School of Management   Edward E. Leamer
8 February 2007

Contents

Part I
Introduction

Chapter 1
Introduction: We Are Pattern-Seeking, Story-Telling Animals

Several years ago, I was listening to NPR on my way to work and I heard a commentator say "Human beings are pattern-seeking, story-telling animals." Those simple words rang off loud celebratory bells in my head, since that was *exactly* the message that I have been trying to get across in my courses, but I had never said it so clearly, and maybe never really understood it. Armed with those powerful words, I promise to take you on a tour of the US macro economic data, looking for clear patterns and telling compelling stories. This is a journey during which we will create knowledge together. When we are done, we will know a lot more about how the US economy has been behaving and why it has its ups and downs. Once we understand the history, we will be ready to look more clearly into the future.

You may want to substitute the more familiar *scientific* words "theory and evidence" for "patterns and stories." Do not do that. With the phrase "theory and evidence" come hidden stow-away after-the-fact myths about how we learn and how much we can learn. The words "theory and evidence" suggest an incessant march toward a level of scientific certitude that cannot be attained in the study of the complex self-organizing human system that we call the economy. The words "patterns and stories" much more accurately convey our level of knowledge, now, and in the future as well. It is literature, not science.[1]

---

[1] The words "theory and evidence" also mislead about the process. These words support the Scientific myth: Formulate hypotheses. Gather experimental data and test. Reject. Formulate new hypotheses. And so on. This positivistic myth may help organize the learning process in the experimental sciences, but it has been harmful in non-experimental economics. Economists are taught that theories are either true or false, when in fact theories are sometimes useful and sometimes misleading. Economists are taught that it is the function of Economic Science to test the truthfulness of the theories, when the real goal is to identify the theory's domain of usefulness. (Theories are neither true nor false. They are sometimes helpful and sometimes misleading.) When Economists "successfully" reject a theory, other economists go on about the business of trying to understand what makes the economy tick with little of no interest in the formal rejection. Once indoctrinated in graduate school, it takes a long time for new Ph.D.'s in Economics to learn that it is only stories and patterns that we do. Until they make that discovery, they waste a lot of time and rhetoric on "theory and evidence," admiring their t-values.

E. E. Leamer, *Macroeconomic Patterns and Stories: A Guide for MBAs.*
© Springer-Verlag Berlin Heidelberg 2009

Theory but no Evidence

New York Times, 5 May 2003

A State Department report issued on the first anniversary of the 9/11 attacks said that development aid should be based "on the belief that poverty provides a breeding ground for terrorism." As logical as the poverty-breeds-terrorism argument may seem, study after study shows that suicide attackers and their supporters are rarely ignorant or impoverished.

Although we worry about the subtle but substantial influence of language, notice that my title has "pattern-seeking" first and "story-telling" second. That order is purposeful. I do not mean to suggest that there is any special time ordering in the tasks needed to create knowledge. I put pattern seeking first to right a wrong: most of what economists believe comes from the stories that we tell each other. Economists are story-telling animals. We do not worry much about patterns.

Take the parable of the "Invisible Hand" for example. Once upon a time there was a world where people did good by being selfish. Here is the way Adam Smith says it:

> Every individual ... neither intends to promote the public interest, nor knows how much he is promoting it ... He intends only his own gain, and he is in this, as in many other cases, led by an invisible hand to promote an end which was no part of his intention. Nor is it always the worse for society that it was no part of his intention. By pursuing his own interest he frequently promotes that of the society more effectually than when he really intends to promote it.
> Adam Smith, "An Inquiry into the Nature and Causes of the Wealth of Nations" 1776.

This very radical idea has become widely believed and highly influential, but not because there is compelling evidence in its support. It is a story whose logic stands on its own. It is a story without a pattern. That is generally the case in economics: lots of theory but not much evidence.

In great contrast, the study of economic cycles has traditionally been mostly pattern-seeking, with very little story-telling. Among the pioneers in pattern-seeking with macroeconomic data was the Russian economist Kondratieff, who in the 1920s saw long waves in the data but struggled to find a good story of why. Furthermore, he had a hard time finding compelling patterns because the data were so limited. But after WWII both US and UK governments started collecting macroeconomic data in earnest, which set off an orgy of pattern-seeking. One of the most important findings was made by the British economist A.W.H. Phillips, who in the 1950s saw a negative relationship between unemployment and inflation, which out of deference to its importance has been called "The Phillips Curve." You can see the Phillips Curve clearly in the figure at the left, which strongly suggests an association between the inflation rate and the rate of unemployment.

The Phillips curve offered governments some very nasty medicine for unwanted inflation: increase unemployment. The good news for workers around the globe is that the story of the Phillips curve was never very compelling and the subsequent

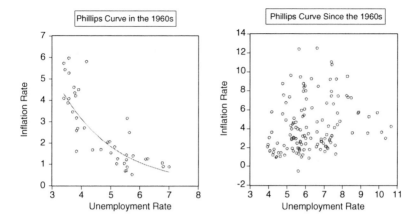

movements in US data made the curve much more difficult to see (see the figure at the right). This has led many academic economists to question whether unemployment is the right medicine for unwanted inflation. The bad news for workers is that, once let loose, a good pattern with even a weak story is very difficult to corral. Virtually as you read these words, a meeting of the Federal Reserve Open Market Committee is discussing whether or not unemployment is so low that a burst of inflation is imminent.

1.1 Advice: Do Both Patterns and Stories

Economists are fond of repeating the sentence "That's an empirical question." meaning "beyond the reach of economic theory," thus establishing the clear importance of pattern-seeking work. But the word "empirical" actually has a checkered past. The *American Heritage Dictionary of the English Language* lists as the first definition

> *Empiric*: One who is guided by practical experience rather than precepts or theory.

That seems like a promising occupation but read the definition more carefully. It may have meant: "One who is guided *only* by practical experience." The second definition sets the record straight:

> *Empiric*: An unqualified or dishonest practitioner; a charlatan.

Like modern economists, medieval doctors divided themselves sharply into two competing groups: those who sought understanding of how to treat disease through rational thought (story-telling) and those who sought understanding through observation (pattern seeking). The theorists were able to turn the word empiric into an epithet that lingers in today's dictionary. The empirics failed linguistically but have established their legitimacy by morphing into Statisticians.

Today, advances in medical science come from the joint effort of both theorists and empirics, working together. That is what we need when we study how the economy operates: theory and empirical analysis that are mutually reinforcing. But I have to warn you: this book is mostly empirical. The theory is important but it mostly lurks in the background.

It is easy to understand why we are so tenacious in pursuit of patterns. There could not be life as we know it without repetitions, without almost everything that happens tomorrow being the same as today. The sun comes up, the sky is blue, sugar is sweet, and so are you. We learn these patterns and we get an evolutionary edge.

Long ago we learned the rules by which almost everything repeats. Most of that understanding is built into our sensory apparatus. But that leaves countless nonrepeating puzzles that need to be solved. Like the days when you are not so sweet. But as I pour over the data in search of a pattern to explain your moods (or is that mine?), I am not making any progress. This is making me feel very frustrated and I am starting to obsess. This is taking time that could better be used in other pursuits. Fortunately, there is a fall-back position: faith-based decision-making. Tell a story. That will help me cope. It is the full moon last night that is making your mood sour.

Belief that the full moon causes abnormal human behavior is very persistent, even in the face of overwhelming evidence to the contrary.[2] The mental health professionals who carry out the moon studies are leading the charge. They are not conducting those studies to debunk the moon myth once and for all. They are looking for the confirmatory pattern that we all know is there.

This is understandable. We need peace of mind. We need to cope. Absent a pattern, we need a good story. That is faith-based decision-making.

Ideally what we should be seeking are clear patterns and corresponding compelling stories. Not one without the other. The problem with patterns without stories is there are way too many patterns that intensive data mining can uncover. Few of these patterns are useful for forecasting because they do not recur, which is one problem, but more importantly, an oddball pattern without a story cannot persuade; it cannot affect the way you think. "Oh, just another oddball pattern," you mutter, as you throw the latest one in the heap of discarded oddballs. The patterns that persuade have some logic behind them. That is the story.

In contrast, a story without a pattern is just as bad for the same reason. A human's ingenuity at concocting stories easily matches a computer's determination at finding patterns. There are consequently as many oddball stories as there are oddball patterns, and there is a heap of discarded oddball stories that is just as high as the heap of discarded oddball patterns. Some really great stories like the invisible hand and moon madness persist without supporting patterns, and some really great patterns like the Phillips curve persist without compelling stories, but those are rare. Better try as hard as you can to get both: patterns and stories, in alignment.

---

[2] Sharon Begley, Wall Street Journal, December 24, 2004, "Full Moon Gets Blame For Many Catastrophes. But Is It Truly at Fault?"

1.2 We Can Also Analyze

Though pattern-seeking and story-telling are important, there is one more trick we can perform. We can think logically and mathematically. We can analyze. We are pattern-seeking, story-telling, *analyzing Homo sapiens*. We were not always so good at this. Primitive humans prayed to the Gods for rain and sacrificed virgins to assure victory over competitors. We do it differently now. To deal with uncertainty we consult Statistical Science. Be careful not to be overly impressed with Statistics. Maybe all that has changed are the robes of the priests and the appearance of the virgins.

Statistical science can in principle help decide which numerical patterns are real and which are flukes. A highly instructive experiment is to have a student (a proto-typical Primitive) write down a "random" sequence of 20 heads and tails, and also have the Computer generate its own "random" sequence. Then, when you compare the two, you can almost always tell which sequence the Primitive made and which sequence the Computer made. Here is an example, with black bars representing tails and white bars representing heads. Is this the work of a Computer or a Primitive?

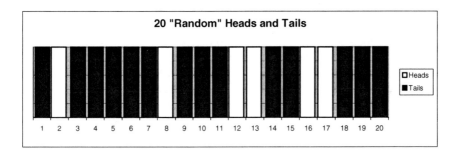

Notice the long run of five tails in a row. That cannot possibly be random, can it? If you were a sports announcer, you would be talking about "hot streaks" of tails and long dry spells. This is clearly not random, and you can be sure that the student will not allow these kinds of runs in the sequence she created. That's how you tell the computer's choices from the student's. This one was generated by a Computer. A Computer likes runs of head or runs of tails. A Primitive does not.

So who is right about the chances of having runs? The Primitive or the Computer? Be careful. Do not automatically choose the Computer. A Computer cannot possibly generate random numbers. What the Computer offers is the precise outcome of a numerical algorithm starting with a first one, called a "seed." If the seed stays the same, the random numbers stay the same too. This fact was driven home to me and my students, when I used Excel to randomly select students to answer questions in class. After three or four classes, the student complained that the Computer always chose the same sequence of students!

Mathematicians work hard to devise numerical algorithms that yield numbers that "seem" random. The sequence does not "seem" random if it does not conform adequately to what we know mathematically about random numbers. Mathematicians counsel us: do not be surprised if two people in a class of 30 have the same birthday. The chance that 30 random birth dates have one day in common is 70%.[3] Do not be surprised to see long runs in random sequences of heads and tails. The probability of at least one run of 4 in a sequence of 20 random tosses is about 80%.[4,5] Thus, the mathematicians explain, the sequence of heads and tails displayed above could easily have come from a purely random experiment.

That's analysis. That's logical, mathematical thinking. That's Statistical Science. To turn numbers into knowledge, we need to combine the pattern-seeking and the story-telling with some hard-nosed mathematical thinking. But mathematical thinking is neither intuitive nor natural. It takes some hard mental work to do it right, years of training and decades of experience. I cannot offer a course in mathematics in this slim volume, but I will do what I can to hit a few of the highlights, when genuinely needed. I will issue one early warning: do not be intimidated by what you don't completely understand. Statistical Science is not really very helpful for understanding or forecasting complex evolving self-healing organic ambiguous social systems – economies, in other words.[6]

A statistician may have done the programming, but when you press a button on a computer keyboard and ask the computer to find some good patterns, better get clear a sad fact: computers do not think. They do exactly what the programmer told them to do and nothing more. They look for the patterns that we tell them to look for, those and nothing more. When we turn to the computer for advice, we are only talking to ourselves. This works in a simple setting in which there is a very well-defined set of alternative theories and we can provide the computer with clear instructions. But in complex nonexperimental settings, Sherlock Holmes admonishes: "Never theorize before you have all the evidence. It biases the judgments."

In this book, you and I are going to explore the US macro economic data in the Holmesian fashion. We are going to look for patterns and tell stories. In this enterprise, the value of the wisdom offered by Statistical Science is pretty minimal.

---

[3] Feller, W. *An Introduction to Probabilty Theory and Its Applications, Volume* I, John Wiley and Sons, New York, 1957, second edition page 32.

[4] Feller, W., op.cit. page 301.

[5] Mathematicians presumably checked to make sure that the random number generator embedded in my Excel program produces sequences which usually have runs of four or more. If they don't, the result doesn't "seem" random, and we need to find another algorithm. Those who wrote the software code to produce random numbers checked and rechecked to assure that their numbers have outcomes that conform with many of the properties of random numbers. Many, but not all.

[6] A fundamental problem with statistical science applied to nonexperimental data is that too much knowledge is presumed. When asking if the coin flips are random, you are expected to be able to define in advance and completely what you mean by nonrandomness. Is it momentum that you are looking for: Is it more likely that a head follows a head? How much more likely? Or is it that the even-numbered flips have more heads than tails? Or what? What exactly is the kind of nonrandomness that you want the computer to look for?

For more on this, take a look at the appendix to this introductory chapter. But if you think you might be intimidated by that material, just move on.

Thus when dazzled by the mathematics, there are three things you need to do: resist, resist, and resist. The mathematically uninitiated begin with a naïve pattern-seeking mentality, and may "see" an obvious pattern in the coin flips, and may then be astonished to discover from the mathematics that this is not a pattern at all. Having made that discovery, many will properly want to reposition themselves in the continuum between naïve pattern-seeking on the one hand, and complete skepticism on the other. But, if you do not resist, you may flip completely over to the other pole, and suppose that there are no patterns at all, and thus no need to look at the data. But then you must rely entirely on stories, if you have any, which is a very bad idea. Your goal should be to anchor yourself wisely between the two opposites of naïve empiricism and incapacitating skepticism.

This is a familiar problem for Wall Street quants. Freshly minted MBAs often arrive on Wall Street with skills at designing Excel spreadsheets and with the anticipation that their superior intelligence and analytical skills will allow them soon to find the pattern in the stock prices that will turn them into multi-millionaires. After a few years of looking at the historical data and finding patterns (NYSE prices always rise between 1PM and 3PM EST on the second Tuesday after the first full moon of each calendar month), and then having their hopes dashed by the failure of the patterns to persist into the future, these analysts tend to get skeptical and flip from the naïve pole to the skeptic's pole. There are even books about being "Fooled by Randomness" and "When Genius Failed" as if to counsel the skeptic's approach.[7] Do not go that far. You do not want to be fooled by randomness but you can do better than simply throwing darts at your difficult decisions. How? "Read" this book, he answered with a quizzical and indecipherable expression on his face.

1.3 Pictures, Words, and Numbers: In that Order

Here is a way to reinforce the message. Repeat with me: "Pictures, Words, and Numbers" – pictures referring to the patterns, words to the stories, and numbers to the numerical (scientific) analysis.

In the first half of the twentieth century, graphical displays (pictures) of the data were routine in economics but in the intervening half century, the economics profession has deluged itself with numerical estimates and t-values. Most statistics courses in business schools also take a numerical approach: the mean, the median, and the standard error. But you and I don't "internalize" all these numbers. We walk through the mist as if it were not there at all.

---

[7] *Fooled by Randomness: The Hidden Role of Chance in the Markets and in Life* by Nassim Nicholas Taleb; *When Genius Failed: The Rise and Fall of Long-Term Capital Management* by Roger Lowenstein; *Liar's Poker: Rising Through the Wreckage on Wall Street* by Michael Lewis.

There are probably many reasons why numbers do not much affect us. One important reason is that humans were not designed by evolution to process numbers. As a species we first learned to process images. Words and language came much later. Numbers came last. As children, we recapitulate our evolution, first peering out of our cribs and learning to process images, then a few years later, words, and last of all numbers. It's not just a sequence in time. We have enormous bandwidth for natural images, and much less for aural information, and hardly any for numbers and symbols. So if you want to persuade, emphasize the pictures and the stories. Put the numbers in a footnote. They will impress someone.

So say it once more: *Pictures, Words, and Numbers*

- Visual displays to help internalize the main messages and to prepare for the subtle messages
- Stories to memorialize the images
- Numerical modeling to force clarity of thinking and communication onto ambiguous settings

1.4 Analytical Thinking: I think I Can Help

With the introduction now complete, I need to reveal that there is a subtext. I am writing in this book about analytical thinking. Some business school graduates are said by recruiters not to be "analytical." I take that to mean that our students learn simple frameworks and hypothetical business problems, and a mechanical mapping of one to the other. That works well on exams when the instructor selects one from the portfolio of problems covered in the class. But when confronted with a new business problem, our students sometimes act as if they were taking a course exam, and they search their internal databases for problems that seem to them to be similar. Finding the closest one, they force the corresponding framework onto the setting, never-mind that it may be a patently silly thing to do. In other words, there is a lack of good judgment, and an inability to think out of the box.

How to correct this problem? How to teach and to learn analytical thinking? There is not just one path toward that goal, but I offer one: Along with your vitamins and aerobics, try daily exercises in pattern seeking and story telling. Be insatiably curious.

1.4.1 Forecasting Is a Participant Sport

By the way, do not expect to get much just from watching aerobics or from watching forecasting. You need to participate.

"It's not the forecast, it's the forecasting," "It's not the model, it's the modeling." That's my way of saying that you cannot get the message unless you participate in creating it. It's the *process* of creating a forecast or building a model that creates the knowledge. Thus do not hire me to do a forecast for you. Hire me to plan a way for us to make the forecast together. Then you will get the message and internalize it.[8]

To encourage your active participation, I have tried to write this in an exploratory way, raising questions and trying to resolve them. I have also sprinkled the text with questions. You should try doing these on your own, but I doubt that will work as well as doing it in a group. The creation of knowledge is a social experience.

1.4.2 Tell Someone About It: It Will Help You More Than Them

Was it Oscar Wilde who said he did not know what he was thinking until he wrote it down? Thinking occurs behind the curtain. If you want to know what's going on there, write it down or explain it to someone. If you worry that there is nothing going on behind the curtain, trying to write it down and trying to explain it to someone else may get something going.

Remember the goal is persuasion. The first step is to persuade yourself. The next, and much larger step, is to persuade others. If you fail to persuade others, it is probably because you have not persuaded yourself.

1.5 What Now?

Before embarking on this journey together say it one more time: Pictures, Words, and Numbers.

We are going to proceed like the best eighteenth century empirics. We will decide first what are good ways to measure the health of our patient – the US economy. There are many possibilities. A modern economy is an organism that turns labor time into goods and services. This organism is healthy when work is plentiful and when production is great relative to the effort expended. Once we have decided on the metrics, we will take a close look at the historical data, trying to determine when the economy was healthy and when it was not. If we can adequately answer the "When?" question, we can turn our attention to the more difficult question: "Why?" If we make some progress on that one, then we may be able to find answers to the two questions that are the reason for studying macroeconmics: What are the circumstances that tell us this patient is starting to fall ill? What can be done to keep this patient healthy?

---

[8] President and General Dwight D. Eisenhower is quoted as saying, "In preparing for battle I have always found that plans are useless, but planning is indispensable." The Columbia World of Quotations. 1996.

ATTRIBUTION: Dwight D. Eisenhower (1890–1969), U.S. general, Republican politician, president. Quoted by Richard Nixon in "Krushchev," Six Crises (1962).

1.6 Preview: The Key Pattern

To set the stage and to get you thinking, here is a key pattern in search of a story. This is US Real GDP, the subject of the next chapter. The US Real GDP has been growing steadily at 3% for 35 years, with a few wiggles here and there. What are those wiggles, and why should we care?

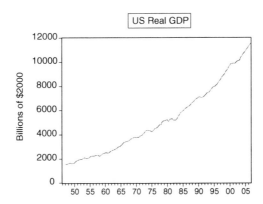

1.7 Data Sources

The data that are used in this book come from the US government. You can get these from some friendly websites.

First try Googling: *Fred*. That's the Federal Reserve Economic Data provided by the St. Louis Fed: http://research.stlouisfed.org/fred2/

> Fred can give you most of the major data series. You can download the data easily and you can make some great graphs too, only a couple clicks away.

For much more detailed macro-economic data try the Bureau of Economic Analysis. For that one, try Googling **BEA**. http://www.bea.gov/

> The BEA provides a massive amount of data. You could spend a week on this site just figuring out what is there. See if you can find Table 1.1.2: Contributions to Percent Change in Real Gross Domestic Product.

The labor market data are collected by the Bureau of Labor Statistics. For that one, try Googling **BLS**. http://www.bls.gov/

> The BLS also provides a massive amount of data. You could spend another week on this site just figuring out what is there. See if you can find the number of employees in Credit card issuing.

For up-to-the minute latest releases, I go to www.briefing.com

For my own downloads, I am a subscriber of www.economagic.com

1.7.1 Updated Displays

For updates of the displays in this book, go to Ed Leamer's personal Web site
http://www.anderson.ucla.edu/faculty/edward.leamer/

1.8 Appendix: Statistical Science Is Severely Limited in Its Applicability

Mathematical analysis for separating real from accidental patterns has one huge shortcoming – the mathematician presumes that the data analyst can fully define the set of alternative nonrandom patterns. Think about that coin-tossing example again. For trying to decide if the observed sequence of tails was produced by a computer or by a human, we made a vague reference to the fact that humans generally do not produce long runs. Humans think that after a couple of heads, a tail "comes due". That's not good enough, the mathematician advises. We have one explicit model of the probability of runs that is prepared by the mathematician. Call that the "random model." We need an explicit alternative model that tells how probable are runs in sequences chosen by humans. We need a two-horse race to decide which horse wins. But now we have a problem: though there is only one "random" model, there are an unlimited number of "nonrandom" "come-due" models, and we are going to have a heck of a hard time deciding which ones to consider. Thus it is not a two-horse race. It is a one plus x-horse race, where x stands for the unknown number of "come-due" models.

One alternative "come-due" model that we might consider is "never more than three," meaning that humans produce what they think of as random sequences but never allow more than three heads or more than three tails in a row-random, except long runs are eliminated. Try running this oddball horse against the random horse given the sequence of heads and tails displayed above. This oddball horse wins by three lengths. If we had more data, we could check this out more thoroughly, but if we are limited to the data displayed above, what are we going to do about this possibility?? This is a real problem. In a race between horse A and horse B, mathematics works great. It tells us which horse won, and by how much. But mathematics cannot tell us if we should include horse C in the race. If C beats both A and B, we obviously have a problem: should we include C or not? If model C is a real oddball, maybe we should find some way to handicap it, and require it to win by four lengths.

1.8.1 Was that 1969 Draft Lottery Random? Was It Fair?

1.8.1.1 The Vietnam Lotteries

A lottery drawing – the first since 1942 – was held on 1 December 1969, at Selective Service National Headquarters in Washington, D.C. This event determined the order of call for induction during calendar year 1970, that is, for registrants born between 1 January 1944, and 31 December 1950. Reinstitution of the lottery was a change from the "draft the oldest man first" method, which had been the determining method for deciding order of call.

There were 366 blue plastic capsules containing birth dates placed in a large glass container and drawn by hand to assign order-of-call numbers to all men within the 18–26 age range specified in Selective Service law.

With radio, film, and TV coverage, the capsules were drawn from the container, opened, and the dates inside posted in order. The first capsule – drawn by Congressman Alexander Pirnie (R-NY) of the House Armed Services Committee – contained the date September 14, so all men born on September 14 in any year between 1944 and 1950 were assigned lottery number 1. The drawing continued until all days of the year had been paired with sequence numbers.

http://www.sss.gov/lotter1.htm

Comment:
A "random" draft lottery would assign to each of the 366 birth dates (one extra for the leap year February 29) a randomly chosen number from 1 to 366. The average number assigned to any of the 12 months of the year would be 367/2 = 183.5, plus or minus the statistical variability. At the right is what actually turned out.

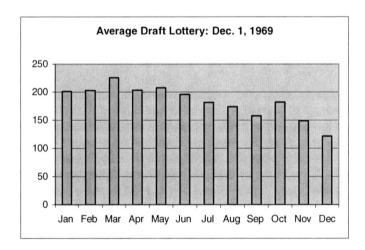

Wow! The outcome seems strange. The early birth months turned out to be the "lucky" ones, with high draft numbers, and a low risk of being drafted. Those unlucky December babies were marched off to Vietnam. But was it really just bad luck, or was the draft lottery nonrandom? And if it was not random, was it unfair? Two very difficult questions. Neither can be answered by Statistical Science.[9]

---

[9] We might pause a moment in the train of thought and talk about the other issue: What is a fair lottery? Clearly it is unfair to send some young men to Vietnam while others stay home. How can

According to Statistical Science, if the lottery were random, then every sequence of the 366 numbers would be equally probable. The sequence that was drawn is highly unlikely, but so are all the others, equally so. No help there at all. For Statistical Science to be helpful, we need to choose some particular kinds of patterns to look for. Was the lottery unfair to Saturdays? Was the lottery unfair to 1969 Full Moon Days? Was the lottery unfair to cold days? Or rainy days? Was the lottery unfair to holidays? And so on, and so on. If you work hard, you are sure to find a pattern in the data that Statistical Science will reveal is highly unlikely. Months-of-the-year does the job just fine. Not only is there surprising variability in the averages across months, there is also a "statistically significant" trend in the averages!

So is this evidence of nonrandomness, or only tenacity in the search for patterns? Sorry there is no way to answer this question. If we knew precisely how tenacious was the search for patterns, then we can make some Scientific progress. If, for example, before we started looking at the data, we had made a full commitment to search only for time dependence of a specific type, then Statistical Science reveals that these data do not appear random. There is statistically measurable time dependence. The difference between the expected lottery number for January 1 and the expected lottery number for December 31 is equal to 83 with an error band of ± 38.[10] That sounds like statistical mumbo-jumbo, but we can translate this into something we can all understand: If, in advance of performing the lottery, we knew what we do now, and if half of the young men had to go to Vietnam, then the *predicted probability* of getting drafted was about 66% for those with January 1 birthdates but only 35% for those with December 31 birthdates.

But the line of premises that leads to a conclusion of nonrandomness includes some demonstrably false sentences. Most particularly, there was never any commitment to look only for that one time-dependence pattern. It was only after-the-fact that someone stumbled on that pattern. Now, there is no way to know how much

---

a randomly chosen unfair outcome be fair? It may be fair in a predictive *ex ante* sense, but the *outcome* is demonstrably unfair. An all-volunteer army might be a better choice, but is it fair that those with wealth and income stay behind while the poor "volunteer" to join the Army?

Secondly, if your standard of fairness is predictive probabilities, then it is fair to say that no one in advance knew that there was time-dependence in the outcomes, and the predictive probability of being drafted was the same for every birthdate. There is no unfairness for something discovered after the fact. Of course, once discovered, we need to eliminate the time dependence for the next lottery, but looking backward there was no unfairness in the sense of unequal predictive risks of being drafted.

[10] Dependent Variable: Lottery Number
Method: Least Squares
Included observations: 366

Variable	Coefficient	Std. Error	t-Statistic	Prob.
C	224.7	10.8	20.9	0
Day of Year/365	−82.4	18.6	−4.4	0
R-squared	0.051	Mean dependent var		183.5
Adjusted R-squared	0.048	S.D. dependent var		105.8
S.E. of regression	103.21			

stumbling was going on and how wide was the search for patterns. Absent that knowledge, Statistical Science is not useful.[11] Statistical Science is useful for confirmatory analysis, when the set of hypotheses can be well defined in advance, but not for exploratory analysis. Time dependence was suggested by an exploratory study of the data, and it is double counting then to act as if that pattern was the only one we were looking for and to use the data to confirm that the lottery was nonrandom.

Thus the problem with pure pattern seeking – you cannot possibly tell the real patterns from the accidental patterns. What to do? Story-telling is the answer. If you want to persuade, tell a compelling story that is well aligned with the pattern you discovered. Here is a good one. Workers who filled the glass containers put the capsules in one day at a time, beginning with January 1. When they turned the container over and over to produce a "random" lottery, the layering was disturbed but not eliminated. Mostly they just flipped the whole mass upside down, making it relatively easy to grab a December capsule right a way and relatively hard to grab a January.

1.9 Conclusion

Mathematical analysis works great to decide which horse wins, if we are completely confident which horses are in the race, but it breaks down when we are not sure. In experimental settings, the set of alternative models can often be well agreed on, but with nonexperimental economics data, the set of models is subject to enormous disagreements. You disagree with your model made yesterday, and I disagree with your model today. Mathematics does not help much resolve our internal intellectual disagreements.

---

[11] The "width" of the search needs to be defined in a way that makes reference to the *a priori* plausibility of the models under consideration. If you look at one plausible nonrandom model and a lot of odd-ball models then the statistical standard applied to the plausible model is not much affected by the search for odd-ball patterns. See:

Leamer, Edward E. "False Models and Post-Data Model Construction," *Journal of the American Statistical Association*, 69 (March 1974), 122–131; abstracted in *Zentralblatt fur Mathematik*, reprinted in Omar F. Hamouda and J.C.R. Rowley, *Foundations of Probability, Econometrics and Economic Games*, Edward Elgar Publishing Limited, 1995.

Part II
Four Key Variables: Growth, Unemployment, Inflation and Interest Rates

Chapter 2
Gross Domestic Product

We need to start with some basic definitions. This first step may not be all that exciting. But, I remind you, if you expect the paint to last, you will need to spend a lot of time preparing the surface. I know you want to slap on the paint right away, but you will regret it if you do not show a little patience.

Stick with me here. It will get better soon.

2.1 Definitions

2.1.1 GDP Is an Imperfect Measure of Economic/ Material Success

The first focus of our attention is *Gross Domestic Product* (GDP). *GDP is the market value of goods and services produced within a selected geographic area (usually a country) in a selected interval in time (often a year).* Rightly or wrongly, this has become the standard by which we measure the size and health of a country. Big and/or growing are good. Small and/or shrinking are bad. For example, California politicians are fond of informing the voters: If California were a country, it would rank 7th on the GDP list. Whooo, whooo! Go, California.

As we are about to repeat these three letters a couple thousand times, it is wise to put firmly into our consciousness the fact that GDP is a very imperfect indicator of the health of countries. One big problem is that GDP measures only the material, not the emotional or the spiritual, or .... If it is produced and sold, then it is counted; otherwise not. Driving along Sunset Boulevard in your fancy car and wearing your fancy clothes, you probably don't realize it yet, but "You can't buy love." If you could, the accountants would include "love services" in GDP. (I know what you are thinking, but that is not love.)

Another issue is that GDP is about outcomes rather than processes. Most of us do care about *how* we got the goods and services we consume as well as *what* we consume. We think the process out to be just and fair. But GDP does not include justice or fairness. And GDP does not account for the joy of giving. The pleasure I derive from giving you the cookies I baked is not counted in GDP, nor is the extra smile on your face thinking about me baking those cookies for you. Even the cookies do not count unless I sell them to you. There has to be a market transaction. What would be the fun of that?

2.1.1.1 Adjustments to GDP

GDP is not happiness, that's for sure, but even limited to its material domain, GDP *excludes* much that is valuable, and *includes* much that is really unwanted. Most alarmingly, GDP does not subtract the annoyance that you suffer from your long hours of work, or the loneliness of your children. If your health deteriorates, but you stay on the job, GDP will also increase because someone has to produce all those pills and doctor visits that you purchase. Likewise, GDP increases when crime increases, because we have to pay the police for their overtime work. And damage to the environment is not subtracted from GDP. Neither is increased congestion nor the health consequences of more smoking. If some one produced it, and you bought it, it counts. If what you buy has unintended consequences, for you or for the rest of us, that does not matter. It is only the market value that counts. No market, no market value.

There is much that should be subtracted from GDP, of course, but there is something extremely important that should be added – "consumer surplus." When we use market prices to value output, we ignore the fact that items generally are purchased because they are worth *more* than the price we pay. Only "at the margin" is value equal to price. To get this idea of the margin, think about drinking water. The margin is the last glass of water you drink each day – the eighth glass. The first glass of water has virtually unlimited value since you could not live without it. The second glass is less valuable and the third less valuable still. According to an economic model of personal decision-making, you will drink additional glasses of water until the benefits of another glass are less than the cost. Most of us live in communities where water is very cheap. My statement from the Department of Water and Power indicates that I am charged $0.03 per gallon. The half-gallon of water that I drink each day is valued in GDP at the market rate of only about $0.015 per day, when its value to me is staggeringly high. Do you know the old joke: an economist is someone who knows the price of everything but the value of nothing. But, actually, we quite well understand that the price of water is low, but the value is immense.

The difference between the market value and the full value is really dramatic for all the information delivered to you over the Internet. Since it is provided for free, its market value is zero, and it is not included in GDP at all.

2.1.1.2 Gross Domestic Happiness

Clearly, GDP and well-being are not the same. Since GDP was first defined, Social Scientists have been trying to find a useful alternative that accurately measures

Gross National Well-being. Try doing a Web search on "GDP and Happiness" to see the vast sea of possibilities.

The problem is measurement. We can measure pretty accurately the market value of the automobiles produced in the United States, but how much do those new vehicles contribute to well-being? Keep in mind that those cars fundamentally change our lifestyles, confining us alone in metal boxes for many hours of the day. Is that well-being?

But happiness is a slippery concept. What you call happiness may not be anything like what I call happiness. That makes it difficult for me to tell if you are happy. But I can ask. The General Social Survey in the US asks: "Taken all together, how would you say things are these days – would you say you are very happy, pretty happy, or not too happy". When you report to this survey taker that you are "very happy" and I report that I am "pretty happy" whatever does that mean? What does it mean, especially, if you and I come from different cultures and use different languages?[1]

Material Success May or May not Correlate with Happiness

"So what?," most economists would retort. Though "you can't buy love," you can buy a pretty good facsimile. Of course, material well-being is not everything, but for a lot of people it seems pretty close.

But there is a problem with material pursuits. For many of the materialists it is not their material well-being that matters; it is how much better they are doing than their neighbors. Like bird-watching. The pleasure comes from seeing a bird that others have not seen. How mean-spirited is that? If all that matters is where we are in the material pecking-order, then when we all get better off materially, we do not get any happier. Maybe this is what is happening in the data displayed in Fig. 2.1, which contrasts the growing material well-being of the US with the deteriorating happiness levels. Are we making ourselves miserable trying to outdo our neighbors?

A different conclusion comes from the data in Fig. 2.2, which compares across countries GDP per capita with happiness measured by Ingelhart and Klingemann. It looks as though a little extra income for these poor countries matters a lot. But look again. If you put your hand over all those unhappy Former-Soviet-Union countries with low incomes, what remains looks like a pretty straight line: More income, more happiness.[2]

---

[1] Surveys might not work to measure happiness but neuroscience promises to provide "objective" measures. R.J. Davidson finds that positive feelings excited by visual displays create brain activity for right-handers at the left side of the prefrontal cortex and negative feelings in the same place on the right side of the brain. Davidson, R.J. (2000) 'Affective style, psychopathology and resilience: Brain mechanisms and plasticity', *American Psychologist*, 55, 1196–1214.

[2] Incidentally, the horizontal scale in this last figure is not GDP per head but income per head. But double-entry book-keeping assures that production and income are identical. That which is produced and sold generates income for the seller. That which is produced but not sold also generates income for the producer in the form of valuable inventory that can be sold later.

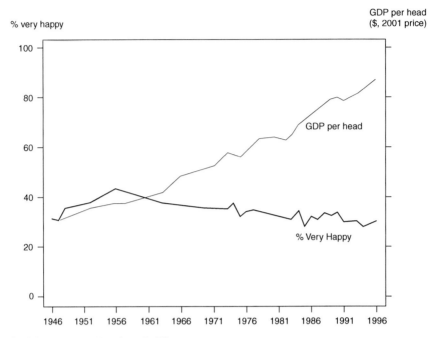

Fig. 2.1 Income and happiness in US

2.1.1.3 GDP Works Fine for us

Though GDP is a problematic measure in many ways, it actually serves our purposes
quite well. This book is not about comparing the happiness of California and France.
This book is about the business cycle. Every country and every community has
periods when GDP is growing nicely, and jobs are plentiful, and also periods when
GDP is declining or growing slowly, and jobs are hard to find. These periods of
weak or negative growth are called "recessions," suggesting an organism like a mold
that generally grows but every once in a while it recedes a little bit. In the popular
press, a recession is defined as "two quarters of negative GDP growth." This is not
a good definition, for reasons I will explain below. But negative GDP growth, like a
high body temperature, is a very important symptom of illness. That's why we are
looking at it closely.

2.1.2 What Do Those Three Letters Stand For?

Make sure you understand each letter: G and D and P.

   "P," for product, refers to the *production* of goods but also to the production of
services. Thus GDP includes both assembling automobiles and giving massages.

Happiness (index)

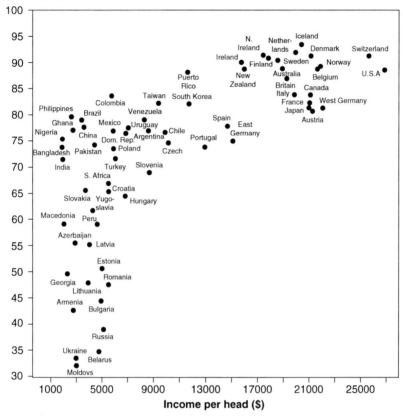

Fig. 2.2 Income and happiness across countries
(Source: Richard Layard, Income and Happiness, Lionel Robbins Lecture, March 2003,
http://cep.lse.ac.uk/events/lectures/layard/RL030303.pdf)

"D," for domestic, means "made in the USA."[3] It does not matter whether the
factory in South Carolina is owned by Ford or by BMW. The auto is still made in
USA. Gross *National* Product, on the other hand, refers to the value of goods and
services produced by Americans, no matter where the production takes place. Part of
the value of that automobile made in Georgia comes from the BMW brand and that
accrues to German owners. That is not included in GNP. Only the part of the value
of that BMW automobile that is attributable to US workers is included in US GNP.

Thus the difference between GNP and GDP is whether the country is defined by
geography or by ownership. For most countries, GDP and GNP are very similar,
and in any case, the concept of GNP is rapidly losing its meaning as corporations
become multinational in ownership and as footloose intellectual service workers
wander the globe in search of the most lucrative contracts. Just for the record, US

---

[3] Forgive the chauvinism. Search and replace USA with Your Country.

Table 2.1 Relation of gross domestic product, gross national product, net national product, national income, and personal income, 2005

Bureau of economic analysis	$billion	%	Per capita
Gross domestic product	**12,456**	**100.0%**	**41,519**
Plus: Income receipts from the rest of the world	513	4.1%	1,711
Less: Income payments to the rest of the world	482	3.9%	1,605
Equals: Gross national product	**12,488**	**100.3%**	**41,626**
Less: Consumption of fixed capital	1,605	12.9%	5,349
Private	1,353	10.9%	4,509
Domestic business	1,059	8.5%	3,530
Households and institutions	294	2.4%	978
Government	252	2.0%	841
Equals: Net national product	**10,883**	**87.4%**	**36,276**

GDP in 2005 was $12.456 trillion while US GNP was $12.488 trillion. That's too small a difference to worry about. Check it out in Table 2.1.

2.1.3 What's "Gross" About Gross Domestic Product?

What about the "G" in GDP? Whatever is gross about Gross Domestic Product, anyway? (Ask your economist friends. A lot of them don't know the answer.) If not "gross," then what? Pleasant?

To an accountant "gross" means including everything and "net" means something has been removed. There are a lot of things that might be "netted" out of GDP, but for us, Net National Product is the value of goods and services produced, net of *depreciation*.

You know about the depreciation of your car. That $40,000 new car you bought last year is worth only $30,000 today. If you have spent all of your earnings this year, your personal wealth has declined by $10,000 because of this depreciation. Just to tread water, you need to put aside $10,000 to offset that depreciation. If you don't, your wealth will deteriorate.

Net National Product is the amount of product left over after enough is put aside to offset the depreciation of our equipment and our buildings.

As can be seen in Table 2.1, in 2005, US depreciation (consumption of fixed capital) was $1605 billion, equal to 12.9% of GNP. That is how much of GNP was needed to maintain and to replace worn-out existing capital. The last column of Table 2.1 has the per capita figure. Notice that household figure of $978 – that is your home and your car depreciating.

2.1.4 What's "Real" About "Real GDP" and What Is "Nominal" About "Nominal GDP"?

Another word puzzle is to figure out what is the meaning of "Real GDP." What's real about real GDP? And what's the opposite of real? Unreal?

Instead of calling it "unreal" GDP, economists call it "nominal" GDP, meaning "in name only." There is *real* GDP and *nominal* GDP.

There can be something unreal or "in name only" about increases in the market value of goods and services, since you can pay more but get less if prices rise. "Real GDP" controls for price differences over time and across countries. It measures the real stuff we are producing. "Nominal" GDP is only the money value of the items, which can go up or down depending on the prices.

To get a clear visual image of the difference between "nominal" and "real" GDP, picture yourself checking out of a grocery store. Pile into your shopping basket all the goods and services that are made in US in a given year. That's "real" GDP. Now go through the checkout line to find out how much these products cost. We need a name for the total cost of the items in your shopping basket. Let's call that "nominal" GDP to draw a distinction with "real" GDP.

Nominal GDP   Real GDP

Understand that Real GDP changes only when the stuff in the shopping basket changes. But nominal GDP can change either because the stuff is changing or because the prices are changing. If prices are rising, you may have to pay more, even though you do not "really" have more. Thus nominal GDP can increase when real GDP stays fixed.

The visual image of real GDP that you constructed for yourself probably has a great variety of products in your shopping basket. We need to summarize all that detail in a single number. The way this is done is by fixing the prices at some base year, say the year 1996. Value the stuff in your shopping cart at fixed prices that do not change each time you check out of the store. If you use 1996 prices, call that "GDP in constant 1996 prices" or "real GDP" for short. Be sure you understand that changes in GDP in constant 1996 dollars cannot be due to changes in prices. Real GDP can change only if the products in the basket change.

Nominal GDP: GDP is the market value *in current prices* of goods and services produced within the geographic borders of the United States.

Real GDP: Real GDP is the value *in base year prices* of goods and services produced within the geographic borders of the United States.

Remember, when you hear an economist say the word "real," visualize a basket of real goods rolling through a checkout line at the grocery store. Contrast that with

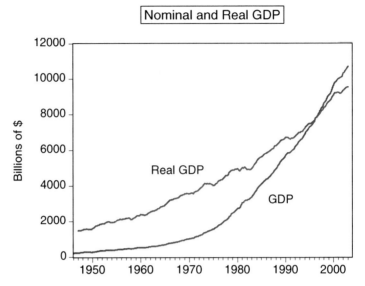

Fig. 2.3 Nominal and real GDP

the money left behind to pay for all that stuff. The money is "nominal" and the goods are "real."

Real and nominal GDP are displayed in Fig. 2.3. Looking at this figure you should be able to answer the following questions:

Why do Real GDP and Nominal GDP cross in 1996?[4]
Why does Nominal GDP rise more rapidly than Real GDP?[5]

Then two last questions:

Why 1996? Why use 1996 prices as the base year?

> As far as I know, that is entirely accidental. This base year changes over time, keeping pretty close to the current year. That makes sense because we want to use prices with which we are most familiar to value GDP. Other than recency, there is not any special reason for the choice of base year.

Does the choice of the base year matter?

> This question has two answers: Yes and NO. Start with No first.

> Take a look at the chart above that compares real GDP and GDP. These cross at the base year 1996. Suppose that we changed the base year to 1980. Then we have to lower Real GDP down to make it cross the GDP curve in 1980. So the base year seems to matter. But the picture of Real GDP stays exactly the same. It has the same growth rate and the same

---

[4] Answer: We are using 1996 prices to evaluate real GDP.

[5] Answer: Prices have always been rising and accordingly the value of GDP rises more rapidly than the real GDP.

wiggles here and there. So the base year really does not matter at all. Granted, if you use 1980 prices to value production, the values will be less than if you use 1996 prices. But there are no questions that we are going to ask that depend on this difference. So forget it.

But this "no" answer is based on the assumption that relative prices do not change very much. If relative prices do change substantially, the base year does matter for GDP growth calculations. The falling price of computers offers a good example. Let us compare 1980 with 2000. Suppose that your 1980 shopping cart had only two items: an automobile and one personal computer, and suppose that your 2000 shopping cart had the same automobile but *two* personal computers. How much more stuff is there in your 2000 basket. In 1980, the automobile cost $5000 and the computer cost $5000. In 2000, the same automobile cost $20,000 and the same computer only $1000. Using 1980 prices, you spent $10,000 in 1980 and $15,000 in 2000, for a 50% increase in "real GDP." But using the year 2000 prices, you spent $21,000 in 1980 and $22,000 in 2000, for a 5% increase in "real GDP." So which is it: Did real GDP grow a lot or only a little? For more on this index number problem, see the appendix to this chapter. Believe me, we have much bigger things to worry about than this. We are looking mostly at short-term ups and downs of real GDP in intervals of time in which relative prices do not change enough to cause a big measurement problem. For longer-term issues, like deciding how much cost-of-living adjustment is appropriate for Social Security recipients, this index number problem is a much bigger deal.

2.1.5 What Does SAAR Mean?

If you visit the Web site of the Bureau of Economic Analysis you will discover that the GDP data come both annually and quarterly. Below is an excerpt from a quarterly table with the data for 2002. Notice that the Real GDP numbers on a quarterly basis are each about the same as the annual number $9,440 billion. How can that be? Should not the amount we produce in a year be about four times what we produce in a quarter? Yes, that is true, but GDP is not how much we produced. Its the *rate* at which we were producing. GDP is the market value of goods and services produced within the geographic borders of the United States *per unit of time*. The BEA alerts us to this by including the acronym SAAR in the table – Seasonally Adjusted at Annual Rates. (Back to seasonal adjustment later.)

Table 1.2. *Real Gross Domestic Product*
[Billions of chained (1996) dollars]
Seasonally adjusted at annual rates

2002			
I	II	II	IV
9,363	9,392	9,485	9,518

Source: http://www.bea.doc.gov/

Notice also in this table the reference to chained (1996) dollars. This is the BEA telling us that they have been working hard trying to adjust for changing relative prices as discussed in the appendix below.

28

2 Gross Domestic Product

2.1.6 What Is an Annualized Compound Rate of Growth?

While we are on this annualization point, we should also discuss "annualized rates of growth." The BEA estimates of Real GDP in 2001 and 2002 were 9,214.5 and 9,439.9, respectively. The percentage difference between these two numbers is 2.4%. That is the rate of growth in Real GDP *per year*. The BEA estimates of Real GDP in 2002 Q1 and Q2 were 9,363.20 and 9,392.40. The percentage difference between these two numbers is only 0.312%. That is the rate of growth in Real GDP *per quarter of a year*. This is going to get hopelessly confusing unless we standardize on the time interval. In the case of interest rates, a year is the standard time period. When the Wall Street Journal reports that the yield on a 10-year Treasury is 4%, that is not 4% over the whole 10 years, that is 4% per year. We will do the same thing for GDP growth. That is the rate of growth per year.

To transform that growth figure of 0.312% per quarter into an annual number, we could just multiply by four to obtain 1.247%. But the annualized rate of growth is just a little bit greater than that because of the effect of compounding. After four quarters of growth at the rate of 0.312% per quarter, the increase in the GDP is actually 1.253%. That is the annualized compound rate of growth.[6]

2.2 What Does Real GDP Look Like?

2.2.1 Does a Logarithmic Scale Help? The Narrow Corridor of US GDP Growth

Real GDP is displayed again in Fig. 2.4. Look at that scale – the distance between 2 and 4 trillion is the same as the distance between 4 and 8. That is a logarithmic scale. In a logarithmic scale, a straight line represents a constant rate of growth. The two straight lines drawn in this figure identify the narrow corridor in which real GDP has been confined since 1970. The floor and ceiling of this corridor grow at the rate of 3% per year and the distance from floor to ceiling is ±3%. Call that the 3–3 rule of US GDP. Notice that the US grew a bit faster than this 3% rate in the 1960s.

You can also see in this figure the periods when GDP was dipping down to the floor of the corridor and when it zoomed back up to the ceiling. The dips downward

---

[6] The formula for computing the growth rate with quarterly data is:

$$\text{Annualized compound rate of growth per year} = -1 + (\text{RGDP}/\text{RGDP}(-1))^4,$$

where RGDP refers to the Real GDP and RGDP(-1) to RGDP in the previous quarter.

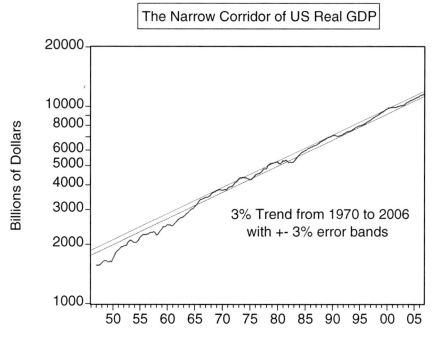

Fig. 2.4 Real GDP grows in a very narrow corridor

are the "recessions." These are followed by "recoveries" when GDP rises above the floor of the corridor.

This figure gives us our assignment. We need to understand why the US GDP has been growing at a 3% rate for 30 years and we need to form an opinion whether or not this is going to continue for the next 30. We need to understand why the GDP occasionally dips down to the floor of the corridor and sometimes rises above the ceiling. We need to know when the next dip is going to occur.

Parenthetically, after Ronald Reagan's death I received an e-mail proclaiming that the Reagan tax cuts had "unleashed a juggernaut of economic growth." Look again at Fig. 2.4 to find that juggernaut of growth. Can you see it? I see the US economy growing persistently at 3%. We had the oil shocks of the 1970s, and still 3%. In the early 1980s, we had the Reagan tax cuts and the subsequent deficit, and still 3%. In the mid-1980s, we had the overvaluation of the dollar and the subsequent depreciation, and still 3%. We had the Internet Rush in the 1990s, the Bush W. Tax Cuts, the Bush W. Deficits, and the Housing Bubble in the 2000s, and still 3%.

If you think this book focuses a lot on recessions and recoveries, the preceding paragraph tells why. It is the ups and downs within the corridor of growth that call out for explanation and control. The remarkable persistence of the long-term rate of growth leaves the clear impression that the long-term trend is just something we have to live with. That long-term growth rate surely cannot depend much on tax rates or interest rates, at least not given the historical variability of these two policy instruments. All bets are off if we had income taxes at 90% or interest rates and inflation at 20%. But within the historical range, Fig. 2.4 suggests that fiscal and monetary policy should be focusing on something they have some hope of influencing: not the long-term trend but the descents that cause distress, and the ascents that lay the foundation for the next descents. That's why we are focusing a lot on recessions and recoveries.

2.2.2 Four Pictures: What Does Growth of Real GDP Look Like?

Remember a theme of this book: pictures, words, and numbers. A persuasive argument requires well-chosen pictures, well-chosen words, and well-chosen numbers. Concentrate on the pictures and words. People do not understand numbers.

We already have learned a lot from Fig. 2.4 and the words that have accompanied it. There are some *other* good pictures of GDP worth looking at. Figure 2.5 is a bar chart that displays the GDP growth rate, quarter by quarter. Figure 2.6 is a moving average of the same data. And Fig. 2.7 illustrates one measure of the volatility of

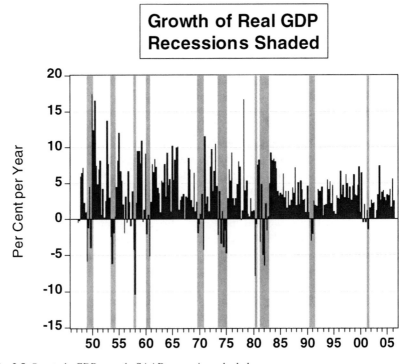

Fig. 2.5 Quarterly GDP growth, SAAR: recessions shaded

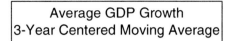

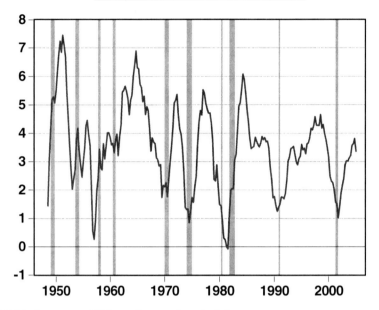

Fig. 2.6 Moving average GDP growth, recessions shaded

GDP growth. Which display is best? Which communicates an important message most clearly?

While the first display, Fig. 2.4, is a good one for depicting long-term movements in GDP, the growth bar chart, Fig. 2.5, concentrates the eye on the quarter-by-quarter differences. Here you can see the 10 recessions very clearly as the periods in which the growth bars dangle downward. Remember that it is only a panel of economists at the National Bureau of Economic Research who have the official function of selecting the quarters in which the economy was in recession. Feel free to question their judgments. Were there really two separate back-to-back recessions in early 1980s? Did they miss the onset of the 2001 recession by a quarter?

The recessions jump out at you from the bar chart Fig. 2.5, but what else can you see? Can you see the rather high volatility of GDP growth from quarter to quarter? This should alert you to the fact that knowing GDP growth in one quarter cannot tell you much about GDP growth the next quarter. We will come back to this later. Also take a look at growth in the Kennedy/Johnson expansion in the 1960s compared with the Bush/Clinton expansion of the 1990s. What differences do you notice? There are two. The Kennedy/Johnson bars are both generally higher and also more volatile. We already learned from the first display, Fig. 2.4, that growth was greater before 1970 than after, so that's not news, and this fact is much more clear in the first display than the second. But that first long-run display does not tell

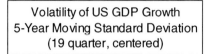

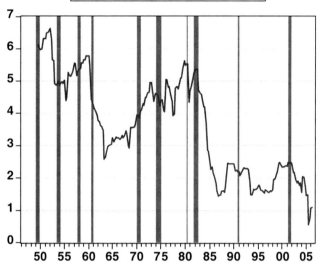

Fig. 2.7 Volatility of GDP growth

us anything about the quarter-to-quarter variability. If you look real close you can
see the recessions in the long-term display Fig. 2.4, but the bar chart Fig. 2.5 makes
the recessions very apparent.

A problem with the growth bar chart, Fig. 2.5, is that GDP is very wiggly. All
those wiggles can be pretty distracting. The long-term display, Fig. 2.4, goes too
far in eliminating almost all the wiggles. A good way to eliminate much of the
variability but to retain some as well is to display a moving average of GDP growth.
A three quarter centered moving average is the average of the current, preceding,
and following quarter's growth number:

$$\text{Moving Average} = (\text{Growth}(-1) + \text{Growth} + \text{Growth}(+1))/3$$

Figure 2.6 illustrates a 3-year (11 quarter) centered moving average of GDP growth.
Here the magnitude of the difference between the 1960s and the 1990s is clear (one
or two percentage points), while the long-term display in Fig. 2.4 tells us nothing of the magnitude. If you need to know the magnitude, the choice of picture is
obvious.

Next, what about volatility? If you look hard at the corridor of growth, Fig. 2.4,
you can see that the US economy was more prone to be at the edges of the corridor
in the 1970s than the 1990s. That's because the more recent recessions have been
much less severe, a point that is apparent in the dangling down bars in Fig. 2.5. It

is very interesting that the smoothed growth rates in Fig. 2.6 tell a different story. The dips in the 1970s were about as deep as the dips in the 1990s but pulling the three-year averages down to about 1.5% per year. It was the double-dip recession of the early 1980s that really knocked down the three-year average growth.

Homework problem: Explain why Fig. 2.5 suggests that recessions are getting milder but Fig. 2.6 suggests there has been little change (or disagree with this conclusion.)

To do better on volatility, we need a numerical measure of volatility. I suggest the standard deviation. The standard deviation is a measure of dispersion of a group of numbers. If the numbers form a bell-shaped normal distribution, then 67% of the numbers are within one standard deviation of the mean, while 95% are within two standard deviations. That is all we need to know for now.

Figure 2.7 illustrates the standard deviation of the GDP growth numbers taken 5 years at a time, rolling that 5-year window over the data. Here you can see the sharp drop in volatility in the early 1980s, but there was a similar drop in the early 1960s.

This decline in volatility is potentially important for business decision-making and for forecasting. Can we expect this stability to continue, or get even better? This matters a lot for inventory policies. Lean inventories and low ratios of inventories to sales work fine in a stable economy, but not well in a volatile one. New Economy advocates in the mid 1990s were promising steady growth forever and indeed there was a significant decline in volatility, which can be seen in Fig. 2.7. But for Cisco in 1999, inventories that were planned to be "just-in-time" turned out "way too early" when sales of routers and servers dropped dramatically and inventories built up.

GDP volatility bumped up again with the onset of the recession of 2001, but subsequently volatility has fallen to an all-time low standard deviation of 1.0. How small is that standard deviation of 1.0? If GDP growth is approximately normal with a mean of 3 and a standard deviation of 2, there is a 7% chance of a negative, but with a mean of 3 and a standard deviation of only 1, the chances of a negative are only about 0.1% (1 in 1000). Are recessions a thing of the past? We need to answer this important question.

Now I ask you to stop looking at these four graphs, and try to remember each of them.

- Which picture is the most memorable?

  ○ You will want to include that one in any presentation

Now you can look at them again and answer two more questions:

- Which picture conveys most clearly the most amount of information?

  ○ You may want to include that one as well since you will be there to explain it.

- Which picture coveys information not conveyed by any other picture?

  ○ If it important to make this point, you will need to include this display.

Make a note of this important point: There are many ways to display the same data, and each can send a different message. *Work hard to find a display that sends the message you intend.*

2.2.3 How Much Is $10 Trillion? Does Dividing by Employment Help?

US GDP is currently about $10 trillion. You really have no idea how much is $10 trillion, do you? It is just a number with a bunch of zeroes. *A number has meaning only when we can compare it with something familiar. If you are going to use numbers to persuade, be sure that your audience has a basis for comparison.* Dividing GDP by the number of workers does the trick quite nicely. That $10 Trillion translates into $70,000 per worker. Now you have a scale of reference. Compare your annual earnings with $70,000. How are you doing? Are you producing more than the average worker?

Real GDP per worker is displayed in Fig. 2.8, again with a logarithmic scale. Back in the early 1950s, it was only $30,000 per worker. Now it is $70,000. We are producing more than twice as much per worker as we did a half-century ago! Figure 2.8 conveys a very different message than the constant rate of growth of Real GDP equal to 3.45% illustrated in Fig. 2.4. Here, in Fig. 2.8, we have a high growth of Real GDP per worker until about 1970s, then slow growth between 1970 and 1980, then what looks like a new trend line after 1980. This is an extremely important fact for thinking about the future.

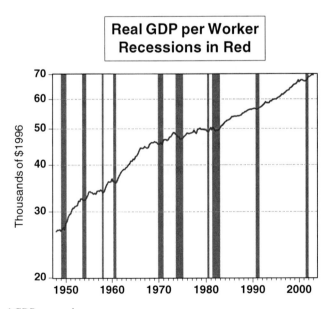

Fig. 2.8 Real GDP per worker

Appendix: The Index Number Problem and Chain Indexes

Suppose that you checked out of a grocery store in January 2000 with $100 worth of groceries. If a year later in 2001 you check out with $117 worth of merchandise, did you get more stuff? Was your shopping basket more full? Not necessarily. Maybe you have the same stuff, and it just cost more a year later. How are we going to figure out if you have more stuff in 2001? Specifically, consider the following details about prices and volumes in the 2000 and 2001 baskets:

Shopping Baskets in 2000 and 2001

	2000			2001		
	Number	Price	Value	Number	Price	Value
Apples	60	1	60	45	1.4	63
Oranges	40	1	40	60	0.9	54
Total			100			117

In 2000, you bought 60 apples and 40 oranges, each at the price of $1. In 2001, the price of apples rose quite a bit and the price of oranges fell. You wisely decided to buy more oranges but fewer apples. You spent more in 2001, but I am not so sure if you bought more. Sure, you have more oranges but you also have fewer apples. How can we compare apples to oranges? I am not so sure but I have an idea. I can compute what it would cost to buy those goods in 2001 if the prices were the same as 2000. That is using constant prices to value the basket. That is a good way to compute the real value of the goods, and that is exactly how real GDP is computed. The problem with the calculation is it depends on which prices you select. If you use 2001 prices it may look like there is more stuff in the basket in 2001, but if you use 2000 prices it may appear to be the opposite. Indeed, that is what happens here:

Values in "Constant Dollars"

	$2000		$2001	
	2000	2001	2000	2001
Apples	60	45	84	63
Oranges	40	60	36	54
Total	100	105	120	117
Change		5%		−3%

First use the year 2000 prices to value the baskets. Those 45 apples and 60 oranges that you bought in 2001 would have cost $105 in 2000, compared with only $100 for the 60 apples and 40 oranges in 2000. Thus you have 5% more "stuff" in your basket in 2001. Next do the same calculation with year 2001 prices. Those 60 apples and 40 oranges that you bought in 2001 would have cost $120 in 2000. That compares with the $117 value of what you bought in 2001. Thus you have 3% less in your basket in 2001. So which is it? Is the 2001 basket fuller than the 2002 basket, or the other way around??

Boy that seems alarming. Never mind. It is a cooked up example with wild swings in prices and quantities. Real movements in prices and quantities make the choice of base year a whole lot less important, and in any case government statisticians work hard devising "chained" or compromise measures. The "chain" compromise between the 5% increase in the basket using intial prices and the -3% reduction using final prices is found by multiplying the two and taking the square root: $1 - ((1 + .05)^*(1 - .03))^{1/2} = 0.9\%$. Forty five apples and 60 oranges is 0.9% "more" than 60 applies and 40 oranges.

This chain compromise makes the problem even less. Especially for our purpose of finding out if the US economy is in recession or not, this measurement issue is virtually irrelevant.

Appendix: The Seasonal in GDP Is Very Large

We need to take a look at the seasonal patterns of GDP growth since they tell an alarming story. The annualized rates of growth of GDP (nominal not real) from 1946 to 2001 are displayed separately for each quarter in Fig. 2.9. There are dramatic

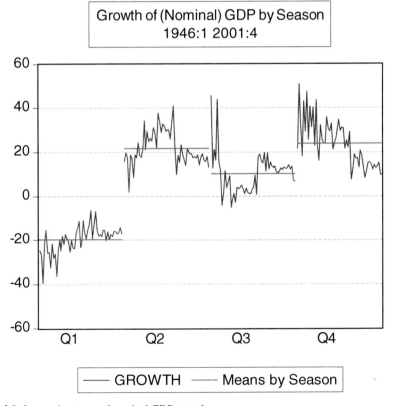

Fig. 2.9 Seasonal patterns of nominal GDP growth

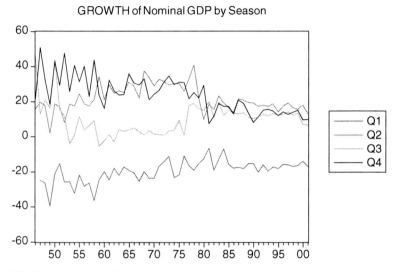

Fig. 2.10 Growth of nominal by season

differences among the quarters! Though on average, nominal GDP has grown at the rate of 9.2%, the January–March first-quarter production has been down compared with the fourth quarter at the annualized rate of about –20%! After working so hard to get those gifts ready for the holiday, Santa and his elves huddle around

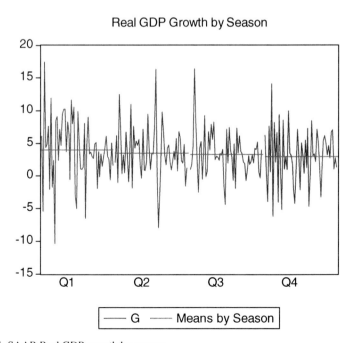

Fig. 2.11 SAAR Real GDP growth by season

the fireplaces in the winter and do not get much done. But the springtime brings a renewal and a complete return to normal, providing a +22% rate of growth. The summer offers normal growth (10%) compared with the Spring, and then that last quarter is when we get the most growth, averaging 24% compared with the Fall.

Note the apparent change in the seasonal pattern over time. You can see this best in Fig. 2.10. The seasonal pattern stabilizes after 1980 with only a first quarter effect, and an effect that is relatively mild. From 1960 to 1980, we had strong fourth and second quarter growth, little growth in the third and a large negative in the first. Before 1960, the fourth quarter was exceptionally strong. I am wondering how the Department of Commerce does their seasonal adjustment. I hope they are not using that old data.

Don't worry. If the Commerce Department were not aware of the changing seasonal, then their seasonally adjusted data would have one seasonal pattern for part of the data and an offsetting pattern for the rest. That isn't the case, as you can see in Fig. 2.11.

Chapter 3
The Components of GDP: C + I + G + X − M

If you want to be an economist, or act like one, you have to be able to say quickly:

C plus I plus G plus X minus M.

That's another way we say GDP.

3.1 How Might GDP Be Measured?

As we learned in the previous chapter, GDP is the market value of goods and services produced during a particular time period in a particular geographic area. Now that we know how GDP is defined, we have to think about how it might be measured. Suppose you were hired to devise a way to measure the value of goods and services produced in the United States in 2006. Could you do it? It is a mind-boggling task that was tackled in earnest in the 1930s by the Department of Commerce and the National Bureau of Economic Research under the leadership of Simon Kuznets, who was awarded the Nobel Prize in 1971 *"for his empirically founded interpretation of economic growth which has led to new and deepened insight into the economic and social structure and the process of development."*

To get you thinking about measuring GDP, start with a simpler problem: how would you measure the market value of the goods and services that you personally produced last year? If you are an attorney, your legal earnings are the market value of the legal services that you produced. Did you make some money some other way? Do not count selling that old car of yours. You did not produce that. When you sell that car, record the transaction as a change in the way you hold your assets: cash not car. That is not income. Its merely a change in the way you hold your wealth. You do need to count the honorarium you earned for giving a speech. Include also the rent that you received for that second home that you own. Do not forget your primary home. It is producing housing services too. Better make a guess of the "market value" of the housing services afforded by the home you own. Consider that "renting to yourself" and include that rent as current production. Now you have

E. E. Leamer, *Macroeconomic Patterns and Stories: A Guide for MBAs.*
© Springer-Verlag Berlin Heidelberg 2009

Table 3.1 Income and employee compensation by sector, 2005

National income without capital consumption adjustment (BEA Table 6.1)
Compensation of Employees (BEA Table 6.2)

	Income $b		Compensation $b		C/I
TOTAL	10,918	100.0%	7,030	100.0%	64%
Domestic industries	10,886	99.7%	7,037	100.1%	65%
Private industries	9,575	87.7%	5,695	81.0%	59%
Agriculture, forestry, fishing, and hunting	88	0.8%	42	0.6%	48%
Mining	159	1.5%	50	0.7%	32%
Utilities	177	1.6%	55	0.8%	31%
Construction	604	5.5%	391	5.6%	65%
Manufacturing	1,366	12.5%	933	13.3%	68%
Durable goods	746	6.8%	613	8.7%	82%
Nondurable goods	620	5.7%	320	4.6%	52%
Wholesale trade	689	6.3%	389	5.5%	56%
Retail trade	825	7.6%	468	6.7%	57%
Transportation and warehousing	306	2.8%	225	3.2%	73%
Information	417	3.8%	240	3.4%	58%
Finance, insurance, real estate, rental, and leasing	1,833	16.8%	640	9.1%	35%
Professional and business services[a]	1,510	13.8%	1,020	14.5%	68%
Educational services, health care, and social assistance	938	8.6%	766	10.9%	82%
Arts, entertainment, recreation, accommodation, and food services	394	3.6%	277	3.9%	70%
Other services, except government	268	2.5%	199	2.8%	74%
Government	1,311	12.0%	1,342	19.1%	102%
Rest of the world	32	0.3%	−6	−0.1%	−20%

Note: Estimates in this table are based on the 1997 North American Industry Classification System (NAICS)
[a]Consists of professional, scientific, and technical services; management of companies and enterprises; and administrative and waste management services

an accounting system for defining your production. There is a line for legal services, and a line for public speaking, and a line for rental income.

3.1.1 National Income and Employee Compensation

Having solved the task of measuring your contribution to GDP, it will be a lot easier to devise an accounting system for a country's GDP. There could be a line for legal services, and a line for public speaking and a line for the rental value of the housing stock, a line for building automobiles and a line for selling at a retail store, and so on and so on. The natural categories are paid productive activities. Table 3.1 is prepared by the BEA along these lines. This table includes "Income" and also "Compensation" of Employees. Total "National Income" is not the same as GDP, but pretty close. Details are in an Appendix.

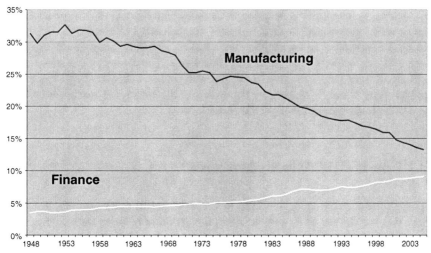

Fig. 3.1 Manufacturing and FIRE employee compensation shares of total

Take a look at Table 3.1 and see if there is anything that surprises you. I am distressed though not surprised that only 12.5% of National Income is earned in Manufacturing. But I am astonished that 16.8% is "burned" in FIRE (finance, insurance, and real estate). That seems like a distressingly small fraction in manufacturing where they actually make stuff, and a surprisingly large fraction in FIRE where they just fill out the paperwork. Not so fast. Somewhere in this table, they have buried the "earnings" of owners of their own homes as well as apartments and office buildings. Can you see those earnings anywhere in Table 3.1? They are in FIRE. According to another BEA table, consumers in 2005 "bought" $1,304 billion worth of housing services, out-of-pocket rent and also the rental value of owner-occupied housing. That leaves for finance as we know it only $528 billion, which is the more sensible 4.8% of National Income.[1] **ALERT: National Income Accounting is a complex business with pitfalls galore for anyone trying to make sense of these data.**

Though perhaps not so dramatic as the income numbers in Table 3.1, the compensation figures do indicate that a surprising large 9.1% of compensation was earned in FIRE in 2005. Figure 3.1 displays the fractions of compensation in manufacturing and FIRE over time. Back in the 1950s, over 30% of compensation orginiated in manufacturing and only 4% in FIRE. With the steady erosion of manufacturing and the steady rise of FIRE, Fig. 3.1 will soon be an ominous X, with FIRE crossing manufacturing. Is that the future? We would not make anything anymore, but instead will celebrate our genius in a gigantic parasitic bonFIRE?[2]

---

[1] Can you figure out why compensation in FIRE was $640 billion but income net of residential housing was $528 billion?

[2] But here is another pitfall: when manufacturing firms outsource finance and various business services to other domestic businesses, it looks as though the nature of jobs is changing when it is only

The last column of Table 3.1, which has the employee compensation fraction of income, is also worth discussing. Remember that the rest of income accrues to owners. For government, with no owners, compensation of employees is 102% of income. At the other end are mining and utilities, with compensation shares of 32% and 31% respectively. You know why, don't you? The capital in the mines and in utilities is very large compared with the workforces. Likewise FIRE has an employee share of only 35% because the owners of the homes and apartment buildings and offices take a large chunk of the rental income.

3.2 How Is GDP Actually Measured?

Though the accounting system used in Table 3.1 seems quite sensible, it isn't the way that the Bureau of Economic Analysis and other national statistical agencies routinely organize the GDP data. It was James Meade and Sir Richard Stone, working for the British Central Statistical Office in the early 1940s, who suggested the four subaccounts that are now the norm.[3] These are households, businesses, governments, and the "rest-of-the-world." Sir Richard Stone, like Kuznets before him, won the Nobel Prize in 1984 *"for having made fundamental contributions to the development of systems of national accounts and hence greatly improved the basis for empirical economic analysis."* James Meade also won the Nobel prize, in 1977, but shared it with Bertil Ohlin, not for national income accounting but *"for their pathbreaking contribution to the theory of international trade and international capital movements."*

The National Income Accounts designed by Meade and Stone were chosen because of data availability. Most of the data are collected by governments at tax time when individuals file personal income taxes and businesses file sales tax receipts. This pushes the government accounts toward what is now the standard, displayed in Table 3.2. This accounting system takes a "direction of sales" approach to measuring GDP. GDP is the sum of the sales to consumers plus the sales to business plus the sales to government. That's a good idea, but be a little careful. There are two problems.

First we don't want to double count. When a textile firm makes cloth and sells it to an apparel manufacturer who eventually sells the cloth to consumers as shirts and blouses, we don't want to count the value of the cloth twice, since it was only produced once. If the cloth isn't sold yet, count it as an increase in business inventories, and otherwise count as the sales to businesses only those items that are retained by businesses – thus investment in equipment and software and structures.[4]

---

the way that business is organized. Some of that decline in manufacturing share of compensation is due to outsourcing.

[3] John W. Kendrick, Economic Accounts and Their Uses, New York: McGraw Hill, 1972, pp. 17–18.

[4] But, a very clever student in my class, asked: "Doesn't this treatment of equipment create a double-counting problem, too. You count as GDP the equipment when it is made and again when the equipment is operated to produce consumer goods." What a great question. This is the very best

Table 3.2 US gross domestic product, 2002
[Billions of dollars]

Line		$Billions	Percent (%)
1	**Gross domestic product**	**10446.2**	**100**
2	**Personal consumption expenditures**	**7303.7**	**69.9**
3	Durable goods	871.9	8.3
4	Nondurable goods	2115	20.2
5	Services	4316.8	41.3
6	**Gross private domestic investment**	**1593.2**	**15.3**
7	Fixed investment	1589.3	15.2
8	Nonresidential	1117.4	10.7
9	Structures	269.3	2.6
10	Equipment and software	848.1	8.1
11	Residential	471.9	4.5
12	Change in private inventories	3.9	0.0
13	**Net exports of goods and services**	**− 423.6**	**− 4.1**
14	Exports	1014.9	9.7
15	Goods	703.6	6.7
16	Services	311.3	3.0
17	Imports	1438.5	13.8
18	Goods	1192.1	11.4
19	Services	246.4	2.4
20	**Government consumption expenditures and gross investment**	**1972.9**	**18.9**
21	Federal	693.7	6.6
22	National defense	447.4	4.3
23	Nondefense	246.3	2.4
24	State and local	1279.2	12.2

Bureau of Economic Analysis Table 1.1.
http://www.bea.gov/bea/dn/nipaweb/TableViewFixed.asp#Mid

There is another problem with the final sales approach to measuring GDP – some of what was sold here was made abroad and some of what was made here was shipped abroad. We need to subtract imports and add exports.

---

experience an educator can have – a question with no off-the-shelf answer, or at least not off-my-shelf. What's your answer to this question? After I thought about the answer, here was my reply. (What do you think of my answer?) Suppose the equipment can produce 100 shirts at the touch of a button, using no electricity and no labor except that effortless touch. Then the equipment is really just a box full of 100 shirts. It is the same as inventory. Since it is the same as inventory, we should be booking the product only when the "equipment" is produced, not again when the shirts are produced. Thus this clever student seems right – there does seem to be a double-counting problem. When the shirts are sold there should be an offsetting entry that represents the drawdown of the "inventory" built into that equipment. But before we claim to have uncovered a fundamental problem with the National Income Accounts, we would better think long and hard about it. A lot of very smart people have spent a lot of time thinking about these kinds of issues. Surely someone noticed the double counting problem before us. Actually, the solution to this puzzle was discussed in the previous chapter. There is an offset to GDP when the equipment is operated. Can you recall what that was? If you need to, go to the footnote.

Thus the way economists recite the letters is "**C plus I plus G plus X minus M**."
Households: "C" stands for goods sold to consumers.

Businesses: "I" stands for investment, including the equipment and software, offices, factories, homes, apartments, and inventories.

Government: "G" refers to the sales to federal and state and local governments.

Rest-of-World: "X" refers to the sales to foreigners (exports) and "M" to the imports.

$$GDP = C + I + G + X - M$$

3.3 How Big Are the Components: C, I, G, X − M?

From Table 3.2 you can see that Consumption in 2002 was 70% of GDP, Investment was 15%, sales to the government were 19%, and net exports were −4.1% of GDP. These shares of GDP vary over time as can be seen in Fig. 3.2. The consumption share of GDP has been on the rise since the 1970s. Since the shares have to add to one, the increasing consumption share must be offset by declining the shares of something else. Which components? Take a look. It is G for government and X − M for exports minus imports.

Wait a minute, I thought the government is on the backs of the people. How can G be a declining fraction of GDP? The answer is that G is government "*production*". G does not include transfers; a transfer occurs when the government takes your tax contributions and merely shuffles the money off to someone else, not for work performed but only because the recipient is worthy. When the government shuffles your tax contribution to a government employee, that is production. That is part of GDP. Likewise, all those smart bombs that we have been dropping on Afganistan and Iraq are part of G. But the tax contribution that I make that is passed on to your elderly parents in the form of Social Security is a transfer and not part of GDP. Bottom line: G is mostly the salaries of government employees.

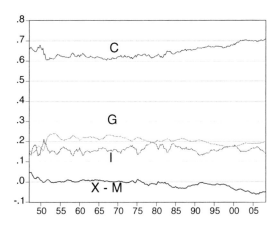

Fig. 3.2 Shares of GDP

As for the decline in X − M as a share of GDP, we are going to need to come back to that too. Like the White Rabbit in Alice's Adventures in Wonderland, we need now to hurry on: "Oh dear! Oh dear! I shall be too late!"

3.3.1 Which Are the Most Volatile Components of GDP?

One of our goals is to understand what causes the recessions when real GDP falls. If we get that understanding, we should be able better to predict when the next recession will occur. Figure 3.2, which illustrates the shares of GDP, is a good place to begin. Here you can see which is the largest GDP share. It is consumption, C. The media quite commonly and accurately report that consumption spending is 2/3rds of GDP, thus suggesting that we should look to the consumers as the driver of the business cycle. But a locomotive makes up only about 1/500th of a modern freight train, yet it is still the driver.

The driver of the recession is not necessarily the largest share; more likely it is the most volatile. During a recession, there are some components of GDP that decline more sharply than the others. These are the ones that have the greatest volatility. These are likely the drivers. Figure 3.2 suggests pretty clear which component is the driver. It is not consumption; the investment. As a share of GDP, investment is the component that varies the most. Investment is a rising share of GDP when investment spending is driving the growth; it is a falling share of GDP when investment spending is slowing the growth.

Do not be too quick to draw conclusions here. This is just a start. Investment includes spending on new homes and remodeling. Homes could be the driver. It could also be that small changes in consumption spending C could be enormously amplified by swings in business investment. Thus we would see the volatility in investment I even though the driver was C, consumption. We will return to this question, I promise. But in the meantime, maybe you should take a look at Fig. 3.3, which has the shares of GDP for the components of investment, plus consumer durables (cars and appliances), which is a form of consumer investment. Generally, the peaks in these figures occur near the ends of expansions and the troughs sometime after the beginning of the expansions. What can you see in these figures? Can you see:

- The building boom in business structures in 1980–1982 and the equipment and software boom in 1996–2000.
- The mildness of the rise in consumer durables and homes in the 1990s expansion compared with earlier expansions.
- The early peaks in consumer durables and homes compared with the peaks in business spending, except for the year 2000 bust in equipment and software.

Figure 3.3 displays most of the volatile components of GDP, but there is one other important component – inventories. The I in $C + I + G + X − M$ is composed

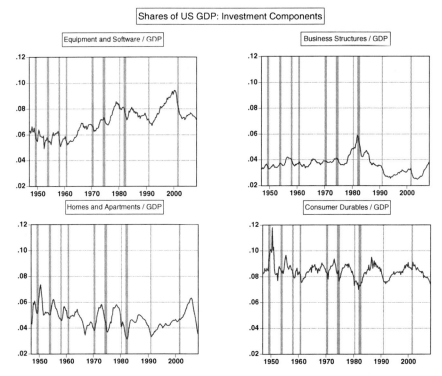

Fig. 3.3 Shares of GDP, recessions shaded

of equipment and software, structures, residences, and *the change in inventories*. Pause a moment and reflect on those last several words. It is not the inventory *level* that is a component of GDP: It is the *change in the level* of inventories. When inventories are increasing, someone had to make the stuff: That's GDP. When inventories are falling, some of the sales are satisfied from inventory, not from the current production. To estimate production from sales data, you thus have to add the *change* in inventories to the sales: Production = Sales + Change in Inventory.

This gets really confusing when we talk about the *growth* of GDP, and virtually incomprehensible when we discuss a *change in the growth* of GDP. Let us see if we can understand it. Remember that it is the *change* in inventories that contributes to GDP. What about the growth of GDP? For GDP to increase because of inventory, we would need a bigger change in inventories. That is a change in the change.

Wow, my head is already hurting, but it gets worse.

Next think about how inventories may have contributed to a fall in GDP growth from 3 to 2%. That is a change in the growth of GDP. For inventories, that is a change in the change of the change. Wow, that seems hopelessly confusing. Fortunately, the Bureau of Economic Analysis does the hard work and reports a number that is the

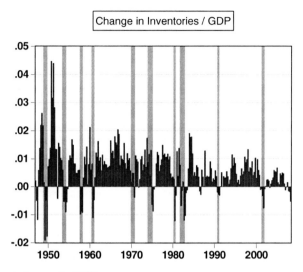

Fig. 3.4 Change in inventories/GDP

contribution of inventories to GDP and to GDP growth. Maybe it is best just to work with those numbers.

The change in inventories as a fraction of GDP is charted in Fig. 3.4. The average is only 0.6% but inventory swings have contributed substantially to the change

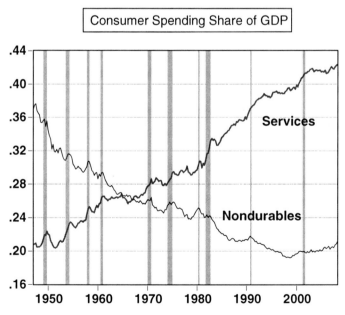

Fig. 3.5 Consumer services and nondurables, services shaded

Table 3.3 Components of services

Components of Consumer Services: 2003		
$ Billions		
$ 4,610	100.0%	**Services**
$ 1,122	24.3%	Nonfarm dwellings: Space rent for owner-occupied dwellings and rent for tenant-occupied dwellings
$ 12	0.3%	Rental value of farm dwellings
$ 785	17.0%	Motor vehicle repair, rental, and other services; other repair services; other purchased intercity transportation; legal and funeral services; barbershops, beauty parlors, and health clubs; nursing homes; laundries; employment agency fees; accounting
$ 578	12.5%	Physicians, home health care, medical laboratories, eye examinations, all other professional medical services
$ 214	4.6%	Private nursery schools, elementary and secondary schools, day care, welfare activities, political organizations, foundations, and trade unions and professional associations
$ 195	4.2%	Financial services furnished without payment by banks, other depository institutions, and investment companies
$ 247	5.4%	Brokerage charges and investment counseling, bank service charges, intercity transportation except "other," and private higher education
$ 19	0.4%	Domestic service
$ 250	5.4%	Public education and hospitals, water and other sanitary services, and lotteries
$ 1,066	23.1%	Insurance, private hospitals, religious activities, cable TV, electricity, natural gas, telephone, and local transport
$ (8)	−0.2%	Foreign travel by U.S. residents ($79.2 billion) less expenditures in the United States by non residents ($86.7 billion)
$ 129	2.8%	Other services: Motor vehicle leasing; parimutuel net receipts; other housing except hotels and motels; bridge, etc. tolls; other household operation except repairs and insurance; travel and entertainment card fees; stenographic and reproduction services

Source: Survey of Current Business
http://www.bea.gov/bea/ARTICLES/2004/11November/1104NIPAMeth.pdf

in GDP, especially in the 1950s. And inventory declines are a feature of every recession.

That leaves only services and nondurables depicted in Fig. 3.5. This figure has two features that deserve comment. First, consumer spending neither on nondurables nor on services seems to contribute much to the recessions. Second, spending on nondurables is steadily declining, which is more than offset by the rise in services, which now makes up about 42% of GDP.

Do you wonder what exactly is in that service category? Table 3.3 from the BEA Website offers an answer. Out of the $4.6 billion of consumer services in 2003, 24% was the rental value of housing, and 12.5% for direct payments for health services, and about 10% for financial services. The rest is a very mixed bag. Take a look and see if you can find your favorite services.

Appendix: GDP and National Income

Relation of gross domestic product, gross national product, net national product, national income, and personal income

	$ Billions
Gross domestic product	**12,456**
Plus: Income receipts from the rest of the world	513
Less: Income payments to the rest of the world	482
Equals: Gross national product	**12,488**
Less: Consumption of fixed capital	1,605
Equals: Net national product	**10,883**
Less: Statistical discrepancy	71
Equals: National income	**10,812**
Less: Corporate profits with inventory valuation and capital consumption adjustments	1,331
Plus: Personal income receipts on assets	1,519
Equals: Personal income	**10,239**

Source: Bureau of Economic Analysis

Appendix: Answer to Footnote Question

It is depreciation. Gross Domestic Product does suffer this double counting problem but it is fully corrected by subtracting depreciation and maintenance and repair of existing equipment to create Net National Product. Homework problem: What about housing? Do the government statisticians allow for depreciation of the housing stock when they compute Net National Product?

Appendix: A Better Way to Treat Imports and Exports

Here is a question that you might imagine would be answered by our GDP accounts: "What was the value of Consumer goods and services produced last year?" Sorry, cannot answer that one. The consumption component of GDP, C, tells us if we *sold* a lot of consumer goods and services, but *production* is different. Some of what was sold was produced elsewhere − imports. In addition, we produced consumer goods here that were shipped to foreigners − exports. So to C we need to add the consumer goods and services that were exported and we need to subtract the consumer goods and services that were imported. But we do not have X and M broken down by product. We only have the total exports and total imports.

It would be much better if X and M were allocated separately to C and I and G, creating an accounting system that includes the domestic production of each of the components of GDP. It would look like this:

	Domestic sales (a)	Domestic sales from foreign sources = imports (b)	Foreign sales = exports (c)	Domestic production $(a) - (b) + (c)$
Consumption goods				
Investment goods				
Government				

The problem with the accounts as currently arranged is that movements in C or I or G need not correspond with the movement in the domestic production. That can easily lead policy makers astray. Suppose for the sake of argument that US manufacturers make machinery to be sold to other businesses, but make no consumer items at all. (That is not so far off, by the way.) Then all of the consumer spending C would come from imports M. In that case, changes in the spending of consumers C would have no effect at all on US GDP, since that spending would be exactly offset by the changes in imports M. If you did not understand what was happening, you might conclude that tax reductions that stimulate consumer spending C would increase US GDP when all they do is to increase the demand for foreign goods M, keeping C-M constant. While that stimulus to foreign production might eventually wash back on US shores in the form of higher sales of US-made business equipment, in the meantime we would be waiting impatiently for the effect of a tax cut to show up.

Chapter 4
Employment

After GDP, employment is the most important macro-economic variable. GDP measures what we are producing. Employment measures the number doing the work. Like GDP, employment moves up and down with the business cycle. Unlike GDP, the employment numbers help to predict where the economy is headed. There is a good reason for this. An employment contract is a forecast. When a firm decides to hire or fire, that is a forecast of good times or bad times ahead; it is not a perfect forecast, but often it is a pretty good one.

Neither GDP nor employment are easily defined or easily measured. Corresponding to each component of GDP, people are making the products or providing the services. Those are the folks who are counted as working. But GDP is what *some* of us produce. Many of the rest of us are working hard too. Some of us produce goods and services that are missed by the government statisticians, such as childcare and work around the home. Some of us are working hard at school. The human capital that we are producing is not included in GDP, though it should be. A few of us are gainfully employed as trophy husbands for rich and powerful women. Those critical services are not part of the recorded GDP either. Some of us are too young or too old or too ill to hold jobs. What remains are those who are not working, some looking for work and others living off savings, either their own or their parents.

Are you getting the point: employment status is a pretty complicated question.

The US government collects a vast amount of information about working and not-working Americans. We do not need to know about all the details, but we need to acquaint ourselves with the surveys used to compile the employment data on which we will rely heavily to track the ups and downs of the economy.

4.1 Labor Market Surveys

The Bureau of Labor Statistics together with counterparts at the State level conduct a number of ongoing surveys of households and establishments to determine how many people are working, and who is doing what task. Here is the current list:

QCEW   Quarterly Census of Employment and Wages
CES   Current Employment Statistics
OES   Occupational Employment Statistics
CPS   Current Population Survey
LAUS   Local Area Unemployment Statistics
MLS   Mass Layoff Statistics
JOLTS   Job Openings and Labor Turnover Survey

Some details about these seven surveys can be found in Table 4.1 at the end of this chapter, but for our purposes we need only to focus on the two surveys that are most widely cited in the media – the monthly survey of households that is used to determine the unemployment rate (CPS: Current Population Survey) and the monthly survey of establishments that is used to determine the number of payroll jobs (CES: Current Employment Statistics). We will also discuss the widely cited weekly figure on Initial Jobless Claims that is provided by the Department of Labor.

4.1.1 CES: Current Employment Statistics

The CES is a monthly survey of over 200,000 *nonfarm establishments* drawn from a "universe" of 8 million establishments determined by the Quarterly Census of Employment and Wages, which covers all employers' subject to the state unemployment laws. This includes 98% of the wage and salary workers, but notably excludes individual entrepreneurs and consultants as well as your gardener and your maid.

The CES collects seven data series for each industry:

1. All employees
2. Female employees
3. Production workers (PW)
4. Average weekly hours of PW
5. Average hourly earnings of PW
6. Average weekly earnings of PW
7. Average overtime hours of PW

Keep in mind that the workers with more than one job are counted more than once, and understand that the geographic reporting is by location of work and not by location of residence. When you see payroll jobs in San Jose plummeting, many of those jobs were held by folks who were commuters and did not reside in high-priced San Jose. Some of these folks who lost a job still had another one. And some may have lost more than one job.

4.1.1.1 250,000 was the Norm in the 1990s, Lately It's Been 190,000

The monthly change in payroll jobs is reported with large headlines in the business section of every newspaper in this country. You need to know what is a big number

Table 4.1 Comparison of labor force programs

	QCEW	CES	OES	CPS	LAUS	MLS	JOLTS
Data collected by	States and BLS	States and BLS	States and BLS ROs	Census Bureau	Input data from CPS, CES, & UI	States	BLS
Data collected from	Establishments	Establishments	Establishments	Households	Input data from CPS, CES, & UI	Establishments, and input from QCEW & UI	Establishments
Estimate or universe count?	Universe	Estimate	Estimate	Estimate	Estimate	Universe	Estimate
Frequency of collection	Quarterly for monthly data	Monthly	Semi-annually	Monthly	Monthly	Monthly and quarterly	Monthly
Frequency of publication	Quarterly & annually	Monthly	Semi-annually	Monthly	Monthly	Monthly and quarterly	Monthly
Major data types published	Total UI covered employment and wages	Nonfarm employment, hours, hourly earnings by industry	Occupational employment and wages by industry	Civilian labor force, employment, unemployment, unemployment rate	Civilian labor force, employment, unemployment, unemployment rate	Number of layoff events and affected workers involving 50+ separations	Nonfarm job openings, hires, total separations (quits, layoffs, & discharges and other separations)
Geographic detail (smallest to largest)	County, MSAs, State, USA	Selected MSAs, State, USA	MSAs, State, USA	USA only	Cities/towns of 25,000+, County, LMA, MSA, State	County, MSA, State, Census Division & Region, USA	Census Region, USA
Demographic detail	None	Female employees until – June 2005	None	Extensive detail	None	Gender, age, race/ethnicity	None
Benchmarked?	No, QCEW is a benchmark	Yes, to QCEW	Yes, to QCEW	No	Yes, to CPS annual averages	No	Yes, to CES employment
Major uses	Sample frame and benchmark	Economic indicator	Planning, training and education programs	Economic indicator	Economic indicator, and to allocate Federal funds	Economic indicator, and to allocate Federal funds	Economic indicator
Time from reference week to publication	6 months or more	USA 3 weeks States 5 weeks MSAs 7 weeks	10 months	3 weeks	States 5 weeks Areas 7 weeks	6 weeks	4–6 weeks after reference month

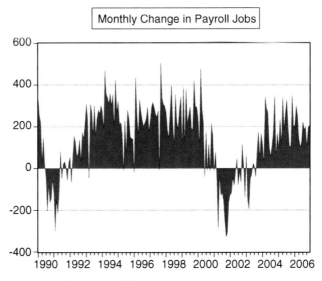

Fig. 4.1 Change in payroll jobs in the 1990s: bar chart

and what is a small number? Think 200,000. Figure 4.1 is a bar chart showing the ups and downs of the payroll numbers since 1990. You can see two recessions very clearly here – that is when the bars dangle down. You can also see that, ignoring the negatives, it looks like payroll jobs have been increasing at the rate of about 200,000 per month. Just to confirm, Fig. 4.2 is a smoothed version of Fig. 4.1, displaying the 12-month moving average of the monthly change in payroll jobs. Here you can see the recovery in the early 1990s, with job increases exceeding 300,000 per month. In

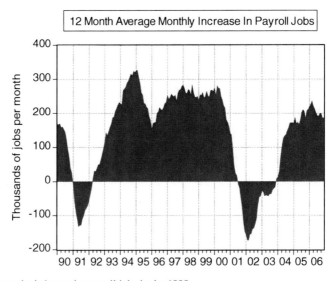

Fig. 4.2 Smoothed change in payroll jobs in the 1990s

Fig. 4.2, you can see the weak period in 1995, followed by four and a half years of powerful job growth at the rate of about 250,000 per month. In the aftermath of that 2001 recession, job growth is now around 190,000 a month. What's happening to those other 60,000?

4.1.1.2 One Monthly Payroll Number Does Not a Trend Make: It Takes Three

An increase in payroll jobs around 200,000 in a month is typical. What is not typical? What is news? Should we jump down with glee if we get 300,000, or is that pretty normal too? This could be a good homework question: Define what is news? And determine when the payroll number is "newsworthy." Here is my answer. (It is not the only one.) News is something that substantially changes the forecast. Using the data from 1990 to form a prediction of next month's change in payroll jobs, I have discovered that one month of data alone is not enough. The best prediction depends on the average of three months data. Figure 4.3 is a scatter diagram comparing the average change in the payroll jobs in the previous three months, with the change in the current month. The figure also has a best-fitting curve in the midst of all these data points. One thing that is remarkable about this curve is that below 200 thousand there is a one-for-one relationship between the three-month average and next month's value, but the curve flattens out above 200 thousand. In other words, overheating is not something to worry about. *Cold streaks continue, but hot streaks do not.*

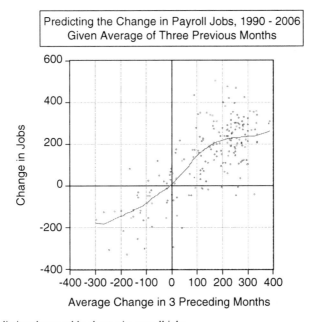

Fig. 4.3 Predicting the monthly change in payroll jobs

Furthermore, since the best predictor is an average of three months of data, this month's data are at most only 1/3rd as interesting as you might otherwise imagine. Moral: When the media reports that the payroll jobs number is disappointing, digest that with 1/3rd a grain of salt.

4.1.2 CPS: Current Population Survey

The Current Population Survey is a monthly survey of 60,000 *households* covering about 120,000 persons aged 16 and older. The survey separates all Americans into three categories:

- Working
- Looking for Work (Unemployed)
- Not working and not looking for work

You would be right to ask if these are well-defined categories. What does it mean to "work," anyway? Isn't taking out the garbage "work"? A broad definition of people "working" would include almost everyone. And "looking for work"; what does that mean? We are all looking for a better situation, are we not?

To deal with the fuzziness in the categories, the Bureau of Labor Statistics uses some clear definitions and uses a top-down approach, first determining whether the respondent is "working" in the survey week, and, if not, if that person is "looking for work." The third category is what remains: not in the labor force.

Here is what the BLS means by "working"[1]

- All persons who did any work *for pay or profit*, during the survey reference week
- All persons who did at least 15 h of unpaid work in a family-operated enterprise
- All persons who were temporarily absent from their regular jobs because of illness, vacation, bad weather, industrial dispute, or various personal reasons

Thus, the words "for pay" have been inserted prominently into the definition of working, which helps substantially to relieve the fuzziness, but some lingering issues remain. For example, what about the self-employed who are promoting their businesses, but who currently have no customers and no revenues? I guess they are employed as they are working for pay, though not receiving any.

But most of the fuzziness in the definition of working has been resolved by adding the phrase "for pay." Fuzziness in unemployment is also relieved by some good choice of words.

"Unemployed" are:

- All persons who were not classified as employed during the survey reference week who made *specific active efforts* to find a job during the prior 4 weeks, and were available for work.
- All persons who were not working and were waiting to be called back to a job from which they had been temporarily laid off.

---

[1] http://bls.gov/cps/cps_faq.htm#Ques3

Though helpful, the key words "specific active efforts" do not relieve as much as the ambiguity as the words "for pay." Though the border between "working-for-pay" and "not" seems pretty well defined, the border being unemployed and not-in-the-labor-force remains more than a little fuzzy.[2] For example, this is a setting in which there are bound to be interviewer effects. Imagine a stern survey taker, as your third grade teacher, looking at you square in the eye and asking if you were making "specific *active* efforts," with heavy emphasis on the word "active." Does that help you remember that you have been sitting on the sofa watching soap operas for the last month?

With all those concerns, we need to look carefully at some of the data collected by the household survey illustrated in Fig. 4.4 – the fractions of the population employed, unemployed, and not-in-the-labor-force. In the period depicted from 1975 to the present, the fraction employed hit its high point of 64.7% in April 2000, at the end of the Internet Rush. Also in April 2000, the fraction unemployed hit its low of 2.58%, and the fraction not-in-the-labor-force hit its low of 32.6%. April 2000 was about as good as it gets for working Americans.

Best to keep in mind that the unemployment rate that is usually reported by the Bureau of Labor Statistics is the ratio of the unemployed divided by the workforce. But to make this figure, we are dividing by the total number of adults, not just those who claim to be in the workforce. As only about 2/3rds of those who are 16 years and above are in the workforce, the usual unemployment rate is about 50% higher than the one displayed in Fig. 4.4. I am not trying to confuse. I am trying to make sure that you understand that some of the movement in the unemployment rate is because of the changes in the labor-force participation, rather than jobs and population. Figure 4.4 works for that because all three variables have the same denominator. The denominator (total adults) moves slowly because of births, deaths, and immigration. It is the numerator where the action lies.

You can see in Fig. 4.4 that the recession of 2001 brought down the fraction working from 64.7% to 62.3% – a drop of 2.5% – in May of 2003. As the fractions add to 100%, that 2.5% of job losses had to be found in the unemployed or in the not-in-the-labor-force. The majority was in the unemployed category. The fraction unemployed rose from 2.6% to 4.1%. The fraction not-in-the-labor-force rose from 32.7% to 33.7%. Not healthy, no matter how you look at it.

The shaded region in Fig. 4.4 from September 2001 to November 2003 is one of those ambiguous periods of time in which the unemployment rate was unchanged at 3.8% but the employment fraction declined. Why? Discouraged workers must be the reason. The fraction not-in-the-workforce increased from 33.6% to 33.8%. I would not call that a healthy labor market, even though the rate of unemployment was constant.

---

[2] The Bureau of the Census does list the "specific active efforts to find a job" but there remains a distressing impermanence in the responses: "Table 4.1 shows that only two-thirds (66.3 percent of people classified as "Unemployed" in the original interview are classified as "Unemployed" in the reinterview."

Data mining the cps reinterview:digging into response error, Pamela D. McGovern and John M. Bushery, U.S. Bureau of the Census, http://www.fcsm.gov/99papers/ mcgovern.pdf

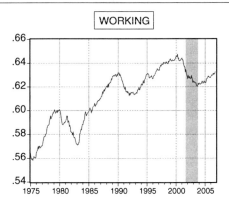

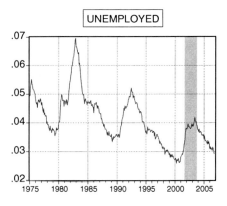

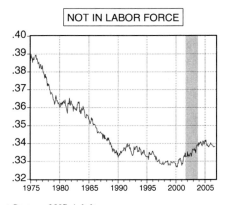

Fig. 4.4 Labor-Market Status of US Adults

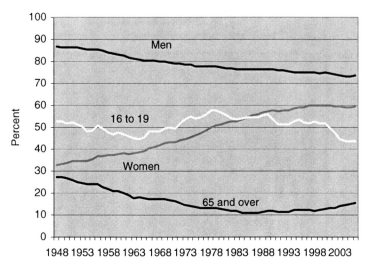

Fig. 4.5 Labor force participation

Labor force participation is the sum of the first two categories (working + unemployed). As labor force participation is an important issue in measuring the health of the labor market, we should take a look at some of the details in Fig. 4.5, which depicts the labor force participation rates of men, women, youth, and the elderly. With the help of this figure, answer the following questions:

- What is the difference between labor force participation of men and women?
- Whose labor force participation fluctuates the most? Who are the newly "discouraged" workers? Can you tell a story about that?
- What about the elderly? Are they working as hard as they used to? Might we expect them to do more?

4.1.3 Initial Jobless Claims

The government indicators are all reported with a lag, some lags greater than the others. The "advance" estimate of the quarterly GDP number comes out a month after the end of the quarter. The "preliminary" estimate comes a month later, and the "final" estimate is reported at the end of the third month.

The hottest most recent number is the weekly initial claims for unemployment insurance reported by the Department of Labor with only a week delay. Figure 4.6 illustrates the data on initial claims for the 1990s. The shaded regions represent the official US recessions. We are going to discuss these carefully soon, but for now just think of them as periods of economic malaise.

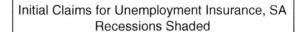

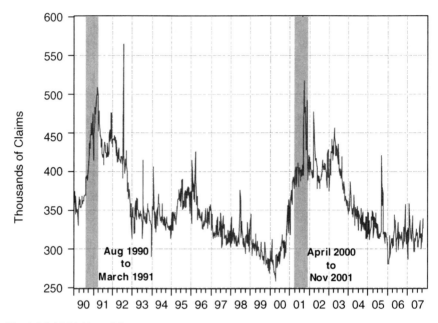

Fig. 4.6 Initial jobless claims

There is a lot of information in this figure, and you should take a good look at it. Here are some things that I see:

- Between 330,000 and 360,000, initial jobless claims seem normal. That is a lot of Americans getting laid off every week. When you hear that Chrysler is laying off 12,000 over the next year, remember that is a tiny drop in the bucket.
- The job market weakened in late 1995 but heated up in 1996, and got really hot in the first part of 2000, when initial claims fell almost to 250,000.
- The labor market was seriously deteriorating in the second half of 2000, well before the official starting date of the recession. Maybe they got that date wrong.
- There is a spike after the 9/11 terrorist attack, which supports the consensus view that the terrorists caused the recession. That view is wrong. The terrorist attack occurred in the midst of an ongoing recession and did not materially affect its course. The impact of the 9/11 attack was confined mostly to the airline carriers and the hospitality sectors, where the effect was substantial.
- Labor market problems lingered on through 2002 and 2003. It was not until 2004 that things got back to normal. That was also true of the 1991 recession. The labor market did not get back to normal until 1993.

• Through October 2007, there is nothing in these data to suggest an imminent recession. The numbers remain at elevated levels of 330, but are far below the recession numbers as 400 or 450.

Table 4.2 Employees on nonfarm payrolls (establishment survey), June 2002–2003 average

Total nonfarm	130,216	100.0%
Goods-producing	22,334	17.2%
Natural resources and mining	571	0.4%
Construction	6,737	5.2%
Manufacturing	15,027	11.5%
Durable goods	9,316	7.2%
Nondurable goods	5,711	4.4%
Private service-providing	86,359	66.3%
Trade, transportation, and utilities	25,391	19.5%
Wholesale trade	5,608	4.3%
Retail trade	15,013	11.5%
Transportation and warehousing	4,173	3.2%
Utilities	597	0.5%
Information	3,351	2.6%
Financial activities.:FIRE	7,895	6.1%
Finance and insurance	5,861	4.5%
Real estate and rental and leasing	2,034	1.6%
Professional and business services	16,003	12.3%
Professional and technical services(1)	6,722	5.2%
Management of companies and enterprises	1,700	1.3%
Administrative and waste services	7,581	5.8%
Education and health services	16,365	12.6%
Educational services	2,690	2.1%
Health care and social assistance	13,675	10.5%
Leisure and hospitality	12,018	9.2%
Arts, entertainment, and recreation	1,779	1.4%
Accommodations and food services	10,239	7.9%
Other services	5,335	4.1%
Repair and maintenance	1,226	0.9%
Personal and laundry services	1,236	0.9%
Membership associations and organizations	2,872	2.2%
Government	21,523	16.5%
Federal	2,774	2.1%
Federal, except U.S. Postal Service	1,942	1.5%
U.S. Postal Service	831	0.6%
State government	4,979	3.8%
State government education	2,205	1.7%
State government, excluding education	2,774	2.1%
Local government	13,770	10.6%
Local government education	7,690	5.9%
Local government, excluding education	6,080	4.7%

4.2 Industry Composition of Payroll Jobs

Before pushing on, we might want to take a brief look at some of the employment detail. Table 4.2 indicates the number of employees by sector of the economy. In 2003, there were 130 million nonfarm jobs. Seventeen percent of those jobs were in the goods-producing sectors, principally construction and manufacturing but also a few in natural resource extraction. Another 17% were in government jobs including education. Most of these government jobs were at the local level. Federal government employment, excluding the Postal Services, was only 1.5% of the jobs. The remaining jobs (66%) were in the private service producing sectors. Getting the goods from them to you (trade and transportation) took 19% of the workforce. Health care was 10.5%. The professional activities of providing information, finance and insurance, real estate, and professional and business services added up to 21% of the workforce.

Appendix: Which to Rely on: Business-Reported Payroll Jobs or Household-Reported People-at-Work

In addition to the unemployment data, the CPS household survey also estimates the number employed, which competes directly with the number of payroll jobs from the CES establishment survey. These two employment totals are illustrated in Fig. 4.7 and the gap in percentage terms is illustrated in Fig. 4.8. Though there is double counting in the payroll jobs, there are still more people at work than there are payroll jobs covered by unemployment insurance. The difference, which had

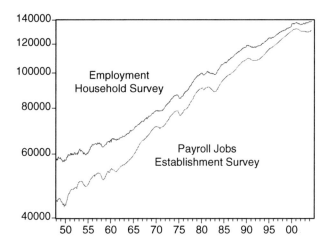

Fig. 4.7 Payroll jobs and number employed

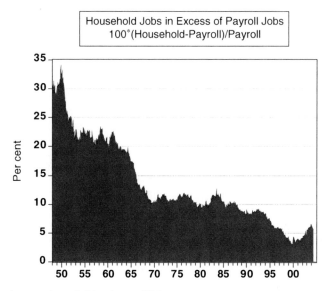

Fig. 4.8 Gap between household and payroll jobs

been 20% in the 1950s, fell to 10% in the 1970s, as the coverage of unemployment insurance increased.

The household and payroll numbers usually move in the same direction, but they sometimes diverge, as they did in the aftermath of the 2001 recession, when the recovery of payroll jobs was notably slower than the recovery of the household employment estimates. This divergence is all the more clear in Fig. 4.8, which illustrates the percentage difference between the two series. In this figure, you can see

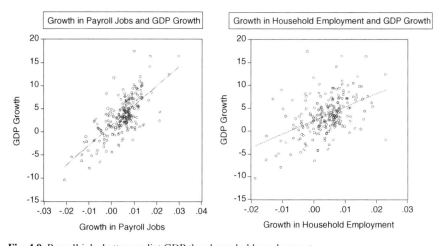

Fig. 4.9 Payroll jobs better predict GDP than household employment

that the aftermath of the 2001 recession was a return to a more normal relationship between the household and payroll numbers. The gap that was 6% in 1995 fell to the historic low of 3% in December 1999, but has since returned to 5.7% in May 2005. Viewed this way, the puzzle is not why payroll job formation was weaker than household employment in the wake of 2001. The puzzle is why payroll job formation was so strong in the Internet Rush from 1996 to 2000? As we shall learn soon enough, what is unique about the Internet Rush is that the US economy was driven by business investment spending, not by consumer spending. That means more business-to-business transactions where the payroll coverage is virtually complete, as opposed to sales to consumers where the payroll coverage is much less (think, for example, of the difference between gardeners working at business sites as opposed to gardeners working at your home.)

It was not only the aftermath of the 2001 recession. If you look hard at Fig. 4.8, you will see that the household jobs have quite a few times accumulated more rapidly than the payroll jobs. So which is better? Some argue that the payroll numbers miss an important and vibrant part of the economy, and it is the household survey that is superior. But speaking as a statistician, it is the payroll numbers that are most informative – they do a better job of predicting GDP growth than do the household data. You can see this in the two scatter diagrams in Fig. 4.9.

Chapter 5
Inflation and Interest Rates

The subject of macro economics is intended to help us understand the movements of five variables:

1. GDP growth
2. Unemployment/employment
3. Inflation
4. Interest rates (short and long-term)
5. Exchange rate

GDP and employment have been discussed in the immediately preceding chapters. We now turn to the inflation and the interest rates. We will do the exchange rates and the external deficit later when we turn to long-run issues like the adequacy of savings to fund our retirements. If our focus were any other country than the United States, the exchange rates and the external deficit would be front and center, but, looking backward, there is very little volatility of the US economy that has come from our economic interrelations with other countries. In that regard, the future is quite likely to be different from the past. As I write these words at the end of 2006, a huge US external deficit that has persisted for almost a decade and an apparently over-valued dollar constitute the greatest threat to the stability of the US economy.

GDP and employment are the measurements of a physical reality: you can touch your new car and you can hug the gal who made it. Prices, inflation, interest rates, and exchange rates are different from GDP and employment. These measure the rates at which the products trade one for another. You cannot see or touch or hug these prices. These are feelings. These are what we think collectively about the relative values of goods and services.

We begin discussing measures of the level of prices at a given point in time, next inflation, which is the rate of change in the level of prices, and next interest rates. None of these alone matters at all. What matters is the real interest rate: the rate of interest minus the rate of inflation. I will explain why.

E. E. Leamer, *Macroeconomic Patterns and Stories: A Guide for MBAs.*
© Springer-Verlag Berlin Heidelberg 2009

5.1 A Price Is a Ratio

When Hillary Clinton was asked by a reporter, "How's your husband?" her reply
was: "Compared to what?"

In discussing prices, the first thing you need to understand is *RATIOS*: it is only
ratios that matter: the price of something *divided by* the price of something else.
Your answer to the question: "What's the price of that?" should be the question
"Compared to what?"

I know you like to talk about the price of milk, but when you say "The price
of a quart of milk is $2.10" that is useful information for me only because I know
something about the price of bread and the price of beer in US dollars. If you told me
that the price of Coca-Cola is 9,640 Ghanaian cedi that would be utterly meaningless
to me. That does not tells me whether Coke in Ghana is cheaper or more expensive
than in LA. It does not tells me whether Coke in Ghana is cheaper or more expensive
than a cup of tea. If I know that the exchange rate is 9,640 cedi to the dollar, then I
can do some math to translate the price into US dollars. Coke in Ghana costs US$
1. Still, I am not done yet. I need to know also that the price of Coke in LA is US$
2. Now I know something. The Coke costs about twice as much in LA as in Ghana.

So let us make sure when we look at prices that we seek an answer to a clear
question "Compared to what?"

5.2 The Consumer Price Index (CPI)

The first "price" that we will take a look at is the consumer price index. The answer
to the question, "Compared to what?" is "compared to the consumer prices at other
points in time." But a visit to the Website of the Bureau of Labor Statistics yields
the following confusing definition of the CPI (italics added):

> "The Consumer Price Index (CPI) is a measure of the *average change* over time in the
> prices paid by urban consumers for a market basket of consumer goods and services.
> "http://stats.bls.gov/cpi/cpifaq.htm#Question_1,

With this definition of the CPI, let us look at the data illustrated in Fig. 5.1. Can
you see in this figure "the average change over time in the prices"? The CPI takes
on the value 29 in 1959. How is "29"? the answer to the question: "What was the
average change over time in the prices paid by urban consumers"? Huh??

OK. I am making a point, which I will make again by asking the following rhetorical question: Tell me one value that a price index takes on at some point in the
series. Can you do this for the GDP of Norway? I do not think so. But you can do
it for the CPI of Norway. Yes you can. An index is set arbitrarily to 100 in some
"base year." When asked "name a value of the Consumer Price Index" say "100",
and you are guaranteed to nail the CPI sometime in the series. The title in the chart
in Fig. 5.1 tells us when: 1982–1984 = 100. Sure enough, look at the data and you
can see that the numbers are about 100 at that point in time.

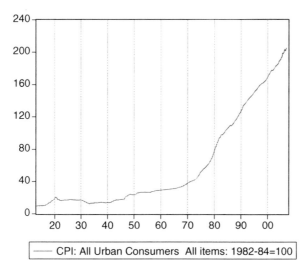

Fig. 5.1 Consumer price index

Since the CPI is arbitrarily set to an average of 100 for 1982–1984 period, the question "What was the CPI in 1982–1984?" has the information-less answer "100." The number 100 has meaning if you know that the CPI was 30 in 1958. That means that from 1958 to 1982–1984, consumer prices have risen by a factor of $100/30 = 3.33$. There's that ratio I promised you: a numerator and a denominator. A comparison.

Now that we know better, we can adopt a much better definition than the one offered by the BLS:

> The Consumer Price Index (CPI) is a measure of the prices paid by urban consumers for a market basket of consumer goods and services. This *index* is normalized to equal 100 in the base year and is designed to compare price levels at one point in time with price levels at another point in time. (For more about the details, take a look at the Appendix to this chapter.)

5.3 Two Views of Inflation

Speaking of comparing prices at different points in time, that's inflation. How much higher were prices at the end of 2004 than they were at the end of 2003?

The percent change per year in the CPI is a measure of the rate of inflation. I am tempted to say that it is the rate of inflation, but there are other price indexes that compete with the CPI, most notably the "GDP deflator," which is a price index of all goods and services produced in the US, not just the stuff bought by consumers. There is also a "Producer Price Index" that measures prices at the factory gate – wholesale prices. There is also the CPI less food and energy, which is a bit more stable than the overall CPI.

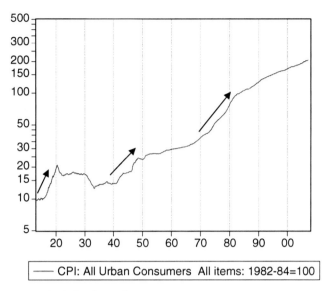

Fig. 5.2 Consumer price index, log scale

Figure 5.2 depicts the level of the CPI with a logarithmic scale that turns constant rates of growth into straight lines. When the level of the CPI is growing rapidly, that's a high level of inflation. Use your mind's eye to put some straight lines into this figure. It looks like there have been three bouts of inflation – in the roaring 1920s, during the war years in the 1940s and during the oil shocks of the 1970s.

We also can look for these three episodes in Fig. 5.3, which displays the rate of change of the CPI, year over year – the rate of inflation. This figure uses exactly the same data but they sure look a lot different when displayed this way. Those three episodes we see in the levels display Fig. 5.2 are not so apparent in the inflation display Fig. 5.3. You can see the inflation in the 1920s but both the 1940s and the 1970s have two mountains of inflation, with much less inflation in the middle of the decades. And then there is the smaller mountain in the late 1960s, leading up to the two larger ones in the 1970s.

You can also see clearly in Fig. 5.3 the deflations (falling prices) in the 1920s and the 1930s, and you can see the happy times in the early 1960s when inflation was low and stable. I wonder if we can expect some of that ahead. We are going to need to try to figure out what is causing the ups and downs in this figure. Foreshadowing: inflation is one of the hardest variables to explain and to predict.

NOTE: This is the second time we contrasted two different displays of the same data. When discussing GDP growth, we also looked at a display of the level of GDP with a logarithmic scale and a display of the quarter-by-quarter rate of growth. Make a mental note of the fact that while these two displays are based on exactly the same data the messages they convey are very different.

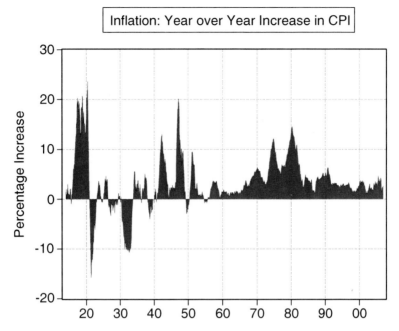

Fig. 5.3 CPI-based inflation rates

5.3.1 *Homework*

What is the news in the following figure? What is the difference between the behavior of the prices of medical care, bananas, and new vehicles, and why? (Make sure you explain why the price of bananas is so wiggly.)

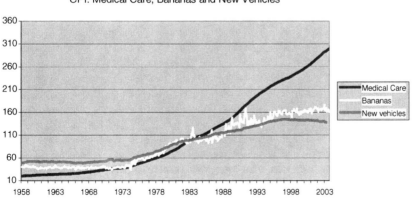

5.4 Interest Rates on Short-Term US Government Securities

We are proceeding here in short steps toward the target: the real rate of interest. We have taken two steps so far: The CPI and the rate of inflation. The next step in the journey is the rate of interest.

Figure 5.4 illustrates the level of two key short-term interest rates: the Federal Funds Rate and the rate on 3-month Treasury "bills." These two interest rates move in a virtual lock step.

Whatever are "Federal Funds?" What is a Treasury "bill"? Why do their interest rates move so closely together? More than the answers to these questions, you need a way to find the answers. You can Google "Federal Funds" on the Internet. I recommend the Glossary of Financial and Business Terms on the New York Times Website compiled by Professor Campbell R. Harvey

http://www.nytimes.com/library/financial/glossary/bfglosa.htm

Here is what Professor Harvey tells us about the Federal Funds:

Federal funds

Noninterest bearing deposits held in reserve for depository institutions at their district Federal Reserve Bank. Also, excess reserves lent by banks to each other.

Federal funds market

The market where banks can borrow or lend reserves, allowing banks temporarily short of their required reserves to borrow reserves from banks that have excess reserves.

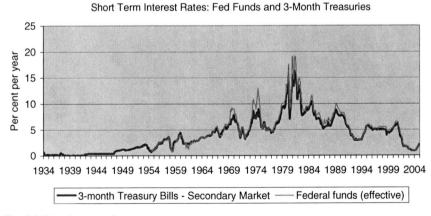

Fig. 5.4 Two short-term interest rates

Federal funds rate

This is the interest rate that banks with excess reserves at a Federal Reserve district bank charge other banks that need overnight loans. The Fed Funds rate, as it is called, often points to the direction of US interest rates.

Here is what Professor Harvey tells us about Treasury Bills:

Treasury bills

Debt obligations of the US Treasury that have maturities of one year or less. Maturities for T-bills are usually 91 days, 182 days, or 52 weeks.

Treasury bonds

Debt obligations of the US Treasury that have maturities of 10 years or more.

Treasury notes

Debt obligations of the US Treasury that have maturities of more than 2 years but less than 10 years.

So there you have it. Banks are required to hold a certain fraction of their deposits in reserve at one of the 12 Federal Reserve Banks (how much? 10% of deposits in excess of $45.8 million.). These reserves stand ready to pay back depositors in the event that there is a significant and rapid withdrawal of funds. Some banks may have more reserves than are required, others not enough. The Federal Funds market is where banks go to borrow or lend excess reserves. The bond market is where the US government goes when it needs to borrow. There the US Treasury issues bills, notes, and bonds, different only in their maturities: bills mature soon, notes later, and bonds latest of all. The bond market is also where you and I and private banks and foreign central banks, and corporations actively trade these bills, notes, and bonds, and establish the market rates of interest – just the right interest rates to get us to be willing to hold all those securities the Treasury has issued, in other words to fund the Government debt.

The Federal Funds rate is also a market-determined rate, balancing the supply of reserves with the demand. In setting monetary policy, the Federal Reserve Board establishes a target Federal Funds rate. To lower the Fed Funds rate, the Federal Reserve buys the US government securities – paying for the bills with "reserves" in the form of cash deposits on the Fed's account. This increases the availability of reserves, which, through the normal market reaction to an increase in supply, lowers the market-determined Fed Funds rate. That's an "open-market operation." It works both ways. To raise the Fed Funds rate, the Federal Reserve sells US Treasuries, reducing the reserves in the system, which increases their scarcity value.

Better pause a moment to get this straight: What happens to the interest rates when the Fed buys bonds? If you like, you can call this an increase in the demand for bonds, which, if the usual logic applies, comes with an increase in the price of bonds. What does that mean about interest rates? Do you know that prices of bonds and interest rates move in opposite direction? Think about that $100 bond issued at the rate of 10% per year. It promises to pay $10 in a year. If the price of the bond is bid up to $110 because the Federal Reserve is actively buying bonds, then it now costs more to get $10 in a year. That's a *decrease* in the interest rate to 10/110 from 10/100. If you prefer, we can tell a story about loanable funds instead of bonds. When the Fed buys bonds it is loaning money to borrowers. An increase in the supply of loanable funds brings down the interest rate. It's the same outcome, just expressed a little differently. Let's write it down to help remember:

$$\text{Buy bonds} = \text{Lending} \rightarrow \text{Interest Rate down, Price of Bonds Up}$$

The Federal Reserve directly controls the Federal Funds rate, and indirectly influences the interest rates on all other short-term debt/deposits. Take a look at Fig. 5.4. Here you can see that the interest rate on 3-month Treasury bills is virtually identical to the Fed Funds rate. Why is that? Why does control over the Fed Funds rate imply control over the market-determined rate on 3-month Treasuries? That's a question for you to answer. (Hint: When you deposit your paycheck in your bank, the banker can use that deposit either to buy Treasury bills or to deposit the cash at the Federal Reserve. What might that do to the supply of reserves?)

5.5 The Real Interest Rate: The Price of Durability and the Compensation for Waiting

We have now the building blocks to look at what really matters: the real interest rate. Neither a price index, nor the rate of inflation, nor the rate of interest by itself is useful for any decisions. What matters is the real rate of interest – the interest rate minus the inflation rate. That's the price of goods later compared with goods today.

Think about giving up that cup of tea today and buying some tea a year from now. Put the dollar that you are about to spend on the cup of tea into the bond market instead. If the interest rate is 100%, that $1 will grow to $2 by the end of the year. Do you think that you can have more tea at the end of the year? Not if the price of a cup of tea has also doubled. Then the real interest rate is zero. Then there is no compensation to you for waiting patiently for that cup of tea. But if the price of tea did not change, you can get two cups at the end of the year if you give up one now. That's the real rate of interest: 100%.

The real rate of interest is equal to the (nominal) rate of interest minus the rate of inflation.

From the standpoint of the lender/consumer, the real rate of interest is the compensation for waiting – if you wait, you can have a bigger meal. From the standpoint of the borrower/investor, the real rate of interest is the price of durability. Durability is cheap when the real interest rate is low.

Let's digress briefly with an historical puzzle. It will help understand why the interest rate is the price of durability.

In the nineteenth century, British goods were made to last while American goods were characteristically "shoddy." The word "shoddy" itself was an American contribution, referring to inferior wool cloth made from scraps used to make military uniforms during the Civil War – shoddy cloth literally fell apart after days of use. It was not just cloth that was shoddy in America – it was virtually everything.

> In contrast with the British, Americans used structures and equipment with shorter service lives, which were run and depreciated more quickly; Americans adopted organization forms that reduced inventories per unit of output and per unit of labor.
>
> American farmers concentrated on grain farming rather than livestock.
>
> British Board of Trade's Enquiry reported that in comparison with England, "the practice of buying clothes that are expected and intended to last for a single season only is much more common . . . noticeable not only in respect to clothing, but also as regards houses in their inferior durability and, as regards machinery, in the greater rapidity with which it is either worn out or discarded."
>
> Alexander James Field, *Journal of Economic History*, Vol 43, Issue 2(June, 1983), 405–431

Now the question: why were British goods durable and American goods shoddy? Does that reflect some deep British cultural superiority? Maybe, but maybe there is a better explanation. Most economists would suspect that the British bought more durable goods because the British price of durability was lower than the American price of durability. So what is the price of durability? It is the real rate of interest.

Think about the choice between buying a shirt that lasts two years vs. buying a less durable shirt that lasts only one year, and another when you need it next year. Suppose the durable two-year shirt costs $15 but the shoddy one-year shirt costs $10, now and $10 a year from now when you need a replacement for the rags. (Assuming no inflation) Which shirt is the better buy? That depends on the rate of interest. To put a shirt on your back for two years you can either make a one-time right-away payment of $15 or you can make two payments – $10 now, and $10 a year from now. Which option is cheaper depends on how much $5 not-spent on the durable shirt will earn you during the first year. If the rate of interest is greater than 100%, that $5 not-spent will grow to more than $10, allowing you to buy another shoddy shirt and have something left over besides. Then it is better to choose shoddy, not durable.

To put it another way, if the real rate of interest is high, you cannot afford to have scarce capital tied up in durable goods and equipment. That is the explanation for the British choice of durability. It is not preferences or culture. Real rates of interest were much higher in the frontier of the New World than in Britain.

Thus there is a good reason to keep track of the ups and downs of the real rate of interest. When the real rate is low, that's a good time to buy durables: land and houses, offices, automobiles, and refrigerators.

5.5.1 A Look at the Data

Now that we understand that the real rate of interest is the price of durability, let us see how it has changed over time. Figure 5.5 illustrates the interest rate on the 1-year Treasury and the rate of inflation. The gap between them is the real rate of interest, which is charted directly in Fig. 5.6. Take a look at these and try to tell a

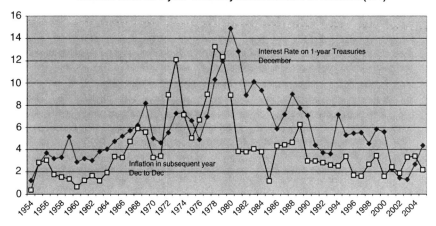

Fig. 5.5 Interest rates and inflation

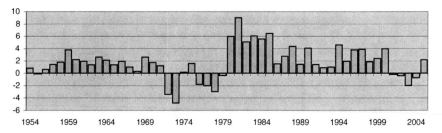

Fig. 5.6 Real rates of return

story why the real interest rate is high and why it is low. You might need two stories. One for the 1970s and another for today's negative real interest rates. The first story begins: Once upon a time there was a tribe of people who looked forward by looking backward. They thought tomorrow would be pretty much the same as today. . . .

Regardless of the story, durability was cheap in the 1950s, really cheap in the 1970s, very expensive in the 1980s, and getting cheaper year after year since then.

5.6 Interest Rates on Long-Term US Government Securities and Monetary Policy

We came easily to the conclusion that the Federal Reserve has control over the interest rates on short-term securities. What about the interest rates on the longer term maturities? Does the Federal Reserve Board control them as well? Figure 5.7

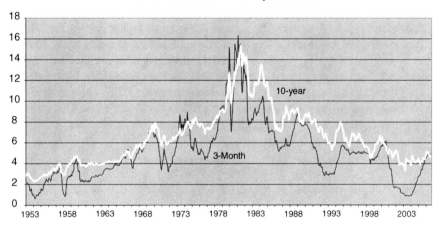

Fig. 5.7 Interest rates on 3 treasury securities

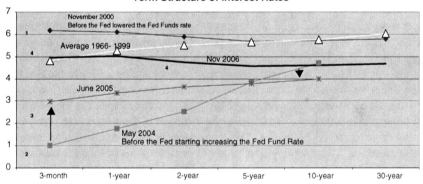

Fig. 5.8 Term structure of interest rates: The yield curve

illustrates the interest rates on the 3-month and 10-year Treasuries. Here we see that the interest rates on the 10-year has a life of its own, sometimes moving with the 3-month rate, but not always. That should make one wonder how much impact the Fed has on the longer-term rates and also wonder how much it matters.

We can look at this a little differently by graphing the interest rates at a particular point in time as a function of the maturity of the bond. This graph of the *term structure of interest rates* is called the *yield curve*. Five different yield curves are illustrated in Fig. 5.8.

The yield curve with the large triangles is the average of the interest rates from 1996 to 1999, which is a period of normal economic growth. This "normal yield curve" is upward sloping with the difference between the 3-month rate and the 10-year rate equal to about 100 basis points. (That is bond market speak for a full percentage point.) Between 1999 and November 2000, the Fed raised the target Fed

Funds rate from 4.75 to 6.5. As always happens, the 3-month Treasury rate moved right along with the target Fed Funds rate. The yield curve number 1 in Fig. 5.8, which occurred in November 2000, accordingly has a higher rate on the 3-month Treasury. But the other end of the yield curve did not move much at all. Actually, the 30-year rate fell a bit. Those movements produced what is called an "inverted yield curve" with a downward slope. (We will discover soon that an inverted yield curve is an excellent predictor of an oncoming recession.) This episode should get you thinking about moving an elephant by grabbing hold of the tail. That effort has a big impact on the tail, but not much effect on the rest of the elephant.

Between November 2000 and May 2004, the Fed reduced the target Fed Funds rate from 6.5% per year to 1.0. This time the reduction in the short-term rates was accompanied by a reduction of the long-term rates, producing the yield curve number 2 in Fig. 5.8. The co-movements of the short-term rates and the long-term rates in this episode might make you rethink the elephant analogy. Maybe the Fed really can affect the long-term rates. But when the Fed starting "tightening" again, and raising the short-term rates between May 2004 and June 2005, the long-term rates continued to fall, thus moving opposite the direction of short-term rates, creating the yield curve number 3 in Fig. 5.8. This movement seemed to astound Mr. Greenspan, who called it a "conundrum." (Picture Mr. Greenspan in his finest circus outfit showing how he can move an enormous elephant in the center ring, left and right, merely by slight movements of its tail. He does this by watching the elephant's eyes, which betray the elephant's intentions. First to the left, and then to the right;. Now to the left again. Whoops, that time the elephant started moving right. No problem. Quick Mr. Greenspan move that tail to the right.) But between June 2005 and November 2006, as the Fed continued to raise the short-term rates, the elephant moved in a more normal way, with long-term rates rising along with the short-term rates.

The yield curve number 4 that applies in November 2006 is just about the same shape, though about a percentage point lower, than the yield curve number 1 in November 2000, just before a recession during which the Fed started lowering rates. I wonder if the bond market in 2006 is sending a message. What do you think??

5.6.1 The Term Structure of Interest Rates: Theory

These data are leaving me completely confused. Now is the time to switch to stories. We need to find a good story titled "Why the yield curve slopes upward." Then we can look for the sequel: "When the Fed affects long-term rates and when it does not."

Hang on tight. We are going to have to do some symbolic manipulation. This is sure to tax your attention span.

Think about the choice between buying one-year bond and a two-year bond. Denote the annualized rate on the two-year bond by the letter s. Take the one-year rate currently available to be r_1 and the one-year rate available at the start of the next year to be $\boldsymbol{r_2}$, where the **boldface** type refers to something you do not know and will have to guess when making your investment decision today.

It is not just the nominal return that matters. Inflation will take away some of your return. Let the first year inflation rate be $\boldsymbol{I_1}$ and the second year inflation rate be $\boldsymbol{I_2}$. These are in boldface too, since, when you are buying bonds today, you don't know either the rate of inflation in the first year or the second.

Table 5.1 below is approximately what you are looking at if you invest $1 in the bond market in one-year Treasuries or $1 in two-year Treasuries. When you see a bold letter, that's not a sure thing investment.

You can see in this table that the real return on the one-year bond is the nominal rate minus the rate of inflation, $r_1 - \boldsymbol{I_1}$, if you sell out after one year, and the sum of two real returns, $(r_1 - \boldsymbol{I_1}) + (\boldsymbol{r_2} - \boldsymbol{I_2})$, if you stick it out for two years. The two-year real return on the two-year bond is the nominal return $2s$ minus the two-year inflation.

The table also includes the real return on the two-year bond after one year. This applies if you discover that you need the money before the two-year bond matures. To get your money back at that point you have to assure the new buyer of that bond that it is just as good as the one-year bond then paying r_2 (the **boldface** has been removed from this rate of return r_2 to indicate that at this point in time you know the interest rate in the second period). Your two-year bond will pay $2s$ at the end of the second year compared with r_2 of a one-year bond. So offer to sell the bond at face value net of the difference in the yields $2s - r_2$.[1] That's your nominal return after one year. You get the first year of interest, s, plus the difference between the locked-in rate s and the going rate when you sell this bond, r_2.

5.6.1.1 Expectations Theory

If there were no uncertainty, and the future one-year interest rate and the future inflation rates were known, then the returns on the one-year bond and the two-year bond would have to be the same at each horizon. Otherwise all the lenders would be in the market for the high-yield maturity and all the borrowers would be in the market for the low-yield maturity, and there would be no way to get borrowers and lenders together. This condition, as you can easily verify, implies that the two-year rate is the average of the two one-year rates:

$$s = (r_1 + \boldsymbol{r_2})/2.$$

---

[1] I know I am ignoring compounding. It makes life simpler.

Table 5.1 Approximate rate of return in the bond market[2]

	End of First Year	End of Second Year
One-year bonds	$r_1 - I_1$	$r_1 + \mathbf{r_2} - I_1 - \mathbf{I_2}$
Two-year bond	$2s - \mathbf{r_2} - I_1$	$2s - I_1 - \mathbf{I_2}$

One-year bond paying r_1 in the first year and r_2 in the second
Two-year bond paying the compound rate s
The inflation rates are I
Boldface type refers to variables that are uncertain when the first
bonds are purchased.

Change that uncertain $\mathbf{r_2}$ into the expected future interest rate and you have one
pretty good explanation for the slope of the yield curve.

$$\text{Expectations Theory } s = (r_1 + E(\mathbf{r_2}))/2.$$

*The formula suggests that the two-year rate is equal to an average of the current
one-year rate and the expected future one-year rate.* If the one-year rate is expected
to increase, then the two-year rate s will exceed r_1 and the yield curve will be upward
sloping. Analogously, if the one-year rate is expected to decline, the yield curve is
downward sloping.

Expectations about future short-term rates are part of the story of the yield curve,
but this expectations theory cannot help explain why the yield curve is *usually* sloping upward – one cannot expect future short-term rates *usually* to be higher than
today's rates. That would be a recipe for ever-higher rates.

5.6.1.2 Risk Theory

Maybe the slope of the yield curve reflects a risk premium for those longer-term
bonds – no sense committing your money to a long-term investment unless there is
some extra return offered. Make sure you understand that we are not talking about
liquidity here. When you buy a long-term bond, you are *not* locking up your money,
since you can sell the bond at any time. The choices described in Table 5.1 explicitly
include selling the two-year bond after holding it for only one year. It's a matter of
risk, not liquidity.

Table 5.1 suggests that what is risky may depend on the investment horizon. For the one-year horizon, it looks like a two-year bond is more risky than

[2] This table approximates the following table using $1/(1+I) = 1 - I + I^2 - I^3 + \ldots$ and $(1+r)/(1+I) = 1 + r - I +$ terms that involve product of small numbers:

	End of First Year	End of Second Year
One-year bonds	$(1+r_1)/(1+\mathbf{I_1})$	$(1+r_1)(1+\mathbf{r_2})/(1+\mathbf{I_1})(1+\mathbf{I_2})$
Two-year bond	$(1+s)^2/(1+\mathbf{r_2})(1+\mathbf{I_1})$	$(1+s)^2/(1+\mathbf{I_1})(1+\mathbf{I_2})$

one-year bond because the real return on the two-year bond has an additional source of uncertainty since it depends on r_2, the future one-year rate. But it also looks like the risk characteristics for the two-year horizon are the opposite – the future value of r_2 affects the one-year return, but not the two-year return. Thus what is risky seems to depend on the investment horizon. For the one-year horizon, it the two-year bond that is risky. For the two-year horizon, it is the one-year bond that is risky.

If that's the way it was, then the slope of the yield curve would depend on the "preferred habitat" of lenders and borrowers. If lenders want one-year bonds, and borrowers want two-year bonds, expect an upward sloping yield curve, with the borrowers having to pay a premium to get lenders to commit to the longer term instruments. More on this below.

But this thinking is ignoring the "covariance" between those uncertain variables. For example, when the inflation rate in the first period I_1 is unexpectedly high, the interest rate in the second period may be adjusted upward. That's positive covariance. That positive covariance would make the two-year bond especially risky for the one-year horizon because the uncertainty in the realized return $2s - r_2 - I_1$ is greater if r_2 and I_1 move together. Then unexpectedly high inflation in the first year subtracts from your real return both directly and also indirectly because it will come with a higher value for the second-year one-year rate r_2, making the second-year return s on the two-year bond less valuable.[3]

For the two-year horizon, things are more complicated and more ambiguous. Positive covariance between r_2 and $I_1 + I_2$ makes the *one-year* bond more attractive for the *two-year* horizon because the real return for the one-year bond depends on $r_2 - (I_1 + I_2)$. On the one hand, positive covariance between r_2 and I_1 is a symptom of monetary policy aimed at inflation control – higher short-term interest rates when inflation is realized. On the other hand, negative covariance between r_2 and I_2 is a symptom of monetary policy that actually works, since the higher rates r_2 bring down future inflation I_2.[4]

---

[3] The variance of the sum of two random variables is the sum of the variances plus twice the covariance:

$$\text{Var}(r_2 + I_1) = \text{Var}(r_2) + \text{Var}(I_1) + 2\text{Cov}(r_2, I_1).$$

[4] Let's make this concrete. Suppose you want to put some money into bonds to pay for your child's college in ten years. Many investment advisors would recommend a ten-year bond, but a sequence of one-year bonds could be a better option. It depends on the extent to which future inflation is mitigated by offsetting interest rate policy by the monetary authorities, which tends to stabilize the real return on one-year bonds. If you think the monetary authorities will keep the real return on one-year bonds reasonably stable but will not be able to control inflation, go for the one-year bonds. If you buy that 10-year bond, inflation might pick your pocket and make the real return lower. That's a risk you could avoid by going for the one-year investments.

On the other hand, if there is no inflation risk in the sense that both I_1 and I_2 are perfectly predictable, then the only uncertainty in Table 5.1 comes from the uncertainty in the future short-term rate, r_2, and there is no covariance issue. Then we do get the result that the risk is lower for

If you have the stamina and the interest and the background, take a look at the appendix to this chapter that tries to make sense out of this covariance issue, allowing for inflation risk. The choice of the bond for the two-year horizon is not clear-cut, since it depends substantially on the rule that the monetary authorities use to select the interest rate and on the impact of that choice on inflation rates. If you look at the appendix and then want to take it to the next level, try dipping into the academic literature on this topic.[5]

5.6.2 Real Returns on One-Year and Two-Year Treasuries

If we cannot figure out theoretically what is risky and what is not, a look at the facts may help. Figure 5.9 illustrates the real rates of return for one and two-year Treasuries for a one-year horizon and a two-year horizon from 1977 to 2004. You can see that for the one-year horizon, it looks like the two-year investment is riskier but also has a higher return. It is more difficult to compare visually the two investments if the horizon is two years. But Table 5.2 helps. This has the means and standard deviations for the two horizons. Indeed, as seemed apparent from Fig. 5.9, if the horizon is one year, the two-year bond is riskier, with a standard deviation of the real return equal to 3.9% compared with the one-year bond of 2.2%. But to take on this extra risk, there is compensation in the form of a higher mean, 4.2% for the two-year bond but only 3.4% for the one-year bond. For the two-year horizon, the two investments are more similar with the means and the standard deviations pretty close, but the ordering is the same. The

---

the bond with maturity equal to the investment horizon: a one-year bond for the one-year horizon and a two-year bond for the two-year horizon.

[5] This is an area that has a large and complex literature in academic journals. I am not doing it justice here and if you want to read more try

Ang, A., and M. Piazzesi. 2001. "A No-Arbitrage Vector Autoregression of Term Structure Dynamics with Macroeconomic and Latent Variables." Working Paper. Columbia University. Forthcoming, *Journal of Monetary Economics*.
      http://www-1.gsb.columbia.edu/faculty/aang/papers/bond.pdf

Dai, Q., and K. Singleton. 2000. "Specification Analysis of Affine Term Structure Models." Journal of Finance 55 (October) pp. 1,943–1,978.

Evans, C., and D. Marshall. 2001. "Economic Determinants of the Nominal Treasury Yield Curve." FRB ChicagoWorking Paper 01–16.
      http://www.chicagofed.org/publications/workingpapers/papers/Wp2001–16.pdf

Fuhrer, J.C. and G.R. Moore, 1995. "Monetary Policy Trade-offs and the Correlation between Nominal Interest Rates and Real Output." American Economic Review 85 (March) pp. 219–239.

Litterman, R., and J. A. Scheinkman. 1991. "Common Factors Affecting Bond Returns." Journal of Fixed Income 1.

Wu, T., 2001. "Monetary Policy and the Slope Factor in Empirical Term Structure Estimations." FRB San Francisco Working Paper 2002–07. http://www.frbsf.org/publications/economics/papers/2002/wp0207bk.pdf

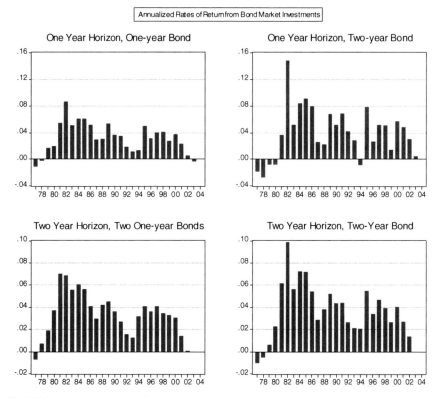

Fig. 5.9 Real returns on one and two-year treasuries by horizon

two-year bond offers a slightly higher mean return and a slightly higher standard deviation.

So there you have it: the bonds with the longer maturity offer higher expected returns but also more risk for both horizons.

Table 5.2 Means and standard deviations of bond market real rates of return, 1977–2004

Real rates of return from bond-market investments, 1977–2004

	One-year horizon			Two-year horizon		
	One-year bond	Two-year bond	Difference	One-year bond	Two-year bond	Difference
Mean	3.4%	4.2%	0.8%	3.4%	3.8%	0.4%
Median	3.3%	4.5%	1.2%	3.5%	3.9%	0.4%
Maximum	8.7%	14.9%	6.2%	7.0%	9.9%	2.8%
Minimum	−1.1%	−2.7%	−1.6%	−0.7%	−1.1%	−0.4%
Std. Dev.	2.2%	3.9%	1.7%	2.0%	2.4%	0.5%
Observations	26	26		26	26	

5.7 What Determines the Shape of the Yield Curve?

Now let's return to the search for an explanation of the shape of the yield curve. The yield curves illustrated in Fig. 5.8 raise three questions:

1. Why is the normal yield curve *sloping upward* with the return on 10-year bonds about a full percentage point higher than the return on the 3-month bills, as it was in 1996–1999?
2. What can make the yield curve sloping *downward* as it was in November 2000?
3. What can make the yield curve *steeper than normal* as it was in May 2004?
4. Why is the *level* of the yield curve lower in some periods than in others, as it was in June 2005 compared with 1996–1999?

We are now in a position to propose answers to these difficult questions.

5.7.1 Why Is the Yield Curve Generally Upward Sloping?

5.7.1.1 Inflation Risk Explanation

It may not have been crystal clear from the discussion of all those formulae describing the real returns to one and two-year bonds, but inflation uncertainty is likely to cause greater real return risk the longer the maturity of the bond. Borrowers have to offer a higher rate of return to offset that inflation risk.

5.7.1.2 Preferred Habitat Explanation

According to the preferred habitat hypothesis, the slope of the yield curve is determined by supply and demand balances at the different maturities. Many lenders have short horizons (think of deposits in savings accounts) and many borrowers have long horizons (think of home mortgages). Because of their short horizons, lenders are unwilling to invest in long-term instruments unless they get a premium. Because of their long horizons, borrowers are willing to pay a premium to lock in that long-term rate. That's what might cause the generally upward sloping yield curve[6] – too much supply of long-term bonds and too much demand for short-term bonds.

---

[6] Banks, for example, take short-term "on-demand" deposits in checking accounts and savings accounts and issue long-term loans, like 30-year mortgages. That's called *intermediation*. The gap between the long-term rate and the short-term rate creates intermediation profits.

5.7.2 Why Is the Yield Curve Sometimes Steep and Sometimes Inverted?

Inflation risk may contribute to the generally upward sloping yield curve but inflation expectations probably cannot change rapidly enough to account for rapid changes in shape of the yield curve. What matters then are either changes in the preferred habitats of lenders and borrowers or changes in bond market guesses about future Fed policy. Let us discuss the preferred habitat hypothesis first.

5.7.2.1 A Change in the Supply and Demand Balance along the Maturity Spectrum Can Alter the Slope of the Yield Curve

The normal balance of borrowers and lenders along the yield curve can be upset by Federal Reserve Board open market operations that involve the direct selling or buying of Treasury Bills. That's the Fed holding onto the tail of the elephant.

The normal balance of supply and demand along the yield curve can also change because of a change in investment opportunities and a strengthening or weakening of long-term borrowing.

In the beginning of an expansion, the investment opportunities are plentiful and the demand for loanable funds is great, which puts upward pressure on the long-term yields. At the same time, the Fed is trying to stimulate the economy and chooses low short-term yields. Thus at the beginning of the expansions the yield curve is steeply sloped.

The ends of the expansions are entirely different in terms of the balance of supply and demand along the maturity spectrum. The ends of expansions often have rising rates of inflation met by "contractionary" antiinflation Fed policy of high short-term rates. Also at the ends of the expansions, most of the good investment opportunities have already been grabbed and the demand for loanable funds is weak, which puts downward pressure on the long-term rates. Thus we get an inverted yield curve.

5.7.2.2 Predictable Changes in the Short-Term Rate Can also Affect the Shape of the Yield Curve

The shape of the yield curve can also change when normal expectations about future short-term rates are disturbed. Remember that in a certain world the two-year rate must equal the average of the two one-year rates, $s = (r_1 + r_2)/2$.

There are several circumstances in which the predicted future short-term rates are different from current rates.

Toward the ends of expansions, the Fed may choose to fight incipient inflation with higher rates, which may flatten the yield curve. Even if the Fed does not actually increase the short-term rates, the Fed in every recession has lowered rates, and the bond market, if it expects economic weakness ahead, will flatten the yield curve in anticipation of Fed actions. After all, if you know that the short-term rates are going to fall, you are going to want to lock in that attractive long-term rate now. When lenders move to lock in the longer-term maturities, they drive down the long-term rates and the yield curve will flatten and possible "invert."

After the Fed has completed an aggressive stimulus of the economy during a recession and has pulled down short-term rates dramatically, the market will expect a rise in the short-term rates and the yield curve will be sloping upward. That happens early in expansions, as we will see soon enough.

5.7.2.3 TIPS: Treasury Inflation Protected Bonds, and the Real Yield Curve

We can confirm that it does not take changes in inflation risks to change the shape of the yield curve by looking at the yields on Treasury Inflation Protected Bonds, which pay a stated rate of interest plus the inflation rate as measured by the CPI. These bonds offer a pretax real rate of interest, though income taxes apply to the total yield including the part due to inflation, which means that Uncle Sam takes a bigger bite out of your return the higher is the rate of inflation. The shape of the yield curve for these bonds should not be dependent on the rate of inflation at least if we can treat the tax issue as a secondary matter. If this real yield curve is flat and unchanging, then it must be that inflation concerns alone are driving changes in the nominal yield curve. If the real curve is sometimes sloping upward and sometimes sloping downward, then preferred habitats and expected future real rates must matter.

The real November yield curves are depicted in Fig. 5.10.[7] (I chose November because as I write, the latest data are November 2006). Take a look: These real yield curves are all over the map.

By using the TIPS rates we have pretty much removed the influence of inflation uncertainty on the slope of the yield curve, leaving only the effects of the other two forces: expectations regarding the course of the economy and preferred habitats. One message of Fig. 5.10 is that it does not take inflation uncertainty to make the yield curve slope upward. The real yield curve had plenty of upward slope to it in 2002, 2003, and 2004. But it is too soon to tell what is "normal" however, because, prior to 2001, the yields for short maturities did not exist and because the period from 2002 to 2004 was a period of aggressive monetary policy aimed at keeping short-term rates low.

Another message of this figure is that the Fed is capable of influencing *real* short-term rates as well as nominal ones. After all, except for the Fed policy change, what else happened to increase the real interest rates on the 3-year debt by 200 basis points from 0.50 in 2004 to 2.5 in 2006? That coincides with an increase in the Fed Funds Rate from 2.0 to 5.25.

---

[7] The Treasury started issuing 10-Year Inflation Indexed Bonds in January of 1997. Those first bonds matured 10 years later on 15 January 2007. A year after the first issuance, the Treasury issued new 10-year bonds that matured on 15 January 2008. At that time the original bonds with a due date of 1/15/2007 had a maturity of 9 years, and by comparing the market yield on those two issues we get two points on the inflation-protected yield curve. Each year thereafter the Treasury has issued new 10-year Tips (and 30-year TIPS as well.) The structure of interest rates across these outstanding bonds with different due dates is what forms the "real" November yield curves.

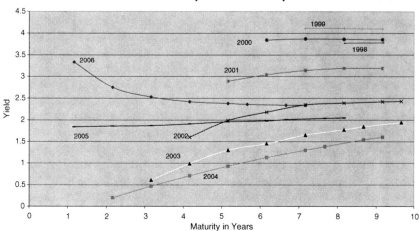

Fig. 5.10 TIPS yield curves

5.7.3 What Determines the Level (Not the Slope) of the Yield Curve?

Speaking of increasing rates, it is not just the slope of the yield curve that varies over time. It is the level too. Take a look at the nominal yield curves depicted in Fig. 5.8. Notice that the June 2005 curve and the "average" have the same shape, but June 2005 is lower by almost 2% (200 basis points). November 2006 and November 2000 also have about the same shape, but the 2006 curve is about 100 basis points lower. Why is that so? Why are these yield curves shifting lower over time?

It might be that inflation is getting more and more under control, and while real rates have stayed about the same, nominal rates that include an inflation premium have fallen. It might be, but it is not so. The real yield curves depicted in Fig. 5.10 have fallen as much or more than the nominal curves. For example, the long-term rates are about 250 basis points lower in November 2006 than they were in November 2000.

Why are real rates of interest so low? Greenspan's successor, Ben Bernanke, has an answer: a global savings glut: too much savings chasing too few investment opportunities. Back in 1998 and 1999, during the Internet Rush, US corporate earnings were disappointing, but the demand for loanable funds to create Websites was intense and the real rate of interest illustrated in Fig. 5.10 was around 4%. The bursting of the Internet stock bubble, the lowering of the growth expectations, a collapse of business investment followed by a sharp increase in corporate earnings dramatically altered the supply/demand balance for loanable funds and brought the long end of real yield curve steadily down, producing long-term yields of 3.2% in November 2001 and 2.4% in 2002, 1.9% in 2003 and a miserable 1.6% in November 2004. Subsequently, and coincidental with an increase in the Federal Funds rate, the long-term TIPS rates have elevated back to almost 2.5% in November 2006. Still 2.5% is not much if you are used to 4.0%.

So why is it that bond buyers have to put up with such low rates of return? No one really knows, but that lack of knowledge does not prevent a confidently expressed opinion. The answer is both supply and demand for loanable funds. A great deal of global growth is now emanating from the high savings countries of Asia, and the world is generating a lot more savings than it did when growth came from US and Europe, where savings rates are dramatically lower. At the same time, as the advanced developed countries experience the shift from an industrial to a postindustrial age, the big capital investments for industrial infrastructure, factories, and equipment are a thing of the past, and the demand for loans to finance the acquisition of these assets has fallen as well. That decline in the issuance of industrial bonds has not been offset by an increase in the issuance of postindustrial bonds because bond financing does not work well for the acquisition of intangible knowledge assets. Physical assets served as collateral for corporate borrowing since they can be seized and sold, but intangible knowledge assets that are the basis for a postindustrial economy are mostly nontransferable, and cannot serve as collateral. For these assets, equity is the only financial option.

Circumstances may also be dictating a flatter "normal" yield curve. Uncertainty in inflation seems substantially reduced and the force for a steep yield curve is lessened. It seems also to be the case that the preferred habitat of these Asian savers is not short-term bills but rather long-term bonds. Much of Asian savings is flowing into US Treasuries through foreign central banks. The flow of Asian savings into long-term bonds holds down the long-term rates and makes the yield curve flatter.

What to expect now for the nominal yield curve? Flatter and lower, for the indefinite future.

Appendix: Q and A from BLS Web Site Regarding the CPI

How is the CPI Market Basket Determined?

The CPI market basket is developed from detailed expenditure information provided by families and individuals on what they actually bought. For the current CPI, this information was collected from the Consumer Expenditure Survey over the three years 1993, 1994, and 1995. In each of these three years, more than 5,000 families from around the country provided information on their spending habits in a series of quarterly interviews. To collect information on frequently purchased items such as food and personal care products, another 5,000 families in each of the 3 years kept diaries listing everything they bought during a 2-week period.

Altogether, more than 30,000 individuals and families provided expenditure information for use in determining the importance, or weight, of over 2000 categories in the CPI index structure.

What Goods and Services Does the CPI Cover?

The CPI represents all goods and services purchased for consumption by the reference population (CPI-U or CPI-W). BLS has classified all expenditure items into more than 200 categories, arranged into eight major groups. Major groups and examples of categories in each are as follows:

- FOOD AND BEVERAGES (breakfast cereal, milk, coffee, chicken, wine, full service meals, and snacks)
- HOUSING (rent of primary residence, owners' equivalent rent, fuel oil, bedroom furniture)
- APPAREL (men's shirts and sweaters, women's dresses, jewelry)
- TRANSPORTATION (new vehicles, airline fares, gasoline, motor vehicle insurance)
- MEDICAL CARE (prescription drugs and medical supplies, physicians' services, eyeglasses and eye care, hospital services)
- RECREATION (televisions, cable television, pets and pet products, sports equipment, admissions)
- EDUCATION AND COMMUNICATION (college tuition, postage, telephone services, computer software, and accessories)
- OTHER GOODS AND SERVICES (tobacco and smoking products, haircuts and other personal services, funeral expenses)

Also included within these major groups are various government-charged user fees, such as water and sewerage charges, auto registration fees, and vehicle tolls. The CPI also includes taxes (such as sales and excise taxes) that are directly associated with the prices of specific goods and services. However, the CPI excludes taxes (such as income and Social Security taxes) not directly associated with the purchase of consumer goods and services.

The CPI does not include investment items, such as stocks, bonds, real estate, and life insurance. (These items relate to savings and not to day-to-day consumption expenses.)

For each of the more than 200 item categories, BLS has chosen samples of several hundred specific items within selected business establishments frequented by consumers, using scientific statistical procedures, to represent the thousands of varieties available in the marketplace. For example, in a given supermarket, the Bureau may choose a plastic bag of golden delicious apples, US extra fancy grade, weighing 4.4 pounds to represent the "Apples" category.

How are CPI Prices Collected and Reviewed?

Each month, BLS data collectors called economic assistants visit or call thousands of retail stores, service establishments, rental units, and doctors' offices, all over the United States to obtain price information on thousands of items used to track and measure price change in the CPI. These economic assistants record the prices of

about 80,000 items each month. These 80,000 prices represent a scientifically selected sample of the prices paid by consumers for the goods and services purchased.

During each call or visit, the economic assistant collects price data on a specific
good or service that was precisely defined during an earlier visit. If the selected item
is available, the economic assistant records its price. If the selected item is no longer
available, or if there have been changes in the quality or quantity (for example, eggs
sold in packages of 8 when previously they had been sold in dozens) of the goods or
service since the last time prices had been collected, the economic assistant selects
a new item or records the quality change in the current item.

The recorded information is sent to the national office of BLS where commodity specialists, who have detailed knowledge about the particular goods or services
priced, review the data. These specialists check the data for accuracy and consis-
tency and make any necessary corrections or adjustments. These can range from an
adjustment for a change in the size or quantity of a packaged item to more complex
adjustments on the basis of statistical analysis of the value of an item's features or
quality. Thus, the commodity specialists strive to prevent changes in the quality of
items from affecting the CPI's measurement of price change.

Appendix: Risk Characteristics of Bonds

ALERT: This section is for aspiring nerds only. This is the kind of exercise that is
needed to decide how inflation risk affects the yield curve. The algebra is messy, but
not really complex.

To get a handle on the complicated covariance questions that affect the risk characteristics of the one-year and two-year bonds discussed earlier, it is useful to build
a model that determines the inflation rate and the short-term interest rates. The point
of what follows is to determine whether inflation uncertainty can cause an upward
sloping yield curve because the inflation uncertainty adds more risk to the long-term
bonds than the short-term bonds. As it turns out, this is not a forgone conclusion,
since it depends critically on the behavior of the monetary authorities and the responsiveness of inflation to monetary policy (interest rates).

Let's work with the choice between a one-year bond and a two-year bond discussed in this chapter. Suppose that the Fed picks the interest rate at the beginning
of the second year according to the formula

$$r_2 = \beta r_1 + \delta I_1 + \varepsilon_r,$$

where β determines the persistence of rates, δ determines the sensitivity of the
interest rate in the second period to the inflation in the first period, and ε_r is the
unpredictable Fed surprise.

We also need a model for inflation. Here is one that allows for persistence and
also an effect of the Fed's interest rate policy on inflation:

$$I_2 = -\lambda r_2 + \theta I_1 + \varepsilon_1,$$

Table 5.3 Variances of return of $1 invested in the bond market

	End of first year	End of second year
One-year bonds	$\mathrm{Var}(I_1)$	$(\delta-1-\theta+\lambda\delta)^2\,\mathrm{Var}(I_1)$ $+\,(1+\lambda)^2\,\mathrm{Var}(\varepsilon_r)$ $+\,\mathrm{Var}(\varepsilon_I)$
Two-year bond	$(\delta+1)^2\mathrm{Var}(I_1)+\mathrm{Var}(\varepsilon_r)$	$(1+\theta-\lambda\delta)^2\mathrm{Var}(I_1)$ $+\lambda^2\,\mathrm{Var}(\varepsilon_r)+\mathrm{Var}(\varepsilon_I)$

where the minus sign in front of λ applies if higher interest rates reduce the inflation rate, as the Fed imagines. Substituting the r equation into the I equation we have:

$$I_2 = -\lambda(\beta r_1+\delta I_1+\varepsilon_r)+\theta I_1+\varepsilon_I = -\lambda\beta r_1+(\theta-\lambda\delta)I_1+\varepsilon_I-\lambda\varepsilon_r$$

Then we can solve for the needed quantities that form the returns in Table 5.1:

$$
\begin{aligned}
I_1+r_2 &= \beta r_1+(1+\delta)I_1+\varepsilon_r\\
I_1+I_2 &= -\lambda\beta r_1+(1+\theta-\lambda\delta)I_1+\varepsilon_I-\lambda\varepsilon_r\\
r_2-I_1-I_2 &= \beta r_1+\delta I_1+\varepsilon_r+\lambda\beta r_1-(1+\theta-\lambda\delta)I_1-\varepsilon_I+\lambda\varepsilon_r\\
&= \beta r_1+\lambda\beta r_1+(\delta-1-\theta+\lambda\delta)I_1+(1+\lambda)\varepsilon_r-\varepsilon_I
\end{aligned}
$$

with corresponding variances

$$
\begin{aligned}
\mathrm{Var}(I_1+r_2) &= (1+\delta)^2\mathrm{Var}(I_1)+\mathrm{Var}(\varepsilon_r)\\
\mathrm{Var}(I_1+I_2) &= (1+\theta-\lambda\delta)^2\,\mathrm{Var}(I_1)+\lambda^2\mathrm{Var}(\varepsilon_r)+\mathrm{Var}(\varepsilon_I)\\
\mathrm{Var}(r_2-I_1-I_2) &= (\delta-1-\theta+\lambda\delta)^2\mathrm{Var}(I_1)+(1+\lambda)^2\mathrm{Var}(\varepsilon_r)+Var(\varepsilon_I)
\end{aligned}
$$

These variances can be used to fill in the variances in Table 5.1

By comparing the two entries in the first column of this table, we can conclude that for the one-year horizon, the one-year bond is less risky than the two-year bond unless the Fed perversely lowers the interest rate when inflation is high, $\delta < 0$ (Table 5.3)

For the two-year horizon, things are more complicated. The variance of the two-year bond is less than two one-year bonds if

$$(1+\theta-\lambda\delta)^2\mathrm{Var}(I_1)+\lambda^2\mathrm{Var}(\varepsilon_r) < (1+\theta-\lambda\delta-\delta)^2\mathrm{Var}(I_1)+(1+\lambda)^2\mathrm{Var}(\varepsilon_r),$$

which can be rewritten as

$$0 < \delta(-2(1+\theta-\lambda\delta)+\delta)\mathrm{Var}(I_1)+(1+2\lambda)\mathrm{Var}(\varepsilon_r)$$

This complicated expression depends on two sources of uncertainty: inflation and Fed behavior. If the Fed is very unpredictable, that is if $\mathrm{Var}\varepsilon_r)$ is large, go for the two-year bond. What about inflation? It depends on the coefficient in front of the inflation variance. If the coefficient is positive, uncertainty in inflation favors the two-year bond. This condition can be written as: $\delta(2\lambda + 1) > 2(1 + \theta)$.

Summary

If you need the money in one year, choose the one-year bond.
If you need the money in two years, go for the two-year bond if:

   Inflation is not very persistent, and θ is small.
   The Fed is unpredictable: large $\text{Var}(\varepsilon_r)$
   The Fed is very inflation sensitive: large δ.
   The Fed can control inflation with high interest rates: large λ.

What does not matter is future unpredictable inflation risk, $\text{Var}(\varepsilon_I)$, since this affects both the one-year and the two-year real return exactly the same. Furthermore, while the amount of initial inflation risk, $\text{Var}(I_1)$ affects the risk differences in the two bonds, it does not affect the ordering. It is the persistence of inflation that matters, not the uncertainty.
   Can you explain why?

Chapter 6
Extrapolative Forecasting

We have already taken a close look on four key macro variables: GDP growth, inflation, interest rates and the unemployment rate. We studied the definitions of these variables, how they are measured, when they were high, and when they were low. For the purposes of understanding and especially for forecasting, we also need to know some of their "intertemporal" properties: If one of these variables shoots up, does it tend to stay there, or does it quickly come back down to normal levels? That's *persistence*. If one of these variables is moving in one direction, does it tend to keep moving in the same direction? That's *momentum*.

Before we study these two properties, we will discuss why they are important for forecasting. The key idea that drives all extrapolative forecasts is "regression toward the mean." Don't forget, when you hire that high-paid consultant to form forecasts, their report is only saying "regression toward the mean." Don't forget to pay them the big bucks for that tidbit of wisdom.

If there is a one-sentence bit of knowledge that you should take from this section, it is: Inflation and interest rates are very persistent, unemployment is moderately persistent, but GDP growth is hardly persistent at all. That makes GDP growth hard to forecast, while inflation and interest rates as they are very persistent, are much easier to forecast from their pasts. You should also realize that when you read in the newspaper that GDP growth was the very high number, 5.6, forget it. It doesn't matter. There is no persistence. But if you read that the unemployment rate jumped up by 0.5% points, that's really important. That jump in unemployment is not going away any time soon.

6.1 Regression Toward the Mean

To uncover the statistical properties of persistence and momentum, we have to turn Excel or some other statistical program loose on the data. We have to "run some regressions."

   Most MBAs learn that "linear regression" means fitting a straight line through
the data. But not many MBAs ask how curve fitting came to be called "regression."
You need to have that kind of curiosity. Ask what is "gross" in "Gross National
Product," and ask what the word "regression" really means. You cannot push back
the boundary between what you know and what you don't, if you don't know where
the boundary is.

   If you asked me, here is what I would say about the word "regression".

   I am sorry, but we have really screwed up our language by calling it "regression."
The correct, but narrower concept is "regression toward the mean" referring to the
fact that offspring tend to have characteristics that lie between the characteristics
of their parents and the average characteristics of the population. Thus tall parents
tend to have children who are tall compared to other children, but not as tall as their
parents. The kids regress toward the mean. They are predictably shorter than their
tall parents.

   Regression toward the mean is illustrated in the picture at the right. The horizontal axis is the parent characteristic and the vertical axis is the offspring characteristic.
The population mean is indicated by the circle in the middle of the figure. The 45°
line applies if inheritability is perfect, that is if the children are identical to their
parents. The "regression line" is what actually happens. Since the regression line is
flatter than the 45° line, parents who have characteristics for tallness that are greater
than the mean tend to have offspring who are shorter than they. (Not shorter than
the average. Shorter than the parents.) If the regression line were perfectly flat, the
parents wouldn't matter at all.

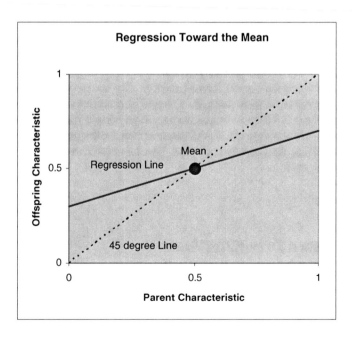

Just to make sure that you understand that this is a statistical property, better realize that it works *both forward and backward* in time. Unusually tall *children* tend to have *parents* who are shorter than them. If you bet on sports, you know this. Remember the year in which your favorite sports team performed really well? They didn't do so well the following year, or the year before either, did they? That is not a causal explanation. That's just a property of data with some variability.

Regression toward the mean was discovered by Francis Galton in 1877 by making a scatter plot comparing the mean diameter of sweet pea seeds with the mean diameter of their offspring. To his astonishment, these data lay along a straight line, flatter than the 45° line. Fat sweet peas had offspring that were not as fat, and scrawny little peas had offspring that were larger. Excited by what he must have thought to be a fundamental law of genetics, he called the slope of the line the "coefficient of reversion". The good news and the bad news are that he had the intellectual firepower to be one of the founders of modern statistical thinking. Soon enough he realized that what he had uncovered was not a new law of genetics but only "Galton's regression fallacy", which has been the source of incorrect inferences countless times. (Give some remedial math training to the students who do the worst on a math test and test them again. Even if the training has no effect, the average test score is sure to improve because of the force of regression toward the mean. If you are not careful, you will think the training made the students better.) To memorialize his improved understanding, Galton changed the name, but only slightly and subtly, from "coefficient of reversion" to "coefficient of regression". But the bad news is that he was one of the founders of modern statistics, and those who came after were greatly influenced by his graphs and his words. He made fundamental contributions to the statistics of curve-fitting, and his word "regression" stuck to all curve-fitting exercises, whether they have to do with inheritability or not.

Sorry that we have to use the word regression, but it is more than a century too late to do anything about it.

Just to make sure you are getting the message, below are two scatter-diagrams comparing parents' characteristics (height and lifespan) with the corresponding characteristics of their children. In each, the best fitting is "regression line." Take a look. You should notice that height is highly heritable: like father like son. But longevity is not. If your parents or grandparents died early, don't worry, that doesn't much affect your prospects.

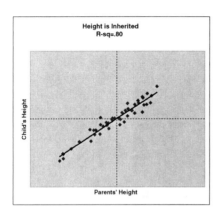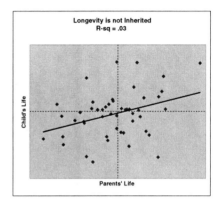

6.2 Forecasting and Regression Toward the Mean

Regression toward the mean is a great forecasting tool. Actually, it is the only forecasting tool. All methods of technical extrapolation are based on regression toward the mean or elaborations thereof. Here is how it works. First, we have to figure out the mean toward which the data regresses. Let's analyze GDP growth. The mean GDP growth since 1970 has been 3.2%. Using the principle of regression toward the mean, the best forecast is then going to be a weighted average of the current growth rate and that historical mean of 3.2%. Denoting the weight on the current value by w, we have the GDP growth forecast equal to

$$\text{GDP growth forecast} = w \times (\text{Current Quarter GDP growth}) + (1 - w)$$
$$\times (\text{Historical Mean GDP Growth})$$
$$= w \times (\text{Current Quarter GDP growth}) + (1 - w) \times (3.2)$$

Next, we have to find the weight w. This is done by curve fitting. The scatter on the right compares GDP growth in one quarter with GDP growth in the next. Into this scatter, I have assigned the computer to insert a best-fitting regression line. It has a slope of 0.25. That's w. Thus, put 25% weight on the current quarter and 75% on the historical mean of 3.2.

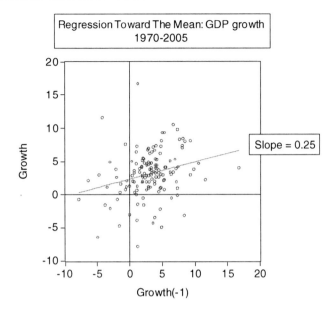

Just to be sure that you understand how this works, suppose that in the current quarter, GDP growth is 4.0%. The forecast for next quarter is then 0.25 times 4.0 plus 0.75 times 3.2, which is 3.4, just a little bit greater than the historical mean of 3.2.

No reason to stop here. We can roll this forward to another quarter by taking a weighted average of the historical mean 3.2 and the one-quarter ahead forecast that we just discovered to be 3.4. So for two quarters ahead, we have 0.25 times 3.4 plus 0.75 times 3.2, which is 3.25, virtually indistinguishable from the historical mean of 3.2. In other words, when it comes to GDP growth, the children (one quarter ahead) retain some similarity of their parents (this quarter's growth) but the grandchildren (two quarters ahead) have completely forgotten who their ancestors are. The children get 25% from their parents; the grandchildren get 0.25 times, 0.25 = 6%, from their grandparents. Thus for GDP growth there is little "inheritability" or, equivalently, little "persistence". When you are forecasting GDP growth, you won't go terribly wrong if you just say 3.2, every time. If your clients find that annoying and wonder why they are paying you the big bucks for creating a forecast, you can spice it up a bit by throwing in a 1.0 or a 4.0 forecast occasionally based on your "intuition" whether you have any or not.

The speed at which GDP growth regresses toward the mean makes these extrapolative forecasts uninteresting, but GDP growth is one of the least persistent of macro economic variables. One of the most persistent is the unemployment rate. Compare the scatter-diagram at below with the one depicting GDP growth. These two are totally different. The quarterly persistence of unemployment is 96%, which means that the children look very much like their parents. Whereas the historical mean of 3.2 is a pretty good forecast for GDP growth, no matter what is current

GDP growth, a good prediction of next quarter's unemployment rate is not the historical mean of 6.2; a much better prediction is this quarter's unemployment rate. It's very persistent.

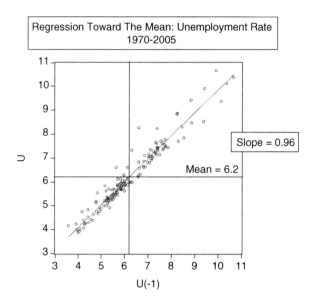

So here is the take-away: Extrapolative forecasts converge to the historical mean. If the persistence is low, the convergence is rapid; if the persistence is high, the convergence is slow. Take a look at Fig. 6.1 that contrasts forecasts of GDP growth and forecasts of the rate of unemployment based on the two regressions just discussed. Period 0 refers to this quarter's data. In the period 0, GDP growth is assumed to be 2% points above the mean of 3.2 as represented by the horizontal white line. Unemployment rate is also assumed to be 2% point above its historical mean of 6.2. Then the forecasts converge to the mean. After two quarters, the GDP growth forecast is indistinguishable from the historical mean of 3.2. But even after five years (20 quarters), the unemployment forecast is noticeably above the historical mean of 6.2. Unemployment is very persistent; GDP growth is not.

6.3 Persistence, Momentum

The power of the personal computer that occupies your desk would completely boggle the mind of Francis Galton, not to mention virtually all the statisticians who worked in twentieth Century. At the press of a button or two, you and your personal computer can make Galton's graphs and estimate his regressions, things that took him hours if not days to do by hand. You can also easily estimate multi-variable

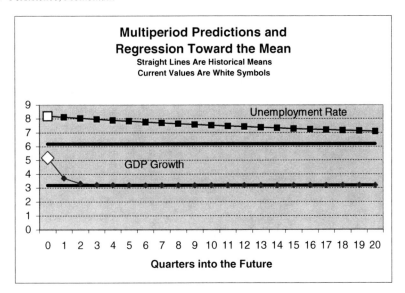

Fig. 6.1 Simple convergence paths for unemployment and GDP growth

regressions, when he was limited to work with two or three variables. To allow for more complicated dynamics, let's do some of these multivariable regressions.

Table 6.1 reports estimated regressions for our four key macro variables: growth, inflation, short-term interest rates and the unemployment rate. These equations allow these variables to depend on four lagged variables: the variable in the previous quarter, two quarters ago, three quarters ago and four quarters ago. If y refers to either growth, inflation, interest rates of unemployment, $y(-1)$ refers to the value in the previous quarter, and $y(-2)$ means a lag of two quarters.

Table 6.1 Time series properties of four macro variables

Regression estimates
Period of estimation: 1970 Q1 to 2005 Q3

		Regression coefficients					
	Mean	$y(-1)$	$y(-2)$	$y(-3)$	$y(-4)$	Persistence[a]	Half-Life[b]
Persistence							
Growth	3.20	0.22	0.15			0.37	1
Inflation	4.10	0.46	0.31	0.16	0.01	0.93	3
			Momentum				
			$y(-1)-y(-2)$			0.95	13
Persistence and Momentum							
Unemployment Rate	6.2	0.95		0.64		0.95	13
3-month Treasury Rate	6.0	0.95		0.23		0.95	13

[a]Persistence is the sum of the coefficients
[b]Half-Life is the number of quarters to eliminate 50% of disturbance.

This table reports two different properties of these variables:

1. **Persistence**: A persistent variable will hang around where it is and converge slowly only to the historical mean. A measure of persistence is the half-life: the number of quarters needed to eliminate 50% of a disturbance from historical levels.
2. **Momentum**: Momentum is the tendency to continue *moving* in the same direction. The momentum effect can offset the force of regression toward the mean and can allow a variable to move away from its historical mean, for some time, but not indefinitely.[1]

Let's start with the GDP growth equation in the first row of Table 6.1. It has a coefficient equal to 0.22 on the previous quarter's growth and a coefficient equal to 0.15 on the growth rate two quarters before. In terms of genetics, these GDP children depend not just on their parent's characteristics, but also their grandparents. The sum of the coefficients is only 0.37, meaning about 37% of the GDP abnormality is passed into the future. The actual path of the variable over time depends on both the sum and how the sum is distributed across the lagged values. The inflation equation reported just below the GDP growth equation includes four lagged inflation variables and has a longer memory and a greater sum of the coefficients than GDP growth. Both these contribute to make inflation much more persistent than GDP growth. Growth has a half-life of only 1 quarter while inflation has a half-life of 3 quarters, although more careful data analysis leads to a much longer half-life of inflation.

Turn your attention now to the unemployment equation[2] and the interest rate equation reported in Table 6.1. In addition to persistence, these variables exhibit momentum, meaning that once they get moving up or down they tend to keep on moving in the same direction. That's the meaning of the positive coefficient on $[y(-1)-y(-2)]$. Thus if the parents are taller than the grandparents, the intergenerational gain is partly passed on to the children who are taller as a result. That's the momentum effect. Can you tell a good story about the way firms hire and fire workers that explains this momentum effect in the unemployment rate? We'll deal this in the next section.

---

[1] Provided that the persistence is less than 100%.

[2] You can get to this result by estimating an equation that depends on U(-1) and U(-2), which has a strange pattern of signs: the coefficient on the first lag of unemployment is positive and bigger than one, and the coefficient on the second lag is negative: $U = c + 1.58U(-1) - 0.64U(-2)$. What kind of inheritability can that possibly represent? It looks like having a tall grandparent is going to make the children short. How weird is that? To make sense out of this equation, we need to shuffle it a bit to write it as a function of the lagged value and the *change* in the lagged value: $1.58U(-1) - 0.64U(-2) = .94U(-1) + .64[U(-1)-U(-2)]$. Confirm that this really is an equality – the expression on the left is algebraically equal to the expression on the right. The point of rewriting it this way is that it helps us put some sensible words onto what is at first a confusing result.

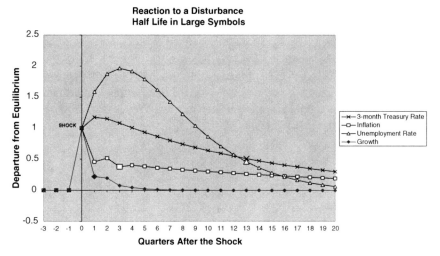

Fig. 6.2 Reaction to a temporary disturbance

6.4 Pictures that Help to Understand the Numbers

Don't forget: Pictures, Words and Numbers.

Those numbers are really tough to understand, aren't they? Pictures that show how these variables move over time may help out. Figure 6.2 displays the reaction to a temporary disturbance, meaning that historically the variable was at its historical mean and then was jumped up to a value of one above the mean for one quarter only. What happens next?

Because of the momentum effect, two of the variables (unemployment and interest rates) continue to rise higher. The extent of the overshooting is not much for interest rates but a lot for unemployment.

All these four variables converge back to their normal levels (zero), some faster than others. When the variable gets below 0.5, half of the disturbance has disappeared. Call that the half-life, which is also recorded in Table 6.1. GDP, the least persistent of the variables has a half-life of only one quarter. Inflation, which is also very persistent, has a short half-life of only three quarters. That half-life is short because inflation is a long-memory process, and the hypothesis illustrated in Fig. 6.2 has zero inflation in the quarters before the disturbance. Then the most persistent variables, unemployment and interest rates, have the same half-life of 13 quarters.

6.5 Stories that Help to Understand the Numbers

Did we learn anything from the numbers and the pictures? To memorialize our findings, lets tell some stories.

Why does unemployment have the momentum effect? Answer: Firms do not hire or fire all in a single quarter. They make an employment plan and phase it in over several quarters. When you see unemployment rising, expect it to rise some more, as those multi-quarter layoff plans are put into practice.

Why do interest rates have a momentum effect? You tell the story about Greenspan and company, if you can. They are the ones setting interest rates. When they move in one direction, they tend to keep moving. Why is that? How about your thermostat? Do you adjust it gradually?

Part III A
Recession Symptoms

Chapter 7
Unwanted Idleness: Recessions and Recoveries

A recession is two quarters of negative GDP growth. *NOT.*

Definition: A *recession* is a market failure, which causes a persistent and substantial increase in *unwanted idleness*. Following a recession is a *recovery* during which idleness returns to normal levels.

Irrigated farmland, industrial equipment office buildings, factories, skills and ideas are the assets that are used to produce GDP. These assets do not work around the clock, 365 days a year. There are normal scheduled downtimes for recuperation, replenishment, maintenance, and, in the case of human skills and understanding, sleep and leisure time. There are unscheduled downtimes because of illnesses or breakdowns or natural catastrophes. There are downtimes when assets are transferred between owners and between functions – when workers move between jobs, and when a San Francisco office building is transferred from dot-com firms to not-for-profits. There are seasonal downtimes. Mechanical harvesters are operated only during harvest time. The last 10% of electric generating capacity is idle except in the peak summer hours.

The greatest amount of idleness of assets is due to scheduling problems. Your bed is used only when you sleep and your TV used only when you are awake. (You could try to rent out your bed when you are not using it, but it may be hard for you to find anyone with a sleeping schedule that is complementary with your own.) Your hammer sits idle when you are using your screwdriver. Your skills in data analysis sit idle when you are composing a document. Airplanes sit at gates waiting to pick up passengers from other flights, or waiting at busy airports for the opportunity to take off again. Your car and your skills and your ideas and the road all sit idle when you are jammed in traffic on the "freeway," trying to get to your job.

Idleness of a productive asset is costly because the owner is paying the capital rental costs around the clock, all year long, whether or not the asset is working. Markets do not like idle assets. By awarding ownership to the highest bidder, markets transfer assets to those who know how to minimize idleness and who can squeeze the most value out of them. Indeed the primary function of the division of labor is to minimize idleness. If you do the hammering while I do the sawing, we can keep the hammer and the saw operating at the same time.[1]

Hard as we might work at it, we should not eliminate all idleness, any more than we should eliminate absolutely all air pollution. There is an optimal level of pollution, which comes from weighing the benefits of a cleaner environment with the costs of making it cleaner. There is also an optimal level of idleness of productive assets – you have long ago stopped worrying about the idleness of your bed when you are at your desk. Some idleness is thus a characteristic of a normal, healthy, and efficient economy. But every modern economy also experiences periods when the level of idleness increases dramatically and stays there for uncomfortably long periods of time. A period of rising unwanted idleness is an economic recession.

Idleness can be measured in many ways, but the three most important indicators are: the unemployment rate, capacity utilization in manufacturing and weekly hours in manufacturing.

7.1 Worker Idleness: Unemployment

The most familiar measurement of unwanted idleness is the unemployment rate: the number seeking work divided by the total labor force. You can see the ups and downs of the US unemployment rate in Fig. 7.1, which has the official "NBER recessions" displayed in white. These are also listed in Table 7.1. These official recession periods have been selected by a committee of the National Bureau of Economic Research, after poring over as much data as they can get their hands on.

7.1.1 The NBER Definition of a Recession Isn't So Great

This committee of the National Bureau of Economic Research magically does their work without benefit of a clear definition of a recession. Here is what their website says.

(http://nber.org/cycles/, June 18, 2003)

"A recession is a significant decline in activity spread across the economy, lasting more than a few months, normally visible in real GDP, real income, employment, industrial production, and wholesale-retail sales."[2]

---

[1] Southwest Airlines, virtually alone among the carriers, has achieved profitability by keeping its expensive fleet of aircraft in the air.

[2] "Because a recession influences the economy broadly and is not confined to one sector, the committee emphasizes economy-wide measures of economic activity. The committee views real GDP as the single best measure of aggregate economic activity. In determining whether a recession has occurred and in identifying the approximate dates of the peak and the trough, the committee

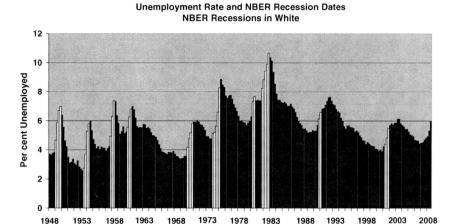

Fig. 7.1 US unemployment rate: Recessions

Sorry, ye wise men of the NBER, this is not a definition of a recession. This is only a list of incidental symptoms. It's like saying SARS is a high fever and a cough. Moreover, when you use the words "significant decline" to define a recession, you presume that the normal state of the economy is a modest level of growth, so that negative growth is an abnormality. That's like saying a period of sustained weight loss is a symptom of a chronic disease, when it's a symptom only in middle-aged adults. For babies, the problem is slow weight gain. For the elderly, the symptom is something else altogether. I give the NBER a grade of B, and encourage them to try again.

7.1.2 Identifying the Recessions in the Unemployment Data Is Child's Play

What the NBER says isn't so clear, but what they do is very transparent. If you ask your 10-year-old daughter to point out the mountain slopes facing west in the unemployment data depicted in Fig. 7.1, she would surely select almost the

therefore places considerable weight on the estimates of real GDP issued by the Bureau of Economic Analysis of the U.S. Department of Commerce. The traditional role of the committee is to maintain a monthly chronology, however, and the BEA's real GDP estimates are only available quarterly. For this reason, the committee refers to a variety of monthly indicators to choose the exact months of peaks and troughs.

It places particular emphasis on two monthly measures of activity across the entire economy: (1) personal income less transfer payments, in real terms and (2) employment. In addition, the committee refers to two indicators with coverage primarily of manufacturing and goods: (3) industrial production and (4) the volume of sales of the manufacturing and wholesale-retail sectors adjusted for price changes."

Table 7.1 US business cycle expansions and contractions[1]

Business cycle reference dates		Duration in months			
		Contraction	Expansion	Cycle	
Peak	Trough	Peak to	Previous trough to	Trough from Previous	Peak from Previous
Quarterly dates are in parentheses		Trough	this peak	Trough	Peak
November 1948(IV)	October 1949 (IV)	11	37	48	45
July 1953(II)	May 1954 (II)	**10**	**45**	**55**	**56**
August 1957(III)	April 1958 (II)	8	39	47	49
April 1960(II)	February 1961 (I)	10	24	34	32
December 1969(IV)	November 1970 (IV)	**11**	**106**	**117**	**116**
November 1973(IV)	March 1975 (I)	16	36	52	47
January 1980(I)	July 1980 (III)	6	58	64	74
July 1981(III)	November 1982 (IV)	16	12	28	18
July 1990(III)	March 1991(I)	8	92	100	108
March 2001(I)	November 2001 (IV)	8	120	128	128
Average,					
1945–2001 (10 cycles)		10	57	67	67

Figures printed in **bold** are the wartime expansions (Korean War, and Vietnam War); the wartime contractions, and the full cycles that include the wartime expansions.
[1] *Contractions (recessions) start at the peak of a business cycle and end at the trough.*
Sources: NBER; the U.S. Department of Commerce,
Survey of Current Business, October 1994, Table C-51.

same periods as the NBER committee. That's when idleness was on the rise. Your daughter might want to color a little more white onto the 1991 recession, extending its length. Maybe the Ph.D's on the NBER committee made a mistake on the timing of that one. High unemployment also persisted quite a while after the 2001 recession.

However, maybe there is a reason for a continued rise in unemployment after a recession. A recession may be only the virulent phase of the disease, when the unemployment rate is rising rapidly. When a recession is over, the economy is not back to normal. It takes a period of recovery, to get back to normal. In the first phase of the recovery, with demand picking up again, firms may adopt a wait and see attitude, and postpone any commitments to new employees until they are sure. In this first phase of a recovery, the unemployment rate can drift a bit higher.

An NBER committee handles the recessions, but there is no official committee that determines when a *recovery* is complete. No problem. You and I and your 10-year-old daughter can look at the pictures and make some guesses. I have shaded in white in Fig. 7.2, which seems like recovery periods to me. Here I am trying to capture the idea that a recovery may begin with a slight increase in unemployment, but soon enough this unwanted idleness is eliminated and the rate of unemployment

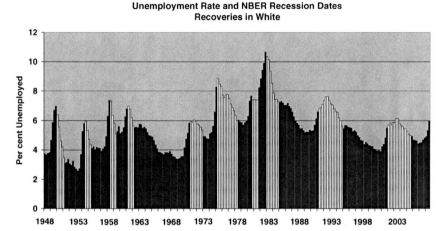

Fig. 7.2 US unemployment rate: Recoveries

is driven down rapidly to a normal level. When the unemployment rate plateaus out, that's back to normal.

7.2 Capital Idleness: Capacity Utilization in Manufacturing

Recessions come with increases in the idleness of capital as well as labor. When the demand for air travel falls, airlines routinely maintain "load factors" (percentage of seats that are filled) by cutting down flight services. As the planes sit on taxiways for longer hours, that's idleness of capital. If the decline in travel persists, aircraft are put "in mothballs" in the Arizona desert. That's idleness of capital.

It's very difficult to measure capital idleness at most worksites, but a manufacturing facility typically has a designed capacity. The capacity utilization rate is the ratio of output to designed capacity, which can sometimes exceed 100%. Now that

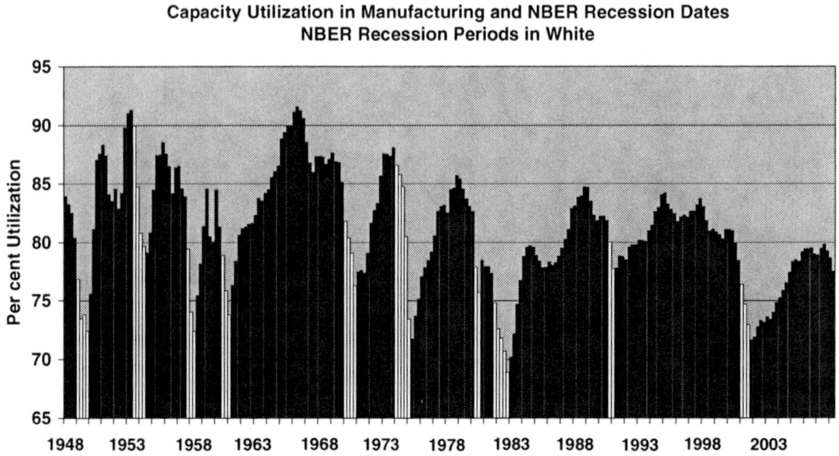

Capacity Utilization in Manufacturing and NBER Recession Dates
NBER Recession Periods in White

Fig. 7.3 Capacity utilization in manufacturing

we have your 10-year-old daughter as a consultant to the NBER, ask her to take a look at Fig. 7.3, which displays capacity utilization in manufacturing. Don't worry her about how capacity utilization is measured. Just ask her to identify the mountain slopes facing east, when capacity utilization was falling sharply. I think that she will pick pretty much the same periods as the NBER committee. That's when idleness of capital was on the rise.

7.3 Work Intensity: Hours per Week in Manufacturing

You don't have to be officially unemployed to be idle. You can sit around the work-site not doing much, but nonetheless draw a paycheck. Idleness on the job is very difficult to measure directly, but an indicator of the intensity of operations is hours per week. When demand is high and it's hard to get the work done in the normal workday, there are three possible solutions: increasing the pace of work, stretching the workday or hiring more workers. This is the typical response ordering: intensity, hours and jobs. The first response to an unexpected increase in sales is to increase the pace of work; the second is to increase overtime hours, and the third is to hire more workers. Going in the other direction, the first response to a *fall* in demand is to slow the pace of work, the second is to reduce overtime and the third is to lay off workers. Though changes in weekly hours often come after changes in work intensity, the delay is not great enough to preclude treating hours as a symptom of intensity.

Weekly hours in manufacturing is displayed in Fig. 7.4 with the official NBER recessions in yellow. Here it is a bit more difficult for your 10-year-old daughter to find the recessions because of the wavering in these data. The unemployment peaks and valleys in Fig. 7.1 are quite smooth, the capacity utilization peaks and valleys in

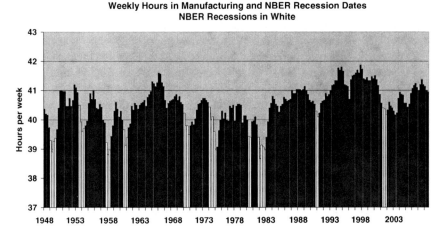

Fig. 7.4 Weekly hours in manufacturing

Fig. 7.3 are less, and the weekly hours least of all. Still, your daughter isn't going to have trouble locating the valleys in Fig. 7.4, but she may see valleys in the middle of some of the NBER expansions, including the 1960s and the 1990s.

7.4 Five Episodes: Normal Growth, Sputters, Spurts, Recessions and Recoveries

This is good detective work that your daughter has performed. We may be on to something. The NBER classification system has only two kinds of episodes: *normal economic growth* (expansions) and *recessions*. After looking at the unemployment graph, we decided that we need another category *recoveries*, when idleness returns to normal.

That's not all. Look again at the hours graph, Fig. 7.4. Can you see the decline in hours in 1967 and in 1995? Confirm in Fig. 7.3 that, at the same time, capacity utilization in manufacturing was also on the decline. Those evident problems in manufacturing didn't lead into recessions. Call those *sputters*, threatened recessions.

Finally, look again at the unemployment data displayed in Fig. 7.2, which has the recovery periods in white. Can you see that during the subsequent expansions, the unemployment rate is fairly constant for a couple of years but sometimes falls sharply to a new, lower plateau. That's a growth *spurt*.

So there you have it: the two NBER categories (recessions and expansions) are not enough. We need recessions, recoveries, normal growth, sputters and spurts. Sometimes a period of normal growth is ended with a sputter that gives way to a recession. Sometimes the sputter is met with a growth spurt.

While we are on discoveries, Fig. 7.4 reveals that the 40-hour week is a thing of the past. The workweek in manufacturing hovered around 40 h from 1948 to the mid 1980s, with a shorter workweek in the recessions and with overtime in the expansions. But since the (from) 1980s, the norm seems to have shifted up to a 41-h workweek. In the expansion of the 1990s, weekly hours reached the record average of 42 per week. What can account for this increase? I thought that increasing wealth and incomes would have led to more leisure time, not less: 60 h in 1900, 40 h in 1950 and 30 h in 2000. One possible reason for the rise in hours is the increase in benefits, especially health care. Now is a good time to digress to the subject of benefits since it fits rather aptly into our discussion of capital idleness. When you rent a moving van by the hour, you pay whether the van is idle or not. That creates an incentive to keep the van operating throughout the rental period. Avoid idleness. The higher the rental price, the greater the pressure to keep it moving. Likewise, when a worker is paid for a fixed benefit per year or per week, there is an incentive to keep her working as many hours as possible to spread that fixed cost over a larger labor input. Thus the deal: more health benefits but longer hours and fewer workers.

Chapter 8
Recession Comparison Charts

The right definition of a recession is a persistent and substantial increase in unwanted idleness. The three most important measures of idleness have been discussed in the previous chapter: the rate of unemployment, the intensity of work (hours per week in manufacturing), and excess capacity in manufacturing. Most other macroeconomic variables also behave differently during a recession, most notably the ones that the NBER has put into their definition of a recession: real GDP, real income, employment, industrial production, and wholesale-retail sales. Let's have a look at some of these series, and a few others too.

By the way, if you are going to read passively, this material will be hopelessly boring, and you might as well skip to the next chapter. You will find this more interesting if you think of yourself as Sherlock Holmes, trying to gather all the facts to figure out which culprit is guilty of causing each recession.

Don't forget: We are pattern-seeking story-telling animals. Find some patterns and tell some stories. Better yet, write it down. How are recessions different from other periods, and why?

8.1 Recession Comparisons: Employment and Output

8.1.1 Payroll Employment

Figure 8.1 displays the level of nonfarm payroll employment with the official NBER recessions colored in white. Here you can see rather clearly the dips of employment in each of these recessions. Though it is good, this kind of display requires you to do a lot of visual work to compare one recession with another. Which recession had the biggest drop in employment? Which one lasted the longest?

Figure 8.2 is another kind of display that allows a direct side-by-side comparison of the 10 recessions since 1948. The horizontal axis is the number of quarters before or after the NBER peak. To the left are quarters before the recessions begin; to the right are the recession quarters. What is displayed is the percentage difference

E. E. Leamer, *Macroeconomic Patterns and Stories: A Guide for MBAs.*
© Springer-Verlag Berlin Heidelberg 2009

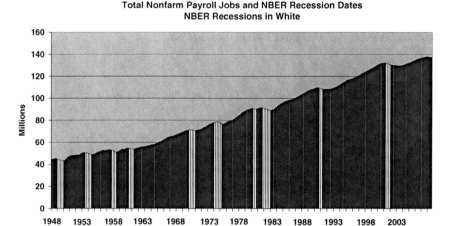

Fig. 8.1 Nonfarm payrolls: Bar chart

between employment and the employment level at the peak, quarter zero. *These recession comparison graphs display the data for each of the recessions until the payroll employment level exceeds the previous peak.* That's why we start with payroll employment.

You need to study this picture. What can you see in it? What is the typical path of employment before, during and after recessions? Which of the recessions was unusual, and how? Next I'll tell you some things I see in this figure, but before you read my discoveries, you need to make some of your own. If you passively read on, and rely completely on me, you will be deprived of a learning experience. If you allow me to carry you everywhere, you will never learn to walk. Incidentally, the greatest joy for me as a classroom teacher is when a student sees something important that completely escaped me.

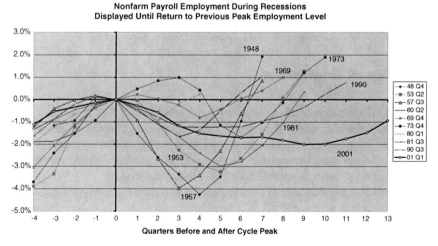

Fig. 8.2 Private payrolls: Recession comparisons

.... Waiting while you look at Fig. 8.2 ....

Here is what I see:

- Employment levels have dipped during recessions by 2–3%. Larger losses of 5% occurred in the long-ago recessions of 1948, 1953 and 1957.
- It has generally taken a little over a year for employment to bottom out.
- Employment regains its previous peak in about two years.
- The rate of growth in employment in the recovery period is more rapid than the pre-recession rate.
- The second most anemic recovery was the 1990 recession when it took 10 quarters (2.5 years) to get back the lost jobs.
- The 2001 recovery was the most prolonged on record. It took 16 quarters (4 years) before we got back to the level of payroll employment in 2001 Q1. We will need to give this recession some very careful scrutiny. It is very different from the others in many ways. For thinking about the future, we may want to toss that one out.
- Based on these employment data, the NBER missed the peak period in two recessions. The recessions on 1957 started earlier and the 1973 recessions started later. The NBER chose the 1973 peak to be the quarter when the growth of employment slowed considerably, but it continued to grow for three more quarters. We will need to look at the other data for these two recessions to decide for ourselves if the NBER made a mistake. (Do you want to be trained or do you want to be educated? If you choose training, read passively and memorize. If you want to be educated, actively question all self-proclaimed experts, including this author. Training will assure that you can solve the problems that are already solved. But electronic computers can do that, much better than you. If you want a good job in the twenty first Century, you have to be able to solve problems that are not yet solved. If you want that skill, opt for education, not training. Find your own patterns, and make up your own stories.)

8.1.2 Real GDP

Now that, you have mastered a recession comparison chart, take a look at the Real GDP (Fig. 8.3), and tell me what you see in it.

Here is what I see:

- Real GDP declines in recessions by about 1–2%. The largest declines occurred in the 1957 and the 1973 recessions.
- In these Real GDP data, there is no evident problem with the NBER choice of peak quarters, though the 2001 recession might have been timed a quarter earlier.
- It has taken about 3–4 quarters for GDP to bottom out, after that there has been very strong economic growth. That's the recovery.
- Real GDP has returned to its onset level in 4–5 quarters. By the "ends" of these events, when employment was back to its peak level, real GDP was 4–6% higher than at the previous peak. Thus the same number of payroll

jobs was associated with substantially high levels of GDP. That means higher productivity.

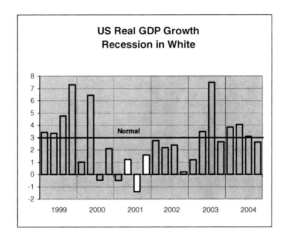

- Using negative GDP growth as an indicator, it looks like the 2001 recession started earlier in 2000 Q3 and ended in 2001 Q3. That period captures all the three negative growth numbers. Too bad, the NBER didn't have these revised data when they made their decision that the recession began in 2001 Q2 and ended in 2001Q3.
- The 2001 recession was very mild and officially short-lived. There wasn't a normal high-growth recovery. It was back to subnormal in 2002. I wonder why. Even though the growth rate wasn't negative, I wonder if we need to stretch that recession into 2002. The employment data would be compatible with that.

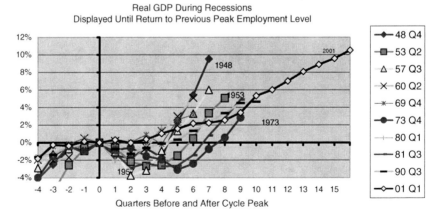

Fig. 8.3 Real GDP: Recession comparisons

8.2 Idleness

Now that we have a new kind of graph for comparing recessions, we can go back and take another look at the three idleness measures: unemployment, capacity utilization in manufacturing and weekly hours in manufacturing.

8.2.1 Household Unemployment Rate

Figure 8.4 compares the rate of unemployment over the ten downturns. I have labeled this the "household" unemployment rate, to remind you that the unemployment numbers are collected in a survey of households. Note that the vertical axis of this recession comparison graph is different from the vertical axis of the employment graph, Figure 8.2. The Figure 8.2 employment graph answers the question: What has been the percentage change in employment since the onset of the recession? Fig. 8.4, however, answers the question: By how many percentage points did unemployment increase since the onset of the recession? The worst recession in this sense was the 1973 recession, which increased the unemployment rate by 4 percentage points. You cannot see it in this figure but the rate of unemployment increased from about 4 to 8%.

Ok, it's time for you to do a little work. Take a look at the picture and tell me what you see. Remember that the data are displayed until the number of payroll jobs recover its value at the onset of the recession.

Here is what I see:

• The unemployment rate increased during recession by 2–3% points. Larger losses of 4% occurred in the 1973 recession, but the recessions of 1948, 1953,

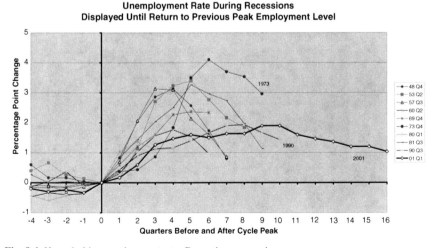

Fig. 8.4 Household unemployment rate: Recession comparisons

and 1957, which had the largest employment loss, do not stand out so much in terms of unemployment.

- It has taken a little over a year from the onset of the recession for the rate of unemployment to reach a peak.
- The last two recessions, 2001 and 1990, were slow and low. The peak unemployment rates took a long time (two years) to emerge and the increase in the unemployment rate was only 2%. Are we starting to experience a different kind of recession? I wonder what the next one will be like?
- Within the time periods displayed, in no case did the unemployment level return to its pre-recession value. The rate of unemployment was typically 1–2% points above that level. This may seem puzzling because the employment levels did return to their prerecession levels. The difference may come from the growth in the number of job seekers during the recession, or from some important difference between the household survey used to measure the number of employed and the payroll survey used to measure the number of jobs.
- Based on these unemployment data, the 1980 and 1990 recessions seem to have started a couple of quarters earlier than the NBER has said – unemployment was already on the rise.

8.2.2 Capacity Utilization in Manufacturing

Next take a look at capacity utilization in manufacturing depicted in Fig. 8.5. What do you see here?

I see:

- The rate of capacity utilization in manufacturing falls during recessions by 5–10% points. The greatest decline in capacity utilization (16%) occurred in the

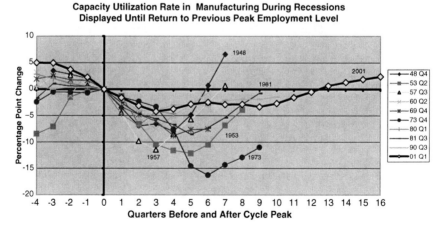

Fig. 8.5 Capacity utilization in manufacturing: Recession comparisons

1973 recession. The recessions of 1948, 1953, and 1957, which had the largest employment loss, also stand out in terms of the fall in capacity utilization.

- It has taken a little over a year for the rate of capacity utilization to bottom out.
- When employment was back to its previous peak level, in seven recessions of ten, the rate of capacity utilization was still below its prerecession value.
- Based on these capacity utilization data, many of these recessions seem to have started a couple of quarters earlier than the NBER has said. Or you can call a decline in the rate of capacity utilization a leading indicator of the onset of a recession.
- The 2001 recession had capacity utilization stalled at the bottom for a full year. This is really interesting to me. What makes this event so different? If this recession is unique, shouldn't monetary and fiscal policy have been different too? Do economists allow the possibility that there is more than one kind of recession? (Answer: No).

8.2.3 Hours per Week in Manufacturing

A decline in capacity utilization in manufacturing is one of the early warning signs of an oncoming recession. Hours per week in manufacturing, displayed in Fig. 8.6, is even better. To interpret this figure, keep in mind that normal hours-per-week is a little over 40. A reduction by one hour may not seem that much, but this kind of reduction is accompanied also by slower pace on the job and by sharp reductions of overtime.

Notice, by the way, the stuttered recovery following the 2001 recession. I wonder what caused the problem in 2002 Q? Was it the ripple effect of the 9/11 terrorist attacks? Following that catastrophe, there was so much agony expressed on

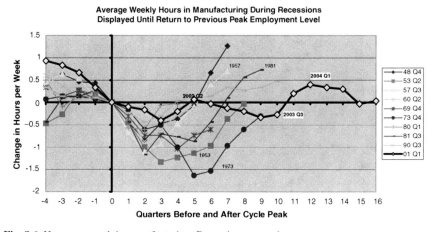

Fig. 8.6 Hours per week in manufacturing: Recession comparisons

the business pages of newspapers that most managers thought they would never make a sale again. Fighting against that possibility, businesses promoted very heavily. Then they were totally surprised by the result. October 2001 had a record sales volume for automobiles and sales were brisk throughout the economy, allowing real GDP to grow at the rate of 1.6 per year in the fourth quarter of 2001 after the dismal −1.4 in the third quarter. To satisfy this unexpected burst in sales, businesses drew down inventories. Then, in the first couple of quarters, businesses fought against this inventory decline by ramping up hours and production. After the ripple of the 9/11-induced sales passed through, the economy returned to its sluggish fundamentals, until 2003 Q3 when an apparent recovery in manufacturing seemed to be on the way. Sorry, down we went again in 2004. (Figs. 8.7–8.9).

8.3 Other Indicators

8.3.1 Industrial Production

Next take a look at industrial production in Fig. 8.7. What do you see? How does it compare with GDP?[1]

The industrial production data extend backward all the way to 1919, which is one of the few available business cycle indicators before the WWII. Take a look at Fig. 8.8 and comment on the volatility of industrial production before and after WWII. Are the cycles more or less extreme now? If you cannot see the answer in this figure, Fig. 8.9. What might explain the differences in volatility of industrial production?

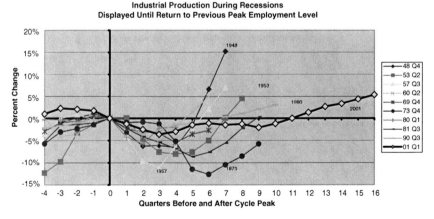

Fig. 8.7 Industrial production: Recession comparisons

---

[1] Answer: industrial production varies a lot more in recessions than GDP. Why is that?

Fig. 8.8 Industrial production: Long view

8.3.2 Employment in Manufacturing and Construction

While we are looking at these data on recessions, I am going to give you one really big clue: Most of the employment loss during recessions comes in two sectors: manufacturing and construction. Figure 8.10 illustrates the sharp declines in manufacturing employment in recessions; Fig. 8.11 illustrates the substantial declines of construction employment during recessions; Fig. 8.12 illustrates the very mild, if at all, declines in employment other than manufacturing and construction. To confirm

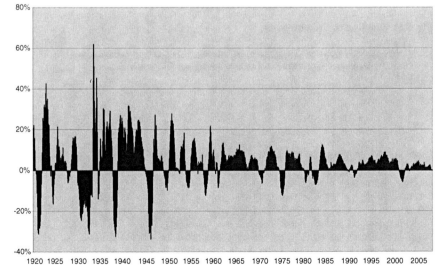

Fig. 8.9 Growth in industrial production

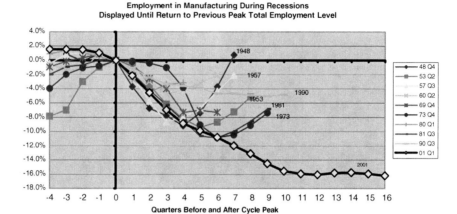

Fig. 8.10 Employment in manufacturing

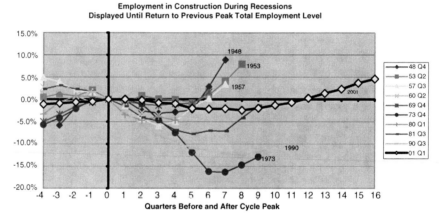

Fig. 8.11 Employment in construction

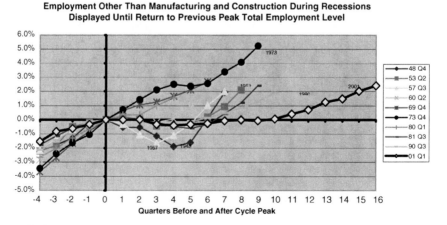

Fig. 8.12 Employment other than manufacturing and construction

how important is this result, compare the total employment in Fig. 8.2 with the employment outside manufacturing and construction.

Obviously, to understand recessions we are going to have to focus a lot of attention on *manufacturing and construction*. That's where most of the unwanted idleness occurs.

8.4 Numbers

We don't refer to "getting the big picture" by accident. Pictures like the ones we have been looking at are designed to convey clearly an overall sense of the data and also to alert us to extreme and unusual events. But if you just look at pictures, you may be making a mistake. Better to confirm what you think you see with some hard numbers like the data reported in Table 8.1.

Table 8.1 Recession properties
Maximum Changes and Quarters to reach the extremes

	NBER	Real GDP		Unemployment		Employment		Capacity Utilization	
Cycle Peak	Quarters	Drop (%)	Quarters	Increase	Quarters	Drop (%)	Quarters	Drop	Quarters
1 48 Q4	4	−1.8	2	3.1	4	−4.3	4	−8.0	4
2 53 Q2	4	−2.7	3	3.4	5	−3.2	5	−12.2	5
3 57 Q3	3	−3.7	2	3.1	3	−4.0	3	−11.5	3
4 60 Q2	3	−1.1	2	1.8	4	−1.7	3	−7.5	3
5 69 Q4	4	−0.2	4	2.4	5	−0.8	4	−8.8	4
6 73 Q4	5	−3.1	5	4.1	6	−1.7	6	−16.3	6
7 80 Q1	2	−2.2	2	1.4	2	−0.9	2	−6.9	2
8 81 Q3	5	−2.9	2	3.3	5	−3.0	5	−8.5	5
9 90 Q3	2	−1.3	2	1.9	8	−1.2	4	−4.1	2
10 01 Q1	3	−0.05	2	1.9	9	−2.0	10	−4.2	3
AVG	3.5	−1.9	2.6	2.6	5.1	−2.3	4.6	−8.8	3.7

	Indust. Prod.		Manufact. Emp.		Construct. Emp.		Other Emp.	
Cycle peak	Drop (%)	Quarters	Drop (%)	Quarters	Drop (%)	Quarters	Drop (%)	Quarters
1 48 Q4	−6.5	4	−9.2	4	−3.2	3	−1.9	4
2 53 Q2	−8.0	4	−9.4	5	−0.8	5	−0.4	3
3 57 Q3	−11.1	3	−8.7	3	−6.0	3	−1.6	3
4 60 Q2	−5.5	3	−4.8	3	−4.1	4	−0.2	3
5 69 Q4	−5.4	4	−7.5	7	−1.4	3	0.0	0
6 73 Q4	−12.7	6	−10.8	6	−16.4	7	0.0	0
7 80 Q1	−5.8	2	−4.5	2	−4.7	4	0.0	0
8 81 Q3	−8.6	5	−10.9	6	−7.8	5	−0.6	5
9 90 Q3	−3.5	2	−5.1	9	−12.5	8	−0.4	3
10 01 Q1	−3.6	3	−16.1	12	−2.5	8	−0.4	4
AVG	−7.1	3.6	−8.7	5.7	−5.9	5.0	−0.6	2.5

Note: The unemployment increase is the per centage points increase in the unemployment rate. Likewise for capacity utilization.

On average, the ten recessions since the WWII have dropped real GDP by 1.9%. The labor markets are generally been harder hit than the product markets. Unemployment raised an average of 2.6% points, while employment fell 2.3%. While it took only 2.6 quarters to hit the product market bottom, it took 5.1 quarters for unemployment to peak out, and 4.6 quarters for employment to hit its bottom. The drop in employment has been a bit more, 3.0%.

While idleness of labor tends to elevate a significant amount in recessions, it is idleness of capital in manufacturing that is especially hard hit among these indicators, dropping an average of 8.8% points, compared with 3% drop in employment overall. But that is the difference between the overall economy and the part of it (industry) that is especially hard hit. The drop in employment in manufacturing averaging 8.7% is about the same as the fall in capacity utilization in manufacturing. That's three times the overall employment decline of 3%. The percentage drop in employment in construction is between these two, about twice the overall decline.

After removing manufacturing and construction, the average job loss in recessions has been only 0.6%.

Message: worry about *manufacturing and construction.*

Chapter 9
Who Struggles and Who Does Well in Recessions?

You should care a lot about recessions.

Recessions are the periods of weak sales, weak cash flows, and weak job markets. The worst way to enter a recession is with a heavy debt load premised on overly optimistic ideas about future growth of sales and earnings. It is doubly bad if that debt is collateralized with durable assets and inventories, whose prices tend to be very soft in recessions, if you can find buyers at all. Thus, in a recession, you cannot get out of debt service problems by growing your income and you cannot get out of debt by selling off assets. Delinquencies defaults and bankruptcy are your only options. In an expansion, the opposite is true. In an expansion, loans backed by hard assets are self-collateralizing as the assets increase in value.

Fortunately, recessions don't have the same effect on all sectors of the economies. Some sectors lose lots of jobs. Some sectors lose their profitability. But there are other sectors that are pretty much recession-proof and there are a few sectors that find prosperity amidst the troubles elsewhere.

If your job is in one of the hard-hit sectors or if your financial assets are concentrated in one of these hard-hit sectors, you need to find some risk-reducing assets that will likely do well when the recession hits.

Don't think that recessions are a thing of the past. That kind of thinking has been prevalent before, and has been proven wrong. With the apparent success of the 1964 Kennedy Tax cut in stimulating the economy, economists had the hubris to host conferences on "The End of the Business Cycle." And again, in the 1990s, businesses and governments and individuals got into a lot of trouble, when they bought into the new economy hype and imagined that there would never be another recession. Here is what Steven Slifer, Chief Economist of Lehman Brothers said:

> Now a growing number of economists are accepting the once-heretical view that the United States may have permanently increased the rate at which its economy can grow without inflation, thanks to advances in computing and information technology.
>
> "Wherever productivity is today, my guess is that in six months or a year, it will be higher still," said Stephen Slifer, the chief United States economist at Lehman Brothers. "About once in 100 years, something really big happens, and this is it."

E. E. Leamer, *Macroeconomic Patterns and Stories: A Guide for MBAs.*
© Springer-Verlag Berlin Heidelberg 2009

Risking the scorn of skeptics, Mr. Slifer added that he had begun to believe that recessions were no longer inevitable. "Is it inconceivable to think this thing can keep going, and in 2010 we could see the 20th year of this expansion?" he asked. "No."

But what about the skeptics, who point to a legion of potential problems, including higher oil prices, the nation's giant trade deficit, the possibility that productivity growth is overstated, and the high prices of many technology stocks? Mr. Slifer advises them to open their eyes.

"They keep trying to find the problems," he said, "and every year comes and goes, and things still look as good as they have before."

New York Times, September 10, 2000, Rising Productivity Challenges Notions on Limits of Growth By ALEX BERENSON

As far as recessions are concerned, be afraid, be very afraid and expect that there will be another sometime in the future.

9.1 Job Losses in Recessions Affect Some Sectors More than Others

Maybe you remember the quip: A recession is when you lose your job; a depression is when I lose mine.

During a recession, your job would be a lot more secure if you were a member of the California Teachers Association than the United Auto Workers.

Table 9.1 reports the percent of jobs lost in each of 16 major sectors during the last seven recessions. These are arranged in order by the averages from worst to best. In a recession, you want your job to be in the bottom of this list, not the top. The maximum in each row is printed in bold.

The best sector is education and health services, which has never had a net reduction of jobs in any of these seven recessions. The worst sector is durable manufacturing (think automobiles and washing machines). Durable manufacturing has lost an average 10.6% of its jobs in these recessions, but was especially hard hit in the 2001 recession, when 17.6% of jobs disappeared.

Table 9.2 offers a somewhat different view of the same data, identifying the sectors that contribute most to job loss. These numbers add up to the total job loss in each recession. By that metric, the 2001 recession was the worst ever, with a loss of 4.12% of payroll jobs. Funny, in terms of GDP, the 2001 recession was a very mild event. We will need to take a closer look at this one.

Figure 9.1 illustrates the data for the most cyclical sectors, Fig. 9.2 for the moderately cyclical sectors and Fig. 9.3 for the least cyclical sectors. Take a look at durable manufacturing in Fig. 9.1 and education and health services in Fig. 9.3. Quite a difference there!

The contribution to total job loss reported in Table 9.2 reveals that it is mostly manufacturing and construction where the job losses occur. On average about 70% of the job losses occur in these sectors, which currently make up only about 20% of employment, a fraction that is declining over time. These facts are memorialized in Fig. 9.4, which displays the employment in these critical sectors (manufacturing

Table 9.1 Percent of jobs in each sector lost during and immediately after recessions

	1960Q2 (%)	1969Q4 (%)	1973Q4 (%)	1980Q1 (%)	1981Q3 (%)	1990Q3 (%)	2001Q1 (%)	Average (%)	MAX (%)
Durable manufacturing	-6.7	-10.1	-12.3	-5.9	-14.0	-7.6	**-17.6**	-10.6	-17.6
Nat res mining	-11.5	-8.4			**-20.0**	-12.1	-5.9	-8.3	-20.0
Construction	-4.1	-1.4	**-16.4**	-6.9	-7.8	-12.6	-2.4	-7.4	-16.4
Information	-3.3	-2.8	-5.0	-2.6	-11.6	-2.2	**-15.1**	-6.1	-15.1
Nondurable manufacturing	-2.0	-3.5	-9.0	-2.1	-5.8	-1.7	**-12.9**	-5.3	-12.9
Transport warehousing	NA	NA	-4.9	-2.9	**-6.9**	-0.8	-6.2	-4.3	-6.9
Wholesale trade	-0.8			-0.4	-3.1	-3.9	**-4.3**	-1.8	-4.3
Federal	-2.8	-2.6		-0.3	-1.7	**-3.6**	-0.6	-1.7	-3.6
Utilities	NA		-1.2			-3.4	**-4.8**	-1.6	-4.8
Retail trade	-1.5		0.0	-0.7	-0.6	-2.6	**-2.9**	-1.4	-2.9
Profess bus services						-1.9	**-5.3**	-1.0	-5.3
Leisure hospitality	**-0.8**					-0.7	-0.6	-0.4	-0.8
State local gov				-0.4	-0.2			-0.3	-1.2
Financial activities				-1.0	-1.2	**-1.8**		-0.3	-1.8
Other services						**-1.2**		-0.2	-1.2
Educ health services								0.0	0.0

Table 9.2 Sectoral contribution to total job loss

	1960Q2 (%)	1969Q4 (%)	1973Q4 (%)	1980Q1 (%)	1981Q3 (%)	1990Q3 (%)	2001Q1 (%)	Average (%)	Worst (%)
Durable manufacturing	-1.12	-1.61	**-1.83**	-0.78	-1.79	-0.74	-1.43	-1.33	-1.83
Nondurable manufacturing	-0.24	-0.35	**-0.83**	-0.17	-0.44	-0.11	-0.61	-0.39	-0.83
Construction	-0.23	-0.07	**-0.89**	-0.35	-0.36	-0.60	-0.13	-0.37	-0.89
Information	-0.10	-0.08	-0.14	-0.07	-0.30	-0.05	-0.42	-0.17	-0.42
Transport warehousing	NA	NA	-0.17	-0.10	**-0.22**	-0.03	-0.21	-0.14	-0.22
Retail trade	-0.16		0.00	-0.08	-0.07	-0.32	**-0.34**	-0.14	-0.34
Profess bus services						-0.19	**-0.67**	-0.12	-0.67
Nat res mining	-0.17	-0.08			**-0.27**	-0.08	-0.03	-0.09	-0.27
Wholesale trade	-0.04			-0.02	-0.16	-0.19	-0.19	-0.08	-0.19
Federal	**0.12**	-0.11		-0.01	-0.06	-0.10	-0.01	-0.06	-0.12
State local gov				-0.15	**-0.17**			-0.05	-0.17
Leisure hospitality	-0.05			-0.03	-0.02	**-0.06**	-0.05	-0.03	-0.06
Financial activities						**-0.11**		-0.02	-0.11
Utilities	NA					**-0.02**	-0.02	-0.01	-0.02
Other services			-0.01			**-0.05**		-0.01	-0.05
Educ health services								0.00	0.00
Total	-2.23	-2.31	-3.87	-1.75	-3.86	-2.64	-4.12		

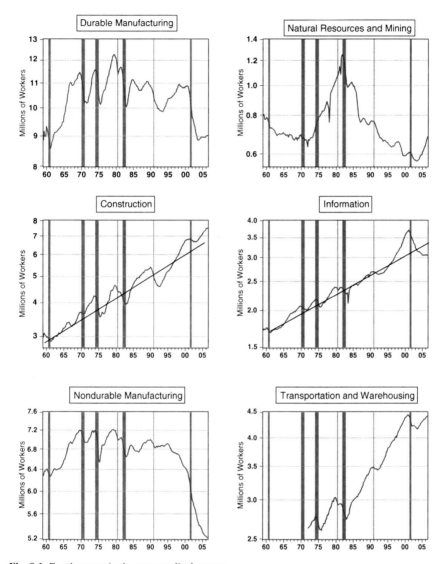

Fig. 9.1 Employment in the most cyclical sectors

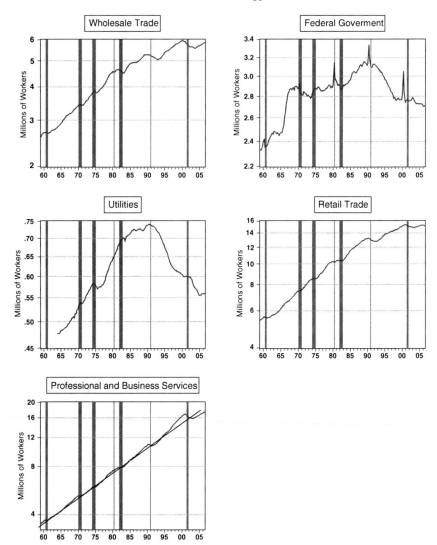

Fig. 9.2 Employment in moderately cyclical sectors

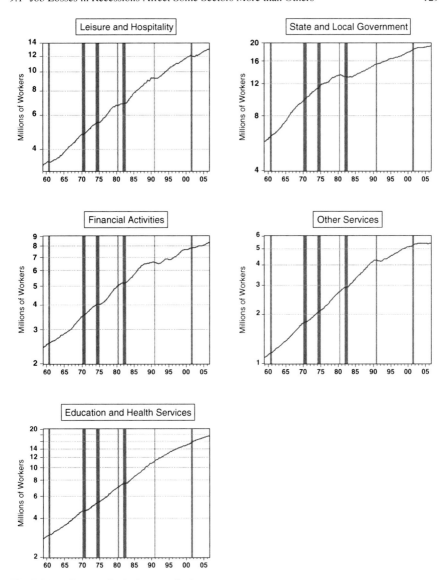

Fig. 9.3 Employment in the least cyclical sectors

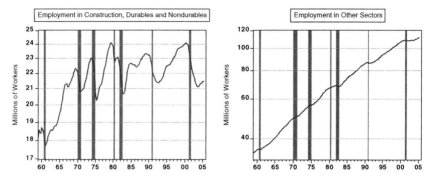

Fig. 9.4 The largest three contributors to the cycle in employment, and the rest

and construction) and employment in the rest of the sectors. There you can see the steady growth in jobs outside the cyclical sectors and the great volatility of jobs in manufacturing and construction.

9.1.1 The 2001 Recession Was an Anomaly

Both Tables 9.1 and 9.2 reveal that the 2001 event was unusual in a number of ways. Manufacturing jobs were especially hard hit, but there were also unusually high losses in "information", professional and business services, retail trade and wholesale trade.

It is tempting to conclude from the contribution of "information" and professional and business services to the 2001 job loss that these peculiarities are the effect of the US shift from an industrial to a postindustrial economy, which might lead one to think that the next recession would also have more contribution from these intellectual service sectors. But if 2001 was the first recession of the postindustrial period, there was sure a lot of job loss in the industrial sectors of durable and nondurable manufacturing! Something strange is going on here.

The reason that 2001 was unusual in several aspects is that 1997–2000 was unusual in the opposite way. Two unusuals add up to usual. That's what happen in 2001, back to usual.

The "information" sector is a good example. Why is information a "cyclical" sector, with 15.1% job loss in the 2001 downturn? Take a look at the data displayed in Fig. 9.1. This is a pretty big sector, with 3.1 million workers after the decline in the 2001 recession. The vertical scale in this figure is logarithmic, and the straight line that is drawn on the figure represents a constant rate of growth. With the aid of this straight line, you can see very clearly the run-up in information jobs during the Internet Rush in the late 1990s beyond the long-term trend. Thus the big decline in jobs in this sector in the 2001 recession was created in the 1998 and 1999 and 2000 when the number of jobs expanded well beyond the normal trend. 2001 was back to normal.

What exactly is "information" anyway? That can't be just information operators, can it? Table 9.3 has the subcodes of this information category. I didn't know it, but

Table 9.3 2002 NAICS Subcodes, 51: Information

51	Information
5111	Newspaper, book, and directory publishers
5112	Software publishers
5121	Motion picture and video industries
5122	Sound recording industries
5151	Radio and television broadcasting
5152	Cable and other subscription programming
5171	Wired telecommunications carriers
5172	Wireless telecommunications carriers
5173	Telecommunications resellers
5175	Cable and other program distribution
5181	ISPs and web search portals
5182	Data processing and related services
519	Other information services

when I viewed the latest King Kong movie I was receiving "information." This can't be the source of the cycle, can it? Must be advertising revenue is killing the "information" sector in economic downturns. That is the story of 2001. Massive spending on advertising in pursuit of first-mover-advantage on the Web during the Internet Rush from 1997 to 2000 created a correspondingly massive increase in "information" jobs. When Wall Street and Main Street lost interest those jobs had to go.

It wasn't just "information" jobs; it was professional and business services too. The run-up in professional and business services during the Internet Rush is harder to see in Fig. 9.1 especially without the aid of the straightline that is drawn over the data, but with the benefit of the line, there it is – the run-up in jobs during the Internet Rush.

Thus it appears better to treat the loss in jobs in 2001 in information and professional and business services as the consequence of the not-to-be-repeated Internet Rush, and not an indication of the likely contribution of these sectors to the cycles in the future.

In addition to the large loss of jobs in information and business services that was the fallout of the hiring in the Internet Rush the 2001 recession was unusual in that construction contributed only 3% of the job loss, when the average for this sector is 13%. For this, we can thank the 2001 strength of residential construction, supported by the very low interest rates provided by Mr. Greenspan and the dearth of financial investment opportunities other than housing.

But what about manufacturing? Why was it pummeled in 2001? Did that have anything to do with the Internet rush? More importantly, why haven't those manufacturing jobs recovered? These are not easy questions to answer, but the pursuit of market share rather than profitability during the Internet rush probably contributed to the maintenance of jobs in manufacturing in the US, and masked the long-term decline driven by technological change and globalization. Those underlying forces were revealed catastrophically in the 2001 event. But a depreciation of the US dollar relative to the Euro that has already occurred, and the depreciation relative to Asian currencies that is sure to occur in the future will help bring back jobs to the US.

9.1.2 With that Anomalous 2001 Recession, What Will the Next Recession Be Like?

The job cycles in manufacturing and construction have always been coordinated. Not now. Manufacturing is at a trough and construction is at the peak. That makes for a different kind of slowdown, without the normal loss of jobs in manufacturing.

Looking at durables and construction and nondurables in Fig. 9.1 helps to think about the next recession, if it comes soon. As of 2006, there has been no "recovery" of jobs in manufacturing in either durables or nondurables, and employment levels in those sectors are very low by historical standards. Thus it seems unlikely that there could be another bout of substantial job loss in those sectors. Though what goes up, must come down, if it didn't go up, it won't come down.

Among the cyclical sectors displayed in Fig. 9.1, most seem closer to their troughs than to their peaks. Exceptional job growth is confined to construction. If we get a construction correction back to the trend line, this is about half million jobs and if we go to recession levels we could lose something like 1 million construction jobs out of 7 million. That would be tough on construction, but with 133 million payroll jobs, that is only 1/133 = 0.8% of jobs. Is that enough to declare a recession? Not really. The weakest recession in terms of job loss was the 1980 recession that racked up only −1.8%. To get to a real recession, we would need to lose another million jobs or more, but which sectors might they come from? Information illustrated in Fig. 9.2 doesn't seem over-employed and not likely to contribute much job loss. Don't count on transportation and warehousing illustrated in Fig. 9.3 to contribute much either – they aren't out of whack.

Bottom line: it may not be a national recession. It may be sluggish growth but not a formal recession. The job losses may be mostly confined to the construction sector.

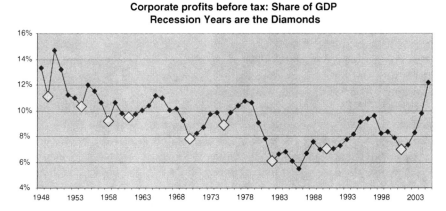

Fig. 9.5 Corporate profits and recessions

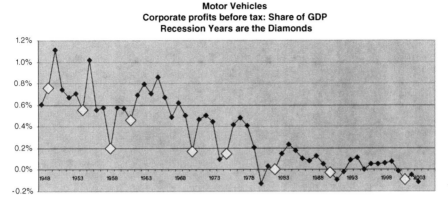

Fig. 9.6 Motor vehicles corporate profits and recessions

9.2 Many Sectors Lose Profits in Recessions

It's not just jobs that are affected by recessions. Prices, wages and profits can all be soft in economic downturns.

Corporate profits annually as a share of GDP is illustrated in Fig. 9.5, where the recessions are indicated by the diamonds. Here you can see the big decline in profits in every recession but the 1990–91 event. There is also the curious weakness in profits during the Reagan expansion and the startling ascent during the Bush presidency.

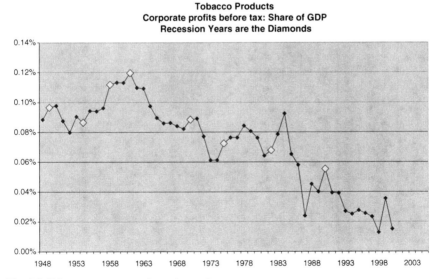

Fig. 9.7 Tobacco corporate profits and recessions

Table 9.4 Sensitivity of Corporate Profits to Recessions

Effects of Recession on Corporate Profits Before Tax

	Recession Year									
	1949 (%)	1953 (%)	1957 (%)	1960 (%)	1970 (%)	1975 (%)	1980/2 (%)	1990 (%)	2001 (%)	Avg. (%)
TOTAL	−17	−2	−15	−4	−11	−2	−27	7	−8	−9
Transportation	−32	−47	−41	−24	−108	−54	−104	−50	−95	−62
Manufacturing: Durable goods	−16	−9	−32	−20	−40	−7	−80	−41	−146	−43
Mining	−32	−13	−34	16	41	0	−161	10	5	−19
Wholesale trade	−36	−18	−16	−13	−2	−14	−22	−16	−22	−18
Agriculture, forestry, and fishing	−23	−35	−13	78	−67	77	−97	−31	−18	−14
Construction	−7	−14	3	−32	−2	14	−54	−30	5	−13
Manufacturing: Nondurable goods	−25	3	−18	−7	−6	0	1	−4	−15	−8
Retail trade	−28	−10	−9	−16	−5	27	−18	−1	14	−5
Services	−9	−5	−6	−5	−7	26	4	28		3
Finance, insurance, and real estate	17	10	5	7	10	1	−43	19	11	4
Communication	6	16	8	7	−12	−2	2	10		4
Electric, gas, and sanitary services	13	6	−1	14	−13	70	25	3	−3	13

Note: 2000 data based on NAICS classification. SIC revised in 1987

Some sectors are especially hard hit in recessions. Figure 9.6 has motor vehicles profits as a share of GDP. For the US auto sector, there has been a distressing decline in profitability to the point of virtual invisibility, but in addition there is a very substantial cycle with profits taking a nosedive in recessions. If you want something that is recession proof, try tobacco products, whose profits as a share of GDP are illustrated in Fig. 9.7. Profits in tobacco, like motor vehicles, is declining as a fraction of GDP, but keep in mind that these are not the global profits of tobacco but only the profits off sales of product made here in the USA.

Table 9.4 provides sectoral detail about the impact of the recession on corporate profits, sorted from worst to best by the average of the nine recessions, counting the 1980–82 as a single dip. The problems are mostly confined to the goods side of the economy: getting the raw materials, building the products, and delivering them. The recession-resistant sectors are services, FIRE (finance, insurance and real estate), communication, and utilities.

Part III B
Recession Stories

Chapter 10
Idleness Stories

Modern industrial economies suffer from a collective bipolar disease, swinging back and forth between manic activeness and depressive idleness, with epsiodes of normality in between. Why is that? Why doesn't the all-powerful market provide only happy outcomes, with each of us enjoying just the right mixture of leisure and work? Is there something that we can do to make the depressive periods of unwanted idleness shorter and less extreme?

There *is* something we can do. When field workers lose their jobs as dry weather destroys their crops, they can visit the temple of the rain god, offer a donation to the priests, and pray for a better outcome. When industrial workers lose their jobs, they have a choice: they can visit the temple of the market, offer a donation to the economists, and pray for a better outcome; or they can visit the temple of government, offer a donation to the politicians, and pray for a better outcome.

The economists teach a simple message: Market good, Government bad. According to their teachings, the market will reward us all with riches beyond our wildest dreams, but *only* if we swear allegiance to the market and disdain for all time the teachings of the politicians, who would have us pray to the false god of government. If we want prosperity, we must leave our fates to the invisible hand of the market. If we allow the perceptible hand of Government to intervene, we will anger the market and find ourselves idle and poor. The medicine, these Economists prescribe for unwanted idleness is, greater faith.

Politicians offer the opposite advice; do not have faith in the impersonal uncaring market: Government good, Market bad. According to the them, if you want the best outcome, the market must be regulated and controlled. Offer a donation in the form of taxes or a contribution or a bribe, and the Politicians will bend the market to your needs. They offer low-interest loans, pork-barrel government spending, minimum wages, tariffs to keep out your foreign competitors, bail-outs for ailing corporations, regulation of big business, your health care paid by unknown future generations, and so on. Rather than relying just on faith in the market, politicians promise that they will make it happen for you. They offer action.

Deciding where to pray is not an easy matter. Some pattern-seeking and some story-telling ought to help.

10.1 How Do Economists Explain Unwanted Idleness?

When you visit the temple of the market, it is considered a sacrilege to ask the question: "Why is there unwanted idleness?" But if you persist, the answer is usually mumbled and not altogether understandable.

Economists' confidence in the market in front of the unwashed is not matched by equal confidence when they are in their ivory towers where they read the scrolls and study the market data. Unwanted idleness is an annoying puzzle to most economists since their simple model of supply and demand leads them to think that the market left alone will find the price that equilibrates supply and demand, producing only the amount of idleness that makes everyone happy. Here is how the Market is supposed to operate: If someone wants to work or if a plant or office building is not used to capacity, then the market will lower the price, generating more demand or less supply until we get the Goldilocks solution: prices not too high, not too low, just right.

Market Equilibrium with Flexible Prices

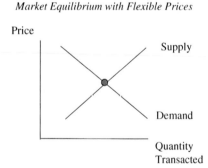

The picture above is the usual supply and demand market model that captures this thinking. The demand curve represents the buyers' willingness to pay for the items for sale. If the price is low, they will buy a lot; if the price is high, not so much. The supply curve represents the sellers' willingness to part with the items – the higher the price, the more offered for sale. The intersection of the supply and demand curves selects the market clearing price at which the willingness to sell exactly matches the willingness to buy. An efficient free market is expected rapidly to find this market equilibrating point, and then every office is rented and everyone who wants work can find it, though not necessarily at a rate of pay that will make them all joyous. The folks "at the margin" in the labor market are indifferent between working and not. The slightest deterioration in wages would make them tell their boss "take this job and shove it."

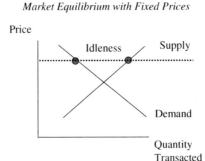

Market Equilibrium with Fixed Prices

In the context of this model, unwanted idleness can be caused only by "sticky prices," namely market failures, which prevent the reduction in prices and wages that would eliminate the idleness. This is illustrated in the figure above, where the price is fixed above the market-clearing price. At this high price, suppliers want to sell more than demanders are willing to buy. If the item in question is office-space or labor-hours, these fixed prices cause unwanted idleness. This unwanted idleness could be eliminated if, somehow, the price were lowered. At this lower price, customers would want to buy more and sellers would offer less. At the market-clearing price, there would be no unwanted idleness: Noone looking for work at the going wage rate and no office looking for someone to rent it.

Unwanted idleness, according to this model, is caused by impediments to the freedom of the market to lower prices. If unwisely impeded, the market could also make the opposite error – prices too low. If prices are below the market-clearing level, then there is more demand than supply. Rather than idleness, this market pathology is *rationing*: some buyers get the item but others are left out.

Many economists are comfortable assuming that it is easy to increase prices but hard to lower them. Looking around for sticky prices, economists have traditionally pointed to the labor market as the culprit. It's wages that are sticky. You know that. When was the last time your boss called you into his/her office and explained that times are tough and your salary has to be cut? It happens, but not that often. So, the story goes, an increase in demand for workers causes higher wages, but when demand falls back again, wages stay at the high level. At that high price with persistent weak demand, there is a gap between the number of people that employers are willing to hire and the number of workers seeking jobs. Thus workers suffer from unwanted idleness.

What does this have to do with the business cycle? The story continues. Wages are bid up when workers are scarce late in expansions, but when demand inevitably falls back a bit, wages do not come down again and workers lose

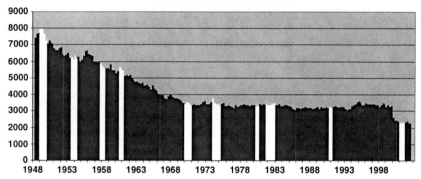

Fig. 10.1 Employment in agriculture

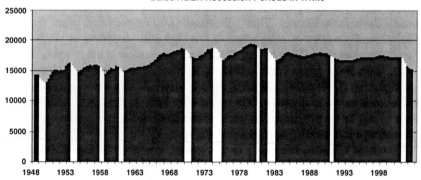

Fig. 10.2 Employment in manufacturing

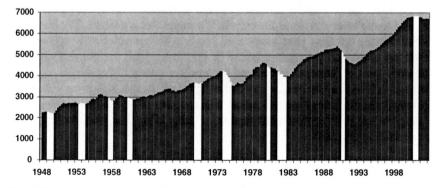

Fig. 10.3 Employment in construction

their jobs as they are unwilling to take the pay cut that the market requires. When some workers lose their jobs, they cut back spending, and others workers lose their jobs too, for the same reason – not enough flexibility in wages.[1]

10.1.1 The Job Cycle Is Mostly Construction and Manufacturing

This's an interesting narrative about wages that can't decline in the face of a fall in demand, but there are some important patterns that any story of cyclical idleness needs to confront. One pertinent fact is that pathological idleness is a problem confined mostly to two sectors: manufacturing and construction. In the great depression, the number of jobs in agriculture held firm though real wages plummeted; at the same time, the number of jobs in manufacturing plummeted though real wages of those who held onto their jobs stayed high. Agriculture has a price cycle, manufacturing and construction a volume cycle.

Figure 10.1 illustrates employment in agriculture, Fig. 10.2 in manufacturing, and Fig. 10.3 in construction. Note the ups and downs in manufacturing and construction, in contrast to the steadiness of agricultural jobs.[2] Is that because wages are "sticky" in manufacturing and construction but not in agriculture? It's those evil unions that are causing the idleness, isn't it? Maybe, but I think we may be able to find some more compelling explanations for the unwanted idleness.

10.2 Broken Relationships

A healthy first step toward understanding the determinants of unwanted idleness is to accept the fact that economists' beloved market model has a limited domain of applicability. Many exchanges are mediated not by "markets" but by "relationships."

A "market" is a time and place, where and when many sellers meet many buyers to haggle over the price. The medieval agricultural landscape was dotted with market towns. On prearranged market days, sellers from the surrounding area would set up

---

[1] One cure for this unwanted idleness of labor is inflation of product prices. Employers' willingness to hire workers depends on the wage rate but also on the price of the products the workers produce. Economists call it the *real wage*: the wage rates divided by the product price. Thus if the Federal Reserve feels the unemployment rate is too high, they can give us a dose of monetary medicine that they think will help to increase product prices and get those laborers back to work. But if the Federal Reserve is not up to the task, there is another way to equilibrate the labor market: wait for productivity gains to work their magic. It's not just real wages that matter; productivity (output per hour) matters too. That's *unit labor costs*: real hourly wages divided by productivity. Unfortunately, the pace of improvement in productivity is pretty slow, so don't expect a lot of quick help from that corner.

[2] The agriculture figure has two distinctly different periods – declining jobs until 1970 and flat thereafter. That last little cliff in agriculture can't be real – it must be a data error. What happened in 2000? I think I know.

stalls in the market square to display their merchandise. Buyers and sellers would haggle out loud and listen to the haggling of others. With all that haggling and listening, and guided by a superior collective intelligence, large differences in the prices offered by competing sellers would quickly disappear, as the market sought the price at which the number of willing buyers exactly matched the number of willing sellers. Having found that price, the transactions were consummated, and the stalls were closed down until the next market day.

The title of this short story is "The Tale of the Walrasian Auctioneer" written by the French economist Léon Walras at the end of the nineteenth Century.[3] Like any good story, this is not a perfectly accurate description of what actually happened. The story is for insight and understanding. If it were perfectly accurate, the story would be impossibly long, and insight and wisdom would be hard to come by. The point of the story is to help us understand the efficiency differences between sales made by itinerant peddlers and sales made on market days in market squares of market towns. Sales made by itinerant peddlers were based on information that was very limited and largely one-sided. Hypothetical market exchanges are based on *all* the relevant information revealed to *all* market participants. Surprisingly enough, the participants don't need to know how each buyer and each seller values the items. All that is relevant is summarized in the market price, which is apparent to all buyers and sellers. This doesn't mean that markets are fair. It only means that markets are incredibly efficient ways of summarizing and communicating vast amounts of information about what we want to buy, how much we are willing to pay, what we are willing to sell and at what price.

If this fictional account were written in words, we would all understand its limited domain of applicability:

> Once upon a time, there was a caring King who wanted his subjects to be as happy as possible. "Wheat is what they want" said one of his advisors; "Meat" said another. A wise Market gathered all the information in the Kingdom, and told the King: "80% Wheat and 20% Meat."

Expressed that way, one might wonder if the market model could be used to understand unwanted idleness. But this isn't the way that economists speak and write. Economists use graphs and math. Indeed, Messieur Walras, was one of the first "mathematical economists," who chose the title *Elements of Pure Economics* for his 1874 book.

Do you wonder what is "pure" economics? It's not an epithet, like pure baloney. "Pure" is a reference to the language in which the argument is expressed. Graphs are the totems of the religion and math the language of the Priests. Unlike accessible prose, which comes with inherent humility, when the Priests pray before their totems and chant in math, it is altogether natural for the rest of us to perceive no limits to their powers. But be careful. Be very careful. Don't be seduced by the language of the story and the confidence of the storyteller. "Pure" is part of the salesmanship.

---

[3] Don't take everything I write literally.

While competitive markets mediate some transactions, many exchanges take place between individuals with long-standing relationships. These relationships help to shelter the participants from the ups and downs of the market. These relationships also serve as ongoing conduits of information and product guarantees, and allow specialized exchanges that a market cannot support.[4]

If you want to get the idea, think marriages. Marriage is a relationship not a market. There is much that the market can provide (Hugh Grant testimonial here), but there are very special benefits that come from committed long-term relationships including security against a "better offer" and insurance against unexpected problems in health or earnings. (You are not supposed to dump your spouse just because the market offers you something better or because your spouse gets ill.) A committed long-term relationship also allows relationship-specific investments, including understanding and children, in the case of traditional marriages. (My colleague, Armen Alchian, on the first day of a Ph.D. class in microeconomics would muse: "I've been thinking. Wouldn't it be better for all if there were a market for children? What do you think, Mr. Smith?" Answer: "With all due respect, the last thing I want to do is take good care of your children, Professor Alchian.")

In the way they handle changes over time, relationships are different from markets. If there is a long-term relationship between buyer and seller, the response by the seller to a surge in demand may not be to raise price but to ration available supplies among regular customers. When a hurricane is expected to come ashore, there is often a huge increase in the demand for bottled water. Stores in the path of the hurricane might jack up the price of those last few bottles of Pelligrino to $100, but their neighborhood customers would never forget that, and might not ever go back to that store again. They might even feel a desire to break some windows and loot the place. Worried about those possibilities, the storeowners are likely not to raise the price but to ration the supply: one to a customer, regular customers to the front of the line, please.

A relationship is a two-way street. When the demand falls, buyers who have relationships with suppliers are expected to maintain their loyalty, and not insist on a price that matches the best offer elsewhere. A disloyal buyer, who tries to get a better deal by threatening to go elsewhere is likely to go without the water when the next hurricane comes along.[5]

---

[4] My former colleague, Axel Leijonhufvud, chose the apt title for his book about macroeconomics – *Information and Coordination*. Markets work efficiently for some rather special information and coordination problems but not for all problems.

[5] What I have just described is an insurance scheme in which buyer and seller commit to helping each other out when circumstances strongly favor one or the other. In principle, one could write a long-term contract that would list all the contingencies. But the possibilities are endless and the number of contracts enormous. When it is hard to form a long-term contract that is written contingent all the possibilities (e.g. a hurricane) an alternative is a relationship that ties buyer and seller together and that promises a fair and reasonable outcome, such as one that might have been negotiated in advance. Beyond insulating buyer and seller from the vagaries of the Market, committed relationships allow relationship-specific investment that otherwise could not occur.

Relationships are very common in the workplace. Though you can hire day-laborers from among the many that linger outside Home Depot stores in Los Angeles, day-by-day hiring doesn't work for jobs requiring trust and understanding and job-specific knowledge. Many jobs therefore are "marriages" between employer and employee, some a matter of months but many lasting for years. In 1998, per the Survey of Consumer Finances, for those who have been in the work force for 16–25 years, the average duration of the current job was 8.6 years.[6] That's about the same duration as many marriages between a husband and wife. According to the 2000 Census, the mean duration of first marriages that ended in divorce was 8 years, followed by 3.5 years until remarriage, followed by 9 years until the second marriage ended.[7]

This gives us a good unemployment story. In recessions with limited cash flows, facing difficulties servicing debt and making payrolls, some employers may simply go out of business, ending forever their relationships with employees. Other employers may continue to operate, but reluctantly sever their relationships with some employees. Employers could try to get employees to take a lower wage to maintain as many jobs as possible, but have you tried that sort of thing with your spouse? "Honey, I am not as happy in this marriage as I used to be, but if you would make better meals more often and take out the garbage like you used to, I am sure we could make it work. And it would be really great, if you lost some of those wrinkles and that potbelly. I am finding those really annoying." If you are thinking of going down that route, better think again. You can't have both a market and a marriage. The contracts are entirely different.

But you might ask: Why are there more broken relationships in manufacturing than in agriculture? Answer: Because there are more marriages in manufacturing than in agriculture. A strawberry picker is a day laborer – no special skills, no special understanding of the job. Pay per basket of strawberries picked. That makes it a market job subject to the ups and downs of the supply and demand for strawberries. Manufacturing is different. Workers have to build up skills to operate the equipment and coordinate with other members of the team. It takes a relationship. In addition, manufacturing firms regularly go out of business, but farms rarely do. A factory making buggy whips may have no more useful life but that fertile agricultural land is a productive asset that is going to be farmed by someone, year in and year out.

10.3 Soaking the Rich When Times Are Bad

"Relationships, not markets" is one reason why some sectors experience a volume cycle not a price cycle. Another important reason why there may not be market clearing and full employment of labor and capital is that "market power" makes a

---

[6] Friedberg, Leora and Michael Owyang, "Explaining the Evolution of Pension Structure and Job Tenure," NBER Working Paper 10714, Aug 2004.

[7] http://www.census.gov/prod/2005pubs/p70–97.pdf

seller willing to tolerate idleness in periods of slack demand. For reasons that may
be made clear below, I am describing this as "Soaking the Rich When Times are
Bad" referring to the possibility that in recessions, the most price sensitive customers drop by the wayside, and what remains are the wealthy who don't care much
about price. Facing that kind of customer base, firms have little incentive to cut
price.

Let's make this more explicit and consider the pricing of office space in that
high-rise office building that you own. Suppose for the sake of argument that there
are no operating costs at all and the demand is so weak that the only way to fill up
the building is to charge a zero rent, that's what a competitive market would do.
The market would keep on lowering price until all the offices are rented. But you
wouldn't want to do that, would you? You'd just be giving away those offices. You
wouldn't make any money at all. If you charge a high price, you will lose some
customers but not all of them. That's what it means to have market power. If you
didn't have market power, the slightest increase in rents would drive all your renters
away and you would be forced by the market to lower your price. But with a little
market power, it is better to leave some of those offices vacant for some of the time.
Of course, to use this strategy, you will need to cut a deal with the workers who
clean and maintain the building. Some of them will need to be idle when demand
is low. You can keep them all on the payroll and reduce the intensity of work when
demand is weak, or you can lay some of them off. If you choose to lay them off,
you will have to pay a premium when they are working, to compensate them for the
periodic unwanted idleness.

Now back to the difference between employment in agriculture and employment
in manufacturing. Why is manufacturing employment cyclical but agriculture is not?
Why are there sharp swings in capacity utilization in manufacturing, but not on
farms? Market power is one big difference. A bushel of wheat from one farmer is
pretty much the same as a bushel of wheat from another, and farmers do not have
significant market power. But branded manufactures are a different story altogether.
Most manufacturers historically have had considerable market power and have not
cut their prices much during periods of slack demand. Take a look at Fig. 10.4,
which compares the producer price indexes for grains and for motor vehicles and
equipment. The market-determined producer price for grains swings wildly up and
down with changes in supply and demand, but the "administered" price of new
vehicles moves very smoothly over time – no substantial price cutting when sales
are slow and no big increases when sales are booming.

You are probably thinking that there is something wrong in these prices of new
motor vehicles, since you could have sworn that when sales are weak, you can really
cut yourself a good deal at the showroom. Of course, Fig. 10.4 depicts wholesale
(factory gate) prices and not retail prices. It might be that the retail markup varies a
lot even though the wholesale price does not. It might be, but it isn't so, as can be
seen in Fig. 10.5, which depicts the retail (Consumer Price Index) for new vehicles
and for used ones as well. It's the used price that is variable, not the new price. That
makes sense, doesn't it? When you and I sell our used cars, we are just like a farmer
selling a bushel of wheat. We don't have much control over the price we receive.

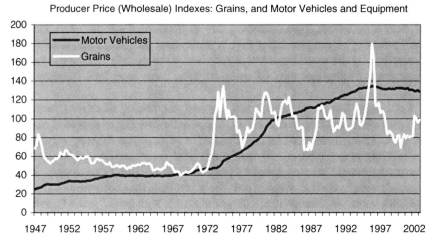

Producer Price (Wholesale) Indexes: Grains, and Motor Vehicles and Equipment

Fig. 10.4 Producer prices of grains and vehicles

Likewise for buyers. No market power on either side of the transaction. Thus there are markets for used cars, and volatile prices. There are no markets for new cars. The manufacturers control prices for new cars and when demand falls, volumes drop, not prices.

To summarize, sellers are going to lower price only when the lower price generates an adequate increase in volume. In periods of weak demand, when the low-income customers may be out of the market, lowering price may have little or no effect on volume. That's one reason why firms don't lower prices, and choose instead the idleness that lower volumes entail.

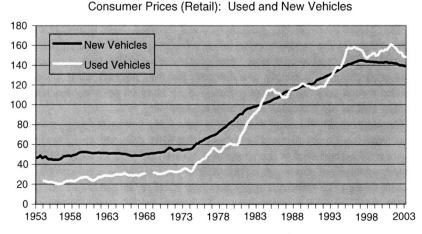

Consumer Prices (Retail): Used and New Vehicles

Fig. 10.5 Consumer price indexes of used and new vehicles

10.4 Making Do with the Old Car

Another important reason why a seller may not cut price in periods of weak demand comes from durability of the item. Think about an automobile manufacturer, who is aware that demand is currently weak because of an economic recession but likely to pick up substantially in a year at most. Aggressive price-cutting now to maintain volume is then doubly bad. It hurts profits today and also hurts profits next year since those customers who get the great deals now will not be ready to buy another car next year.

That's the supply side. There are also demand side reasons why the cycle in durables may be greater than the cycle in nondurables. It is easier to postpone for a year or more the purchase of a new automobile than to postpone your evening meal. Repair and maintenance can keep that old car running another 10,000 miles. Furthermore, in the depths of the economic downturn, the price-sensitive auto buyers are completely out of the market while you rich folks are still buying. That makes price-cutting during the downturns all the more unwise. Maybe, the opposite would be better. Raise those prices and squeeze a little more profit out of the sales to the wealthy.

Thus new cars are not sold in a "market" matching faceless buyers with faceless sellers. It's really a complicated game with buyers trying to time their purchases to get the best deals and sellers trying to entice buyers to buy at the right terms and the best times.

This is an interesting story, but we need to check out the data. If it's right, the volume cycle in durable manufacturing should be greater than the volume cycle in nondurable manufacturing. Check it out! Fig. 10.6 depicts the employment levels in durables and nondurables since 1939 with the white line representing durables and measured on the left scale, and the black line representing nondurables and measured on the right scale. These different scales allow a side-by-side comparison of the two series that reveals which series swings by the largest percentage amount.

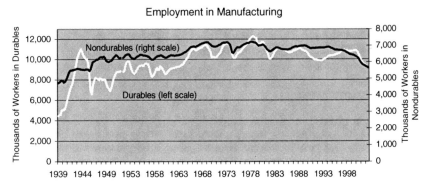

Fig. 10.6 Employment in durables and nondurables

It is clearly the case that the employment cycle in durables is much greater than the employment cycle in nondurables!

10.5 A Pyrrhic Victory of Hope Over Reason

My annoying neighbor sold his $500,000 home last year for $2 million and I am not selling mine for a penny less. I also bought tech stocks when the NASDQ was near 5000, and I am not going to sell until I can get back what my stock is worth.[8]

These are examples of not "marking to market." An asset can be carried on our mental books at the value it used to have, or we can adjust its value up or down depending on market conditions. If assets are not marked to market, there can be extreme swings in transactions volumes. When prices are rising, owners of the assets will be bombarded by what they think to be highly favorable offers above the book value of the asset, and many owners will sell. But when prices are softening, the offers will be below the book value and most owners will refuse to sell.[9]

This is exactly what happens in residential real estate. Sellers look backward while buyers look forward. Sellers remember what they paid for their home or what their neighbors paid. But buyers are thinking what the prices might be in a year or two. When the market is strong and prices are rising, buyers look forward and see higher prices but sellers look backward and see lower ones. Then sales are plentiful since a sale transfers the asset from one who values it less to one who values it more.

But when the market softens, sellers look backward and see high prices but buyers look forward and see low prices. Then there cannot be a sale unless one side caves in. A few buyers will always cave in, and pay at or near the sellers' price. That makes for great persistence in the sales prices even though the market wants a lower price. The market finds its new equilibrium by calling a time-out, waiting for inflation and economic growth to make the homes affordable again. It's a volume cycle, not a price cycle.

Check it out in Fig. 10.7, which has the nationwide volumes of sales of existing homes, the average sales price, and the sales price adjusted for inflation. The volumes numbers go up and down a lot, but nominal prices mostly just go up. It's a volume cycle, not a price cycle. But when sales volumes are low, inflation erodes the real prices making homes more affordable.

---

[8] Just kidding.

[9] Not marking to market can be given some rational justification by referring to option value. When a home is sold, the owner transfers the home to the buyer but also gives up the option of selling a little later, which can be quite valuable when the market is thought to be weak. The option of selling a little later is probably not very valuable to the buyer who would have to bear an extra transaction cost to sell again soon. Thus in times of economic weakness, owners may value the assets because of the option value more than prospective buyers. "You can't get what its worth" is the way to say it. When owners value the item more than prospective buyers, no transaction can occur.

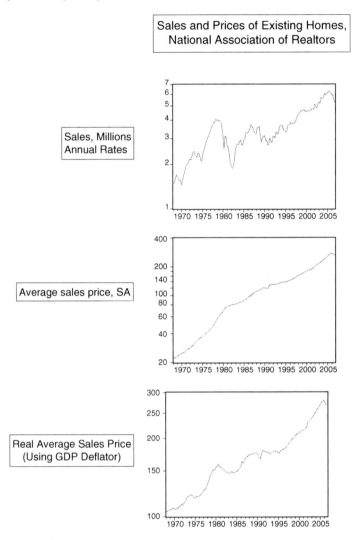

Fig. 10.7 Existing home prices and volumes

Many homes for sales sit vacant waiting to find a buyer. That's unemployment of physical capital. It is even more common for human capital to sit idle because its owner cannot stand to "mark to market."

Most of us love our homes, and have a hard time dealing with the idea that the market value is less than we think. To adjust to a reduced market price can be tough emotionally, but it's much tougher to accept the possibility that all that your education and training aren't nearly as valuable as you might have thought. That can produce some major, long-lasting denial and a substantial period of unemployment while the psychological adjustment is occurring. It isn't surprising then, when the defense cutbacks in the early 1990s greatly reduced the demand for laser engineers who knew how to shoot missiles out of the sky, many of these engineers preferred unemployment to taking a job that didn't use their skills.

Do you understand why I am calling this a Pyrrhic victory of hope over reason? When hope wins the internal struggle over reason and you insist that your asset is worth more than the market thinks, the cost of that victory is unwanted idleness.

Appendix: Supply and Demand Models of Unemployment

For those familiar with the workings of supply and demand models, it may be useful to show in diagrams the difference between a business cycle in a competitive market and a business cycle for a firm with market power.

A competitive market produces a price and profit cycle, not a volume cycle. Depicted below are two market equilibria for a hypothetical office building in which the supply is horizontal to begin with to reflect the operating costs (cleaning and utilities) and then vertical to reflect the fact that there are a fixed number of offices available. In the diagram at the left, the demand is strong and these offices are fully rented at a price above operating costs. The shaded rectangle represents the profits = volume × (rental price-operating costs). But when demand is weaker, as at the right, the price has to be bid down to the operating cost, to fill the building. At this low price, there are no profits at all even though the building is fully occupied. Thus this competitive market has a price cycle, not a volume cycle. The potential loss in volume that might come from the fall in demand is fully eliminated by the extra volume that comes from the lower market price.

Price and Profit Cycle in a Competative Market

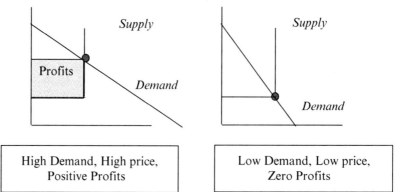

A noncompetitive market has a volume cycle, not a price cycle. Contrast the competitive market model above with the case illustrated below, in which the seller is free to set the rental price of the offices. Here, I have added a dotted line that reflects the "marginal revenue," which is the increase in revenue that comes from each extra office that is rented. Since to rent more offices, the owner has to charge a lower price, revenue that comes from the rental of an extra office is offset by reductions in the rental from the already-rented offices. Profits are maximized by setting marginal revenue equal to cost. You can see in the diagram on the left that when demand is strong the market power is irrelevant and the price is chosen high enough to set the demand for space equal to the available office supply, just as in the competitive case. But when demand is weak, illustrated at the right, the optimal response is not to lower price but instead to put up with the unused offices. If the price were lowered, you would rent out a few more offices, but the revenue gained on those extra units would be more than lost as a consequence of the lower rental value of the other units. Better not to cut the rents, and merely put up with the vacancies.

Firms and market power stabilize prices and profits by varying volume.

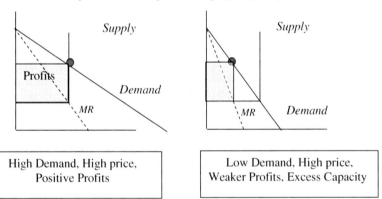

High Demand, High price,
Positive Profits

Low Demand, High price,
Weaker Profits, Excess Capacity

Chapter 11
Cycle Stories

The previous chapter has four stories about unwanted idleness: "Broken relationships, soaking the rich when times are bad, making do with the old car, and a pyrrhic victory of hope over reason". These help us to understand why unemployment is so persistent. This chapter has four stories about economic cycles. These stories help us to understand the ebb and flow of spending on the components of GDP, which drive the business cycle: homes, cars, equipment, offices, and factories:

1. The supply chain bull-whip
2. Rushes to exploit new ideas
3. Social-psychological abnormalities
4. Over-indulgent first-time parents (the Federal Reserve Board)

Parenthetically, the word "cycle" comes with considerable intellectual baggage. It suggests an event that regularly repeats like the hand on your clock going round and round, winter every year and the seventeen-year locusts. But you don't talk about the "cycle" of your health. You have long stretches of well-being interrupted by episodes of illness. What's the difference? It's what econometricians call the "hazard rate" – the probability of transitioning from one state to another, from healthy to ill, from normal economic growth to recession. Your probability of getting ill is pretty constant over time – just because you have been well for a long time doesn't mean that you are coming due for a bout of illness. (Maybe the opposite is true.) That's not a cycle. For a cycle, the hazard rate increases over time, sharply so when the event is "due". The more time that has passed since the last winter, the greater is the chance that the next winter will be here soon. That's a cycle. The jury is still out whether the US economy experiences a cycle with an increasing chance of a recession, the longer the time from the last one, or only periods of healthiness punctuated by occasional recessions.

E. E. Leamer, *Macroeconomic Patterns and Stories: A Guide for MBAs.*
© Springer-Verlag Berlin Heidelberg 2009

Given our limited state of knowledge, we should be adopting a word that is more neutral than "cycle," but we can stick with current usage if we understand that this cycle isn't all that cyclical. Some "cycle" stories are:[1]

(1)   The supply chain bull-whip and self-fulfilling expectations:

The capacity to produce and deliver goods and services has to be created, years in advance. Capacity creation is therefore premised on expected need not actual need, yet it is hard to predict economic growth even a year ahead, let alone a decade or more. The investment spending that creates this new capacity can thus occur in fits and starts with periods of self-fulfilling optimism involving heavy capital outlays supporting high rates of growth, and periods of self-fulfilling doubt involving little capital spending producing low rates of growth. Evidence: *Look for greater swings in production of the more long-lived assets.*

(2)   Rushes to exploit new ideas:

   a. First mover advantages

The railroad, the electric motor, the internal combustion engine, the Internet, and the California gold fields all created vast new profit opportunities for the first to get there. The mad dash for these riches created economic booms, which inevitably turned to bust when most of the real gold was discovered and what remained was only fool's gold. Evidence: *Look for investment surges not matched by profitability.*

   b. Network externalities

The railroad, the telephone, the telegraph, and the Internet all provided dismal returns for the first investments that connected points A and B: the first miles of track, the first miles of wire, and the first miles of fiber optic cable. But with A and B already connected, the investments needed to connect points B and C would also connect A and C. Thus, twice the return. Once A and B and C are connected, the investments needed to connect A and D also connect B and D, and C and D. Thus, thrice the return and so on. That's what economists call a network externality.

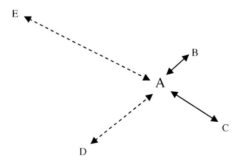

---

[1] The number of stories of the cycle is far greater than the number of actual cycles. A good website that provides a categorization and ample references is http://cepa.newschool.edu/het/schools/business.htm.

The second investors in a network are often surprised by the returns they receive, and the third and fourth even more so. This creates a frenzy of building. But inevitably, the network reaches its economically optimum size and disappointing returns force a halt to the rapid expansion of the system. *Look again for investment surges that are not matched with profitability.*

(3)   Social-psychological abnormalities:

   a. Ponzi schemes: Asset market bubbles

Easy access to cheap credit early in an expansion can set off an asset market bubble with market valuations of homes and businesses greatly exceeding their real intrinsic values. The sky-high valuations of existing homes and businesses produce a frenzy of home building and business formation, which lowers the real values of existing assets and increases further the gap between valuations and values. But as long as there is a buyer willing to pay more, this Ponzi scheme can continue. Evidence: *Look for asset price appreciation not matched by appreciation of real underlying values.*

   b. The madness of crowds[2]

When Alan Greenspan finished a question and answer session, he explained that he had another meeting to attend, and to the crowd, he said "Bye." Two attendees blurted out the question "Buy?" Four yelled "Buy" and all the attendees rushed from the room to place their buy orders. A year later, Mr. Greenspan was explaining his personal philosophy of reward for hard work: "It's not easy to excel" Two attendees blurted out the question "Sell?" Four yelled "Sell" and all the attendees rushed from the room to place their sell orders.

(4)   Over-indulgent first-time parents

In the economics sphere, our Daddy is the Chairman of the Federal Reserve Board and our parents, the members of the Federal Open Market Committee (FOMC), who select the target interest rate for Federal Funds. Our parents really love us, and want us to do well, but few of them have much experience on the job because they come and go so frequently. Like many new parents, they overindulge us with large helpings of ice cream and candy and low interest rates. Sometime later, aghast by the weight we put on after years of this fare, they force us on a diet of vegetables and high interest rates designed to put a halt to the inflation.

The most recent episode of poor parenting began when the FOMC stayed up late in December 2001 and watched on the Sci-Fi channel "How Godzilla and Deflation

---

[2] Charles MacKay, Extraordinary Popular Delusions and the Madness of Crowds, with a foreword by Andrew Tobias (1841; New York: Harmony Books, 1980). But for a contrary view see: Peter M. Garber, Famous First Bubbles: The Fundamentals of Early Manias (Cambridge, MA: MIT Press, 2000), or the popular version: James Surowiecki The Wisdom of Crowds: Why the Many Are Smarter Than the Few and How Collective Wisdom Shapes Business, Economies, Societies and Nations (2004).

destroyed the island of Japan." For over two years, our parents had terrible night-mares over this movie and to make sure that neither Godzilla nor Deflation would every get to the shores of the United States, they gave us candy and ice cream and extraordinarily low interest rates in all of 2002 and 2003. As a result, we grew a se-riously bloated housing sector. When this Deflation Dread Disorder finally wore off in mid 2004, our parents put us on a very restrictive diet of high interest rates, which is causing a very painful reduction of our housing sector as I write these words at the end of 2007. But our parents are now saddened by how hard this dieting is on us, so now they are dishing out ice cream and candy again, in the form of sharply lower interest rates.

By the way, I don't mean to suggest that these are mutually exclusive stories of the business cycle. On the contrary, every cycle probably has aspects of all. For example, early in an expansion, monetary authorities are often accomplices to Ponzi schemes by making credit readily available, but eventually they pierce the bubble with the pin of elevated interest rates, which puts an abrupt halt to home-building and business capacity formation.

11.1 The Harrod-Samuelson Multiplier-Accelerator Model

Before we get to the details of some of these stories, we need to do a little formal modeling to try to think clearly about the kinds of phenomena that might cause cycles. One thing to look for is features of the system that amply the reactions to natural changes in direction. Though "amplifiers" might be the word, Samuelson used "accelerator" instead. Maybe you might pause a moment and think about the difference between those two metaphors. What an amplifier does is to cause an overreaction when a change in direction is called for. This creates overshooting followed by a cyclical return to the new equilibrium.

An early and simple formal model of an economic cycle is the 1939 Samuelson multiplier-accelerator model.[3] The Samuelson model begins with the "Keynesian

---

[3] P.A. Samuelson (1939) "Interaction Between the Multiplier Analysis and the Principle of Ac-celeration", *Review of Economics and Statistics*. Vol. 21 (2), p.75–8. (This model has rather direct precursors in work by Harrod and by Hicks.) Samuelson began with a Keynesian consumption function expressing consumption C as a linear function of income Y in the previous period.

$$C_t = C_0 + cY_{t-1}$$

Here the parameter c is the marginal propensity to consume. To this Samuelson adds an investment "accelerator" based on the assumption that the level of investment spending I depends on the *increase* in consumption

$$I_t = I_0 + b(C_t - C_{t-1})$$

With total GDP equal to $Y = C + I$, you can do the simple substitutions to solve for the "equation of motion" of the system:

$$Y_t = C_t + I_t = (C_0 + cY_{t-1}) + (I_0 + b(C_t - C_{t-1})) = C_0 + cY_{t-1} + I_0 + bc(Y_{t-1} - Y_{t-2})$$
$$= (C_0 + I_0) + (1 + b)cY_{t-1} - bcY_{t-2}$$

multiplier." In response to a jump in purchases of consumption goods or investment goods, businesses, if they have the capacity, will increase production. The proceeds from these new sales are then distributed to labor, capital, and management. Thus the increase in sales, for example, by $100 billion, causes an increase in income by the same amount. That increase in income in the next period generates more spending, not $100 billion but something less as some of the increase in income "leaks" into savings accounts and spending on products made in other countries. If the marginal propensity to consume (MPC) is 80%, then the additional spending in the next round is $80 billion. This stimulates another increase in production and income. And then that $80 billion of new incomes stimulates a $0.8 \times 80 billion = $64 billion of new spending. And so on and so on. That's the Keynesian multiplier: the total increase in the level of GDP is a multiple, 1/(1-MPC), of the initial increase in demand.[4]

This Keynesian multiplier process has a GDP that smoothly rises to a new level as depicted in the figure to the left below, which assumes a marginal propensity to consume (MPC) of 0.80 and an increase in the level of "autonomous demand" equal to $100 billion. The increase in GDP in the new equilibrium is $100 billion times the multiplier 1/(1-MPC) = 5. Thus GDP goes smoothly from $10 trillion to $10.5 trillion.

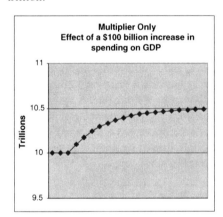

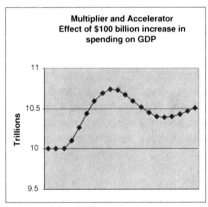

To get some cycles, you need something to cause some overshooting. That requires an amplifier, or in Samuelson's words, an accelerator. An amplifying effect can come from a component of demand that responds positively to *changes* in income. The multiplier, in contrast, has demand depending on the *level* of income – spending is a fraction of current income. When the economy is growing smartly, a component of spending that depends on changes in income gives the economy a special kick, and accelerates the expansion. But when the economy is contracting, this component of spending, subtracts from demand, and amplifies the downward fall of GDP. Then we get a cycle like the one above at the right.

This equation takes values of GDP(Y) in the two previous periods and generates a value of GDP in the next period. This equation is capable of producing a wide variety of dynamical paths including constant oscillations, damped oscillations and explosive oscillations.

[4] Did you recall the formula: $1 + x + x^2 + x^3 + \ldots = 1/(1-x)$?

   This simple technical model serves as a foundation for our search for cycle stories and cycle patterns. We should be looking for economic activities that tend to
occur when *growth* is strong and tend not to occur when *growth* is weak. These will
amplify any changes in direction, the economy may be experiencing. Any ideas? I
am thinking of capacity-creating investment. When growth is strong and capacity is
fully used, firms will feel compelled to make capacity-creating investments to prepare for further increases in sales that may come later. But when sales have fallen
and there is excess capacity, there is no need to make capacity-expanding investments at all. That is exactly what Samuelson thought. His accelerator is investment
spending.

11.2 Some Acceleration Facts

We can pause now to look at some acceleration facts. The diagrams below compare
the contribution to GDP growth of a component in one period with the contribution
to growth in the previous period. Make sure, you understand the words "contribution to growth." These "contributions" add to total GDP growth, which averages
3%. When we say that consumer spending accounts for 2/3rds of GDP growth, that
means the contribution of consumer spending to growth is 2% and the rest is 1%.
Do you get the idea?
   We are looking here for accelerators, brakes, and neutral components of GDP. A
component of GDP that operates to brake the system has a negative correlation with
the past, meaning that a strong quarter is followed by a weak one. A component of
demand that is neutral has a zero correlation with the past, meaning that a strong
quarter is followed by a normal quarter. An accelerator has a positive correlation
with the past, meaning that a strong quarter is followed by another strong quarter
and a weak quarter tends to be followed by another weak one.

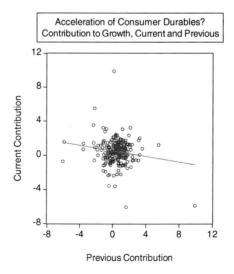

So take a look at the contribution of consumer durables to economic growth depicted above. The horizontal axis is the contribution in one quarter and the vertical axis is the contribution the next quarter. In this scatter diagram, there is a
best-fit regression line. So what is it? Accelerator, brake or neutral? That downward sloping regression line makes it appear that consumer durables operate to
brake the system. We can support that finding with a good story. If you bought a
new car, one quarter you don't need to buy another one the next quarter. Right?
Promotions that ramp up sales this quarter are only cannibalizing sales later on.
Right?

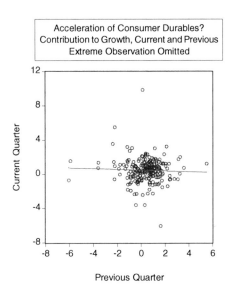

Not so fast, says Yuri Diomin, a student in my Executive MBA class. It looks
to him like there is one observation at the lower right that is dragging down the
regression line. Moreover, the fit of this regression looks so bad and is hard to imagine relying on it. Better check this out. Look at the picture above. Sure enough, if
you drop that one extreme observation, the regression line completely flattens out.
Consumer durables are neither an accelerator nor a brake. (LESSON: Beware of
numerical regression analysis backed up with compelling stories. You need to look
at the pictures too.)

But what about business spending on equipment and software and consumer
spending on new homes? Those might be brakes for the same reason. If you bought
a home or a computer one quarter, why buy another the next? But what do you see
in the diagrams below?

You are supposed to see in these diagrams that both equipment and homes
are accelerators, more for homes than for equipment. For those with the technical background and interest, a regression analysis in a footnote reveals that it is
homes and durables that predict GDP growth, not equipment or structures. But

homes are accelerators while durables are neutral.[5] As we study these US cycle data more and more, we are going to come back many times to a five-letter word: HOMES.

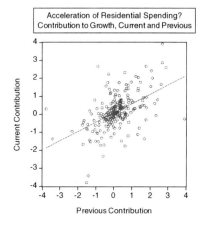

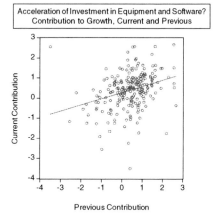

11.3 The Supply Chain Bull-Whip

We make the goods.
We make the tools that make the goods.
We make the factories that make the tools that make the goods.

---

[5] The data are real GDP growth and the contributions to growth of investment in residences, equipment/software, structures (factories and office buildings), and consumer durables.

Vector Autoregression Estimates
Sample (adjusted): 1947:3 2003:2
Included observations: 224 after adjusting endpoints

	Estimates					t-values				
	GDP	RES	EQUIP	STRUCT	DUR	GDP	RES	EQUIP	STRUCT	DUR
GDP(−1)	0.20	0.00	0.07	0.01	0.06	2.4	0.0	4.0	1.3	2.1
RES(−1)	1.88	0.59	0.32	0.02	0.68	6.2	8.8	5.0	0.5	6.3
EQUIP(−1)	0.26	−0.11	0.11	0.11	−0.04	0.8	−1.4	1.5	3.1	−0.3
STRUCT(−1)	−0.54	−0.52	0.07	0.27	−0.41	−0.8	−3.7	0.5	4.1	−1.8
DUR(−1)	−0.47	−0.06	−0.13	−0.01	−0.47	−2.2	−1.2	−2.8	−0.4	−6.0
C	2.64	0.18	0.10	−0.02	0.39	8.1	2.5	1.4	−0.5	3.3
R-squared	0.26	0.36	0.30	0.23	0.24					
Adj. R-squared	0.24	0.34	0.28	0.22	0.22					
S.E. equation	3.64	0.80	0.78	0.38	1.30					
Mean dependent	3.47	0.16	0.39	0.08	0.45					
S.D. dependent	4.18	0.99	0.92	0.43	1.47					

> We make the tools that make the factories that make the tools that make the goods.
> And so on ...

The long supply chain characteristic of industrial economies necessitates the creation of capacity to produce consumer products many years before actual sales are made. With such long lead times, there is little possibility in a vibrant and growing economy that actual capacity will match actual sales month after month. That makes the system seems very fragile, but there are inventories at each point in that long supply chain that will help to smooth out fluctuations. Further, with overtime and higher pace, most operations can squeeze out a lot more production on a temporary basis, which makes the capacity constraints soft, not hard. But when sales are ramping up rapidly and unexpectedly, there may be some intense make-up work to create the additional capacity as quickly as possible, and when demand is not meeting expectations, capacity formation may be weak or non-existent. In the extreme, this can create what operations specialists in business schools call the "bull-whip" effect in which small changes in final demand generate amplified responses as we go further and further back along the supply chain.

Supply chain management issues produce a cycle with expansions characterized by high levels of activity in the capital goods sectors and recessions characterized by low levels.

As an example, think of aircraft, which are capital goods that last for 30 years. In the midst of an economic expansion, airlines place orders for aircraft based on anticipated growth in airline passengers and they need to be thinking as clearly as possible about what the next 30 years might bring. Mistakes are inevitable, which means that the production of aircraft is very cyclical, with boom periods of production up against capacity, and bust periods when airlines aren't placing many orders.

Take a look at the figure below to see what aircraft manufacturers have to put up with. The index of industrial production in aircraft and parts swings between 80 and 120 about every ten years. This figure has the official US recessions in white. You can see that the aircraft cycle is not the same as the US business cycle. That is true for other long-lived assets too, including offices and factories.

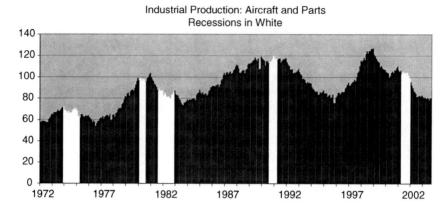

The highly cyclical behavior of industrial production of aircraft contrasts greatly with the very smooth path of the industrial production of food and tobacco, as illustrated below.

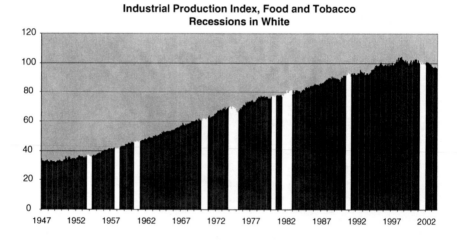

11.4 Rush to Exploit New Ideas

A rush to exploit new opportunities is another reason for a boom/bust cycle. An economic boom can occur both because of the rush itself and also because the first deployment of the new ideas tends to add the most to growth. Before we get into that idea, we need to add a couple of words to your vocabulary: the intensive margin and the extensive margin.

11.4.1 The Intensive Margin and the Extensive Margin

A farmer who increases the crop by cultivating more land is said to be operating at the extensive margin. To get the meaning of these words, visualize the farm as a plot of land and the farmer *extending* the area under cultivation – adding more land at the *margin* of the existing farm. That's the *extensive margin*.

A farmer who increases the crop by using the same land more intensively is said to be operating at the *intensive margin*.

The great march west of American farms during the nineteenth Century was growth at the extensive margin. While unimproved land was free for the first arrivals on the Western frontier, the push west eventually exhausted the free land, and the price of farmland everywhere in the US began an inexorable march upward. At the beginning of the twentieth Century, American farmland was already priced at over $500 per acre. By the end of the century, the price had risen to $1000, thus increasing about 0.4% per year in real terms, with a depression of land prices in the 1930s and a land price bubble in the 1970s along the way.

Agricultural Land Prices
Price Per Acre, Constant $1996 (CPI)

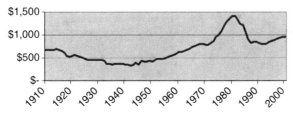

The rising price of land during the nineteenth and twentieth Century revealed a powerful message to every farmer: improve yields. And farmers have responded famously. In the twentieth Century, the enormous growth in agricultural output has not come from adding more farmland but by increasing yields: better land-use, better seeds, better equipment and better fertilizer. That's the intensive margin, not the extensive margin.

http://www.pbs.org/goldrush/intro.html

It was here, in this sleepy valley, that the American dream was re-defined. An accidental discovery near the obscure American river would forever change a young nation. The simple life would no longer be enough. In its place would come a new kind of lifestyle: entrepreneurial, wide-open, free. The new American dream: to get rich; to make a fortune – quickly.

Instant wealth was here for the taking. All across America, young men made the decision to go to California.

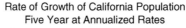

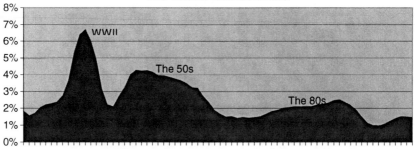

California, Here I Come. Since the Gold Rush of 1849, California has offered abundance – limitless sunshine and plentiful land and personal freedom and opportunities and wealth. The big growth of the California population came during the World War II and in the 1950s, when Americans flocked to California not for gold but for a sunny bungalow in the suburbs. New freeways and new cars year after year extended the reach of home builders, keeping the price of the residential land "at the margin" within reach of the middle class. But California "filled up" in the 1980s when congestion turned freeways into no-ways, making the land at the margin affordable only for those who don't value their commute time. Land-use patterns shifted at a painfully slow pace from single-family homes at the periphery to multi-family buildings at the center. It wasn't just land that had run out. It was water and even sunshine itself, as the sun turned that exhaust from all those cars into noxious smog and the extraordinary growth at the extensive margin turned into slower and more difficult growth at the intensive margin.

11.4.2 The Simple Agronomy of an Idea Rush

It's not just land that has an intensive margin and an extensive margin. It's also ideas. A major technological innovation such as the railroad or the electric motor or the Internet opens up a vast frontier of new business applications. There is naturally a burst of growth as entrepreneurs rush to exploit the new opportunities. Inevitably, high growth at the extensive margin of ideas gives way to slower growth as the ideas mature and the applications become more mundane and less revolutionary. We can tell a story of the cycle around a swing back and forth from the extensive to the intensive margin.

Begin the story with an orchard full of ripe ideas. At the start of the recovery, businesses rush out to pick the low-hanging fruit. Inevitably, the opportunities get harder to find, and firms are forced to seek credit to finance the building of ladders that let them pick from the higher branches. The first businesses to turn to the credit markets find the terms very favorable, with creditors offering low interest rates and expecting little collateral. But all this picking can increase the cost of labor and the cost of ladders. As more and more firms seek more and more credit to build ladders higher and higher, the banks and other credit sources start to worry about bankruptcies and start to insist on higher interest rates, more collateral and more clear evidence of high quality fruit on the branches. When credit gets too tight, labor too expensive and the remaining opportunities too meager, the expansion ends, the businesses abandon the picked-over trees, leaving the orchards time to replenish themselves. And the cycle starts all over again, with entrepreneurs, in the words of Schumpeter, moving "like swarms," when the tree appears to be full of fruit again.[6]

The basic economic pathology that this model embodies is a lack of property rights. No one owns the orchards of opportunities. If the orchard were owned, the picking would be controlled at a sustainable rate.[7] A second pathology is the swarming or contagion, which is characteristic of the pursuit of new opportunities. (I am not sure, if there is gold over there, but when I see you running in that direction, I decide I'd better start running pretty fast, pretty soon.)

Monetary policy, according to this view, should not attempt to extend an expansion beyond its normal life, but instead should limit access to the commons with appropriately high real rates of interest, attempting to keep the harvest rate equal to the replenishing rate, and thus allowing an expansion to live forever. This task may be relatively easy when technology has been constant and when history can serve as a guide for the optimal harvesting rate, but the optimal control of access to the commons following bursts of new technologies like the Internet requires a level of clairvoyance about the nature of that orchard of opportunities that is unlikely to be available. Still, we knew that the Internet orchard was being seriously over-harvested, didn't we?

---

[6] Schumpeter(1939) *Business Cycles: A theoretical, historical and statistical analysis of the Capitalist process*. New York and London: McGraw-Hill. This story of the cycle has much in similarity to the more complicated offering of Zarnowitz(1999) who "ties together profits, investment, credit, stock prices, inflation and interest rates."

[7] Essentially the same idea is embodied in the predator/prey cycles in Smith(1974). Here the prey are business investment opportunities and the predators are entrepreneurs. The Volterra(1926) equations of a predator and prey model, with E standing for entrepreneurs and O for investment opportunities, are

$$\dot{O} = aO - bO^2 - cOE$$
$$\dot{E} = -eE + c'OE,$$

where investment is OE. These equations are descriptive and not necessarily a solution to an optimization problem. Another biological reference is Diamond's (1982) coconuts model, which is a solution to an optimization problem of when to pick the coconuts, when there are improved possibilities of finding a trading partner when the picking is intense.

11.4.3 Kondratieff Long Waves[8]

The swing between the extensive and the intensive margin is part of the Kondratieff long waves. In the 1920's, the Russian economist Nikolai Kondratieff studied two centuries of data stretching from 1700 to 1920 on commodity prices, interest rates, wages, foreign trade and production/consumption of coal and pig iron, and the production of lead and gold. From these data and from the timing of major wars, Kondratieff came to the conclusion that the capitalist economies had 50-year cycles layered on top of the shorter frequency business cycles. The "story" that was offered (rather tentatively) to explain this cycle, combines geopolitical competitive shocks with a propagation mechanism.[9]

Nikolai Dmitrijewitsch Kondratjew (1892–1938)

A war for scarce resources produces a clear victor but a depleted capital stock. Two decades of robust growth follow the war as the global capitalist system pursues the investment opportunities created by the war's destruction. Profits and growth during the long upswing come at the extensive margin, and recessions are brief and mild. But inevitably, scarcity switches the focus from the extensive margin (finding more resources and labor) to the intensive margin (using the resources and labor

---

[8] Photo from http://faculty.washington.edu/~krumme/207/development/longwaves.html
Kondratieff, Nikolai D. "Bol'schije cykly konjunktury" ("The Major Economic Cycles" or "Long Economic Cycles"), Voprosy konjuktury (Problems of Economic Fluctuations) 1(1) 1925.
——. "Die Langen Wellen der Konjunktur" ("The Long Waves in Economic Life"), Archiv fur Sozialwissenschaft und Sozialpolitik (Archives of Sociology and Social Legislation) 56(3) 1926: 573–609. German translation of "Bol'schije cykly konjunktury" ("The Major Economic Cycles" or "Long Economic Cycles"), Voprosy konjunktury (Problems of Economic Fluctuations) 1(1) 1925.
——. "The long waves in economic life," Review of Economic Statistics. 17(6) Nov 1935: 105–15. English translation by W.F. Stolper of "Die Langen Wellen der Konjunktur" ("The Long Waves in Economic Life"), Archiv fur Sozialwissenschaft und Sozialpolitik (Archives of Sociology and Social Legislation) 56(3) 1926: 573–609.

[9] "Although the period embraced by the data is sufficient to decide the question of the existence of long waves, it is not enough to enable us to assert beyond doubt, the cyclical character of these waves. Nevertheless, we believe that the available data are sufficient to declare this cyclical character to be very probable.

more efficiently). The focus on the intensive margin and the competition for scarce resources during the long downturn leaves technological breakthroughs, which create new extensive margins unexploited and ready to produce new sources of growth, when the next long upswing begins.[10]

11.5 Ponzi Schemes and Asset Bubbles

Ponzi schemes are another cycle story.

Carlo "Charles" Ponzi, discovered that postal coupons purchased in Spain for about one cent US could be used to buy 6 cents worth of US stamps. If one could find buyers for those stamps in the US, this was a money machine. You want to invest in this enterprise, don't you? Before you do, maybe you should find out just how easy it is to buy the postal coupons in Spain and to cash them in the US and then to find buyers for the US stamps. Even better, maybe you should ask why Mr. Ponzi needs your hard-earned money to perform this trick and why he would be willing to share the guaranteed profits with you. The answer is that when he tried it out on his own, it didn't work so well – too much red tape and too many long delays to make any money. But by selling the ideas to initial investors (promising a return of 50% per 90 days) and then using the cash contributed by later investors to pay off the first investors, he created enormous interest in his scheme.

See http://home.nycap.rr.com/useless/ponzi/

"An estimated 40,000 people had entrusted an estimated $15 million (about $140 million in U.S. funds today) in Ponzi's scheme. A final audit of his books concluded that he had taken in enough funds to buy approximately 180,000,000 postal coupons, of which they could only actually confirm the purchase of two."

Hyman Minsky has produced a story of the financial cycle that culminates in Ponzi finance.[11] For Minsky, a Ponzi loan is collateralized by an asset that doesn't generate enough earnings to draw down the debt or even to service the debt. The viability of this loan depends entirely on appreciation of the value of the collateral. This is a Ponzi scheme because it relies on ever more buyers to bid the prices of the assets higher and higher. Here is how it works over the business cycle. Early in an economic expansion, default risks on loans to homeowners and businesses are low, because the homes and hard business assets that serve as collateral experience elevating real values and elevating valuations – as the economy grows, they have special scarcity value. (Be sure you understand that values and valuations are not

---

[10] Each wave starts with a trough war and ends with a peak war. In the United States, trough wars include the French and Indian War (1754–59), the Tripolitan War (1801–05), the Mexican War (1846–48), the Spanish American War (1898), and the Korean Conflict (1950–53) and the Persian Gulf Conflict (1991–1992). The peak wars include the American Revolution (1775–81), the War of 1812 (1812–15), the American Civil War (1861–65), World War I (1914–18), and the Vietnam War (1964–72).

Dr. A. Joyce Furero, http://www.drfurfero.com/books/231book/ch20.html

[11] Longer waves in financial relations: Financial factors in more severe depressions", 1964, *American Economic Review*.

always the same. "Real value" refers to the value of the services that these assets provide in the context of a growing economy that is putting pressure on housing stocks and business capacity. "Valuation" refers to the dollar number that we record for the assets in our financial statements.) Early in an expansion, value and valuation conform. But with the low default risk, lenders aggressively pursue borrowers and the consequent easy access to credit to support the acquisition of existing homes and businesses allows the valuations to grow more rapidly than values. Meanwhile, the construction of new homes and new business capacity lowers the scarcity value of the existing assets, further enlarging the gap between valuations and values. The asset bubble may burst on its own, or be pricked by monetary tightening, which makes credit less available.

11.5.1 Housing Bubbles

Homes are the favorite Ponzi scheme of the US economy. The usual fiction that supports a housing asset bubble is that there is only so much residential land, and Americans desperately need more housing, therefore the price can only go up. Beyond the complete illogic of that argument, the facts are otherwise, as you can see in the price data at the right, which reveals price declines in real terms during every recession but one. Buyers couldn't create these price cycles alone. They need a lot of help from lenders. Lenders help out by valuing homes at the prices of "comparable sales" and by offering highly leveraged loans (0% down) up to 2 or more multiples of "stated" (aka falsified) income. Better yet, an option ARM loan allows you to choose your monthly payment – if it doesn't cover the interest charges, the lender (aka loan shark) will just add that to your outstanding balance. Try asking for that kind of loan to invest in the stock market!

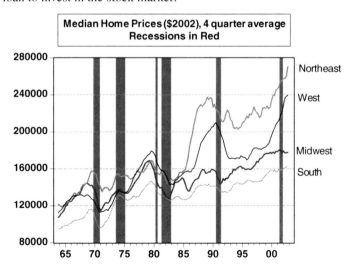

Part III C
Recession Early Warning Signs

Chapter 12
Clues: Temporal Ordering of Components of GDP

It is time now to start doing some detective work to figure out what causes recessions and then to figure out some suitable treatments and preventative measures.

A sensible first place to look for the cycle drivers are the investment components of GDP: inventories, business spending on equipment and software, business spending on structures (office buildings and factories), consumer spending on durables, and consumer spending on new homes and home improvements. These are quite likely to be volatile because they can all be postponed. You can hold on to that car for another year, and you can put off building a new home. Businesses do not have to buy that new computer today, and they can put off for a while their plans to build new offices or new factories. If we all do our postponing at the same time, we will probably have a recession, since the workers and capital that are normally used to produce these investment items may be idled, until we finish our waiting.

12.1 Help from Sherlock Holmes

Holmes: "So, Dr. Watson, what should we be looking for?"

Watson: "That's easy, Mr. Holmes. Find out if these investment items decline a lot in the quarters before the recession. Those early declining expenditure items are the causes of the recession."

Holmes: "You are looking in the right place for clues, Dr. Watson, but be very careful before you jump to conclusions. The temporal ordering of variables is relevant but not conclusive. As you know, correlation does not imply causation. If we discover, for example, that declines in business spending on equipment and software regularly precede recessions, it is of course a perfectly valid conclusion that business spending *predicts* recessions, but to conclude that business spending *causes* recessions is something else altogether, something ever so much more subtle. After all, the mere fact that weather forecasts routinely precede the weather is not conclusive evidence that the forecasts cause the weather. Business investment might be like the weather forecast, merely predicting a fall in consumer demand that has it's own causes."[1]

Watson: "Well, Mr. Holmes, if correlation does not imply causation, what does??"

Holmes: "Listen, carefully, Dr. Watson, since what I am about to tell you is not widely understood, least so by those with Ph.D.'s in Economics. Correlation is in the data. Causation is in the mind of the observer."

Watson: "I listened carefully, but I haven't the slightest idea what you are talking about."

Holmes: "The word "cause" is a reference to some hypothetical intervention, like putting a gun to the head of the weather forecaster, and making her say "sunny." If we actually carried out this experiment, we could get some direct evidence whether or not weather forecasts cause the weather. But we detectives are forced to work with the evidence we have, which is only correlations. To make causal inferences from nonexperimental data we rely on causal models that are in our heads, not in the data. Thus, you and I have some scientific training, a.k.a. indoctrination, which makes us highly doubtful that weather forecasts cause the weather. We don't think the historical correlation between the forecasts and the weather would be preserved if the forecaster had a gun to her head."

"For the sake of clarity, it is very important that we be explicit about the intervention. We should not say that multinational corporations cause lower wages in the United States since whether or not we have multinational corporations is not under our control. The hypothetical of no multinationals is vague, if not better described, and absurd if clearly defined.[2] We might hypothesize that aggressive taxation of foreign-source earnings of US multinationals would raise earnings of

---

[1] Sadly, economists confuse temporal orderings with causality when the test for "Granger Causality," C.W.J Granger. "Investigating causal relations by econometric models and cross-spectral methods." *Econometrica*, 37:424–438, 1969.

[2] McCloskey, D, "Counterfactuals" *The New Palgrave Dictionary of Economics*, Vol. 1, 1987, pp 701–703. "What if Columbus had not discovered America?" is a counterfactual that is either vague

our high school graduates. That would be a perfectly good causal statement since it refers to something under our control."

Watson: "My head is spinning. What does this have to do with finding the causes of recessions?"

Holmes: "Best to understand that the instruments that are available to affect the course of the economy are very limited indeed. The Federal Reserve can influence interest rates, and Congress can alter government spending and taxation. The Treasury can buy or sell US dollars. Chairman Bernanke can proclaim and President Bush can prognosticate. That's about it. We will need to reserve the word "cause" to refer to one of these interventions. If we conclude that declines in spending on homes causes recessions, that is a reference to our belief that changes in interest rates or exchange rates or government spending or government taxation or official utterances can change spending on homes and through that route alter the course of the economy."

Watson: "Is that it? Is there anything more we need to worry about?"

Holmes: "That's it. Let's look at the data."

12.2 Contributions to GDP Growth

Whew, that's heavy stuff. Don't worry. We will come back to it, when and if we need to. For now let's just look at temporal orderings. Let's find out which of the investment items moves first and which moves second.

The first item of business is to choose a suitable scaling of the GDP components to allow us to compare one component with the other. The BEA creates a table that is very useful in that regard. Here it is:

Contributions to Percent Change in Real Gross Domestic Product
Seasonally adjusted at annual rates
Bureau of economic analysis

Line		2004-I	2004-II	2004-III	2004-IV
	Percent change at annual rate:				
1	**Gross domestic product**	**4.5**	**3.3**	**4**	**3.8**
	Percentage points at annual rates:				
2	**Personal consumption expenditures**	**2.9**	**1.1**	**3.57**	**2.89**
3	Durable goods	0.19	−0.02	1.37	0.27
4	Nondurable goods	1.33	0.03	0.94	1.21
5	Services	1.39	1.1	1.26	1.41
6	**Gross private domestic investment**	**1.86**	**2.85**	**0.4**	**2.13**
7	Fixed investment	0.69	2.07	1.37	1.52
8	Nonresidential	0.42	1.21	1.27	1.4
9	Structures	−0.19	0.16	−0.03	0.03
10	Equipment and software	0.61	1.05	1.3	1.37

or absurd. See Preston McAfee, "American Economic Growth and the Voyage of Columbus", *American Economic Review*, September 1983, 735–740

Line		2004-I	2004-II	2004-III	2004-IV
11	Residential	0.27	0.86	0.09	0.12
12	Change in private inventories	1.17	0.78	−0.97	0.6
13	**Net exports of goods and services**	**−0.76**	**−1.06**	**−0.1**	**−1.43**
14	Exports	0.7	0.7	0.59	0.24
15	Goods	0.6	0.41	0.64	0.13
16	Services	0.1	0.3	−0.06	0.11
17	Imports	−1.46	−1.77	−0.69	−1.67
18	Goods	−1.43	−1.52	−0.62	−1.85
19	Services	−0.03	−0.25	−0.07	0.18
20	**Government cons. exp. and gross invest.**	**0.48**	**0.41**	**0.13**	**0.22**
21	Federal	0.48	0.18	0.33	0.12
22	National defense	0.47	0.09	0.45	−0.02
23	Nondefense	0	0.1	−0.12	0.14
24	State and local	0	0.23	−0.2	0.1

In this table we see that GDP growth in 2004 Q4 was estimated to be 3.8. That 3.8 is the sum of contributions for each of the components: 2.89 for consumption spending, 2.13 for investment, 0.22 for government minus 1.43 for net exports. This information is dramatically displayed in the normal growth profile, Fig. 12.1, which is based on historical data only in the "normal" growth phases, not the recessions, recoveries or spurts, that we will discuss in Chap. 16. At the bottom of this pyramid is the largest contributor to normal growth: consumer services. Services contribute 1.15 to the total normal growth of 3.3. Next comes consumer nondurables, then equipment and software. Moving farther up the chart, we see that defense spending

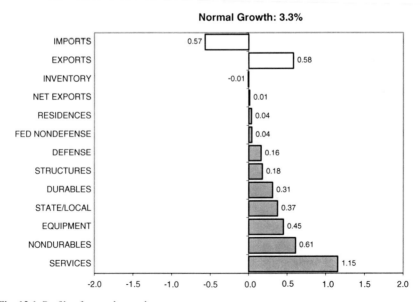

Fig. 12.1 Profile of normal growth

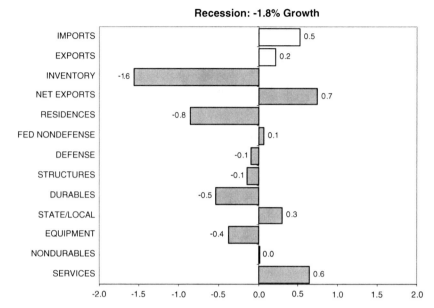

Fig. 12.2 Recession profile

is rather unimportant, while federal nondefense, homes, net exports, and inventory hardly matter at all. Incidentally, at the top of this figure I have displayed imports and exports separately, but shown them in white bars. Thus the 0.58 contribution of exports is almost perfectly offset by a −0.57 from imports.

Note by the way that the consumer components, services (1.15), nondurables (0.61), and durables (0.31) add to 2.1 out of the total 3.3. Thus when commentators say that consumer spending is 2/3rd of GDP, that's about right: (2.1)/(3.3).

We are trying to figure out what causes recessions, and a first step is to ask how recessions are different from normal. Compare the recession profile in Fig. 12.2 with the normal profile in Fig. 12.1. They are dramatically different. A recession has a big negative from inventory, while normal growth has virtually none. A recession has a big positive from net exports, while normal growth has virtually none. A recession has a big negative from homes (residences) while normal growth has a very small positive.

The comparison of the recession with normal growth is much easier if we look at the difference between the two, illustrated in Fig. 12.3. This tells us very clearly how a recession is different from normal. On the negative side, the biggest problem is inventory. Next comes homes, then consumer durables (cars and washing machines) and business equipment. That's an important clue. Put it in your head: *Inventories, homes, cars, and equipment.*

The only bright part of a recession is the positive contribution of net exports. That is mostly due to imports. Why do imports contribute positively to GDP growth? I thought we subtracted imports when finding GDP? That's true, but we are dealing

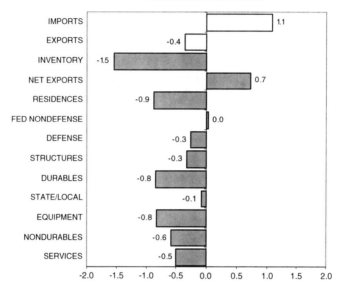

Fig. 12.3 Recession profile: difference from normal

here with the *growth* of GDP, not the level of GDP. Thus these contributions to GDP refer to the *change* in the component. Imports, which subtract from GDP, can make a positive contribution to the *growth* of GDP if imports are declining.[3] Can you understand that confusing arithmetic?

Inventories are even more confusing. It is not the level of inventories that contributes to GDP. It is the increase or decrease in inventories. Then for the growth of GDP, it is the change in the increase or decrease – the change in the change. That is mind-boggling. Do not worry about it. Let us move on and trust that the government statisticians did their job right.

12.2.1 Normal Trend Contributions to GDP Growth

The figures just discussed that contrast the contributions to GDP growth during recessions from the contributions during normal periods do not allow for the possibility that the normal contributions have changed over time. But weakness in a component of GDP in 2001 may be rather different from weakness in 1948 because

---

[3] A much better way of saying this is that some of the weakness in spending is aimed at foreign sources of supply. If you add up the tradables abnormal contributions: nondurables (−0.6), equipment(−0.8), durables (−0.8), and inventory(−1.5), that comes to −3.7. With imports equal to +1.1, about 1/3rd of the decline in demand during recessions leaks to foreign sources of supply, 1.1/3.7.

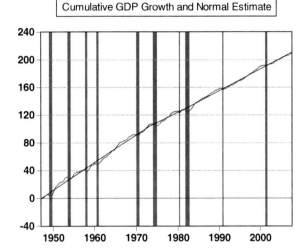

Fig. 12.4 GDP growth cumulative and "normal" cumulative

of potentially substantial changes in the structure of the economy over that half-century.

The goal here is to produce unforgettable images of the timing of the components of GDP. This is going to take a little work, and you will need to bear with me. I know this is hard going for a while, but if you stick with it you will be rewarded with some highly memorable data displays.

I have explored many possible ways of allowing the normal contributions to change over time but the one that seems best is a piece-wise regression of the cumulative contributions on a time trend, allowing for three different trends. The two break-points in these trend lines have been chosen to maximize the fit of the regression, with the restriction that each episode must be at least ten years in length. The results of this exercise for GDP are displayed in Fig. 12.4, which depicts the cumulative GDP growth figures (divided by 4 to turn the quarterly numbers into annual), and the three-trend line that best captures changes in the trends in this series. You can hardly see it in the figure, but this "normal contribution" has breakpoints in both 1973Q1 and 1983Q3. The breakpoints for all the series and the corresponding means and standard deviations can be found in the appendix Table 12.3.

The three-trends "normal" cumulative does not fit so well the defense spending cumulative instead I have chosen a single trend commencing in 1955.

Figure 12.5 displays the three-part trends for all the cumulative contributions to growth. Keep in mind that what matters here are the slopes and not the levels of the curves. It is these slopes that are the normal contributions, and it is the difference between the actual contributions and these slopes that is the abnormal contribution. Many of these normal cumulatives are virtually straight lines, meaning that there is only one normal contribution. However, the rapid rise in both imports and exports after 1987 and the more sluggish growth of exports after 1997 are quite evident.

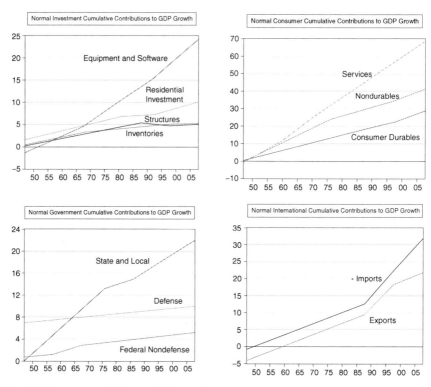

Fig. 12.5 Normal cumulative contributions: three periods

12.2.2 Abnormal Cumulatives

The next step is to subtract from the actual cumulative the "normal" cumulative to get to the abnormal cumulative. For example, the GDP abnormal cumulative, which is the difference between the two lines displayed in Fig. 12.4, is displayed in Fig. 12.6 with the recessions shaded. To understand this figure you need to only think: flat, rising or declining. When the line is flat that means the growth is normal, quarter after quarter, since to get a cumulative abnormal that does not change, it is necessary to have the abnormal be zero, and thus actual equal to normal, quarter after quarter. When the curve is rising, growth exceeds normal; when the curve is declining, growth is less than normal.

The official recessions are shaded in this figure and the weakness of GDP growth is evident as the curve dives sharply in every one of the recessions. Generally, after a few quarters of diving down, the curve shifts in the other direction and rockets skyward. That is the better-than normal growth recovery. There are hardly any flat segments here, and thus few extended periods of normal growth, but you can see two near the end of the series: the early 1991–1995 and 2002–2007.

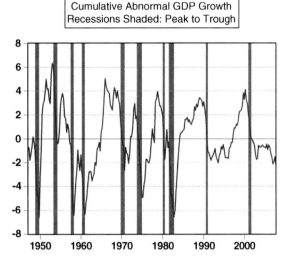

Fig. 12.6 GDP deviations from normal cumulative

The next step will be to look at these cumulative abnormals to see if they are behaving in some special way immediately before the recessions, and can therefore be used to issue an early warning signal of troubles ahead. Figure 12.6 reveals that GDP growth softens dramatically in the recessions, but the weakness immediately before recessions is not so distinct that it can be relied upon to predict recessions.

12.3 Average Temporal Orderings: It's a Consumer Cycle, Not a Business Cycle

We already have some good clues about what causes recessions. The big four problems *during* recessions are: *Inventories, homes, cars, and business equipment.* The next step is to look at temporal orderings: which comes first? Which is soft before recession? Which is a leading indicator?

To explore the temporal orderings, we will first look at the cumulative abnormal contributions to GDP averaged across seven recessions and then look at each of the ten recessions separately. Excluded from the averages are three recessions that are different: the 2001 Internet Comeuppance, the 1953 Department of Defense Downturn, and the 1948 ancient consumer downturn, which is a typical consumer downturn but with an atypically strong recovery. We will look at each of these recessions separately soon enough.

The *average cumulative abnormal contributions* of the investment components of GDP growth during the seven consumer recessions are illustrated in Fig. 12.7. The corresponding data for the other components of GDP are displayed in Fig. 12.8. These data are computed in several steps. First, using the contribution table created by the Bureau of Economic Analysis, we find the cumulative contribution,

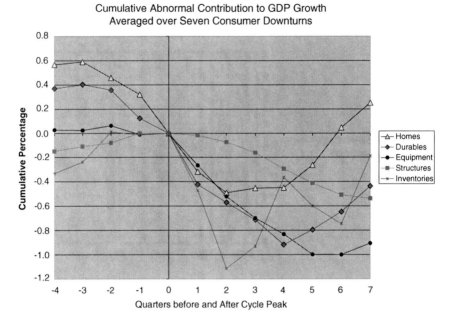

Fig. 12.7 Investment components of GDP during seven consumer downturns

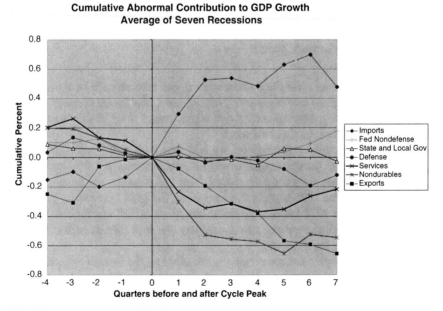

Fig. 12.8 Other components of GDP during seven consumer downturns

accumulating across time but adjusting for the difference between annual and quarterly data by division by four. Second, the normal contribution is found by the regression of the cumulative actual on three optimally selected trend lines. From the actual cumulative contribution, we subtract this normal three-trend to find the cumulative abnormal contribution. Third, we extract the cumulative abnormal data from around each of the ten recessions and normalize by subtracting out the value from the cycle peak. Fourth, we average the resulting numbers for seven of the recession. Thus we compute the average cumulative abnormal contributions around recessions. This seems complex, but you only have to remember one thing: when the displayed line is flat that represents a sequence of normal contributions, since the abnormal must be zero to make the cumulative have no change. FLAT = NORMAL. RISING = GREATER THAN NORMAL. DECLINING = LESS THAN NORMAL.

Take a look at Figs. 12.7 and 12.8. Can you see flat, or rising, or declining? The horizontal scale in these figures is the number of quarters before and after the official NBER peak. Period 0 is the peak and period 1 is the first quarter of the recession. The period zero data is zero in every case by construction: from the data around each recession, we subtract out the value at the cycle peak. Please understand that the vertical scale indicates the cumulative effect of the item on GDP compared with the cycle peak period.

There are big differences in the timing and the amplitude of each of these average contributions. The housing peak occurs three quarters before the official cycle peak, and the decline in spending on homes reduces GDP by about 0.6% before the recession officially begins. (Can you see that number in the figure?) In the first two quarters of the recession, declines in spending on homes reduces GDP by another 0.5%, but strong growth thereafter has home spending exceeding the value at the cycle peak in the sixth quarter of the recession.

Contrast homes with the pattern of spending on equipment and software. In equipment and software, there is just a tiny bit of weakness prior to the onset of the recession – the equipment line is virtually flat to the left of zero. Spending on equipment and software gets very soft immediately at the onset of the recession, and does not return to normal again until the fifth quarter of the recession when the line bottoms out. The cumulative impact of weakness in spending on equipment and software is to knock a full percentage point off of GDP. And even after the seven quarters, the lost growth due to weakness in equipment and software has not been recovered.

So who moves first: businesses or consumers? It is consumers. *It is a consumer cycle, not a business cycle*! Businesses wait to see what consumers are doing. Businesses are the passenger, not the driver.

What about consumer durables and business structures? They tell a similar story. Spending on consumer durables softens considerably two quarters before the official cycle peak. The consumer durables downturn is closely aligned with the decline in residential investment, but the total reduction in GDP is greater for consumer durables (1.4) than for residential investment (1.0), and the bottom in consumer durables is one or two quarters after the bottom in residences. On the basis of these averages, it appears that weakness in consumer durables is as good a predictor of oncoming recessions as weakness in residential investment, but when we look at all the recessions separately another conclusion emerges – the averaging has masked considerable noise in the consumer durables numbers across recessions. Rely on homes not durables to predict recessions.

The cycle in business spending on structures has the smallest amplitude and is the most delayed of these four, not returning to normal until the seventh quarters of the recession.

The inventories component deserves some special attention since the cumulative abnormal is rising smartly several quarters before recessions. Possibly, prior to recessions, businesses are building up inventories in anticipation of exceptional growth ahead, but more likely the softening economy produces an unexpected and unintended buildup of inventories, and when the recession begins in full measure these inventories are drawn down and are a substitute for current production, which makes the production swing greater than the swing in demand. Thus it appears as though inventory management, rather than softening the cycle in production, as it should, is actually amplifying it.

The other components of GDP displayed in Fig. 12.8 reveal additional softness before recessions on the consumer side: consumer nondurable and consumer services. Each of these shaves about 0.2% points off of GDP in the three quarters before recessions. Nondurables during the recessions shave another 0.6 off of GDP and services −0.4.

One thing that really jumps out of Fig. 12.8 is the help during recessions that comes from imports. The weakness in demand for imports in recessions is a plus for GDP because imports subtract from GDP. In other words, we export our troubles by importing less. But we also import troubles too, in the form of weaker exports. Why is that? Why might weakness in the US lead to weakness in our exports? Is that exports of parts made in US for assembly overseas and later reimport into the United States? Or is that a general slowdown in the economies that deliver goods to US because demand in US is weakening? Or some of both?

Don't forget: Its a consumer cycle, not a business cycle. Business is the passenger, not the driver.

12.4 Eight Consumer Cycles, a Disarmament Downturn, and an Internet Rush Comeuppance

Though many of the recessions are preceded by significant weakness in houses and consumer durables, all ten recessions have not been the same, and the averaging masks important differences. We need to take a close look at each of the ten events.

Figure 12.9 displays the cumulative abnormal contribution of residential investment averaged across seven consumer downturns and all ten downturns individually. Here you can see why we have excluded the 1953 and 2001 recessions (no warning

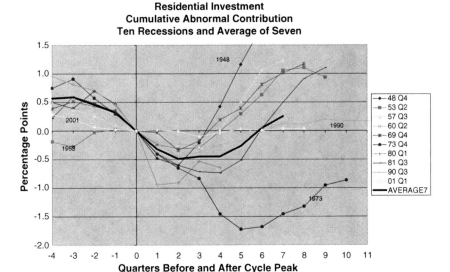

Fig. 12.9 Residential investment during ten recessions

from housing) and the 1948 recession (exceptionally strong recovery). The others closely follow the average, though the dip in 1973 was very extreme.

Figures 12.10–12.15 are similar displays for consumer durables, equipment and software, structure, inventories, defense and export. Take a close look at these. There is a lot of information here. Here is what I see:

- There is a lot of noise around the averages for consumer durables and especially for inventories. This noise greatly reduces the reliability of these components of GDP for forecasting recessions.
- Though equipment and software reliably is weak during the recession, prior to the recession it has a mixed outcome.
- Business structures (offices and factories) are late to the recession party and rarely matter very much.
- There was an exceptional negative contribution from equipment and software before and especially during the 2001 recession.
- The 1953 recession was unusual in that there was no weakness prior to the recession in any of these displays. Though normal until the recession officially began, defense spending subtracted almost 4% points from GDP in eight quarters. With normal GDP growth of 3 in 4 quarters, that is a huge blow.
- The defense display is dominated by the 1953 event but there was considerable weakness in defense spending also in 1969.
- Exports were a problem especially in the 2001 recession.

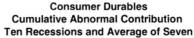

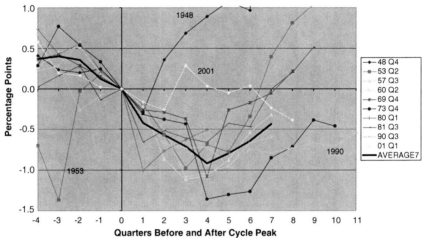

Fig. 12.10 Consumer durables during ten recessions

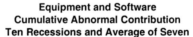

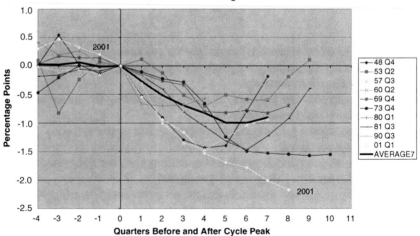

Fig. 12.11 Equipment and software during ten recessions

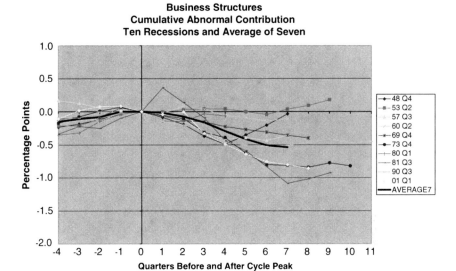

Fig. 12.12 Business structure during ten recessions

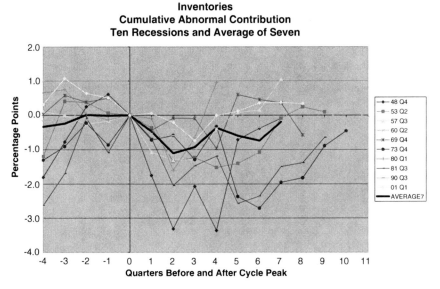

Fig. 12.13 Inventories during ten recessions

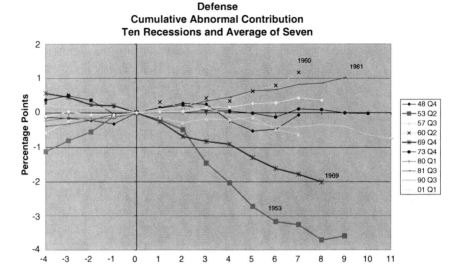

Fig. 12.14 Defense spending during ten recessions

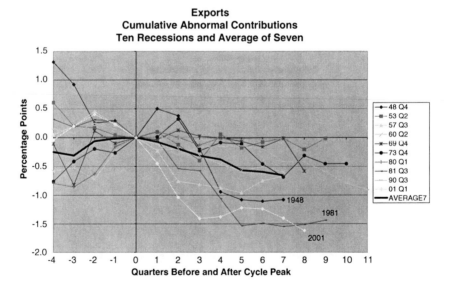

Fig. 12.15 Exports during ten recessions

12.4.1 The 1953 Department of Defense Downturn

The cumulative abnormal contributions of the volatile components of GDP during the 1953 recession are displayed in Fig. 12.16. Notice that there were no alarm bells rung out in any of the spending items prior to the onset of the recession. The Korean

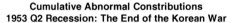

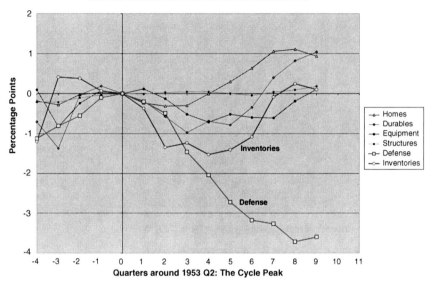

Fig. 12.16 The 1953 DOD downturn

Armistice was signed on 27 June 1953, and the official recession began in the very next quarter, 1953 Q3. Prior to that quarter, defense spending was powering the economy forward with abnormally high positive contributions to GDP growth, but that turned around on a dime with the armistice and defense spending became as strong a drag on the economy at it had been a driver. Most of the action initially came from a drawdown in inventories, which had been building up earlier in the year in anticipation of continued hostilities. Once the armistice was signed, inventories subtracted almost 1.5% points from GDP in only two quarters, presumably in anticipation of the defense cutback that was sure to come in the months ahead. At an annual rate that is 3% points, almost all of normal growth. Through eight quarters the defense cutback reduced GDP by almost 4% points. The multiplier effect of this fiscal cutback is evident in the weakness during the recession in homes, durables, and business equipment.

This 1953 DOD downturn was a great reverse test of "Keynesian" reliance on government spending to pull the economy out of recession, complete with an apparent multiplier effect on consumer spending and also an accelerator effect on inventories and business equipment.

12.4.2 The 2001 Internet Comeuppance

The cumulative abnormal contributions of the volatile components of GDP during the 2001 recession are illustrated in Fig. 12.17. Here you can see how much drag

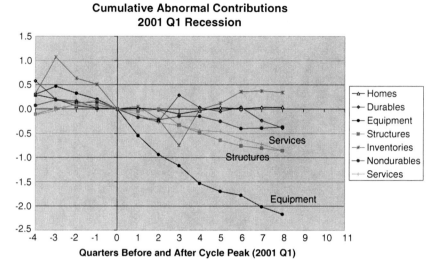

Fig. 12.17 Cumulative abnormals: The 2001 internet comeuppance

came from equipment and software both before and during the recession and from
a drawdown of inventories prior to the recession. You can also see problems in
business structures starting three quarters into the downturn. There is no weakness
in either residential investment or in consumer durables.

This 2001 event was our only business downturn.

12.4.2.1 Recession or Structural Adjustment?

We call it a business cycle but usually it has not been. Since World War II we have
had eight consumer recessions, one DOD downturn, and one business downturn.
Notice that I wrote eight "recessions" and two "downturns." That is foreshadowing
a point that I will now get to. A recession is a V-shaped pathology. During the first
stroke of the V there are massive layoffs. That lasts only a few quarters. During the
second stroke of the V, most of these folks get rehired doing the same thing they did
before. When the illness is over, the economy looks pretty much like it did prior to
the recession. To get the idea, think of members of the United Automobile Works
or the Building Trades Union. Those folks are completely familiar with temporary
layoffs during recessions.

But in addition to V-shaped recessions, there are structural adjustments that entail
a fundamental change in the GDP mix, and no return to the predownturn economy.
The Korean War disarmament is an obvious example. Members of the Army who
got "laid off" did not get "rehired." Defense contractors did not experience a filling
up of their order books soon after the 1953 recession. This was a structural adjustment from a wartime economy to a peacetime economy.

The 2001 downturn was also partly a structural adjustment. I call it the 2001
"Comeuppance" referring to the exuberance that drove the Internet Rush from

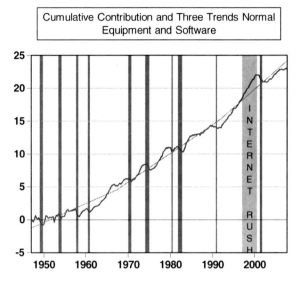

Fig. 12.18 Equipment and software cumulative contribution to GDP growth

1996 to 2000 when every business in the United States had to have the coolest Website, or advertise on one. Figure 12.18 illustrates cumulative contribution of equipment and software to GDP growth. Here you can see the exceptional contribution of equipment and software during the Internet Rush, and the subsequent collapse. The cycle story that best fits this episode is the rush to exploit new ideas.

You can see in Fig. 12.17 that nondurables and services were a bit weak during the 2001 Comeuppance but homes and durables were not. Weakness in nondurables and services is not surprising in light of the job loss that occurred, but it is surprising that neither consumer durables nor residential investment was weak at the same time. What kept two consumer spending items (homes and cars) strong, while the other two consumer spending items were weak (services and nondurables)? The answer is very low interest rates, courtesy of Mr. Greenspan.

The uniqueness of the 2001 Comeuppance is important because it greatly reduces the relevance of the historical evidence for forecasting what was likely to have happened in 2002/3/4. You can see from the normal cycles illustrated in Fig. 12.7 that during the recovery quarters 5–7, homes and consumer durables are usually making a greater-than-normal contribution to GDP growth – they are climbing out of the trough into which they had fallen during the recession. During this recovery period, GDP growth is exceptional (5%), the job market is improving and profitability is strong. But the 2001 comeuppance could have no recovery in consumer durables or homes since there was no consumer dip. If there were a "recovery" on the business side in 2002 or 2003, it would have required someone in a Palo Alto garage to figure out how to squeeze profits off the Internet. That did not happen. Bottom line: we did

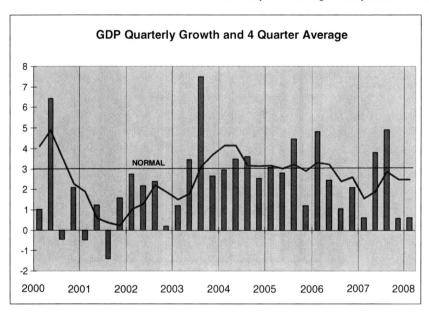

Fig. 12.19 GDP growth, 2000–2008

not think there could have been the usual high-growth recovery from the 2001 recession. Indeed, that is exactly what happened, as you can see in Fig. 12.19. Growth in 2002 and the first half of 2003 was below the normal rate of 3%. But in 2004 and 2005, the US economy kicked into a higher gear with growth averaging above normal. I wonder why? Think interest rates. Think housing.

The uniqueness of the 2001 Comeuppance raises issues for monetary policy as well as for forecasting. A different disease requires a different treatment. Stimulating consumer spending by low interest rates and income tax reductions in 2001 was treating a disease from which the economy was not suffering. Listen up, Drs. Greenspan and Bush. You need to understand that interest rates affect the timing of homes and autos, but not the totals. In a normal consumer recession, weakness in spending on homes and autos creates pent-up demand, and the low interest rates in the aftermath of a recession move sales *forward* in time, capturing sales that had not been made during the recession. But there were no lost sales of homes and autos during the 2001 Comeuppance. So where do you suppose the sales in 2003–2005 came from? They came from the future. Dr. Greenspan was moving sales backward in time, not forward. That created economic strength in 2003–2005, but inevitable weakness later when there were fewer potential home and auto buyers. To put this another way, monetary policy needs to be conceived explicitly as an intertemporal control problem, with the decisions made today affecting the options later on. You can stimulate now or later, but not both. After all, even with low interest rates, how many new cars can you fit in your garage?

In other words, Mr. Greenspan screwed up. His low interest rates in 2001 helped to isolate the disease to the business side, but after 2001 he should have been providing interest rates that would support sustainable sales rates of homes and automobiles, and sustainable rates of appreciation of home prices. But Mr. Greenspan and his band of happy trolls had a bad case of Deflation Dread Disorder, and they swung their interest swords wildly in the air in hopes of slaying a phantom deflation enemy. While they swung their swords and proclaimed ongoing victory over deflation, they were laying the foundation for the troubles we are experiencing in 2006 and 2007 and 2008 and. . . .

The problem started in 2002 when the economy was pulling out of recession. One cold winter night Mr. Greenspan and the folks on the FOMC stayed up late and turned on the Sci-Fi channel that was playing the classic horror film: "How Godzilla and Deflation destroyed the island of Japan." For years after that, no one on the FOMC had a decent night's sleep. Bleary-eyed, but determined to prevent Godzilla or Deflation from successfully attacking US, they voted for lower and lower interest rates. What they failed to understand is that general deflation is a symptom of a sluggish economy, not a cause. The deflation that needs to be prevented is asset price deflation. Asset price deflation can cause serious problems, of which we became painfully aware in 2007 and 2008 when home prices were declining. Though the rental market for homes in many parts of the United States in 2007 and 2008 has been strong and has been crying out for more building, declining home prices from their stratospheric levels has made it impossible to build and sell new homes, since it is usually much better to rent an existing home than to buy a new one that is eroding in value. Keep in mind that even if the interest rate is lowered to zero, you are still out of pocket the loss in value of your home. If you expect a new $1 million home to lose 10% of its value in a year, you have to include that $100,000 loss in the cost of ownership to compare against the cost of renting an equivalent house. With the high price of homes, taxes, and maintenance, the breakeven appreciation that determines whether it is better to own than to rent is usually a healthy positive number.

12.5 Housing False Positives and False Negatives

We have already learned that declines in spending on homes preceded eight of the ten recessions since WWII and contributed substantially to the 1953 decline as well. But how many other times did problems in housing suggest that a recession was imminent?

Figure 12.20 answers this question by displaying the cumulative abnormal contribution to GDP growth of both residences and defense, with the recessions highlighted. Indeed eight of the ten recessions were preceded by declines in housing. The two false negatives labeled FP in the figure were the disarmament downturn of 1953 and the Internet Comeuppance of 2001.

There were only two false positives. Housing was very weak late in 1951 but there was no recession. Why? That was the Korean War, which broke out in

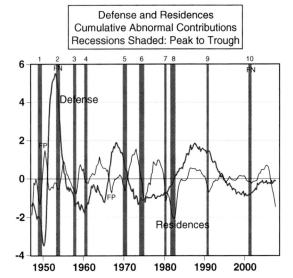

Fig. 12.20 Investment in residences

June 1950. Take a look at the huge contribution of defense spending at that time, completely offsetting the weakness in housing. Housing was also weak in 1966 and 1967. Again it was the Department of Defense that came to the rescue, this time to fight the Vietnam War.

12.6 A Story of the Consumer Cycle: Our Collective Bipolar Disease

It's homes. We need a good story now to memorialize this finding. Here is mine.

As far as homes are concerned we suffer from a collective bipolar disease, swinging back and forth between manic buying and depressed waiting.

In both the manias and depressions, the housing market does not work right. The economists' model of the efficiency of the market hinges in a critical way on "downward sloping demand curves": when the price is reduced, more is sold. If demand curves are downward sloping, and builders experience an unwanted increase in unsold homes, they can cut the price and sell more. When builders are having a hard time keeping up with the demand, they can raise the price and reduce the sales rate. But in both the manias and the depression, demand is upward sloping not downward sloping. When the price is rising in a mania, a higher price suggests even higher prices later on, and buyers rush in before it is too late. Thus higher prices lead to more buyers. When the price is falling during the depressions, a price cut suggests more cuts are on the way, and buyers decide to wait to get a better deal. Thus lower prices lead to fewer buyers.

From these upward sloping demand curves, we suffer terrible overshooting, with prices rising high enough to shock buyers out of their manias, and prices falling low enough to coax the buyers out of their depressions.

Home buyers do not suffer from manias and depressions without the support of the enablers who issue the mortgages. When homes are appreciating in value, home loans are self-collateralizing and anyone who can crawl off the street can get a loan and buy a home. But when home prices are flat or declining, the loans are not self-collateralizing and lenders are forced to look at default risks much more carefully, and to screen out suspicious borrowers.

This creates an inevitable boom and bust cycle in residential real estate. This cycle affects the whole economy, since, during the boom, there are substantial income accruals to everyone involved in the building homes or selling homes, including brokers and bankers. The increase in home values also puts phantom assets onto the personal balance sheets of homeowners who use that paper wealth to finance the purchase of cars and other durables. The income and the phantom assets disappear when the real estate bust occurs, precipitating some serious belt-tightening.

Businesses, meanwhile, merely react to what is happening on the consumer side. They are the passengers, not the drivers. They, like the rest of us, cannot tell when the Ponzi scheme will collapse, and they wait until they are sure to react. The amount of delay on the business side depends on the longevity of the business asset. Shorter-lived assets like equipment and software adjust most rapidly. The long planning process and the long building process and the long lives of factories and offices make these structures the component of GDP that has the most delayed adjustment to the consumer cycle swings.

12.7 Numbers, If the Pictures Are Not Enough

12.7.1 Regression Analyses to Support What the Pictures Say

These images promise that movements in the components of GDP can presage an oncoming recession, but we need to confirm these impressions with some numerical analysis. Let us first try to find out how well we can predict GDP growth from its own past behavior. Is there momentum? Does one weak quarter portend another? Or is GDP growth more like the flips of a coin – a couple of heads in a row having no effect on the probability of another head? The answer is that GDP growth is pretty much like flips of a coin. The fraction of the quarter-to-quarter variability of GDP growth from 1948 Q2 to 2004 Q4 that can be explained by the previous four quarterly numbers is only 14.1%, which is reported at the top of Table 12.1. This is what statisticians call the R^2 – the "r-squared". The R^2 statistic goes from 0%, for perfectly unpredictable, to 100%, for perfectly predictable. An R^2 statistic of 14.1% is going to lead to such terrible prediction errors, and anger your clients so much, that you might as well treat it as a zero and conclude that GDP growth cannot

Table 12.1 Percent of variance of GDP growth explained by previous contributions to growth

Quarterly data: four lagged values of all variables, cubic equations for first lag 1948 Q2 to 2004 Q4	
	R-squared
GDP predicted from Itself	14.1%
GDP Predicted from Components	
Consumption	
Nondurables	15.0%
Durables	9.1%
Services	17.4%
Investment	
Equipment and Software	14.1%
Inventory	5.1%
Residences	30.2%
Structures	6.6%
Net Exports	
Exports	6.2%
Imports	7.5%
Government	1.6%

be predicted from its past. There is no momentum, no coming due. It is a random variable, like flips of a coin.

Also reported in Table 12.1 are R^2 statistics for explaining GDP growth as a function of past behavior of the components of GDP. Next quarter's GDP is predicted from six variables: this quarter's component contribution, the square and cube thereof, and also from the previous three quarters. This allows us to pick up long lags and also nonlinearities, like threshold effects in which small values do not matter much but big ones matter a lot.

The message of this Table 12.1 is: *It's HOMES*, stupid.[4] What's good for KB Homes is good for the country.

The past spending on homes can explain 30% of the variability of GDP growth. That is getting big enough to make the frown on your client's face fade a bit. It is a long way from 100%, but a lot better than 14.1%. The next best number is for consumer services, but it is only 17.4%, not much better than GDP itself. Everything else is a dismal failure. *Residential investment, and only residential investment, helps to predict GDP growth consistently over this long period from 1948 to 2004.*

In summary, although spending on residences makes a rather unimportant contribution to *normal* growth, it is spending on residences that is the most important of the GDP components for predicting the highs and lows: the recessions and the recoveries.

---

[4] For what might be the first discovery of this, see Green, Richard K. "Follow the Leader: How Changes in Residential and Non-residential Investment Predict Changes in GDP", *Real Estate Economics*, V. 25, 1997, 253–270.

So say it again: homes, cars, machines, and factories. That is the order of the downturn. That is the order of the recovery. Homes, cars, machinery, factories.

And if you are interested in GDP prediction, just say HOMES. Or, in the rhetoric of my Jackson Hole paper: Housing is the Business Cycle.[5]

12.7.2 A Summary Table

With all these images filtering into our consciousness, it is time to do some numerical summaries just to make sure that we have seen all there is to see, and we have not seen things that are not really there. Table 12.2 has summaries of the cumulative abnormal contributions to GDP of each of the components before and during the ten recessions. A component that is contributing to the onset of the recession has the cumulative abnormal contribution to GDP declining prior to the official start date of the recession. The amount of this decline from the previous peak is recorded in the *top* panel of Table 12.2. The components that are contributing negatively *during and after* the recession are noted in the *bottom* panel. The numbers reported here are the largest cumulative amount that the component subtracted from growth since the onset of the recession. The blank components in this table are making an abnormal positive contribution to GDP growth. You can't find many of these during the recessions, when softness was very widespread.

I have separated inventories from the other components in this table because weakness in inventories is a symptom of weakness elsewhere in the economy and should not be treated as a driver. Imports are also separated from the other components for the same reasons: a rise in imports that might look like a negative contribution to GDP growth is a symptom of something else going on in one of the other components of GDP.

In both the panels, the biggest negative for each recession is shaded in dark red and items close to this extreme are shaded in light yellow. The column in this table at the far right reports the seven quarter average of the table entries, with the first two recessions and the last one excluded, for reasons already explained.

Looking at the averages column of the top panel, we discover something we saw in the charts: weakness in spending on homes precedes the official onset of the recessions. On average, declines in home building have been the most important reason for economic weakness prior to the official start of the recession, reducing real GDP to 0.66%. Next come inventories (−0.62) and consumer durables (−0.53).

The details in this table leave an impression that is sometimes at odds with our look at the graphs. Maybe that 1969 recession should be called a defense downturn like the 1953 event! Maybe the classification of eight consumer recessions, one DOD downturn and one Internet Comeuppance isn't so clear! Maybe exports need to be understood better.

The table reveals that declines in spending on homes was the greatest contributor to prior weakness in three of the ten downturns. Consumer durables were most

---

[5] "Housing and the Business Cycle," in Housing, Housing Finance and Monetary Policy, A Symposium Sponsored by the Federal Reserve of Kansas City, August 2007.

Table 12.2

Abnormal Contributions to Economic Growth										
	48 Q4	53 Q2	57 Q3	60 Q2	69 Q4	73 Q4	80 Q1	81 Q3	90 Q3	01 Q1	Avg7

Prior to the Recession

Negative of maximum cumulative prior to period 0, if negative

	48 Q4	53 Q2	57 Q3	60 Q2	69 Q4	73 Q4	80 Q1	81 Q3	90 Q3	01 Q1	Avg7
Durables	−0.41	−0.18	−0.52	−0.28	−0.43	−0.77	−0.74	−0.28	−0.68	−0.58	−0.53
Nondurables	−0.25	−0.07		−0.14	−0.30	−0.79	−0.21	−0.17	−0.20	−0.18	−0.30
Services	−0.11	−0.02	−0.30	−0.07	−0.09	−0.28	−0.52	−0.79	−0.03	−0.18	−0.30
Residences	−0.70	−0.02	−0.49	−0.69	−0.51	−0.91	−0.95	−0.60	−0.48	−0.29	−0.66
Equipment	−0.54	−0.10			−0.17	0.00	−0.41		−0.61	−0.47	−0.30
Structures			−0.17		−0.06	−0.07				−0.08	−0.10
Defense				−0.52	−0.56	−0.49			−0.22	−0.03	−0.45
Exports	−1.31	−0.61	−0.45		−0.11			−0.31	−0.25	−0.40	−0.28

Other components shaded if less than minimum of first eight

	48 Q4	53 Q2	57 Q3	60 Q2	69 Q4	73 Q4	80 Q1	81 Q3	90 Q3	01 Q1	Avg7
Inventories	−0.61	−0.41	−0.10	−1.47	−0.58		−0.75		−0.21	−1.07	−0.62
Imports	−0.33	−0.40	−0.05	−0.01	−0.52		−0.03	−0.54			−0.23

During the Recession

Minimum cumulative after onset of the recesssion, if negative

	48 Q4	53 Q2	57 Q3	60 Q2	69 Q4	73 Q4	80 Q1	81 Q3	90 Q3	01 Q1	Avg7
Durables	−0.29	−0.98	−1.12	−1.09	−1.08	−1.36	−1.00	−0.66	−0.95	−0.39	−1.04
Nondurables	−0.73	−0.99	−0.89	−0.68	−0.54	−1.65	−0.61	−0.26	−0.84	−0.40	−0.78
Services	−0.78	−0.51	−0.16	−0.45	−0.28	−0.45	−0.66	−0.53	−0.77	−0.86	−0.47
Residences	−0.61	−0.31	−0.28	−0.27	−0.34	−1.73	−0.94	−0.74	−0.44	−0.10	−0.68
Equipment	−1.43	−0.71	−1.47	−0.81	−0.83	−1.55	−0.71	−1.47	−0.83	−2.17	−1.09
Structures	−0.49	−0.04	−0.44	−0.14	−0.40	−0.84	−0.15	−1.09	−0.53	−0.86	−0.51
Defense	−0.52	−3.71	−0.63		−2.01	−0.12			−0.41		−0.79
Exports	−1.11	−0.40	−0.96	−0.60	−0.58	−0.68	−0.13	−1.55	−0.42	−1.62	−0.70

Other components shaded if less than minimum of first eight

	48 Q4	53 Q2	57 Q3	60 Q2	69 Q4	73 Q4	80 Q1	81 Q3	90 Q3	01 Q1	Avg7
Inventories	−3.36	−1.52	−1.31	−1.55	−0.97	−2.71	−1.60	−2.58	−0.64	−0.75	−1.62
Imports	−0.24		−0.22		−0.03	−0.01		−0.78			−0.26

Cycle Driver

	48 Q4	53 Q2	57 Q3	60 Q2	69 Q4	73 Q4	80 Q1	81 Q3	90 Q3	01 Q1
Prior	X	X	D/R/X	R	W/R/D	R/D/N	R	S/R	D/E	D/E
During	E	W	E	D/E	W/D	R/N/E	D/R/E	X/E	D/N/E	E

D durables; *E* equipment; *N* nondurables; *R* residences; *S* services; *X* exports; *W* war

Largest Negative in Red

Close to largest in Yellow

important in three more. The other largest contributions to weakness prior to the recessions were services (1981), exports (1948 and 1953), and defense (1969). Inventories contribute negatively prior to eight of the recessions and were bigger than the other components in three of them.

Turning now to the averages column of the bottom panel, we see that these recessions involve significant negatives from almost all the components of GDP, though equipment and durables are slightly ahead of the others, except inventories. Three times durables was the biggest problem in recessions, three times equipment and software, twice defense, once exports and once residences.

At the bottom of Table 12.2 are two rows that indicate the components of GDP that drove us into the recessions and the components that contributed the most during recessions. In the "Prior" row, there are six R's, meaning residences. In the "During" row, there are eight E's meaning equipment and software.

12.8 Summary

To get a recession, one or more components of spending have to plummet rapidly and subtract about a full percentage from GDP growth. Then this problem has to continue and infect other segments of the economy.

Not all recessions have begun in the same way. The pictures suggest that we had eight consumer recessions, a disarmament downturn, and an Internet comeuppance. The numbers offer a more nuanced story.

Since World War II, US had six pure consumer downturns that got started with troubles in housing, consumer durables, and services. (1957, 1960, 1973, 1980, 1981, 1990)

The 1969 recession had a big disarmament contribution as well as a big consumer contribution.

We have had one Disarmament Downturn (1953), and one Business Comeuppance (2001).

The 1948 recession was a general malaise, with a big contribution from exports. (What is that, anyway? What were we exporting in 1947?)

Appendix: Normal Contributions in Three Episodes

Table 12.3 Three periods of growth

Begin	End	Mean	Std. Dev.	Obs.	Begin	End	Mean	Std. Dev.	Obs.
		GDP							
1947Q2	1972Q4	4.00	4.85	103					
1973Q1	1983Q2	2.50	5.00	42					
1983Q3	2007Q4	3.24	2.19	98					
		3.44	4.05	243					
	Consumer durables					Equipment and software			
1947Q2	1987Q3	0.47	1.68	162	1947Q2	1967Q1	0.26	1.12	80
1987Q4	1997Q3	0.34	0.76	40	1967Q2	1991Q4	0.36	0.81	99
1997Q4	2007Q4	0.55	0.77	41	1992Q1	2007Q4	0.57	0.70	64
		0.46	1.44	243			0.38	0.90	243

Table 12.3 Continued

Begin	End	Mean	Std. Dev.	Obs.	Begin	End	Mean	Std. Dev.	Obs.
Consumer nondurables					Inventories				
1947Q2	1975Q4	0.78	1.13	115	1947Q2	1968Q1	0.16	3.50	84
1976Q1	1996Q3	0.55	0.55	83	1968Q2	1997Q3	0.08	2.45	118
1996Q4	2007Q4	0.64	0.40	45	1997Q4	2007Q4	−0.05	1.40	41
		0.68	0.86	243			0.08	2.72	243
Consumer services					Residential investment				
1947Q2	1959Q4	0.93	0.62	51	1947Q2	1980Q4	0.18	1.21	135
1960Q1	1969Q4	1.29	0.42	40	1981Q1	1992Q2	0.09	0.75	46
1970Q1	2007Q4	1.16	0.56	152	1992Q3	2007Q4	0.10	0.50	62
		1.13	0.56	243			0.14	0.99	243
Defense					Business structures				
1947Q2	1957Q4	0.72	2.69	43	1947Q2	1987Q3	0.12	0.46	162
1958Q1	1976Q4	−0.06	0.89	76	1987Q4	1997Q3	0.01	0.31	40
1977Q1	2007Q4	0.12	0.48	124	1997Q4	2007Q4	0.05	0.36	41
		0.17	1.30	243			0.09	0.43	243
Federal nondefense					Imports				
1947Q2	1957Q1	0.12	1.02	40	1947Q2	1987Q3	−0.36	1.13	162
1957Q2	1967Q1	0.17	0.72	40	1987Q4	1997Q3	−0.77	0.75	40
1967Q2	2007Q4	0.05	0.31	163	1997Q4	2007Q4	−0.85	1.05	41
		0.08	0.57	243			−0.51	1.08	243
State and local					Exports				
1947Q2	1975Q3	0.46	0.39	114	1947Q2	1987Q3	0.24	1.15	162
1975Q4	1985Q4	0.19	0.49	41	1987Q4	1997Q3	0.88	0.60	40
1986Q1	2007Q4	0.29	0.27	88	1997Q4	2007Q4	0.43	0.87	41
		0.35	0.39	243			0.38	1.06	243

Chapter 13
More Clues: Episodic Forecasting with Components of Conference Board's Index of Leading Indicators

We have found some clues regarding the causes of recessions in the temporal orderings of the components of GDP: homes, cars, equipment, and structures. That is the order of declines going into recessions and the order of the recovery as well; Usually, but not always. The recession of 1953 was different, and so was 2001.

The components of GDP are not the only place to look. There is a vast set of additional variables that might be studied for additional clues regarding the causes of recessions. Fortunately, statisticians and economists at the Conference Board have been mining these data for a very long time, and have produced a "short list" of variables that they have combined into an overall "Index of Leading Indicators."

The behavior of the overall index is illustrated in Fig. 13.1, where the US recessions are shaded. It looks like this index gives some warning of the coming of recessions on the basis of the decline in the index before the recessions, but there are quite a few other dips that are not followed by recessions. Those are called false positives. It is possible that we can improve on this index by treating the components differently. Thus let us have two goals in this chapter: find the early warning signs of oncoming recessions and also see if we can beat the Conference Board at their own game.

13.1 Components of the Leading Indicator Index

Table 13.1 below reports the components of the Conference Board's Index of Leading indicators. To be evocative, I have sorted the components into groups: labor market, housing market, financial markets, manufacturing order books, and man-on-the-street predictions.

The names of these components are generally clear enough except possibly the vendor performance deliveries diffusion index:

"Vendor performance is based on a monthly survey conducted by the National Association of Purchasing Management (NAPM) that asks purchasing managers whether their suppliers' deliveries have been faster, slower, or the same as the

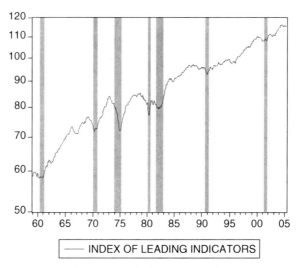

Fig. 13.1 Conference Board index of leading indicators, log scale, recessions shaded

previous month. The slower-deliveries diffusion index counts the proportion of respondents reporting slower deliveries, plus one-half of the proportion reporting no change in delivery speed."

You can find out more about this and the other components in an Appendix to this chapter.

Table 13.1 Components of the index of leading indicators and standardization factors

Leading index	Standardization factor
Labor market	
1. Average weekly hours, manufacturing	0.1963
2. Average weekly initial claims for unemployment insurance	0.0255
Housing market	
3. Building permits, new private housing units	0.0205
Financial markets	
4. Interest rate spread, 10-year Treasury bonds less federal funds	0.3295
5. Stock prices, 500 common stocks	0.0291
6. Money supply, M2	0.2778
Manufacturing order books	
7. Manufacturers' new orders, consumer goods and materials	0.0587
8. Manufacturers' new orders, nondefense capital goods	0.0149
9. Vendor performance, slower deliveries diffusion index	0.0293
Man-on-the-street predictions	
10. Index of consumer expectations	0.0185

13.2 Forget that Expectations Variable

That "man-on-the-street" label for the "index of consumer expectations" is intended
to be derogatory since, without looking at the data, we should begin with a high
state of doubt regarding the predictive value of survey responses to questions about
the future state of the economy. The Conference Board's Index of Consumer Expectations is built from answers to three questions regarding:

(1) The economic prospects for the respondent's family over the next 12 months
(2) The economic prospects for the Nation over the next 12 months
(3) The economic prospects for the Nation over the next five years

That's strange. Why on earth would we be interested in the man-on-the-street's
opinion regarding the Nation's economic prospects over the next 12 months and
even less so, the next five years? After all, professional forecasters have a heck of
a poor track record anticipating recessions, and even Mr. Greenspan, in the midst
of the 1990 recession, prognosticated: "The economy has not yet slipped into a
recession."[1] Why would the man-on-the-street know anything special about where
the economy is headed? There is possibly some value in the first question regarding
the respondent's family, since the respondent might have some knowledge on that
subject that goes beyond ours, but the other questions are only asking what is in the
newspaper lately. We already know that.

But we will need to look at the data to see if this is right or not. As it turns
out, this expectations variable by itself is not the worst of the leading indicators
for predicting recessions, but whatever small amount of information it contains is
embodied in other variables.

I doubt that you will be convinced by the econometric analysis that is reported
later, but I think there is something in the data that is really compelling. The 9/11
terrorist attack offered what is probably the best test of the usefulness of these consumer sentiment variables. The Conference Board index of consumer expectations
plummeted after the terrorist attack, as can be seen in Fig 13.2, which has the 2001
recession shaded.

If consumer psychology matters, this national funk should have presaged a
deeper and longer recession, but in fact the recession ended officially a couple
of months later. If consumer psychology matters, the plummet in the index after
9/11 should have been evident in retail sales. But, while retail sales, displayed
at the right, tumbled in September 2001, those lost sales were completely recap-
tured in October, a record-breaking month, and then sales were back to their normal
trend.

There's a very good reason why these surveys are not very useful. It is not how
you feel that matters, or what you say about how you feel. It's what you do. If you

---

[1] 'By the middle of 1990, the economy was in a full scale recession. Everyone knew it except Greenspan. As late as October of that year, he told his fellow Fed members, "The economy has not yet slipped into a recession." http://www.townhall.com/columnists/brucebartlett/
bb20001226.shtml

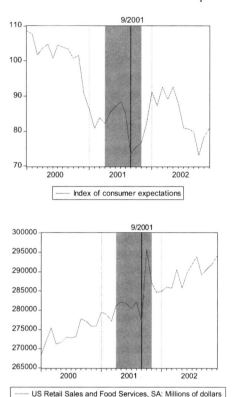

Fig. 13.2 The 2001 Recession and the 9/11 Effect

feel great and you shop, that's good news for the economy. If you feel lousy and you shop, that's good news too.

Why then is the latest release of the consumer expectations index so prominently displayed in the business sections of every newspaper, and sometimes even on the front pages? Might as well print a picture of Chuck the groundhog.

We know the reason. The newspapers need to put words between those ads. And good stories have a life of their own, never mind the absence of support- ing data. The story of bipolar consumers, experience periods of manic-shopping, frenzied-work intermixed with depressions spent at home alone is a pretty good one, is not it?[2] It is worth repeating over and over and over and over....You can imagine the headline: Rising crude oil prices blamed for the epidemic of depression.

---

[2] After all, when the recession gets severe we do call it a "depression." That's seems like a psy- chological metaphor, but maybe it's a journey metaphor, like a "soft landing" or a "pothole in the road" – A depression in the road.

13.3 Only a Few of Those Components Predict Oncoming Recessions

I am suspicious about the use of that consumer expectations variable, and it troubles me that there does not seem to be anything in the Conference Board methodology that would root out irrelevant indicators. All they do is "standardize" the variables to have the same degree of volatility. The last column of Table 13.1 reports the "standardization factor" which multiplies the component to standardize its volatility – the more volatile components have lower standardization factors and less weight in the Index. But volatility is not the issue. The issue is predictability. A low volatility indicator might be a terrible predictor.[3]

We can do some numerical analysis to separate the wheat from the chaff. To get started, look at the index again in Fig. 13.3 but this time with the years before the recessions shaded and with the recessions and first year of every expansion omitted. The statistical analysis that is next discussed asks the question: how different is the index in the shaded area compared with the rest of the data? If the answer is "very different" then this index can be used to forecast a recession in the next twelve months. You can see in Fig. 13.3 that the index of leading indicators does behave very differently in the shaded regions than in the rest of the periods. Although the index is generally growing, it is declining sharply in the years before recessions. A decline in the index has to be a pretty good predictor of an oncoming recession.

Be sure you understand why the recessions and the first years of expansions are omitted. The problem is to forecast an oncoming recession *while we are well into an expansion*. To do that, we need to compare the data at the ends of the expansions with what comes immediately before. At that time, the previous recession and recovery are ancient and irrelevant history. If we include those data, we will wreak havoc on the estimation. Although it is difficult to separate the ends of expansions from the recessions, because the index is declining in both, that is not our task. Though it is very easy to separate the ends of expansions, when the index is

---

[3] In an appendix to this chapter there is a description taken from the Conference Board Website of how these components are combined into a single index. That language is a bit mysterious, but think of it in the following way.

First note that many of these components tend to grow over time but others are percentages that do not grow. The two percentages are the diffusion index and the interest rate spread. Everything else has units that are not percentages, and many of those grow with the economy. Label the stable "percentage" components as Z and the other components X. Then let the logarithm of the index I be a function of components X and components Z per the following formula:

$$\log(I_t) = \sum_i s_i \log(X_{it}) + \sum_t s_j Z_{jt},$$

where s is the standardization factor which makes changes in $s_i \log(X_{it})$ and changes in $s_i Z_{jt}$ all have the same standard deviation (equal to one). This mysterious looking formula just implies that the percentage change in the index can be written as

$$\frac{I_t - I_{t-1}}{(I_t + I_{t-1})/2} = \sum_i s_i \frac{X_{it} - X_{i,t-1}}{(X_{it} + X_{i,t-1})/2} + \sum_t s_j(Z_{jt} - Z_{j,t-1})$$

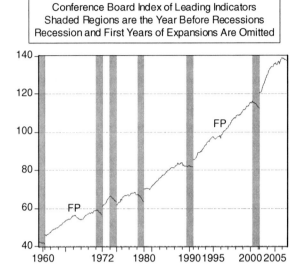

Fig. 13.3 Index of leading indicators with recessions and first year of expansion omitted, ends of expansions shaded

declining, from the first (recovery) phase of expansions, when the index is rebounding rapidly, that also is not our task. We need to exclude the recessions and the recoveries.

We can do with statistical analysis what you have just done with your eyes. The results are recorded in Table 13.2, which reports a "probit" model that predicts the ends of expansions on the basis of the logarithm of the index of leading indicators. Do not be frightened by the word "probit." Regular regression analysis uses dependent variables that are assumed to vary over unconfined ranges, while probit analysis uses a binary variable like ours that takes on two values: one in the year before recession and zero otherwise. The variables used to predict this binary variable are the index in the current month, and six, twelve, and

Table 13.2 Predicting a recession using the leading indicator index Dependent variable: REC_12MO_BEFORE Method: ML - Binary probit (quadratic hill climbing) Recessions and first years of expansions excluded 382 monthly observations

Variable	Coefficient	Std. error	z-statistic
C	0.2	1.5	0.1
Log(index)	−40.1	5.0	**−8.1**
Log(index(−6))	32.8	8.7	**3.8**
Log(index(−12))	0.2	9.9	0.0
Log(index(−18))	7.0	6.1	1.2
McFadden R-squared		0.34	

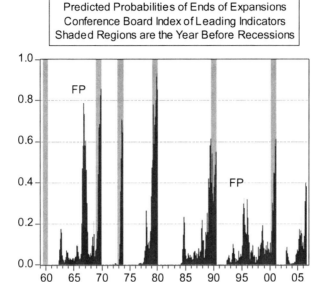

Fig. 13.4 Predicted probabilities of imminent recessions based on overall index

eighteen months previously. The "z-statistic" indicates the statistical significance of each variable and the ones in excess of two are in boldface. These are the coefficients judged by statisticians to be "statistically significant." The message from these boldface labels is to focus on the last six months. If the index is declining over the last six months, worry about a recession. Can you see that in Fig. 13.3?

This statistical analysis can be used to form the predicted probabilities of the ends of expansions illustrated in Fig. 13.4. These predictive probabilities have always elevated in excess of 50% in the years preceding recessions. There is one clear recession false alarm in 1967 and another mild false alarm in 1995.[4]

Here's a summary of the accuracy of this prediction of recessions:

	No recession	Recession occurred
Not predicted	0	0 false negatives
Predicted	2 false positives	5

Another summary is reported in Table 13.2: the McFadden R-squared. This measures the overall fit of the model. You only need to know that this is a number between zero and one; zero is bad, one is good.

---

[4] Figure 13.2 suggests that the index may have missed the 1960 recession but our model requires data 18 + 12 months before recession begins, which are not available.

Table 13.3 Predicting recession, one predictor at a time

14 Models for predicting recessions
Dependent variable: one in 12 months preceding recession, zero otherwise
Time period for which the leading Indicator is available: 1959 M01 to 2005 M03
Excludes recessions and the first year of expansions: 382 monthly observations

	Probit estimates z-statistic significant ones in bold				McFadden
	x	x(−6)	x(−12)	x(−18)	R-sq
1 Spread	**−5.8**	**−2.8**	0.9	−1.6	0.59
2 log(index)	**−8.1**	**3.8**	0.0	1.2	0.34
3 log(claims)	**5.8**	−1.9	**−2.3**	**−2.1**	0.26
4 log(permits)	**−4.4**	1.4	0.0	**3.9**	0.22
5 Confidence	**−6.3**	1.6	1.3	1.6	0.18
6 U	**4.2**	**−2.9**	−0.8	0.1	0.16
7 Crude	**3.3**	−0.4	0.6	**−4.2**	0.13
8 Hours	**−5.4**	1.3	1.1	1.0	0.11
9 log(M2)	**−4.0**	**2.8**	−1.6	1.7	0.08
10 log(Ordrs_cap)	0.1	**2.0**	1.4	**−3.4**	0.07
11 PMI	**−2.8**	**2.2**	0.7	1.9	0.06
12 log(Ordrs_cons)	**−4.3**	**2.3**	0.9	−0.2	0.06
13 Deliveries	1.8	1.6	0.0	0.6	0.06
14 log(S_and_P)	**−3.9**	**3.3**	−0.4	−0.3	0.05

Table 13.3 reports the same analysis for the index overall, the ten components separately, the unemployment rate, the real price of crude oil, and the Purchasing Managers Index, which is said to be Chairman Greenspan's favorite. That includes just about everything you read about in the newspapers, about which the talking heads opine wisely. These 14 models are ordered by the McFadden R-sq, with the best predictor of recessions on top. It is the interest rate spread that does the best, considerably better than the overall index, which comes in second place. Next in accuracy of prediction are claims for unemployment insurance and building permits. Surprisingly enough, consumer confidence is number 5, though well behind the winner in terms of that McFadden R-sq.

The predicted probabilities of recessions from the best model on the basis of the interest rate spread are illustrated in Fig. 13.5. Compare this with the same result using the overall index, Fig. 13.4. The probabilities based on the interest spread are closer to 1.0 in the (shaded) years preceding recessions, and the probabilities are closer to 0.0 otherwise, which is what we want, of course – a model that perfectly discriminates the ends of expansions from the rest.

But the spread is not perfect. The interest rate spread has the 1967 false alarm, has a very mild alarm in 1995, and has a new false alarm in 1998, in the midst of the Long Term Capital crisis and the Russian default. That is one of those rare cases in which the 10-year rate led the way, leading to an inverted yield curve, and the Federal Funds rate followed along behind with some rate cuts to get that curve normal again.

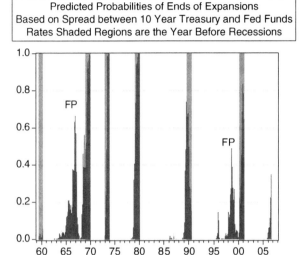

Fig. 13.5 Predictive probabilities of imminent recessions based on interest rate spread

13.4 Combining the Components into an Overall Index

We ought to be able to do better by combining the components into one overall index. The Conference Board combined them, but was not able to produce an index that gives a better recession prediction than the interest rate spread. That's terribly disappointing. But we should be able to do better.

One thing we need to allow for is that some of the components help to predict recessions but others do not. The ones at the top of the list in Table 13.3 do the best individually, and we may want to concentrate on them. The Conference board ignores that possibility altogether, and instead "mushes" the components, combining them with the weights equal to the standardization factors reported in Table 13.1. This standardizes the components all to have the same variance (one). Those weights have very little to do with the accuracy with which the components can predict recessions, and we can easily improve on that approach.

But just grabbing the variables at the top of Table 13.3 is a bad idea too, since the two best individual predictors, the spread and initial unemployment claims, may contain essentially the same information. It might be better to combine the spread with something farther down the list, even the last one, the stock market performance.

Furthermore, the Conference Board "mushing" does not deal with the fact that the predictive time patterns in Table 13.3 are not the same for all the variables. What predicts an oncoming recession is

- An inverted yield curve in the *last 6 months*
- A *decline* in the Leading Indicators in the *last 6 months*
- A *rise* in unemployment claims over the *last year or year and a half*

- A *decline* in building permits over the *last year and a half*
- *Low current* consumer confidence
- A *rise* in the unemployment rate in the *last six months*
- A *rise* in real crude oil prices in the *last year and a half*
- *Low current* weekly hours in manufacturing
- *Falling* monetary aggregates over the *last six months*
- A *peak* in orders for capital goods *six months ago*
- A *fall* in the PMI in the *last six months*
- A *fall* in consumer goods orders in the *last six months*
- *Rapid* deliveries in the *last six months*
- A *fall* in the stock market in the *last six months*

We thus need a method that deals with the differences in timing and differences in accuracy of these 13 potential predictors of recession. One method of combination

Table 13.4 Four models that combine 13 possible indicators

Four models for predicting an oncoming recession
Dependent variable: REC_12MO_BEFORE
Method: ML – binary probit (quadratic hill climbing)
Recessions and first years of expansions excluded 382 monthly observations
Two lag structures, best two models from each
Number of models 3432

| | "Z-statistics" | | | |
	1	2	3	4
SPREAD	−4.2	−4.2	−5.0	−4.5
SPREAD(−6)	−4.5			−3.7
SPREAD(−12)	−1.5	−4.3	−4.7	0.6
SPREAD(−24)		0.3	3.5	
LOG_CRUDE	−1.9	3.3	2.8	−0.2
LOG_CRUDE(−6)	3.2			2.7
LOG_CRUDE(−12)	−3.8	−0.8	0.7	−3.4
LOG_CRUDE(−24)		−3.8	−4.1	
LOG_PERMITS	0.5		3.5	
LOG_PERMITS(−6)	2.5			
LOG_PERMITS(−12)	1.0		1.0	
LOG_PERMITS(−24)			−0.6	
CONFIDENCE		−1.4		
CONFIDENCE(−6)				
CONFIDENCE(−12)		−1.4		
CONFIDENCE(−24)		−3.1		
DELIVERIES				4.5
DELIVERIES(−6)				−2.0
DELIVERIES(−12)				−2.6
DELIVERIES(−24)				
McFadden R-squared	0.827	0.796	0.787	0.784

is just to dump all the variables into the equation and let the data speak. That cannot work here because there are not enough data for them to communicate coherently. We are going to have to help out if we are going to make any sense out of the mutterings from this weak data set. One way we can help out is to restrict our model to include only three of the predictors at a time. It seems likely that three should suffice to capture most of the information. But which three? That's easy. Let's try them all, and see if some clear champion combinations arise.

The number of three-variable models that can be formed from 13 variables is $13 \times 12 \times 11 = 1,716$. As it turns out, if we use the same lag structure as in Table 13.4 with four lagged values for each indicator [x, $x(-6)$, $x(-12)$, and $x(-18)$] the computer hangs up and says: not so many variables please. For that reason, I have tried two different lag structures, a one year structure with x, $x(-6)$, and $x(-12)$ and a two year lag structure x, $x(-12)$, and $x(-24)$.

The best and second best models for each lag structure are reported in Table 13.4. These are sorted by the McFadden R-sq, with the best models on the left. All four of these models include the interest rate spread and the real price of crude oil, which are number 1 and number 7 in the horse race reported in Table 13.2. (If you want to form the best team, do not just choose the two best individual athletes.) The very best model uses the one-year lag structure and includes as third variable the level of permits. The third variable for the second best model is, of all things, the consumer confidence index! Permits show up again in the third model with the one-year lag, but it is the deliveries index that is picked for the fourth best team. That deliveries index was next to last in the head-to-head competition.

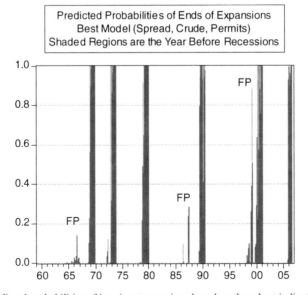

Fig. 13.6 Predicted probabilities of imminent recessions based on three best indicators

Figure 13.6 illustrates the predicted probabilities of recessions coming from the best model reported in Table 13.4. Compare this figure with the predicted probabilities based on the interest rate spread alone, Fig. 13.5, and on the Conference Board combination, Fig. 13.4, to see how much better this model is doing than either of them. Here it is hard to see the shaded years-before-recession because the probabilities jump up virtually to one. Otherwise the probabilities are mostly close to zero. Here we see a mild false alarm in 1965 and in 1987, and a short-lived major alarm in 1998.

Notice, especially that in 2006, a loud alarm has been sounded, making a recession in 2007 a virtual certainty.

I don't think so, but that is what these data suggest.

Appendix: Description of Leading Indicators

Source: http://www.conference-board.org/economics/bci/component.cfm
Leading Index Components

BCI-01 Average Weekly Hours, Manufacturing

The average hours worked per week by production workers in manufacturing industries tend to lead the business cycle because employers usually adjust work hours before increasing or decreasing their workforce.

BCI-05 Average Weekly Initial Claims for Unemployment Insurance

The number of new claims filed for unemployment insurance are typically more sensitive than either total employment or unemployment to overall business conditions, and this series tends to lead the business cycle. It is inverted when included in the leading index; the signs of the month-to-month changes are reversed, because initial claims increase when employment conditions worsen (i.e., layoffs rise and new hirings fall).

BCI-08 Manufacturers' New Orders, Consumer Goods, and Materials (in 1996 $)

These goods are primarily used by consumers. The inflation-adjusted value of new orders leads actual production because new orders directly affect the level of both unfilled orders and inventories that firms monitor when making production decisions. The Conference Board deflates the current dollar orders data using price indexes constructed from various sources at the industry level and a chain-weighted aggregate price index formula.

BCI-32 Vendor Performance and Slower Deliveries
Diffusion Index

This index measures the relative speed at which industrial companies receive deliveries from their suppliers. Slowdowns in deliveries increase this series and are most-often associated with increases in demand for manufacturing supplies (as opposed to a negative shock to supplies) and, therefore, tend to lead the business cycle. Vendor performance is based on a monthly survey conducted by the National Association of Purchasing Management (NAPM) that asks purchasing managers whether their suppliers' deliveries have been faster, slower, or the same as the previous month. The slower-deliveries diffusion index counts the proportion of respondents reporting slower deliveries, plus one-half of the proportion reporting no change in delivery speed.

BCI-27 Manufacturers' New Orders and Nondefense Capital Goods (in 1996 $)

New orders received by manufacturers in nondefense capital goods industries (in inflation-adjusted dollars) are the producers' counterpart to BCI-08.

BCI-29 Building Permits and New Private Housing Units

The number of residential building permits issued is an indicator of construction activity, which typically leads most other types of economic production.

BCI-19 Stock Prices and 500 Common Stocks

The Standard & Poor's 500 stock index reflects the price movements of a broad selection of common stocks traded on the New York Stock Exchange. Increases (decreases) of the stock index can reflect both the general sentiments of investors and the movements of interest rates, which is usually another good indicator for future economic activity.

BCI-106 Money Supply (in 1996 $)

In inflation-adjusted dollars, this is the M2 version of the money supply. When the money supply does not keep pace with inflation, bank lending may fall in real terms, making it more difficult for the economy to expand. M2 includes currency, demand deposits, other checkable deposits, travelers checks, savings deposits, small denomination time deposits, and balances in money market mutual funds. The inflation adjustment is based on the implicit deflator for personal consumption expenditures.

BCI-129 Interest Rate Spread and 10-Year Treasury
Bonds Less Federal Funds

The spread or difference between long and short rates is often called the yield curve. This series is constructed using the 10-year Treasury bond rate and the federal funds rate, an overnight interbank borrowing rate. It is felt to be an indicator of the stance of monetary policy and general financial conditions because it rises (falls) when short rates are relatively low (high). When it becomes negative (i.e., short rates are higher than long rates and the yield curve inverts) its record as an indicator of recessions is particularly strong.

BCI-83 Index of Consumer Expectations

This index reflects changes in consumer attitudes concerning future economic conditions and, therefore, is the only indicator in the leading index that is completely expectations-based. Data are collected in a monthly survey conducted by the University of Michigan's Survey Research Center. Responses to the questions concerning various economic conditions are classified as positive, negative, or unchanged. The expectations series is derived from the responses to three questions relating to: (1) economic prospects for the respondent's family over the next 12 months; (2) the economic prospects for the Nation over the next 12 months; and (3) the economic prospects for the Nation over the next five years.

Part III D
Recession Causes

Chapter 14
The Art of Drawing Causal Inferences from Nonexperimental Data

Our next item of business is to try to figure out what *causes* recessions.

In chap. 12, we discovered that housing often declined before the recessions officially began. In chap. 13, we learned that an "inverted" yield curve and a drop in weekly hours in manufacturing often preceded recessions. Before discussing those important findings we issued the warning not to jump to causal interpretations merely from those temporal orderings. Movements in these early warning signs can *predict* the recessions, but that is not the same as saying they "cause" the recessions. We know that weather forecasts do not cause the weather, even though the forecasts regularly precede the weather. Nor does the flowering of plants cause Summer to arrive, even though Summer has always been preceded by a period of exceptional plant flowering that poets call the "Spring."

14.1 Post Hoc Ergo Propter Hoc

The Greek word "empiric" refers to ancient physicians who based their medical advice on experience, not theory. Medieval empirics came to the conclusion that blood-letting caused improvements in health because the health of the patients often improved after the blood was let. But we know now that temporal orderings do not imply causation, even though we give Nobel prizes to folks who use temporal orderings to infer causation.[1] Just to make sure, we call it a fallacy and express it in Latin: *Post Hoc Ergo Propter Hoc:* After that, because of that.

For scientifically valid causal inferences, we need an experiment; we need a control group and a treated group. Then the difference between the outcome for the treated group and the outcome for the control group is a measure of the effect of the treatment.

In the area of macroeconomics, experiments are hard to come by. What we have are only temporal orderings: first this and then that.

---

[1] Granger, C. W.J. (1969), "Investigating causal relationships by econometric models and cross-spectral methods," *Econometrica* 37: 424–438.

With only temporal orderings and no experimental evidence, we do what humans do: we rely on stories. To each temporal ordering, we attach a predictive narrative or a causal narrative or both. We draw firm causal conclusions from the temporal orderings when the causal narrative is compelling and when there is no equally compelling predictive narrative. This is literature and wisdom, not science.

Take interest rates, for example. A pretty good predictive story is that the arrival of the storm we call recessions is met by a reduction of interest rates. When the storm inevitably dissipates, we cannot conclude that the interest rates caused the recovery merely because of the causal ordering: first the lowering of interest rates and then the recovery. We sometimes suggest that the umbrellas we carry stop the storms too, but I think we are only joking, aren't we?

We economists have a deep dislike for predictive narratives. Predictive stories eat away at the very foundation of our craft. Economics, unlike the other social sciences, is a self-consciously interventionist discipline. Although the other social sciences are content to describe, we the high priests prescribe. We offer our advice to businesses on how to set prices and to governments on how to choose tax rates and interest rates. For the design of these interventions, we must have firmly held causal beliefs. We cannot abide the ambiguity and uncertainty that predictive narratives engender. Thus, so as not to confuse the initiates, our economics textbooks never mention the predictive story that reductions in interest rates are like weather forecasts, predicting but not causing the recoveries from recessions, but instead we indoctrinate our students with the causal narrative of the IS-LM model. (If the symbols IS-LM are completely meaningless to you, don't worry. That's only a reference to an economic model in which cuts in interest rates can "stimulate" the economy and increase GDP.) For some, the force of the causal story of the IS-LM model has been offset completely by the power of the predictive narrative of the Lucas Critique, which is the Economics equivalent of Nietzsche's "God is Dead".[2]

Lucas argues that since we are all guessing the next interest rate move of the Fed, the predictable part of the movement in interest rates must be already accounted for and cannot have real effects. For most empirical economists, the knowledge assumptions of the Lucas Critique make that story more than a little far-fetched and we file it in the gruesome fairy-tale section of our personal hard drives. Probably because beliefs follow needs, IS-LM causal thinking is very much alive, and practiced by fiscal and monetary authorities around the globe.

Best to remember: When we study nonexperimental data, correlation is in the data while causation is in the mind or heart of the observer. That's where considered judgments and wishful thinking originate.

So there you have it: Its faith-based decision making, which is very much influenced by the rhetorical skills of the advocates. I would be conveying accurately the scientific validity of the causal opinions expressed here if, in the printed version, about 50% of the pixels were removed so you could hardly read what I write,

---

[2] Lucas, Robert (1976). Econometric Policy Evaluation: A Critique. *Carnegie-Rochester Conference Series on Public Policy* 1: 19–46.

and, in the spoken version, if I slurred my speech to the point that you could hardly understand the words I speak.

DISCLAIMER: POST HOC ERGO PROPTER HOC

Please delete the previous paragraphs. Wipe from your personal hard drives any caveats about drawing firm causal conclusions from temporal orderings. It is what we are going to do. We are going to draw firm causal conclusions from temporal orderings, and offset the fundamental weakness of the conclusions with rhetorical flourishes.

14.2 Cause = Intervention

The stories that we tell to turn temporal orderings into causal conclusions are often very vague. An essential step toward a persuasive causal inference is to get clear that the word "cause" refers explicitly or implicitly to an *intervention, a hypothetical change, a but-for*. When we say that weather forecasts do not cause the weather, we may be imagining a bribe for a favorable forecast, and when we say that flowers do not cause the Summer, we may be imagining cutting off the tops of the flowers in the Spring. We have not done the test, but most of us firmly believe that the weather will not be much affected by a bribe and that Summer will still follow Spring even if the flowers are cut. We hold this opinion, even in the face of the very clear temporal ordering: first the forecast, then the weather; first the flowers then the Summer.

Do not get disheartened by the ambiguity. You make nonexperimental inferences all the time, with a pretty good success rate. And do not forget that we have already found what "in my mind" is a clear cause of recessions. Not the decline in spending on homes. No clear but-for intervention there. The cause we have uncovered is spending by the Department of Defense. That's a cause because we can imagine a reasonably clear but-for hypothetical regarding DOD spending: If DOD spending had not been cut dramatically in 1953, then . . . .

This but-for the defense cutback hypothetical seems clear enough, but it is not. There are many possibilities, each of which might have produced a different outcome. It is possible that the end of the War might have come earlier or later, in which case the recession might have come earlier or later. It is possible that US might never have entered the Korean War, and might never ramped up defense spending in 1951. Then the incipient recession in 1951 deterred by the Korean War armament might have come to fruition instead of the 1953 disarmament downturn. It is also possible to have had a more measured reduction in spending by the DOD after the war ended. That slower pace might have allowed the labor and capital released from defense work to be absorbed elsewhere and we might not have had the 1953 recession or any other recession soon thereafter. Although each of these scenarios is different, they all have one important feature in common: no 1953 recession. That's the sense in which we can feel pretty comfortable saying: the DOD caused the 1953 downturn.

To see why housing cannot be said to *cause* recessions, try to create a clear but-for hypothetical that refers to spending on housing. What exactly does it mean to hypothesize that spending on housing did not decline in 1981? There are literally billions of levers pulled by tens of millions of actual and potential buyers and builders that determine the amount of spending on homes. Do you have in mind the government controlling all those levers and deciding exactly how much each of us will spend on housing? Probably not. That's absurd. This is not the Soviet Union. That's the problem with counterfactuals that underlie many causal conclusions – they are either vague or absurd.[3] They start out being vague, and when we try to clarify them, they often become absurd. We can do better. We should refer to the causes only if there is a clear and plausible but-for intervention.

14.2.1 Our Hypothetical Interventions Are Very Few

For our purposes, the list of interventions is really very short. The Federal government might have chosen a different level of spending, or a different level of taxation. The Federal Reserve Board might have chosen different short-term interest rates. That's about it. For these, we will try to establish causality in two steps. First, we will look for temporal orderings – a policy change followed by a recession. Second, we will look for causal paths. That means housing especially. We will want to know how much influence these policy levers have on the housing cycle. If we can trace the policy choices through housing to the overall economy, then we will say that the policy caused the recession.

In addition to the fiscal and monetary policy, we will include on the list of causes of recessions crude oil prices. We will not include US exports because it is too hard to come up with a compelling intervention story.[4] A but-for hypothetical regarding crude oil is a stretch but still within reach. Swings in crude oil prices could be influenced by variable external tariffs – high tariffs when crude oil prices are low, and low tariffs when the prices are high. That's not too bad a but-for.

---

[3] See McCloskey, D, "Counterfactuals" *The New Palgrave Dictionary of Economics*, Vol. 1, 1987, pp 701–703.

[4] If a falling value of the dollar can help increase US exports, then but for properly refers to US monetary and fiscal policies that affect the value of the dollar. Then exports are not a cause; they are only a link in the causal chain. But maybe it's the fiscal and monetary policies elsewhere that we have in mind when we say exports cause US growth. This does not work too well either. Some components of the variability of exports might be linked to these foreign policies but not all of them. For example, some US exports are destined indirectly for the US marketplace and are shipped abroad only for some processing. These exports are a symptom of strong US demand, and have little to do with the fiscal and monetary policies elsewhere. You can begin to sense the complexities. Drawing causal conclusions about exports is possible, but beyond the scope of this enterprise.

14.3 There Are Many Roadblocks in the Way of Causal Inferences

The unfortunate reality is this: Finding the causes of recessions is a task that cannot be accomplished with a high degree of confidence. After all, we only have ten recessions to look at. The causality might be the same for all, or each could have its own characteristics. For each of these ten nonexperiments, there are hundreds, possibly thousands of variables that might be examined.

Its not just the lack of data that causes problems. There are a host of difficulties.

A search for causes of recessions among the policy levers needs to include errors of omission as well as errors of commission. The doctor who refused to give you a flu shot can be said to have caused your illness – but-for your doctor's error you never would have been ill. And when our leaders hold steady the fiscal and monetary levers when some change would have been helpful, they can be said to have caused the recessions from their inattentiveness.

A search for causes of recessions needs to look well before the year immediately preceding the recession. The right time to cool the housing passions is when the suitors are arduous but not frenzied. The right time to rekindle the housing desires is when the eyes start to wander, not when the suitors have completely lost interest. When our leaders in Washington wait until the highest housing peaks and the deepest housing valleys to try to influence the passion cycle, they have caused the cycle by their lack of foresight and attentiveness.

A search for causes of recessions also needs to deal with the indirect and possibly unintended consequences of policy changes. Think about a tax cut that "gives the people back their hard-earned money." According to Keynesian thinking, a tax cut provides a "fiscal stimulus," which gets consumers to spend more and thus generates more economic growth. But if the people thought it through, they would recognize that there cannot be a tax cut without a spending cut. There can only be a tax postponement. Sooner or later current government spending is going to have to be paid for. If the people thought it through carefully, they would take the entire tax cut and put it in the bank, saved for the day when the taxes will have to be raised to pay down the debt and the interest charges too. If the people put all the money in the bank, the tax cut has no effect. That is called Ricardian Equivalence.[5]

More generally, when we claim to have found a cause of recessions we need to be very clear what is held constant when our favorite policy lever is pulled. For example, if we are planning a tax cut, for any level of GDP, it is logically impossible to hold fixed both the government spending and the government deficit. If we claim that a tax cut stimulates the economy, we need to make clear whether that tax cut comes with a reduction in spending over time or a change in the deficit. Although not stated explicitly, it is pretty clear what tax-cutters have in mind: more debt now and lower spending later. Deciding what to hold constant when we design monetary policies is more difficult. Our monetary authorities have control over short-term

---

[5] Robert J. Barro (1974) "Are Government Bonds Net Wealth?" Journal of Political Economy 82: 1095–1117.

interest rates, but what about the long-term rates? When we try to trace the effect of some hypothetical change in short-term rates, should we hold the long-term rates constant? Empirically, we have discovered that long-term rates have often moved with the short-term rates, but sometimes have gone the opposite way. So what long-term rates should be assumed when we plan the next change in short term rates? And what about inflation and inflation expectations? What should be held constant and what should be allowed to respond when we imagine changes in the historical values of the short-term interest rates or other policy instruments?

That is not the end of the difficulties. The biggest problem may be what is known as the Lucas Critique, which allows the economy to change as the policy rule changes, an unfortunate possibility that makes it extremely difficult to explore historical data to discover the impact of policy.[6] For this bit of wisdom, Robert Lucas was awarded the Nobel Prize in Economics.[7] The story is pretty straightforward. If it were a durable mechanical system we were dealing with, the response to pulling a lever would change slowly over time as the mechanism slowly wears. In that case, the historical correlations between policies and consequences can be used to plot future policies. But for the organic human system we call the economy, any attempt to control it immediately changes the way it behaves. That makes causal inferences very difficult, since looking backward at what policies seemed to have worked provides no assurance that those same policies will work in the future. If you are a parent you know all about this. The point of a parent's discipline is partly to have an immediate effect on unwanted behavior but more importantly to plant firmly in the child's mind the awesome consequences of actions the parent wishes to deter. Once the rules are understood, child and parent live happily ever after; child never misbehaving and parent never needing to mete out discipline. But if you are a child, you know all about the Lucas critique too. The point of a child's misbehavior is partly to enjoy the moment, but more importantly to put firmly in the parents' minds the awful consequences of the parents' unwanted discipline. Once the parents understand the consequences of their attempts to control the child, the parents will back off, and everyone will be happier.

This complex game between a parent and a child makes it very difficult for the parent to figure out what works and what does not. Worse still, for the parent, the child is constantly changing, from infant to terrible two to youngster to teenager. If you had to rely on only your own experience, the situation would be pretty hopeless, but fortunately millions of parents over many centuries have been accumulating evidence that is collected in numerous (but ever-changing) how-to books for parents in distress.

For us, trying to figure out what causes US recessions, we have only one child to observe, and only ten episodes of bad behavior, several of which occurred in infancy in the 1950s and in the terrible two's in the 1980s. What should we be doing now that we are dealing with a young adult?

---

[6] Lucas, Robert E., Jr., (1976), "Econometric policy evaluation: a critique," Carnegie-Rochester Conference Series on Public Policy, 7–33.

[7] Actually: The Sveriges Riksbank Prize in Economic Sciences in Memory of Alfred Nobel.

14.3.1 We Can Pretend to Draw Causal Inferences, Even If We Cannot Do It

Offsetting these words of caution is our desperate need to think that our leaders are in control of this complex and ambiguous setting. When the crops fail, we are happy to swear allegiance to the great Priest Greenspan, and to sacrifice a virgin or two, if required. When the crops are abundant, we are equally happy to bring gifts of gratitude to the Board of Governors, which houses the Pope and the Cardinals of the Fed.

It is easy to see why we might make the wrong conclusion about Mr. Greenspan's powers. A boat that randomly drifts back and forth across a predetermined path might have a captain who pulled the helm left when the boat drifts right. Since the boat corrects itself following that action, the captain and the passengers would naturally both come to the conclusion that the captain was in control. This is made all the easier, if the captain has Greenspan's remarkable gifts of verbal ambiguity and theatrical flair. After a year in office, Mr. Bernanke seems like a different kind of performer.

Thus since the Fed has lowered interest rates early in a recession, we all conclude that the Fed caused, or at least, contributed to the recovery. But we do not know what kind of recovery there might have been if the Fed had behaved differently. When the Fed raised interest rates and a recession soon follows, we are compelled to the same conclusion: it was the Fed that caused that recession. But we do not know what would have happened if the Fed had not raised the rates.

Like the primitive beings that we all remain, we find it much more comfortable to pin the recession on the Fed, or on Arab oil producers or terrorists, than to admit that as far as treating and preventing recessions are concerned, we are still at the leeches and bloodletting phase.[8]

Pigeons and humans are not that much different. Here is what I wrote in my 1978 book, *Specification Searches,* page 319:

> "I describe (with some literary license) Skinner's[9] (1948) experiment of randomly induced behavior. Hungry birds fed at random intervals are observed to adopt the peculiar behavior of odd head movements, hopping from side to side, and the like. The apparent explanation is that on receipt of the seed, the bird hypothesizes that the seed is a reward for the most recently antecedent trick. If the bird happened to have twitched his head just before the seed arrived, the bird naturally tries twitching his head again. The increased frequency of head twitching makes more likely the event that a twitch will precede a seed, and eventually the bird is twitching frequently with seeds always following twitching. The belief in this relationship is so strong that even after the seed stops arriving altogether, the bird may twitch as many as 10,000 times."

What are we going to do about all of these complexities? Humility is the answer; Three-valued logic. Traditional logic is two-valued: yes or no; true or false.

---

[8] It took a lot more than 10 patients before the doctors came to realize that bloodletting wasn't working that well.

[9] Skinner, B.F. (1948), "Superstition and the pigeon," *Journal of Experimental Psychology,* 38: 168–172.

There is a third option: undecidable. When we try to draw causal inferences from nonexperimental data, we ought to admit that there are many questions in that third, undecidable category. I know you do not like it, but that is the way the real world is.

If you do not like that outcome, you can go for the Wizard of Oz approach, and listen in rapture to every utterance of High Priest Greenspan and his successors.

14.4 Use Biological, Not Mechanical Metaphors

The stories we tell are what turn temporal orderings into causal conclusions. Economists' stories about the economy are built on two different kinds of metaphors: biological and mechanical. It matters greatly which kind of metaphor we use because these metaphors have a subtle and substantial impact on the way we think. When you hear an unfamiliar metaphor, you would be wise to think carefully about the intellectual baggage that comes with it, before you adopt the metaphor as your own. When I say that the economy has a normal state with jobs for all who want them but occasionally suffers from a bout of illness we call recession, do not let me slip unnoticed into our conversation, a disease metaphor for a recession.

"Modern" macroeconomists prefer to pull their metaphors from physics and from engineering. Macroeconomists today routinely speak of the "laws of motion" of the economy. They look for "shocks" that are transmitted through the system according to complex dynamical equations.[10] This was not always the case. John Maynard Keynes gave his name to a sect of business cycle analysts to which even President Richard Nixon in 1969 declared his allegiance: "We are all Keynesians now." The narrow meaning of this quotation is that Nixon had come to believe that a recession is a disease that is treatable by wisely chosen government tax and spending policies. The more important broader meaning is that Nixon was rejecting the bedrock principle of the Republican Party that markets left alone function efficiently, and that governments should minimize their interventions. It is a slippery slope from Keynesian counter-cyclical policy to government supplied medical care and then to totalitarianism. You surprise me, President Nixon!

Lord Keynes was a logician and mathematician, and though he chose English not Mathematics as the language for *The General Theory*, his words suggested to some a set of equations.[11] John R. Hicks (a mathematics specialist at Oxford) and Paul Samuelson (B.A. in physics) translated Keynes explicitly into mathematics. Economics remained a fuzzy verbal discipline until it was mathematized with extraordinary success in the 1940s and 1950s under the leadership of Kenneth Arrow (B.S. and MA. in mathematics) and Paul Samuelson.

Parallel with the adoption of mathematics as the language of economics came an enormous increase in the 1950s and 1960s in the availability of economic data. Build it and they will come. These data supported a vast expansion of economic

---

[10] When I was Chairman of the Economics Department at UCLA, I would frequently get long and complicated letters from engineers who thought that they had uncovered the "laws of motion" of the economy.

[11] The General Theory of Employment, Interest, and Money, 1936.

data analysis and introduced into our vocabulary a new word – econometrics – referring to the measurement of economic "constants" just like physicists do when they estimate the rate of acceleration in a vacuum.

The theory of econometrics uses a mechanical/engineering metaphor not a biological metaphor. Econometrics is premised on the assumption that one can write down the "laws of motion" that describe the economy.[12] But the first analysts of these new data ignored the econometric theory and took an "epidemiological" approach – looking for patterns, and making up stories later. The greatest success of the time was probably the discovery of the Phillips Curve and the Natural Rate of Unemployment. Below is a scatter diagram illustrating the relationship between the rate of unemployment (percentage out of work) and the rate of inflation (rate of change of prices), quarterly from 1955 to 1970. In this scatter I have asked my computer to draw a curve that best summarizes these data. This curve begins at an inflation rate of about 4.5% per year and steadily declines to about 1.5% per year were it levels off. The unemployment rate at which this kink occurs is about 5.5%. **Eureka!** We have discovered the "Natural Rate of Unemployment." When the unemployment rate falls below 5% inflation rises. This deserves an impressive acronym. We can change the idea just a bit and call it the "Nonccelerating-Inflation-Rate of Unemployment," which is a mouthful, but which has the mellifluous acronym "NAIRU." Pronounce it NIGH-ROO and impress your friends.

The Phillips' curve is a pattern in search of a story. Exactly why the rate of unemployment would influence the inflation rate in this way (say NAIRU here) was and continues to be a matter of debate among economists. There is a pretty good story why high rates of unemployment might affect wage bargaining and therefore limit "cost-push" inflation, but the story of that kink in the curve is a real stretch. We need to understand what determines inflation, but right now I only want to alert you to the metaphors that drive the data analysis. On the one hand, we have mechanical/physical/experimental metaphors in which the theory straightjackets the data analysis, and the problem is only to estimate the unknown constants that determine the laws of motion of the system. On the other hand, we have biological/medical/nonexperimental metaphors, which allow a much looser connection between the framework and the data analysis. Data analysis driven by medical metaphors is mostly looking for patterns. It is exploratory, not confirmatory.

Both approaches are right and both are wrong. A theory-driven confirmatory data analysis greatly narrows what one looks for in the data, and precludes any real discoveries. With this approach, you can program the data analysis in advance and get the results merely by pressing the go button on the computer keyboard. You can even wear a white smock and horn-rimmed glasses and look like a Scientist. That's a really cool outfit, but you are not going to learn very much about how an economy works unless you "explore" the data. Exploratory data analysis is a dirty blue-collar job. When, after days of wallowing, you pull from the muck a pattern that you think is a FINDING, how are you possibly going to convince me? I have seen way too many patterns masquerading as FINDINGS already. If you expect to

---

[12] The term "econometrics" as originally conceived by the Econometric Society covered both the mathematical modeling and the data analysis. The term has since evolved to refer only to the data analysis, taking the mathematical model as a literal and accurate description of the actual economy.

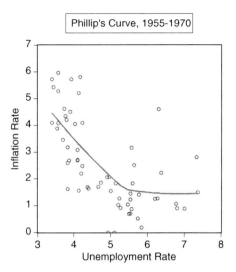

persuade me, you will need a good story, a compelling story. Looking for patterns without backing them up with compelling stories is a big mistake, since you will be sure to find patterns that are not really there.[13]

The Phillips' Curve is a good example of exploratory data analysis gone awry. The figure below displays the data since 1970. No NAIRU there that I can see!

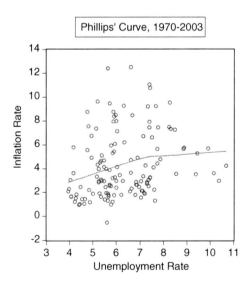

---

[13] Looking for patterns without stories has been called "data mining," which was a pejorative when I was writing my book, *Specification Searches*, in the 1970s, but which has been adopted as a favored activity by the Association of Computer Machinery. They call it KDD (Knowledge Discovery and Data Mining). Who's KiDDing whom?

With that digression over, it is time to turn to the choice: mechanical or biological metaphors. As for myself, I prefer not to talk about the "laws of motion" of my life, which is my way of saying that adopting a mechanical metaphor for making decisions that affect my life seems counterproductive. The same is true, I think, for the complex human system that is an economy. An economy is not a system of pulleys and motors. It is an organic, evolving, self-healing system. A recession is not the propagation over time of a "shock." A recession is disease. Our job is not to find the "shocks" and the propagating mechanism. Our job is to determine the symptoms and the causes:

- The defining symptoms which are always present (e.g. rising unemployment)
- The incidental symptoms which are often present (e.g. negative GDP growth)
- The causes (We will be looking for these.)

The reason why we pursue these three items is to plan actions that make recessions less extreme and less frequent. Thus the goals of the whole enterprise are two:

- Find a treatment (A massive injection of monetary and fiscal medicine?)
- Find a prevention (Regular but low doses of monetary and fiscal medicine?)

As we look at data displays that illuminate features of recessions, we will need to keep in mind these targets. Can we find in the macro economic data what are the symptoms, the causes, the treatments, and the preventions?

Chapter 15
In Search of Recession Causes

The message of the last chapter is that a persuasive causal inference from nonexperimental data requires the following:

(1) Statistically clear temporal orderings from historical data (first this, then that)
(2) An unambiguous but-for hypothetical (an intervention, a change of the past)
(3) A compelling story that turns observed correlations and temporal orderings into beliefs about what might have been

Let us see if we can find these three ingredients and cook up some conclusions about the causes of recessions. This is not going to be easy. We are entering a land ruled by Uncertainty and Ambiguity. If you expect to be comfortable here, you will need Faith.

For most economists, Faith comes from intense studying of the teachings of the Priests of the Orthodox Economics Church, which has large cathedrals in the two Cambridges and in Chicago, and smaller churches scattered all over the globe. While the Initiates study and pray, the Priests of the Economy meditate for countless hours in front of blackboards and personal computers in hopes of enlightenment regarding the Causal Structure of the Economy. When the visions arrive, the Priests are proud to pass the Wisdom on to the adoring Faithful.

I recommend a different approach – the path of Martin Luther – the priesthood of all believers. I think you are capable of reading and discussing the stories and the patterns, and then forming your own beliefs about the causal structure of the economy. I realize this will be really unsettling for some of you. I understand that you came to the university to study the Ancient Texts and to absorb the Received Wisdom. The last thing you expected to hear is that there is no Wisdom, with a capital W. You hate it when you hear that knowledge is your responsibility, not your Professors'. But I think your life will be much richer if you feel empowered to create knowledge on your own. For one thing, it will make you a much more interesting person to be around. It will also get you a better job. Electronic computers are very much better than you at absorbing the Received Wisdom and spouting it back at just the right time. But most of all, the Priests of the Orthodox Economics Church

E. E. Leamer, *Macroeconomic Patterns and Stories: A Guide for MBAs.*   231
© Springer-Verlag Berlin Heidelberg 2009

largely ignore the real world data and instead rely on deep meditation in pursuit of Wisdom. How silly is that?

But this is not going to be easy or comfortable. You cannot create wisdom by stumbling aimlessly around the data.

> "In human endeavor, chance favors the prepared mind."
> Louis Pasteur.
> "Genius is one percent inspiration and ninety-nine percent perspiration."
> Thomas A. Edison

To these pearls of wisdom, I would like to add my own advice. It is not just hard work. It is dogged determination in the face of countless setbacks.

> "Success is ninety-nine percent disappointment and one percent triumph."
> Edward Leamer

15.1 What Are We Looking for?

As we try to figure out what causes recessions, we need to keep in mind that spending is the fuel that keeps the engine of the economy going. Deprived of that fuel, the engine will grind to a halt. Let us look for rapid and substantial reductions in spending by some part of the economy, and let us try to guess what might have been done differently that would have prevented that spending reduction.

Keep in mind that it is not your spending alone that matters. You are important, but not that important. What is needed is belt-tightening by tens of thousands of spenders all at the same time, adding up to more than $100 billion reduction in single year. For that to happen, there has to be some coordinating force that gets large numbers of spenders to do a coordinated belt-tightening. One spender is big enough to matter all by himself: Uncle Sam.

Also, in searching for the causes of recessions, it may be helpful to recall the cycle stories discussed in Chap. 11:

- The Supply Chain Bull Whip
- A Mad Dash to Exploit New Ideas/Network Externalities
- Ponzi Schemes and Asset Bubbles/The Madness of Crowds
- Overindulgent First-Time Parents

According to the story of the Supply Chain Bull Whip, the building of long-lived assets like office buildings, homes, and aircraft is inevitably a boom and bust kind of business – lively when offices, homes, and aircraft are full but quiescent, when vacancies are plentiful. These assets can tip from full to vacancies when that latest office building is completed, or that latest tract of homes. That is when building plummets.

Nice try, but not a very good story. Offices and homes are being completed at entirely different rates on different blocks of different cities of different states. It seems more than a little unlikely that all these locales would experience overbuilding at just the same point of time. For the supply chain story to work, we need a coordinating mechanism. What might that be? Maybe interest rates. When the price of durability is low, the economy will want to build up the stock of durables including homes and offices, and increase the capacity of supply chains that provide those products. If interest rates jump up in an unexpected way, the desired stock of durables falls, and all of a sudden we can find ourselves in an overbuilt situation in homes, autos, and offices.

For the Supply Chain Bull Whip, we might say that lack of information is the cause of the cycle: if the builders and investors could see the future more accurately, overbuilding would be less pronounced. But to say that lack of information is the cause of the cycle, we would need to imagine an intervention that would alleviate the information problem. Perfect foresight is one assumption, but it's a silly hypothetical, as it is impossible. Maybe we need an investor's certification test that includes some forecasting questions, or, best of all, a required subscription to the UCLA Anderson Forecast. That seems pretty silly too, but not so silly compared with ideas being floated in 2007 to prevent another subprime mortgage meltdown. One commenter on Bloomberg news said, "we need to add 10 points to the IQ scores of all Americans." (Leamer the wise guy, at it again!)

There is one intervention that is more within the realm of reason – we could have had different interest rates chosen by the Federal Reserve. If Fed, *paternalistically*, came to the conclusion that overbuilding was starting to be a problem, they could pull in the reins a bit with higher interest rates. The cause of the Supply Chain Bull Whip would then be an error of omission – not raising rates when things were getting out of control. But do you really want the Fed to behave this way? What do they know? Who's your Daddy?

The Fed can commit errors of commission as well as errors of omission. If overbuilding is a result of a Fed Funds rate held too low for too long, which is brought to a screeching halt with an increase in rates, that is an error of commission, two in fact. (Rates held too low for too long, and then raised too rapidly.)

A Mad Dash to Exploit New Ideas has a similar diagnosis – not enough information. A Mad Dash occurs when gold is discovered on an offshore island, which stimulates the rapid building of bridges to allow some miners to get to the island before others. There is plenty of work when the bridges are being built but not much to do when the bridges are completed and when the gold is depleted. That is when the recession begins. What is the cure for this? Higher interest rates and higher tax rates would slow down the race for that gold. More than in the case of the supply chain bullwhip, our monetary and fiscal officials have no special knowledge of how much gold is out there and how many bridges to that gold we need. I am thinking of the Internet Rush. Remember that Mr. Greenspan was a latecomer to the Internet Party and made his famous "irrational exuberance" remark in 1996. Left to follow his own instincts, he might have tried to prevent the Internet Bubble with aggressive increases in interest rates in 1996, which might have slowed the adoption of the Internet and all the benefits that it has bestowed.

A Ponzi scheme is another informational problem. When we play musical chairs, we all expect to find a chair when the music stops, but everyone knows someone will not find a chair. The expectations do not add up. Likewise, when we buy an asset at an inflated price, each of us are expecting to find someone else to pay even more, though we know someone will be left holding the bag when the music stops. To prevent this from happening, we need to rely on Daddy to increase the admission price to the game of musical chairs by raising interest rates at just the right time.

Compared with a Mad Dash to Exploit New Ideas, the excesses of a Ponzi scheme are easy to spot. When, from 2002 to 2006, we marked up the value of US residential land from $4 trillion to $8 trillion that is not a dash to exploit new ideas. Walk around your property and see if you can figure out why it is "worth" more than twice the value of a few years earlier. Does it have a better view? Is it closer to good schools? No, not really. That residential land is providing the same service flow that it did years ago and will do years from now. Why the big increase in the accounting value when the real value is completely unchanged? The change in the accounting value of the land came mostly from easier and cheaper mortgages and from an out-of-control Ponzi scheme.[1]

Real rates of interest are lower in 2007 than in 1999, and innovations in finance have increased access to mortgage loans, both of which support higher valuations. Many economists have such a high level of faith in the collective rationality of the market that they thought these financial innovations completely justified the run-up in prices. The capacity for rationalization is unlimited, as is the clarity of hindsight. For the few, with their foresight[2], and for the many, with their hindsight, it was/is clear that we were in the midst of a massive Ponzi scheme to which Daddy contributed with a very low Fed Funds rates for a very long time.

Not surprisingly, Daddy does not want the parenting job, neither the responsibility, the credit, nor the blame:

Governor Ben S. Bernanke
New York Chapter of the National Association for Business Economics
October 15, 2002

"I think for the Fed to be an "arbiter of security speculation or values" is neither desirable nor feasible"

Governor Frederic S. Mishkin
Forecaster's Club of New York
January 17, 2007

A special role for asset prices in the conduct of monetary policy requires three key assumptions. First, one must assume that a central bank can identify a bubble in progress. I find this assumption highly dubious because it is hard to believe that the central bank has such an informational advantage over private markets.

---

[1] Other possibilities are increased demand by foreigners or a wave of new family formation, neither of which has changed enough to account for the doubling of prices or even to contribute significantly the price increase.

[2] Don't necessarily include Greenspan's "irrational exuberance" remark in 1996 as an example of accurate foresight, since his concern was raised too early and was withdrawn soon thereafter as Greenspan himself succumbed to the allure of New Economy irrationality. Likewise, Robert Shiller in various reincarnations of his *Irrational Exuberance (Princeton University Press)* issued the alarms too early and too loud. Had one followed his advice,

A second assumption needed to justify a special role for asset prices is that monetary policy cannot appropriately deal with the consequences of a burst bubble, and so preemptive actions against a bubble are needed.... Yet there are several reasons to believe that this concern about burst bubbles may be overstated. To begin with, the bursting of asset price bubbles often does not lead to financial instability.... *There are even stronger reasons to believe that a bursting of a bubble in house prices is unlikely to produce financial instability.*

A third assumption needed to justify a special focus on asset prices in the conduct of monetary policy is that, a central bank actually knows the appropriate monetary policy to deflate a bubble. The effect of interest rates on asset price bubbles is highly uncertain.

(*my italics, an award for the worst forecast of 2007.*)

Though Daddy does not want the job, I am going to give it to him, and look for causes of the recessions in Fed interest rate errors of omission and errors of commission. Why on earth did they hold interest rates so low for so long in 2003/2004? What might have happened had they made different choices??

15.2 Fiscal Policy Seems to Both Cause and Prevent Recessions

Let's start with the easiest cases – taxes and spending by the Federal Government.

The big swings in Federal spending since 1940 have been for defense. Rapid rearmaments when the Korean and Vietnam Wars commenced seemed to have saved us from two incipient recessions and rapid disarmaments after the Korean War and the Vietnam War are implicated in two recessions.

The data also include three big cuts in Federal tax rates: The Kennedy Tax Cut, the Reagan Tax Cut, and the Bush Tax Cut. The Kennedy Tax Cut came early in the Kennedy expansion when growth was weakening and that tax reduction might have helped to keep the economy growing. The Reagan Tax Cut and the Bush Tax Cut came during recoveries from recessions, and the subsequent growth may have been only normal during recoveries.

15.2.1 The Department of Defense Is Implicated in the 1953 and 1969 Downturns

We have already unearthed the apparent cause of the 1953 recession, and we should see if the DOD played some important role in any of the other downturns. Let us be sure to look for "false positives" – periods in which sharp reductions in defense spending did not come with an official recession. If sharp reductions in defense spending sometimes cause recessions and sometimes do not, we will need to know why.

Defense spending as a share of GDP is illustrated in Fig. 15.1 – 14% at the height of the Korean War, and down to only a little more than 4% today, though on the rise

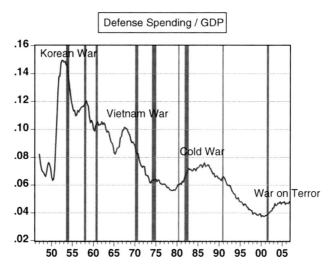

Fig. 15.1 Defense spending share of GDP

again as a consequence of the war on terror. Layered onto that general downward trend have been some pretty big ups and downs.

A better sense of the importance of the DOD for GDP growth is offered by Fig. 15.2, which displays the cumulative contribution of defense spending to GDP. When this cumulative is growing, defense spending is contributing to growth. When

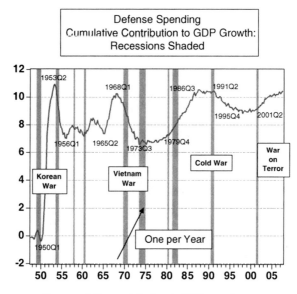

Fig. 15.2 Defense spending cumulative contribution to GDP growth

the cumulative is falling, defense spending is subtracting from growth. Remember that GDP grows at about 3% per year, so a cumulative contribution that is rising at the rate of 1% per year is accounting for about 1/3rd of normal growth. An arrow in this figure indicates this rate of ascent.

The total defense cumulative from 1947 to 2004 was only 10% points, or roughly 0.18 per year, pretty small compared with the normal GDP growth of 3.0% per year. Actually, since the end of the Korean War, defense spending has not contributed at all to total GDP growth. There were periods of disarmament in which declines in spending subtracted from GDP growth, and these were more-or-less perfectly offset by periods of rearmament in which defense spending contributed to growth.

In both of these charts, you can see the enormous run-up in defense spending during the Korean War and the dramatic turnaround starting the third quarter of 1953, exactly the first quarter of the official recession. In that case, disarmament was coincident with the downturn. Blame that 1953 recession on the DOD.

The timing of the Vietnam disarmament was different. The Vietnam disarmament started in 1968 Q2, a couple of years before the 1970 recession. The Vietnam disarmament was comparable in magnitude to the Korean disarmament but stretched over a longer time period – 22 quarters instead of 11. That's probably why the Kennedy/Johnson expansion lasted another two years after the disarmament began. Slow is good, fast is bad. But the declining DOD spending in the midst of that 1970 recession could not have been helpful and that raises the possibility that had the pace of disarmament been slower in 1970, that mild recession might have been even milder.

The Cold War disarmament had yet another timing – not before, not during, but after the 1990 recession. We need to look to other sources for an explanation of that downturn. However, Southern California and some other parts of the country experienced a very prolonged recession lasting into the mid 1990s because of the disappearance of many high-paying defense jobs. From the perspective of Los Angeles, the Cold War disarmament in the 1990s definitely was a drag on growth. This brings up an important point that will not distract us here: The US data are the sum of data from many different regions with different economic cycles: The Farm Belt, the Rust Belt, the Sun Belt, and the Borscht Belt, to name a few belts. If we had the interest and energy, we would be looking carefully at each of these regions.

Pictures, stories, and numbers; What we have seen in Fig. 15.2 and discussed above is summarized numerically in Table 15.1, which reports the effects of DOD spending on GDP growth. The item of importance is in bold: the rate per year. A large change spread over a very large number of quarters is a small rate per year and is not going to matter much, like slowly moving over a lane when your car going 50 miles an hour. But an abrupt turn to the left is going to roll the car and tip the economy into a recession.

The Korean War armament began in 1950 Q2 and peaked in 1953 Q2, contributing in that period a total of 11.30 to GDP growth. That occurred in 13 quarters, thus the very large number of 3.48 per year. Remember that normal GDP growth is only in the 3–3.5% per year range, so when you get 3.48 from defense alone, you can be sure that economic growth will be robust.

Table 15.1 Wartime contribution of defense spending to US GDP

Effect of department of defense spending on US GDP growth				
	Korea	Vietnam	Cold War	War on Terror
Armament				
Trough quarter	1950 Q1	1965 Q2	1979 Q4	2001 Q3
Peak quarter	1953 Q2	1968 Q1	1986 Q3	2007 Q3
Amount	11.30	2.89	3.23	1.30
Quarters	13	11	27	24
Rate per Year	**3.48**	**1.05**	**0.48**	**0.22**
Disarmament				
Peak quarter	1953 Q2	1968 Q1	1991 Q2	
Trough quarter	1956 Q1	1973 Q3	1995 Q4	
Amount	−3.90	−3.62	−1.37	
Quarters	11	22	18	
Rate per Year	**−1.42**	**−0.66**	**−0.30**	

What goes up also comes down. The Korean War disarmament shaved 3.9 off GDP growth over 11 quarters, dragging down growth at the −1.4% per year, rapid enough and long enough to tip us into a recession.

The subsequent armaments and disarmaments have been growing smaller in magnitude and slower in pace, and therefore less and less important as a determinant of the economic health of the US. Most recently, the War on Terror has contributed to GDP growth, the amount 1.3 spread over 24 quarters. The defense contribution to growth of 0.22 per year supports economic growth, but is not much compared with the rate during Korean War armament of 3.48 per year or the Vietnam armament of 1.05 or the Cold War armament of 0.48.

15.2.2 Federal Taxation Might Matter

Wartime surges in spending are equivalent to randomized experiments for which the causal effects, if any, can be expected to be evident in the data. The same is true, but less so for tax policies, which can respond to weakness in the economy. But by the time significant legislation passes through the stages of awareness, deliberation, bill passing, Presidential approval, and implementation, whatever conditions got the discussion started are long gone. That makes tax cuts behave like randomized experiments, at least to some extent (Waffle, waffle).

Federal revenue as a fraction of GDP is illustrated in Fig. 15.3. An increase in the federal tax bite occurred late in several of these expansions, most notably the Kennedy-Johnson expansion of the 1960s and the Bush/Clinton expansion of the 1990s. Most of that increase is not from increases in tax rates, but rather is a consequence of strong economic growth that produces capital gains and income for people

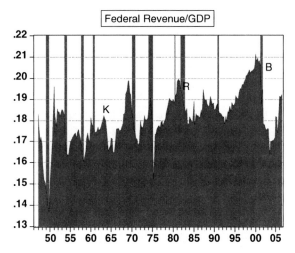

Fig. 15.3 Federal revenue/GDP

at higher tax brackets. This tends to disappear with the onset of the recession, which helps automatically to stabilize the economy.

In this figure, you can see the Kennedy tax cut in the mid 1960s, which actually seem very small compared with the Bush tax cut since 2001, though as much as half that decline in revenue in 2001 was due to the recession, especially the collapse in stock-market earnings.

The impact of these tax cuts is hard to determine. In Chap. 16, I will argue that the Kennedy/Johnson expansion was weakening in 1963 and was kept alive by the Kennedy Tax Cut. The Reagan and Bush Tax cuts came in the wake of recessions, and it is hard to know what would have happened in the absence of the cuts, as a recovery was in the works even without the tax cuts.

15.3 The Causal Path Through Houses and Cars

By now we understand that a causal conclusion needs a clear hypothetical intervention. In that regard, it makes good sense to argue that defense spending is a cause of the 1953 recession because the several ways in which the decline in DOD spending in the second half of 1953 might not have occurred all seem to lead to the same conclusion: no 1953 recession.

Next we need to move on to a harder nut to crack: consumer spending on homes and cars. Here we have a problem. There are countless ways in which the path of housing and automobile spending might have been different, and those many hypotheticals may not all lead to the same consequences for the recession risks. For that reason, it seems *inappropriate* to conclude that "houses and cars cause recessions." That's like saying the clouds cause the rain. Even something as specific as "excessive home price appreciation" cannot comfortably be called a cause of the recession without careful attention to the but-for hypothetical that might have produced a different path of home price appreciation. Was it the low Fed Funds rate, the exclusion of appreciation from capital gains taxation, the Chinese accumulation of $1 trillion in reserves, or what?

We are going to focus on one variable, selected by a committee of elders, as the way housing and cars might have been different: that's the short-term interest rates chosen by the Federal Reserve Board. We will be exploring the hypothesis that it is the Fed that causes recessions, with the effects of monetary policy working through the channels of homes and cars. Of course the Fed's job includes keeping inflation in check, and we need to be sensitive to the possibility that the cycle in homes and cars is an unintended by-product of the Fed's properly conducted anti-inflation policies. More on this below.

This exercise is going to leave some confident and some confused. That's an accurate summary of the professional opinion. Peter Temin in a paper titled "The Causes of American Business Cycles: An Essay in Economic Historiography" begins with a quotation from Rudiger Dornbusch: "None of the US expansions of the past 40 years died in bed of old age; every one was murdered by the Federal Reserve." That clarity of thinking and language stands in stark contrast with John Cochrane, also quoted by Temin: "[N]one of the popular candidates for observable shocks robustly accounts for the bulk of business-cycle fluctuations in output."[3]

As for myself, I continue to swing from elation to despair and back again. Sometimes I think I understand; sometimes I do not. What you read below depends much on my mood when I wrote it.

15.3.1 Housing Predicts Recessions

The first step in thinking about housing and recessions is to determine whether housing is important enough. Figure 15.4 illustrates the cumulative contribution of housing to US GDP growth. The total cumulative for this whole period is 10, the same as defense spending. That is only about 0.18 per year, not enough to matter much in an economy growing in the range of 3–3.5% per year. But there are plenty of ups and downs along the way.

You can see in this figure that housing is a great predictor of US recessions. Almost every time there has been a sharp housing decline, there has been a national recession. And almost every recession has been preceded by a sharp housing decline. What is very ominous is that, as I write this, we are in the midst of a housing decline that is every bit as severe as the ones that led into recessions.

Housing is not a perfect predictor of recessions. Figure 15.4 has two "false negatives" – recessions not presaged by a housing decline. Problems in housing

---

[3] Temin, Peter, "The Causes of American Business Cycles: An Essay in Economic Historiography," NBER Working Paper 662, 1997.; Dornbusch, Rudiger, "How Real is US Prosperity?" column reprinted in World Economic Laboratory Columns, MIT, December 1997; Cochrane, John H., "Shocks," in *Carnegie Conference Series on Public Policy*, 41(1994), 295–364.

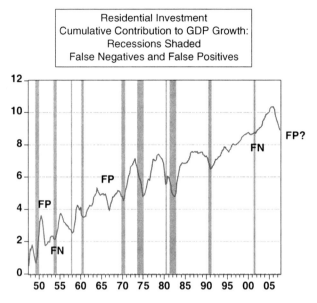

Fig. 15.4 Cumulative contribution of housing

did not warn in advance that the 1953 recession was coming, though housing was weak coincident with the recession. We understand that one. It was a disarmament downturn. And housing played no role, whatever, in the 2001 recession. We understand that one too. That was the Internet Comeuppance. But we still need to know why housing kept afloat during 2001, in the face of a $7 trillion loss of paper wealth in the stock market. Best to keep that in mind when we weave our causal story.

Figure 15.4 also has two "false positives" – housing alarms that did not lead into recessions. One was in 1951, and the other in 1967. These were not false alarms. These were valid alarms that revealed the weakness in the economy that was offset, however unintentionally, by a big ramp-up in spending by the Department of Defense for the Korean War and the Vietnam War.

If pictures do not work for you, Table 15.2 has the numbers: the contributions to GDP from residential investments in each of the US housing downturns. The table indicates the housing peak and trough quarters, (mountain top and valley floor in the figure), the amount of GDP growth that was lost due to housing, the number of quarters of decline, the rate of loss per year, and whether there was a recession immediately after or coincident with this housing problem. The declines are sorted by the total decline, led by the current housing downturn that how shaved 2.44 off of growth in the 9 quarters of decline, thus at the rate of −1.09 per year.

Excluding the contraction that is occurring as I type, there have been 15 previous housing downturns. Ten have led into recessions. The third greatest housing contraction occurred from 1950 Q3 to 1951 Q3, but no recession followed. You

Table 15.2 Housing downturns

	Peak	Trough	Contribution	Quarters	Rate per Year	Recession?	Lag*
1	**2005Q4**	**2008 Q2**	**−2.44**	**9**	**−1.09**	**????**	**8+**
2	1973Q1	1975Q1	−2.33	8	−1.16	1974 Q1	3
3	1950Q3	1951Q3	−1.91	4	−1.91	no	
4	1978Q3	1980Q2	−1.86	7	−1.06	1980 Q2	6
5	1980Q4	1982Q3	−1.24	7	−0.71	1981 Q4	3
6	1955Q2	1958Q1	−1.21	11	−0.44	1957 Q4	5
7	1948Q2	1949Q2	−1.15	4	−1.15	1949 Q1	2
8	1988Q4	1991Q1	−1.08	9	−0.48	1990 Q3	2
9	1966Q1	1967Q1	−1.04	4	−1.04	no	
10	1959Q2	1960Q4	−0.70	6	−0.47	1960 Q3	4
11	1969Q1	1970Q2	−0.66	5	−0.53	1970 Q1	3
12	1964Q1	1964Q4	−0.45	3	−0.60	no	
13	1994Q2	1995Q2	−0.33	4	−0.33	no	
14	1953Q2	1953Q4	−0.24	2	−0.47	1953 Q3	0
15	2000Q1	2000Q3	−0.14	2	−0.27	2001 Q2	4
16	1984Q2	1985Q1	−0.05	3	−0.07	no	

*Lag is the number of quarters from the housing peak to the GDP peak.

remember why, don't you? That was the Korean War. There was also a substantial housing contraction from 1966Q1 to 1967Q1, but no recession followed. It was the same story – the Department of Defense came to the rescue because of the Vietnam war.

There were also less-serious housing problems in 1964, 1984, and 1995 that did not lead into recessions. These occurred in the middle of three long expansions: The Kennedy/Johnson expansion, the Reagan expansion, and the Bush/Clinton expansion. These are what I will call in Chap. 16 the "sputters" in which threatened recessions did not materialize. Why? The Kennedy tax cut, stimulative monetary policy, and the Internet Rush. More on this later.

15.3.2 Consumer Durables Spending Predicts Recessions

The other big contribution to weakness prior to recessions comes from consumer durables. If we are going to prevent recessions, it seems wise to focus on both homes and durables. The cumulative contribution of consumer durables to GDP is illustrated in Fig. 15.5 and the major periods of decline are listed in Table 15.3.

There are important differences and similarities between housing illustrated in Fig. 15.1 and durables illustrated in Fig. 15.5.

Table 15.3 Consumer durables downturns

The US consumer durables cycle
Housing contribution to US GDP growth
Major contractions: sorted by contribution to GDP per year

Peak	Trough	Contribution	Quarters	Rate per year	Recession?
1950Q3	1952Q3	−3.19	8	−1.60	no
1960Q2	1961Q1	−0.76	3	−1.01	yes
1955Q3	1956Q3	−0.90	4	−0.90	no
1957Q1	1958Q2	−1.09	5	−0.87	yes
1990Q1	1991Q1	−0.84	4	−0.84	yes
1981Q1	1981Q4	−0.61	3	−0.82	yes
1973Q1	1974Q4	−1.36	7	−0.78	yes
1953Q1	1954Q1	−0.72	4	−0.72	yes
1978Q2	1980Q2	−1.35	8	−0.67	yes
1969Q1	1970Q4	−0.73	7	−0.42	yes
2007Q4	data forthcoming....				

(1) Durables are three times more important for long-term growth, with an average contribution almost 0.5 per year in contrast to residential investment, which has averaged only 0.15 per year.
(2) Like housing, durables are often weak, going into recessions. Though the pictures suggest that the durable cycle is less pronounced than the cycle in residential investment that is a consequence of the difference in the scales. The

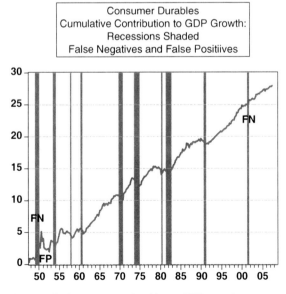

Fig. 15.5 Cumulative contribution consumer durables to GDP growth

numbers in Table 15.3 reveal that the consumer durables contribution to recessions is every bit as important as residential investment.

(3) As I write this at the end of 2007, a major housing decline starting early in 2006 has not been matched by a like decline in consumer durables, which is one reason we are not in recession.

15.3.3 Housing and Consumer Durables Are Predicted by Interest Rates

We may be feeling pretty smug now that we understand so much about the housing cycle and the durables cycle, but remember that neither housing nor durables can be said to be a "cause." They are symptoms of the underlying cause, which might be monetary policy. We need to return to the difficult task of linking monetary and fiscal policy choices to the ups and downs of the economy.

One thing we can do to link homes and durables to interest rates is to estimate "regressions" like those reported in Table 15.4. This table reports estimated equations for the thirteen components of GDP and for GDP overall. Each regression includes the value of the component in the previous quarter, the change in the Federal Funds rate in the preceding quarter, and the quarter before that, and also a constant, C. Thus, we are exploring the possibility that changes in the Fed Funds rate predict (cause?) changes in the contributions to GDP.

The first column in Table 15.4 reports the equation for GDP growth overall. The coefficient of 0.25 on GDP(−1) means that about 25% of one quarter's abnormal GDP growth is passed on to the next. This coefficient is printed in bold to indicate that it is statistically distinguishable from zero, misleadingly described by statisticians as "statistically significant." The change in the Federal Funds rate lagged one quarter is not statistically significant but the change lagged twice is. This equation thus suggests that a change in the Federal Funds rates takes a couple of quarters to take hold, when rising Fed Funds rates are bad for (predict weak?) growth but falling rates stimulate growth.

The components of GDP are sorted in this table by the sum of these two Fed Funds rates coefficients. This puts residential investment and consumer durables at the extreme left – the ones that seem most favorably affected by a reduction in the Fed Funds rate.

The take away from this table is: worry about cars but worry especially, about homes. Among the components of GDP,

Residential Investment:

- Is the most predictable (The highest adjusted R-squared.)
- Is the most persistent (The largest coefficient on *(−1).)
- Has the greatest sensitivity to the changes in the Fed Funds rate. (The largest coefficients on the Fed Funds variable.)

Table 15.4 Regressions explaining contributions to GDP

Sample 1970Q1 2007Q3
Statistically Significant Coefficients are in Bold

Dynamics	Components of GDP												
	GDP	RES	DUR	NONDUR	SERV	STATE	DEF	NONDEF	EQUIP	STRUCT	IMP	INVENT	EXP
*(−1)	**0.25**	**0.55**	−0.15	**0.20**	**0.34**	**0.18**	0.15	−0.25	**0.39**	**0.35**	**0.30**	−0.25	0.09
D(RATE_FF(−1))	0.27	−0.29	−0.12	−0.06	−0.17	0.01	0.00	0.01	0.11	0.03	−0.17	**0.87**	0.23
D(RATE_FF(−2))	**−1.08**	−0.11	−0.28	−0.10	0.05	−0.03	0.01	0.01	−0.08	**0.10**	**0.30**	−0.68	0.02
C	**2.30**	0.04	**0.51**	**0.45**	0.77	**0.23**	0.02	**0.08**	**0.27**	0.04	−0.45	0.07	**0.48**
Adjusted R-squared	0.16	0.48	0.10	0.07	0.17	0.02	0.00	0.05	0.18	0.22	0.15	0.27	0.09
Mean dependent var	3.09	0.11	0.46	0.57	1.16	0.27	0.03	0.06	0.45	0.05	−0.65	0.05	0.53
Sum of Rate FF coeffs	−0.82	−0.40	−0.40	−0.16	−0.12	−0.02	0.01	0.02	0.03	0.13	0.13	0.19	0.25

Definitions
*(−1) is the contribution in the previous quarter
RATE_FF = Federal Funds Rate
D(RATE_FF(−1)) = RATE_FF(−1)-RATE_FF(−2)
Components: residential investment, durables, nondurables, services, state and local government, defense, federal nondefense, equipment and software, structures, imports, inventories, exports

15.3.4 Not So Fast

Worry is one thing. Belief is something else. We have discovered that changes in the Fed Funds rates help to *predict* changes in spending on homes and durables. We have *not* discovered that changes in rates *cause* change in spending. To leap scientifically to that causal conclusion, we would have to imagine that the rate changes were randomized, but they do not flip coins to set rates, do they? The Fed's job is to anticipate problems in the economy and lower rates when things are likely to get worse. For that reason rates may be like weather forecasts – predictions but not causes.

We can make this weather forecast idea very concrete by creating an example from the real data. This is a story about how an otherwise intelligent economist came to the conclusion that the Fed matters, even though it does not. Let us start with one sector of the economy that really has to worry about forecasting. Success in home building depends on an accurate forecast of the labor market, as it is hard to sell homes when unemployment is rising. That's when delinquencies and foreclosures skyrocket, and when lending standards tighten. So let's estimate a simple equation that explains the contribution of residential investment to GDP as a function of the unemployment rate and the change in the unemployment rate, to see if we can confirm that homebuilders are predicting the labor market by their decisions to build or not to build. Let us try to explain the contribution of residential investment to GDP, denoted by I_RES, as a function of the residential investment in the previous quarter, I_RES(-1), the unemployment rate in the previous quarter U(-1), and the change in the unemployment rate D(U(-1)) = U(-1) $-$ U(-2). The details are in the footnote.[4] Here is the equation:

$$\text{I\_RES} = 0.60^*\text{I\_RES}(-1) + 0.11^*\text{U}(-1) + 0.52^*\text{D}(\text{U}(-1)) - 0.6$$

As we will be using this notation often, make sure you know that for a variable X, D(X(t)) = X(t) $-$ X(t-1); D stands for change.

Do you see anything weird in this equation? It says building is predicted to strengthen when unemployment is high and rising. (Those coefficients on U(-1) and D(U(-1)) are positive.) Can you tell a story that makes any sense out of that? I can. My story depends on that big coefficient on the previous quarter's residential investment: 0.6^*I_RES(-1). That coefficient 0.60 means that residential investment

---

4

Dependent Variable: I_RES Sample (adjusted): 1970:1 2007:3				
Variable	Coefficient	Std. Error	t-Statistic	Prob.
I_RES(-1)	0.600	0.076	7.85	0
U(-1)	0.106	0.040	2.63	0.009
D(U(-1))	0.517	0.185	2.79	0.006
C	-0.610	0.250	-2.44	0.016
R-squared	0.39	Mean dependent var		0.11
Adjusted R-squared	0.38	S.D. dependent var		0.82

is quite persistent – if firms ramp up building one quarter they follow through with heightened building the next quarter. There's a very good reason for that. Getting from unprepared land to a finished home takes a year or more, and once the process is started it is pretty irreversible. Because of the long delays, building needs to get going again when the market is dark but there is light at the end of the tunnel. That's during the darkest days of a recession, when unemployment is high and getting worse. That's why high and rising unemployment predict future building.

Into this reality, enter the Ed Fed. The Ed Fed is very concerned with unemployment, and accordingly, lowers the interest rate when the unemployment rate is high and rising. Through a trial and error process, the Ed Fed stumbled on the following rate change rule:

$$D(RATE\_ED) = RATE\_ED - RATE\_ED(-1) = -0.11 \times U(-1)$$
$$-0.52 \times D(U(-1)) + 0.67.$$

Confirm that this equation does call for rate reductions when unemployment is high and rising. You may also notice the similarity between the Ed Fed rule and the estimated equation for residential investment. It looks like the Ed rule is just the piece in that equation related to unemployment. If unemployment worked to predict residential investment, then the Ed Rate should too. Ed did not know that. He proceeded on the assumption that the Ed Rate influenced the economy. To confirm that his rate-setting rule was having the desirable effect on residential investment, Ed estimated the following equation for residential investment as a function of the change in Ed's interest rate D(RATE_ED):[5]

$$I\_RES = 0.60 \times I\_RES(-1) - 1.0 \times D(RATE\_ED)(-1)) + 0.06.$$

(Make sure you understand why the coefficient of the Ed Fed variable is exactly -1.0. This is a consequence of the way that the Ed Fed chooses the interest rate.) This equation makes the Ed Fed very happy because, it "confirms" that a cut of interest rates by 100 basis points increases the contribution of residential investment to GDP by 1.0 in the following quarter. This has been confirmed with the scientific pizzazz offered by the tool of ordinary least squares regression, which has provided a high R^2 and coefficients that are highly statistically significant. No one knows

---

5

Dependent Variable: I_RES
Method: Least Squares
Sample (adjusted): 1970:1 2007:3

Variable	Coefficient	Std. Error	t-Statistic	Prob.
I_RES(−1)	0.60	0.07	9.2	0
D_RATE_ED(−1)	−1.00	0.23	−4.4	0
C	0.06	0.05	1.1	0.26
R-squared	0.39	Mean dependent var		0.11
Adjusted R-squared	0.38	S.D. dependent var		0.82

quite what that all means, but it sounds really great, and everyone can go home happy. This is the Wizard of Oz in operation.

I hope you understand the problem. The Ed Fed got fooled into thinking they were influencing the economy because they used a rate-setting rule that mimicked the forecasting rule used by a forward-looking sector in the economy – the housing sector. I warned you that we are entering the world ruled by Uncertainty and Ambiguity, where complex nonexperimental data can easily mislead.

Maybe you think you can make some progress by estimating an equation for residential investment that includes both unemployment and the Fed Funds rate, to see if the Fed Funds rate predicts changes in housing after controlling for the level and change in unemployment. That's like including the cloud coverage in a model that predicts rain on the basis of the rain forecast. If after controlling for the clouds, we find that the weather forecasts help to predict rain, then that must be a causal effect, right? Wrong. That merely suggests that the forecasts and the rain both depend on some other common variables, like the barometric pressure. It only gets worse as we layer in more and more assumptions about how expectations are formed and what kinds of delays are present in the responses, and what is observable by whom. At this point, the usual solution is to roll out some very heavy and very loud econometric cannon to shoot at the causal target. The noise and the brilliance when these cannon are fired utterly disguise the fact they widely miss their mark. But this econometric performance is only a slideshow. The Priests of the Orthodox Economics Church meditate so deeply in pursuit of Enlightenment about the Causal Structure of the Economy that they do not even hear the noise or notice the cannon flashes. Meanwhile, the Fed's belief in their own importance is not at all affected by the cannon blasts or the meditative chants of the Priests.

This is so annoying. Let us forget these subtle issues altogether and see if we can convince ourselves that the Fed causes recessions. We will do this by studying the Fed behavior prior to recessions. If the Fed could accurately predict the oncoming recessions they would presumably be lowering the interest rates, and not raising them. If we find interest rates rising at the ends of expansions, that is evidence of either perverse forecasting or a causal effect. (I think. Maybe not. I don't know. . . .)

15.3.5 The Fed Raises Short-Term Interest Rates
at the Ends of Expansions

On the basis of the circumstantial evidence, the Federal Reserve Board, by raising rates late in expansions, can take some blame for almost all of our recessions.

Take a look at Fig. 15.6, which illustrates the behavior of short-term interest rates during the 10 expansions since 1947. The vertical line on the right of this graph is the cycle peak to which the labels in the legend apply. To the right of the vertical line are the data during the recessions. Focus on the expansion data to the left. There you can see that the Bush/Clinton expansion that ended in 2001 Q1 was the longest expansion, lasting 40 quarters. You can see the other long expansions too:

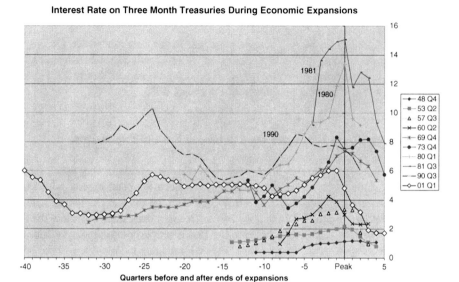

Fig. 15.6 Short-term interest rates increase at ends of expansions

the Kennedy/Johnson expansion that ended in 1969 Q4 and the Reagan expansion that ended in 1990 Q3.

Now look at the behavior of interest rates preceding the cycle peak. In every case, interest rates were rising in the two-year period before the recessions began. That makes me imagine that those rising rates choked off growth and tipped the economy into recession.

The three expansions beginning with 1954 show pretty steady increases in interest rates followed by sharp reductions as soon as the recession hit, as if to say "Sorry about that; we turned that screw a little too far." The 1973 downturn and the 1980 downturn were preceded by very sharp increase in rates, 400 basis points in 1973 and 800 basis points in 1980. When that huge increase in rates in 1979 led to the downturn of 1980, the Fed said "Whoops!!" and lowered the rates by 400 basis points. But as soon as the economy started to grow again, rates increased immediately by 450 basis points and added another 150 basis points in the next three quarters. "WHOOPS!!!" again, and the severe recession of 1981 was off and running.

What kinds of doctors dish out medicine like that? This was administered in the short-lived era when the Fed targeted the "monetary aggregates," including the cash in your wallet and the balance in your checking account. The theory at the time was that if you had a big checking account balance, you would soon go out and spend it, thereby causing inflation. If those balances were growing more rapidly than the economy, the Fed felt compelled to take the balances from us by selling to us bonds at attractively high rates of interest. (To buy these bonds, we had to draw down our checking account balances.) This theory did not work out so well in practice. The attempt to control the monetary aggregates produced those wild swings in interest rates, and the Fed wisely abandoned monetary targeting in the early 1980s only a few years after the experiment began.[6]

Figure 15.6 does reveal that some doctors are better than others. Dr. Greenspan seemed to have anticipated the 1990 recession with rate reductions starting six quarters before the recession officially began. He did not do so well in the 2001 recession, as he was still jacking up rates until the end of 2000.

15.3.5.1 Long Term Rates also Tend to Rise at Ends of Expansions

But, you may object, the rates on short-term bonds cannot matter very much for the economy, can they? Housing, until recently, has been financed mostly with loans with fixed long-term rates. The Fed's influence over the rates at the longer maturities may be pretty minimal. When the 10-year Treasury does seem to follow the Fed Funds rate, perhaps that is only because the Fed is properly anticipating where the longer-term rates are going, and setting the Fed Funds rate to keep up with the bond market. For example, in a recession, weak demand for loans and low inflation because of weak demand for products both allow a fall in long-term rates, completely independent of whether or not the Fed gets a little ahead of the game with early reductions in the Fed Funds rate. After all, we do not think that the Fed's rate cutting necessarily causes the recovery merely because those rate cuts happen in the early stages of a recession before the recovery. Likewise for bloodletting.

The rates on 10-year Treasuries are illustrated in Fig. 15.7. There are a couple of missing expansions because 10-year Treasuries were not issued until 1953. For the expansions you can see, long-term interest rates were generally elevating at the ends. Maybe that was what killed off housing. Maybe that would have occurred even if the Fed had not taken action.

15.3.5.2 The Interest Rate Spread May Be the Key
Determinant of Recessions

Though the rates of interest on bonds with longer maturities are not necessarily much influenced by the Fed behavior, by rapidly changing short term rates, the Fed does control the steepness of the yield curve – the spread between the long-term rates and the short-term rates. This spread is important because the business of retail banking is to take short-term deposits and make long-term loans, what is known as financial intermediation. When the spread is great, banks make substantial intermediation profits on every loan they place. When long-term rates are falling, the banks also make capital gains off their outstanding loans, which were placed at higher interest rates. Offsetting these profits are losses from nonperforming loans. But delinquency and default risk are low for borrowers with strong income flows and

---

[6] Remarks by Chairman Ben S. Bernanke At the Fourth ECB Central Banking Conference, Frankfurt, Germany November 10, 2006 "Monetary Aggregates and Monetary Policy at the Federal Reserve: A Historical Perspective". http://www.federalreserve.gov/Boarddocs/speeches/2006/20061110/default.htm

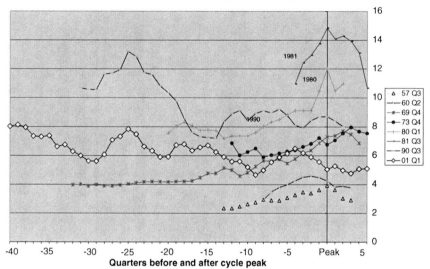

Fig. 15.7 Long-term interest rates increase at ends of expansions

low for houses with appreciating values. Thus give the banks a steep yield curve, falling long-term rates of interest, rising incomes of loan applicants and housing appreciation that makes the loans self-collateralizing, and the banks will be very happy indeed, and will compete intensely to find someone who wants a mortgage loan. When all these good things are happening, anyone who can crawl off the street and fill out the application can get a loan.

But if the yield curve flattens, or if overall income growth slows down or if home price appreciation stops, banks do not make intermediation profits and they must perform a different function – they must carefully identify borrowers with low default risk. When this happens, loan approval can get much more difficult. If there are a lot of loan denials, it is called a "credit crunch," which can put a big crimp in housing sales.

Be sure you understand what a credit crunch is. In a normal market, even very risky borrowers with high delinquency and default risk have access to credit, if they are prepared to pay the interest rate premium that their riskier loan commands (e.g., the subprime mortgage market). In an exuberant market, the lending standards can get very relaxed. But during a credit crunch, many borrowers are simply shut out of the market and denied credit. One reason for tightening of lending standards and denial of credit is doubt about the value of the collateral that supports the loan. Take the housing market, for example. When home prices are elevating, there is little doubt about the home as collateral for a home loan, but when prices soften or decline, lenders are going to insist on seeing more than just the house standing behind the debt. They are going to have verification of good income and good credit scores.

A credit crunch may be the reason why one of the best early warning signals of an oncoming recession is an inverted yield curve, with the short-term rates higher than the long-term rates. We already have covered this ground but it is worth repeating.

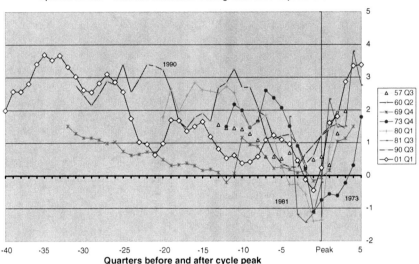

Fig. 15.8 Interest rate spread at ends of expansions

As you can see in Fig. 15.8, an inverted yield curve or a very flat yield curve has preceded every recessions, and monetary loosening with the onset of the recession has always greatly steepened the yield curve.

By creating a credit crunch, an inverted yield curve can be said to cause a recession as well as to predict one. Nothing stays the same, and history is not necessarily a guide of the future.

A very big forecasting question in 2007 has been whether the latest inversion of the yield curve illustrated in Fig. 15.9 is going to cause a credit crunch and possibly lead into a recession. Some held out hope that the old days were a thing of the past. In the dark past, lender and borrower met at an office in a bank, shook hands and looked each other in the eye. When the housing market was soft and the yield curve was flat or inverted, the lender was nervous and sweaty, wondering if the borrower would really pay back that loan, and the borrower was nervous and sweaty, wondering if too much was offered for the house. With all that nervousness and sweating, the loan was not granted, to the great relief of the prospective borrower, who could straightforwardly get out of the contract to purchase the home, and to the relief also of the loan officer, who did not have to worry about another nonperforming loan on the books.

In 2003–2005, however, most mortgage loans were packaged in "mortgage-backed securities" and sold to willing Wall Street investors eager to eke out another 50 basis points in return in a low rate environment. As mortgage brokers made "transaction fees" off every loan originated, and, as their institutions did not retain the loan on their books, these mortgage brokers were rather indifferent to default and delinquency risk. In part because of that indifference, instead of a face-to-face meeting, loan applications were taken over the Internet based on the borrower's "stated"

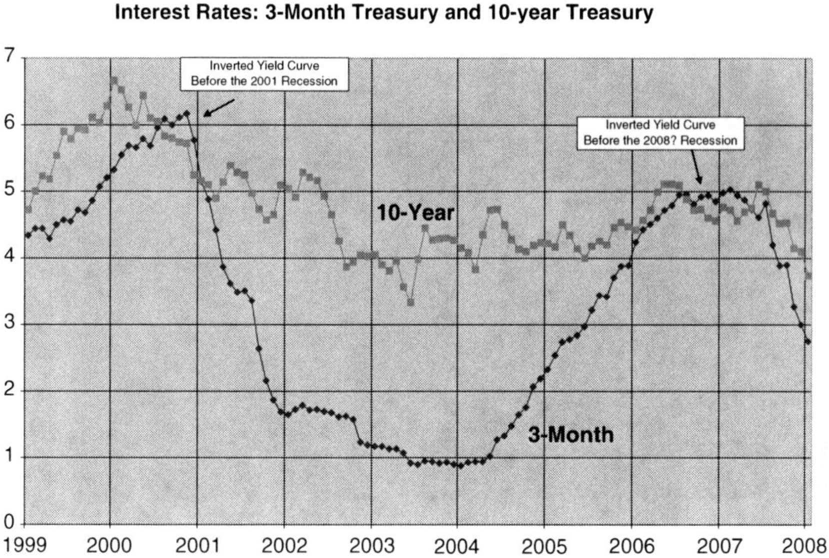

Interest Rates: 3-Month Treasury and 10-year Treasury

Fig. 15.9 Short and long-term interest rates, 1999–2008

income (a.k.a. falsified income). Without the traditional face-to-face nervousness, there may have seemed little possibility of a credit crunch in which access to mortgage loans would be closed off for large number of buyers. The risk spreads might widen a bit if things got bad, but the mortgage window would remain open for business for all.

But when the Fed raised interest rates in 2005 and 2006 and created an inverted yield curve guess what happened? That's right, a credit crunch affecting especially the subprime mortgage market:

Real Estate Articles from Inman News

Subprime lenders hit Wall Street funding wall
Wednesday, January 03, 2007

As I write this in early 2008, there continues to be great concern that the credit crunch will spread beyond housing, as banks try to improve their balance sheets after very substantial losses in the mortgage markets. We shall see on that one . . .

15.3.5.3 But Did Inflation Drive the Bond Market and Force the Fed's Hand?

Into the causal story of recession, we now need to add the real villain: inflation. It is inflation that causes the rise in the long-term rates and also forces the Fed to increase

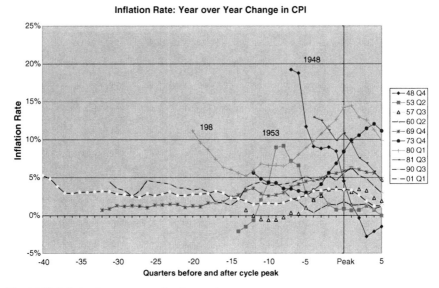

Fig. 15.10 Inflation Increases at ends of expansions

short-term rates. Figure 15.10 illustrates the inflation rate at the ends of expansions. Except for those early episodes in 1948 and 1953, inflation is generally increasing at the ends of expansions.

Though inflation concern at the ends of expansions might have forced the fed to raise interest rates it is not some mysterious extraterritorial force that allowed inflation to raise. It was the fed's attentiveness earlier in the expansion.

15.3.6 Spillovers from Housing: The Wealth Effect or Not?

Though changes in short-term interest rates help to predict weakness in housing, and problems in housing predict recessions with near-perfect accuracy, that is not enough to create a compelling causal story. We cannot have a recession with weakness *only* in housing. Remember the order we discussed in Chap. 12: homes, cars, equipment, and structures. Much of the weakness preceding recessions is in homes, but consumer durables are also weak before recessions. *During* the recessions, the weakness comes from consumer durables, business equipment, and business inventories.

Thus, if we conclude that the monetary policy that smoothed the housing cycle would prevent recessions, we need to explain how that policy would also affect spending on durables and equipment and inventories. Otherwise, with a new kind of monetary policy we may just be creating a new milder kind of recession.

It is easy to deal with declines in spending on equipment and inventories – that is a reaction to weak consumer spending. A policy that maintained consumer spending is likely also to support spending on equipment and software.

It is more difficult to put weakness in the consumer components of GDP into our causal narrative. Why do these components of GDP turn down just a little later than homes? If we kept spending on homes with a different interest rate policy, would that also hold up durables and other consumer items?

There are at least three possibilities here:

1. The furniture component of durables is directly related to homes: no new homes means fewer new appliances.
2. Vehicles, which are the larger and more volatile components of consumer durables, are driven partly by a housing wealth effect, particularly for credit constrained households, which without home price appreciation could not get a new car loan.
3. Interest rate policy that controlled the housing cycle would also work well for controlling the cycle of consumer durables, as spending on both homes and cars are influenced by the same cycle in interest rates and lending standards.

We probably should be exploring these three possibilities, but I have the impression you are getting impatient for the last chapter of this novel. So here it is.

15.3.7 Two Stories of How Monetary Policy Causes Recessions

First a confession: With all these patterns, it is a mystery whether monetary policy can be said to cause anything or merely reacts to things that would have occurred anyway. But if I felt the need, I could suppress the doubt and tell with confidence the following story.

15.3.7.1 My Story

Inflation is tame early in expansions as the economy has plenty of room to grow – offices and factories are far from capacity, and qualified workers seeking jobs are plentiful. With that excess capacity, firms respond to increases in demand by increasing output and not prices.

Inevitably, demand grows faster than capacity formation and firms start to bump up against capacity constraints. When this happens, firms have pricing power and, in the face of increases in demand, they raise prices and contribute to inflationary pressures.

But the Fed fiddles as inflation smolders. The ever-so gradual increase in inflation is not enough to get the Fed to respond, but like a small brush fire, inflation soon enough gets out of control. Meanwhile, housing has started to enter the Ponzi period in which home purchases are contingent on expectations of further increases in home prices. By the time the data are in, and the Fed rate-setting committee has deliberated enough to make absolutely sure that it is time to make a change in monetary policy, inflation is burning fiercely and it takes a heavy spray of higher interest

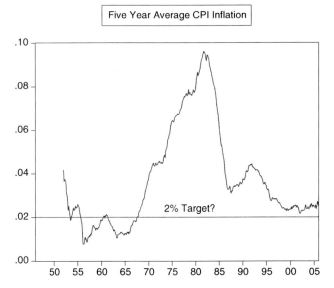

Fig. 15.11 Five-year average inflation

rates to put the fire out. That creates an inverted yield curve, a credit crunch for
housing, and an unpleasant recession. Oh, Oh, we're sorry, say the Fed Governors,
who knock down interest rates to try to get housing and the rest of the economy
back on their feet.

So how might the Fed do it differently? Call it the "Leamer rule," to coin a phrase
revealing the author's uncontrollable immodesty. The "Taylor rule" proposed by
John Taylor[7] has the Fed Funds rate depending on deviations of inflation from an
inflation target and deviations of GDP from trend GDP growth. There are two problems with the GDP part of this rule:

- The comparison of GDP with trend GDP is ambiguous because of problems in
  defining trend GDP.
- There is a difference between being above the trend while growing farther above
  the trend vs. being above the trend while falling back to the trend. The first calls
  for the breaks to be applied, but the second does not.

The Leamer Rule has the Fed Funds rate depending on deviations of a long moving
average of inflation from the target inflation rate (2%), deviations of housing starts
from normal (about 1.5 million per year), and the direction that housing starts are
moving over the last year. Inflation determines the long-run movement in rates and
housing the short-run movement.

Figure 15.11 compares the five-year average inflation with a target of 2% per
year, suggesting tight monetary policy when inflation is well above the target. When
the gap between the target and the realized inflation is pretty constant, as it has been

---

[7] Taylor, John B. (1993): Discretion versus Policy Rules in Practice, Carnegie-Rochester Conference Series on Public Policy 39, 195–214.

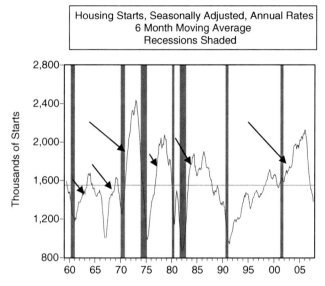

Fig. 15.12 Apply the breaks when housing starts are high and rising

from 1999 to 2008, the variability of the Fed Funds rate should be driven completely by changes in the housing market.

Controlling housing is a lot like pushing your daughter on the swing. You time your intervention at one special point in the cycle when your pushing has the greatest effect. For the Fed, interest rate policy is especially important when housing is strong and growing stronger. That's when the Fed has the opportunity to put on the breaks and prevent a mountain of homes from being built, a mountain that inevitably leads into a valley. This rule is illustrated in Fig. 15.12, which compares housing starts with the historical average of 1.55 million. The arrows identify when housing is strong and getting stronger. That is when we need higher interest rates to cool off the housing sector, and to prevent the mountain of homes from being built.

What lies behind the Leamer rule is the realization that the Fed can affect the timing of the building of new homes, but cannot much affect the total. Thus, after a normal housing-led recession, interest rate cuts are especially effective because building can be moved forward in time – capturing the sales not made during the recession. But following a recession as the one we had in 2001 in which housing plowed ahead with little notice of the softness in the economy, subsequently low levels of interest rates inevitably transfer sales backward in time, encouraging sales that might otherwise have been made years later. This sews the seeds for a housing collapse later on, when there are fewer sales left to make.

15.3.7.2 Your Story

This section is for you to write.

Appendix: Two More "Causes"

I am tired out from all these fiscal and monetary causes of recessions, and I suspect that you are exhausted, but if you want more, we can devote a bit of time to oil prices and exports.

Oil Price Increases Preceded Some of the Recessions

Rasche and Tatom(1977) and Hamilton(1983) were among the first to discover that sharp increases in oil prices have preceded many recessions.[8] That has led to a debate among economists as to whether increases in oil prices can be said to have caused the recessions, and if so, how. One view is that sharp increases in oil prices are like a tax increase that reduces the ability of consumers to buy other things. Another view is that a sharp rise in oil prices encourages buyers of automobiles and buildings to postpone their commitments until they are sure whether energy efficiency is really important or not. A third view is that the rise in energy prices tips the Fed into an inflation-fighting frenzy, which leads to unwise increases in interest rates, the exact opposite of what the tax-increase view would call for. This third Fed folly view was endorsed by none other than Chairman Ben Bernanke.[9]

Figure 15.13 illustrates the path of real crude oil prices since WWII. You have to look pretty long and hard through colored glasses to come to the conclusion that oil prices predict recessions. Oil prices did rise significantly at the ends of three of the ten expansions: 1948, 1980, and 2001, but by the official recession of 2001 crude prices were falling nicely. Crude oil prices were rising moderately prior to the 1973 recession, but then jumped by 135% in January 1974, though according to the NBER, the downturn had begun in the previous month in December 1973. Credit this price "shock" with making the downturn worse than it might otherwise have been, if you wish. Otherwise there are lots of ups and downs of real crude prices that do not seem to bear any relationship with the recessions.

Weakness in Exports Has Not Caused US Recessions

Recessions in most countries can get started because of problems in exports, possibly a result of recessions in trading partners. This idea is memorialized by comments

---

[8] Rasche, R. H., and J. A. Tatom (1977), "Energy Resources and Potential GNP," *Federal Reserve Bank of St. Louis Review*, 59 (June), pp. 10–24.

Hamilton, James D. (1983), "Oil and the Macroeconomy Since World War II," *Journal of Political Economy*, 91, pp. 228–248.

[9] Bernanke, Ben S., Mark Gertler, and Mark Watson (1997). "Systematic Monetary Policy and the Effects of Oil Price Shocks," *Brookings Papers on Economic Activity*,1:1997, pp. 91–142.

Bohi, Douglas R. (1989), *Energy Price Shocks and Macroeconomic Performance*, Washington D.C.: Resources for the Future.

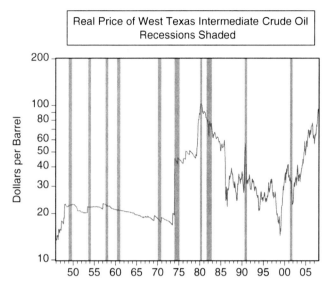

Fig. 15.13 Crude oil prices

like: When the United States sneezes, Canada catches a cold. The US is different. Most of its problems are home grown. This is confirmed by Fig. 15.14, which compares real exports over the expansions. Exports were plummeting prior to the 1948 and the 1953 recessions. What were we exporting back then, anyway? (when the Department of Defense ships tanks and guns and food to our soldiers abroad, that's counted as an export). Other than those events, there is not much happening to exports leading into recessions, though weakness in sales of exports was a contributing factor during several of the recessions.

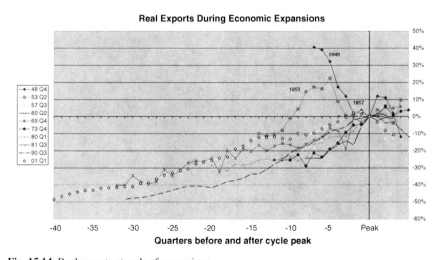

Fig. 15.14 Real exports at ends of expansions

Part IV
Expansions: With and Without Spurts

Chapter 16
The Life Cycle of US Expansions:
Sputters and Spurts

In the previous chapter, we have examined the data as if the US economy experiences normal growth, punctuated by occasional downturns. We were not looking for a cycle. We looked closely at the data before, during, and after the recessions to try to discover the virus that caused them.

We are now going to look at the very same data from a very different perspective. We will turn our focus to the expansions, thus shifting the question from what causes the recessions to what keeps the expansions going. This small change in the framing of the question has big effects on how we think about the economy. Looking at these patterns, we will tell stories about the "life cycle" of expansions: a robust youth, a normal middle age, and a tottering old-age. Rather than looking only for the shocks or diseases that tip the economy out of its normal growth and into recessions, we will look also for rejuvenating tonics that can extend the life of an already old expansion.

We will find evidence about the phases of the life cycle of the expansions especially in the labor markets: A vigorous youth comes with frenetic activity: long hours of work and declining unemployment. Middle age has a normal job market that is good enough to keep the unemployment rate pretty level, but not good enough to drive it down rapidly. Then, age inevitably takes hold and the pace of life slows, symptomized by a decline in weekly hours worked. Absent a rejuvenating tonic, the expansion becomes fragile and soon dips into recession, with rising idleness.

In five cases, expansions were sputtering and appeared near their demise but experienced a second wind and a spurt of growth. Here they are:

	Truman	Kennedy	Johnson	Reagan	Clinton
Last quarter of sputter	1951 Q4	1963 Q1	1967 Q2	1985 Q1	1996 Q1
Driver of the spurt	War	Tax Cut	War	Rates	Animal
				Crude oil	Spirits

The Truman and Johnson spurts were driven by massive increases in spending by the Department of Defense for the Korean and Vietnam War. The Kennedy spurt was caused by the 1963 Kennedy tax cut that reduced federal revenues as a share of GDP

by 2% points. Call those "fiscal spurts," referring to the tax and spend policies of
the Federal government. The Reagan spurt was slow to form and never that strong.
It was caused by a massive reduction in the interest rates by the Federal Reserve
Board, and by a sharp drop in crude oil prices. Call that the "monetary" spurt. Last
was the Clinton spurt that was symptomized by a vast increase in the spending by
business on equipment and software during the Internet Rush. You probably do not
remember, but even the word "Internet" was quite unfamiliar in 1995. A few years
later, there was hardly a business in US, from Fortune-500 down to Mom-and-Pops,
that did not have a Website, and there were innumerable dot-com firms that had
sprung up specifically to look for profits on the Web. Call that the "Animal Spirits"
spurt.

16.1 Production and Employment During Expansions

16.1.1 Real GDP Grows During Economic Expansions

The behavior of real GDP over the ten economic expansions since WWII is displayed in Fig. 16.1, which shows the cumulative growth of real GDP. Period zero in
the horizontal scale is the official NBER trough, and period one is the first period of
the expansion. These data are displayed until the official NBER peak quarter, after
which the economy dips into an official recession. This graph is a great way to see
how long and how strong are the various expansions. Can you see which were the
longest and which were the strongest?

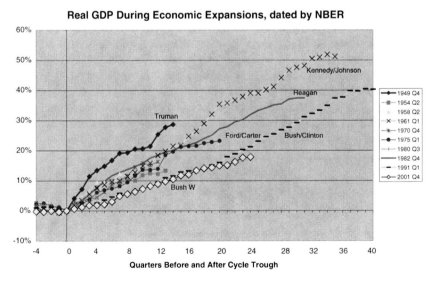

Fig. 16.1 Real GDP during expansions

Table 16.1 Real GDP growth over US expansions

		Fed Chairman	NBER Trough	NBER Peak	Qrts	Growth rate Mean	Std. Dev.	TOTAL
1	Truman	McCabe/McMartin	1949 Q4	1953 Q2	14	6.2	5.4	28.8
2	Eisenhower I	McMartin	1954 Q2	1957 Q3	13	3.3	4.5	13.3
3	Eisenhower II	McMartin	1958 Q2	1960 Q2	8	4.7	5.2	12.3
4	Kennedy/Johnson	McMartin	1961 Q1	1969 Q4	35	4.6	3.3	51.6
5	Nixon	Burns	1970 Q4	1973 Q4	12	4.0	4.3	16.4
6	Ford/Carter	Burns/Miller	1975 Q1	1980 Q1	20	3.8	4.8	23.7
7	Carter/Reagan	Volcker	1980 Q3	1981 Q3	4	1.3	6.3	4.3
8	Reagan	Volcker	1982 Q4	1990 Q3	31	4.0	2.7	36.9
9	Bush/Clinton	Greenspan	1991 Q1	2001 Q1	40	3.4	1.9	39.4
9a	Pre-Rush	Greenspan	1991 Q1	1995 Q4	19	3.0	1.5	
9b	Internet Rush	Greenspan	1996 Q1	2001 Q1	21	3.9	2.2	
10	Bush/?+	Greenspan/Bernanke	2001 Q3		24+	2.8	1.6	15.9
All					201	3.9	3.6	

Data on the growth of real GDP for these economic expansions are summarized in Table 16.1, which contains the length in quarters, the average growth, the standard deviation of growth (a measure of volatility), and the cumulative growth. This summarizes numerically what you should have been able to see in Fig. 16.1:

- The Bush/Clinton expansion was the longest and the smoothest
- The Truman expansion was the strongest and the most volatile
- The Kennedy/Johnson expansion provided the most cumulative growth
- The Carter/Reagan expansion was so short that it hardly counts

16.1.1.1 Slower and Steadier

We need to pause a moment to mark down our discovery about average growth and volatility measured by the standard deviation. Generally, the last 50 years have come with slower but more stable growth, which you can see in Fig. 16.2, which compares average growth with the volatility of growth in each of the expansions. Over time the economy has moved to the lower left in this scatter diagram producing expansions with lower average growth and less volatility.

I have included in Fig. 16.2 two points that represent the two halves of the Bush/Clinton expansion: the first half from 1991 Q2 to 1995 Q5 and the Internet Rush from 1996 Q1 to 2000 Q1. The Pre-Rush 1990s produced the numbers at the lower left of the figure with a low mean and a low standard deviation. This outcome suggested to many analysts that US had entered a mature phase and that the opportunities for exceptional growth lay outside the borders of US, in the emerging markets. But during the Internet Rush, US seemed to have been rejuvenated, and

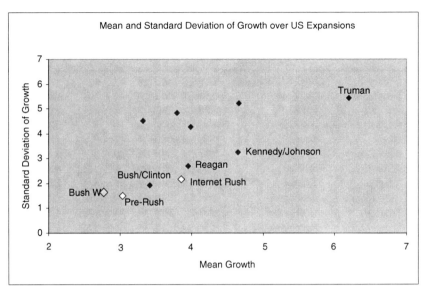

Fig. 16.2 Mean and standard deviation of growth during expansions

produced numbers that were very similar to the Reagan numbers. There are a lot of Fed officials, corporations, government groups, and individuals, who placed very heavy bets on the continuation of that performance. Sadly, the economy has not delivered. The Bush W numbers are the weakest so far with a low mean but also a low standard deviation.

16.1.2 Labor Markets Sometimes Tighten Twice During Expansions

The tightening of the labor markets that is characteristic of an expansion is illustrated in Figs. 16.3 and 16.4, which display the unemployment rates compared with the level in the sixth quarter prior to the beginning of the expansion, roughly the unemployment rate at the end of the previous expansion. Figure 16.3 depicts the data for the short expansions and Fig. 16.4 for the three long expansions. We can see in these figures that unemployment rises during the recession, prior to the onset of an expansion, but it often continues to rise even during the first quarters of an expansion. After a quarter or two of good sales, firms start to hire aggressively and the rate of unemployment starts to drift downward. The slow GDP growth during the beginning of the Bush/Clinton expansion was not enough to turn the unemployment rate around until the sixth quarter, about four quarters late.

After a period of rapid decline in the unemployment rate, the rate of job formation slows to match the increase in the labor force, and the rate of unemployment plateaus

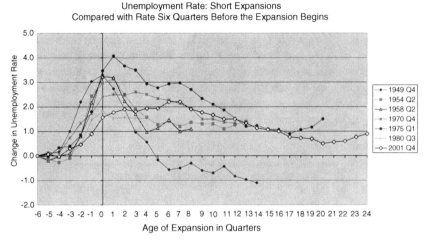

Fig. 16.3 Unemployment rate during the short expansions

out at a level that is sometimes higher and sometimes lower than the prerecession level. The long expansions illustrated in Fig. 16.4 have a first plateau followed by what I will call a spurt of growth and a decline of the unemployment rate to a second plateau.

16.1.3 Cycles in Hours and Unemployment

Unemployment is one kind of idleness. Slow pace of work, while on the job is another kind of idleness. A symptom of the pace of work is weekly hours in

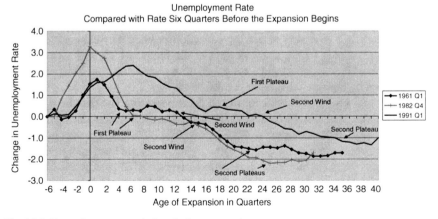

Fig. 16.4 Unemployment rate during the long expansions

manufacturing.[1] When sales growth is exceptional and unexpected, manufacturers increase the pace of work and overtime hours at roughly similar times.

The life cycle of expansions is best depicted in cycle diagrams that illustrate the movement of unemployment and weekly hours. With the horizontal axis indicating hours and the vertical axis indicating the unemployment rate, an expansion generally takes the economy in the southeast direction, with higher weekly hours and lower rates of unemployment; a contraction takes the economy in the opposite direction, with lower weekly hours and higher rates of unemployment.

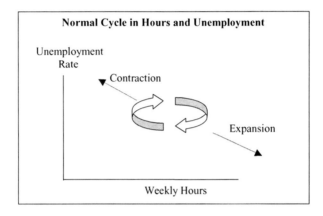

The typical path of the data over an expansion begins at the top of this circle with a movement to the right with the unemployment rate fairly stable and with increasing hours. Next is the movement down with the hours stable and the unemployment falling. Then, a move to the left when the demand slackens, the hours decline but unemployment stays low. Finally, the cycle completes, when the bad news is evident, and unemployment rises. This shape comes from the fact that firms first adjust the hours and then employment. The expansion begins with a sharp increase in the hours, which will give way to a sharp reduction in unemployment, soon enough. The expansion ends with a sharp decline in the hours, which will give way to a sharp increase in unemployment during the subsequent recession. You are going to be surprised by how well this figure works.

Figure 16.5 depicts this cycle for five of the expansions. The dark lines with diamond markers represent the data on the hours and unemployment during the expansion from the NBER trough to the NBER peak. The NBER trough date is indicated in the title, for example, 1954 Q2 in the first figure. The light lines with square markers represent the data during the contractions, from NBER peak to NBER trough. In four of these cases, these data begin at the upper left in these diagrams with high

---

[1] The focus here on manufacturing is for two reasons: It is manufacturing that contributes most to the layoffs during recessions and in many sectors outside of manufacturing it is difficult to measure hours worked.

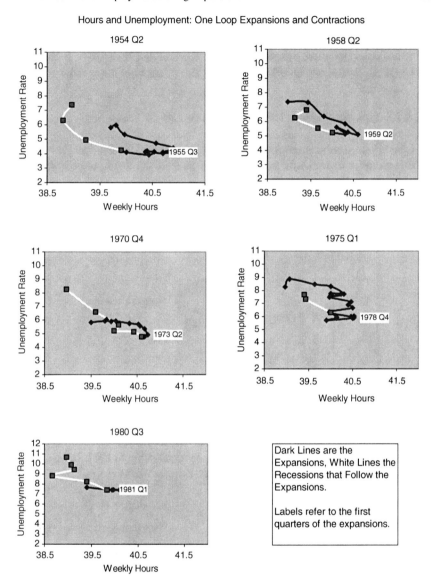

Fig. 16.5 Cycles in weekly hours and unemployment

unemployment and low weekly hours. As the expansion progresses, the numbers find their way toward the lower right, but at the end, turn toward the lower left, tracing out the promised lying-down U. The unemployment plateaus that we discovered in the previous chapter are the strings of quarters at the ends of these expansions when the unemployment rate is constant but the weekly hours are declining. Since the weekly hours are declining, we need a better word than "plateau," which

suggests stability. Call it the Autumn of the expansion. A time when everyone is
still working, but not as hard as during the Spring planting and Summer harvesting.

One exception to the general pattern of renewal and senescence is the aborted
1980 Q3 expansion, which did not last long enough to trace out a path.

16.1.3.1 Four Expansions have Extra Loops

For the US economy, autumn is not always followed by winter. The three long expansions had a second Life tracing out the path of the hours and unemployment
depicted in the figure below.

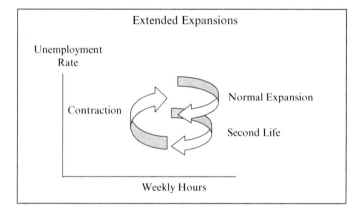

It was not just the three long expansions that had a second Life. The Truman
expansion depicted in Fig. 16.6 appeared to be terminating in 1951, but experienced
a rebirth in 1952. Are you thinking about the Korean War? I am.

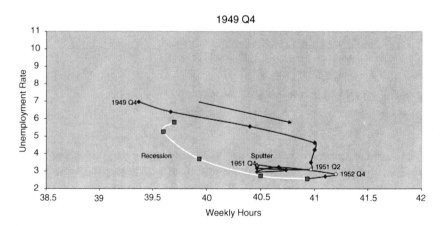

Fig. 16.6 Truman cycle

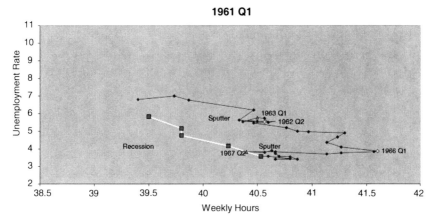

Fig. 16.7 Kennedy/Johnson cycle

The Kennedy/Johnson Expansion depicted in Fig. 16.7 had some troubles in 1962/1963, which I will count as loop. This was a three-loop expansion. The Reagan Expansion in Fig. 16.8 had a second loop, and the Bush/Clinton expansion depicted in Fig. 16.9 had three loops, though the third is not as well defined as the first and second.

What caused these extra loops? We need to find an answer.

And just when you think you understand, something different happens. The Bush W. expansion depicted in Fig. 16.10 is different from the others in two respects. First, the variability of unemployment and the hours is much more compressed than in the previous expansions and I have used a different scale, so we can see what has been happening. Second, the loops created by the relatively rapid and early

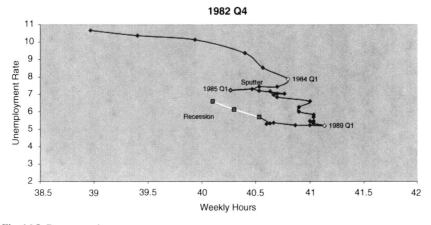

Fig. 16.8 Reagan cycle

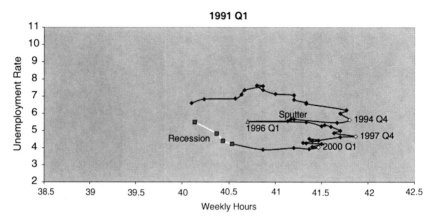

Fig. 16.9 Bush/Clinton cycle

movement of hours per week in manufacturing are not so evident here, especially in the lower right, which has the unemployment rate in 2006 elevating before a decline in weekly hours in manufacturing. We have been arguing since December 2005 that something new is happening. If you recall, we discussed in Chap. 8 the fact that most of the job loss in recessions comes from manufacturing and construction. The recession story in manufacturing is V, V, V... Trim and fatten, trim and fatten... The first stroke of the V is layoffs of about 8% of workers, and the second stroke is hiring them all back a year or two later. The 2001 downturn gave us an L, not a V. We trimmed 3 million jobs in manufacturing but not one of them has come back. Without the fattening, it does not seem likely that manufacturing is positioned to contribute much to the weakness in the labor market if we have a

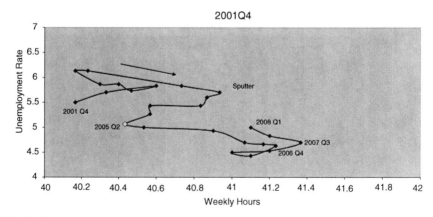

Fig. 16.10 The Bush W. Cycle, through 2008 Q1

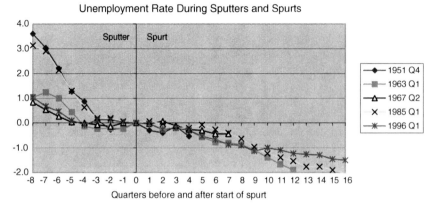

Fig. 16.11 Unemployment rate during sputters and spurts

recession in 2008, which is unlikely to occur without a contribution of job loss from manufacturing.

16.1.4 Spurt Comparison Graphs

16.1.4.1 Unemployment

To study these sputters and spurts, we will use side-by-side comparison graphs with period 0 representing the trough of the sputter and period 1 representing the first quarter of the spurt. The first two comparison figures provide another look at the unemployment and hours data we have already explored with the cycle diagrams. These two spurt comparison graphs reveal things that we have already learned, but something new as well. What we did not learn from the cycle diagrams is the extreme similarity of the paths of the unemployment rate over the five sputters and spurts depicted in Fig. 16.11. Prior to the sputter, the unemployment rate was falling rapidly but stabilized during the sputter. It remained at about the same level for several quarters into the spurt, and then fell rapidly for a couple of years.

16.1.4.2 GDP

It should be expected that GDP growth was weak during the sputters and strong during the spurts. Indeed that is the case, but not so much as you might expect. Figure 16.12 has 5-quarter moving averages of GDP growth. As we take a look at GDP growth depicted in this figure, we should keep in mind that US growth has averaged a little less than 3.5% since 1948 and a little more than 3% per year since

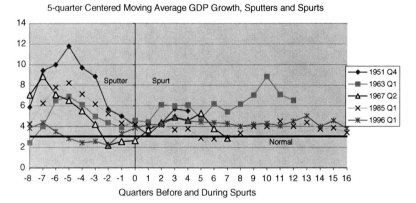

Fig. 16.12 GDP growth during the sputters and spurts

1970. The corresponding numbers for employment growth are 1.6% since 1948 and 1.7% since 1970. Thus a normal growth in the range of 3–3.5% is enough to generate increases in jobs at the rate of 1.6–1.7% and to keep the unemployment rate about constant. Economic growth in excess of 4% would normally be strong enough to encourage firms to hire more workers more rapidly than normal and the unemployment rate would fall. Growth much less than the 3% figure is too weak for the jobs to keep up with the new entrants into the labor market, and unemployment has a tendency to rise. This 3% normal growth is depicted in the figure with a solid horizontal line. Surprise, the 5-quarter moving average is above the 3% line almost always during the sputters as well as the spurts. But the sputter is not an actual downturn. It is a threatened downturn. In every case, there is a sharp drop in growth going into the sputter. The leveling off of the unemployment rate in the year before the spurt was presumably caused by this sharp drop in GDP growth, though the growth numbers in two of these episodes were still around 4%. The spurts had GDP growth at 4% and above, though the Reagan Spurt took a couple of years before those numbers were achieved. Look back at Fig. 16.11, and you can see that the Reagan spurt did not really get going for about 8 quarters, even though weekly hours started to drift upward in 1986 Q1.

16.2 What Caused the Spurts?

The first step toward finding what caused the spurts is to settle on the dates at which the spurts commenced. The National Bureau of Economic Research cycle peak and cycle trough dates and my spurts dates from the previous section are recorded in the table below for the four expansions with spurts. For example, a cycle trough of 1949 Q4 and a cycle peak of 1953 Q2 define the Truman expansion per the NBER. But this Truman expansion was sputtering from 1951 Q2 to

Table 16.2 Four Expansions with sputters and spurts

	Youth	Spurt	Demise
Truman expansion			
Trough	**1949 Q4**	1951 Q4	
Peak	1951 Q2	1952 Q4	**1953 Q2**
Kennedy/Johnson expansion			
Trough	**1961 Q1**	1963 Q1/1967 Q2	
Peak	1962 Q2	1966 Q1/1969 Q1	**1969 Q4**
Reagan expansion			
Trough	**1982 Q4**	1985 Q1	
Peak	1984 Q1	1989 Q1	**1990 Q3**
Bush/Clinton expansion			
Trough	**1991 Q1**	1996 Q1	
Peak	1994 Q4	2000 Q1	**2001 Q1**

Note: The dates of the 1951 Q4 trough and the 2000 Q1 peak are somewhat ambiguous
Official NBER cycle trough and cycle peak in bold.

1951 Q4, when it was rejuvenated by the Truman spurt, which peaked in 1952 Q4, at which time the expansion started a decline from which it never recovered. The NBER official death notice for this expansion is dated two quarters later in 1953 Q2 (Table 16.2).

16.2.1 A Big Fiscal Stimulus Has Three Times Rejuvenated a Sputtering Economy

16.2.1.1 Department of Defense Spending Drove the Truman and Johnson Spurts

Fig. 16.13 illustrates two of the most important sources of growth surges and slow-downs: residential investment and defense spending. The shaded regions represent the contribution of residential investment to GDP growth and the line the contribution of defense spending. These numbers should be compared with normal growth of about 3%.

The housing contribution in almost all the recessions has been about -1%. Two of the ten recessions occurred without a big drag from housing: the 1953 Department of Defense downturn and the 2001 "business" downturn. (You can see in this picture: a huge -2.5 from the DOD in 1953/1954.)

The housing sector has been troubled three different times (1951, 1963, and 1967). In 1951 and 1967, the spending by the DOD completely offset the weakness in housing.

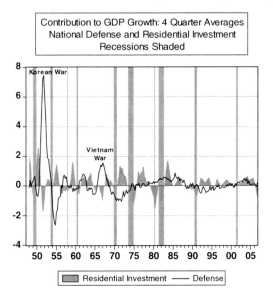

Fig. 16.13 Defense and housing contribution to GDP

16.2.1.2 A Tax Cut Played a Role in the Kennedy Spurt

In the fourth quarter of the Kennedy spurt, there was a massive tax cut, reducing revenues by 2% of GDP. Figure 16.14 reveals that this was the only tax cut that occurred during a spurt. The timing of this tax reduction seems a little off, but maybe you can tell a story about how the economy anticipated the stimulus by a couple of quarters. After all, it was not a mystery that it was in the works.

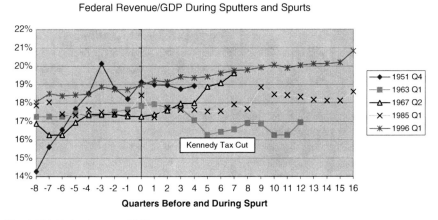

Fig. 16.14 Federal revenue/GDP

To put that into perspective, the Kennedy Tax Cut of 1964 was 1.9% of National Income. That compares with 1.4% of National Income for the Reagan Tax Cuts of 1981 and 2% for the Bush cuts of 2001–2003. It seems as though the Kennedy Tax Cut might have helped a sputtering economy, but the Reagan and Bush cuts came at the very beginning of economic expansions. If you look very closely at the real GDP display in the previous chapter, you will notice that the Reagan expansion got off to a pretty good start, possibly stimulated by the tax cuts, but the Bush expansion has been weak and is hardly a poster child for the effects of tax cuts on economic growth. Remember that GDP growth has been in a very narrow corridor rising at 3% per year. It appears as though fiscal and monetary policy have an impact on the timing of recessions, but they have no discernable effect on the long-run growth.

Tax legislation	Tax cut in billions of current dollars[a]	Tax cut in billions of constant 2003 dollars	Tax cut as a percent of national income[b]	Surplus or deficit (−) as a percentage of national income[b]
The Kennedy Tax Cuts – Revenue Act of 1964	−$11.5	−$54.9	−1.9%	−1.0%
The Reagan Tax Cuts – The Economic Recovery Tax Act of 1981	−$38.3	−$68.7	−1.4%	−2.8%
The Bush Tax Cuts –				
The Economic Growth and Tax Reform Reconciliation Act of 2001	−$73.8	−$75.8	−0.8%	1.5%
The Job Creation and Worker Assistance Act of 2002	−$51.2	−$52.0	−0.6%	−1.7%
2003 Bush/Thomas Proposal (as of May 5, 2003)	−$60.3	−$60.3	−0.6%	−3.2%
The Bush Tax Cuts if Combined in 2003	NA	−$188.1	−2.0%	—

[a] First year estimate
[b] National Income as measured by Net National Product
Source: http://www.taxfoundation.org/ff/taxcutperspective.html

16.2.2 The Reagan Spurt Was Helped by Falling Interest Rates, Falling Oil Prices and a Falling Value of the Dollar (Which Stimulated Exports)

Figure 16.15 compares the short-term interest rates during the sputters and spurts. Only once was there a reduction of interest rates coincident with a spurt. That was during the Reagan spurt, when monetary policy was highly stimulative, reducing short-term rates by 300 basis points (3 percentage points).

Figure 16.16 reveals that a fall in crude oil prices helped the Reagan spurt, and possibly the Clinton spurt too.

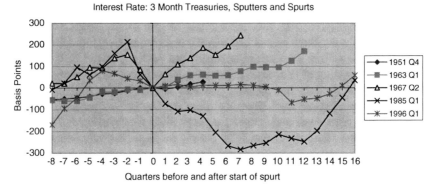

Fig. 16.15 Interest rates on 3-month treasuries

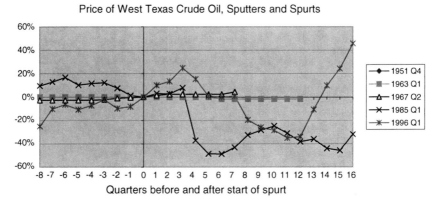

Fig. 16.16 Oil Prices during sputters and spurts

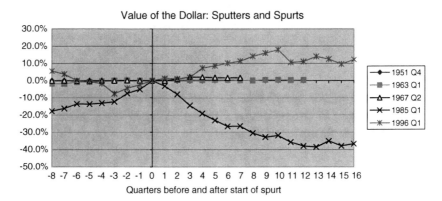

Fig. 16.17 Value of the dollar

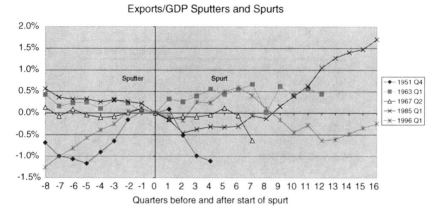

Fig. 16.18 Exports during sputters and spurts

A declining value of the dollar by 40% during the Reagan spurt (Fig. 16.17) helped US exports/GDP grow by 2% points late in the Reagan spurt (Fig. 16.18).

16.2.3 Animal Spirits and the Mad Dash for the Web Drove the Clinton Spurt

The share of spending on equipment and software (Fig. 16.19) rose by 1% point during both the Kennedy and the Clinton spurts. The Kennedy investment boom may have come from the Kennedy tax cut. The Clinton investment boom was surely a search for profits on the Internet.

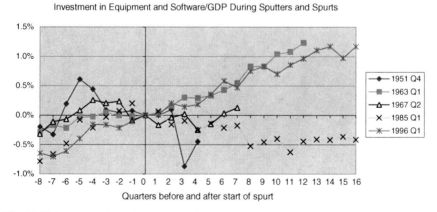

Fig. 16.19 Investment in equipment and software

Appendix: Presidents and Fed Chairmen

	Start year/Start Date
Presidents of the United States	
Harry S. Truman	1945
Dwight David Eisenhower	1953
John Fitzgerald Kennedy	1961
Lyndon Baines Johnson	1963
Richard Milhous Nixon	1969
Gerald Rudolph Ford	1974
James Earl Carter	1977
Ronald Wilson Reagan	1981
George Herbert Walker Bush	1989
William Jefferson Clinton	1993
George W. Bush	2001
Chairmen of the Federal Reserve	
Thomas B. McCabe	15 April 1948
Wm. McC. Martin, Jr.	2 April 1951
Arthur F. Burns	1 February 1970
G. William Miller	8 March 1978
Paul A. Volcker	6 August 1979
Alan Greenspan	11 August 1987
Benjamin Bernark	1 February 2006

Part V
The Longer Run: Savings, Investment, Government Borrowing, Foreign Lending and Your Home

Chapter 17
Savings and Investment

Up to this point, we have been looking a year or two ahead, trying to figure out when that next recession will arrive, and what the downturn is going to do to your pocketbook, if you are not prepared. Now we put on a different pair of glasses and look farther into the future, focusing on your retirement, and on the well-being of your children and your grandchildren.

We prepare for the future economically by saving and investing. If we are worried about the future, instead of spending all of our earnings on wild parties and the latest fashion, we may choose to put a little away for future purchases. That is savings. When we put that money into a savings account, it will find its way to the investors who use the loans to finance the creation of new productive assets such as new factories, office buildings, and shopping centers. That is investment.

17.1 The NIPA Definition of Savings: It Is Not What You Think

17.1.1 Investments Are New Homes, New Offices, New Factories, and New Equipment

Our first order of business is to get clear the difference between financial investments and real investment.

When it comes to preparing for the future, there is something very different between an individual and us collectively. You, as an individual, can prepare for the future by growing your financial assets – your bank account, your mutual funds, your 401 K, and other retirement accounts. But the values you place on those financial assets are just numbers on your computer hard drive. We cannot collectively prepare for the future merely by growing numbers on our computer files. We need real productive assets to back up those numbers. We need factories, office buildings, homes, and knowledge. It is these real assets that will allow workers in the future to produce enough to support your lavish life styles when you retire and to leave enough leftover to take care of the working people and their children.

E. E. Leamer, *Macroeconomic Patterns and Stories: A Guide for MBAs.*
© Springer-Verlag Berlin Heidelberg 2009

Although they are just numbers on computers, we rely on the accounting numbers collectively to tell us whether we are saving enough to prepare for rainy days and for our retirements. Those accounting numbers are pretty much all we have. For that reason, we are totally at the mercy of the financial system, when we prepare for the future. Those numbers should grow only as we accumulate the real productive assets that will contribute to greater material well-being in the future. But in a financial bubble, financial wealth can grow rapidly even though the future is not all that great.

In addition to telling us how wealthy we are, when we put aside some money each year into our retirement accounts, we rely on the financial system to use that money to fund new investments in real assets – factories and homes and office buildings – to grow our wealth as rapidly as possible. More important than that, we rely on the financial system accurately to predict the effect of today's investments on GDP 20 years from now, or 30 years, depending on when we are retiring. That's the real rate of return. To decide how much savings is adequate, we need to know the real rate of return. As a forecaster, I can tell you it is hard to see more than a year ahead, and 20 is far into a foggy future.

It is not surprising that the financial system does not always do a great job at its three primary tasks: accurately valuing current assets, finding the best investments, and telling us what is the real rate of return for new savings. During the Internet Rush, our hard-earned savings funded lavish parties in Las Vegas to promote the latest dot-com business plan, and equities markets told us to expect rates of return as high as 20% per year or more. With those rates of return, we could support our future retirements with very little savings.

Reality and reason reappeared eventually. When the stock market correction occurred in 2000 and 2001, newspapers reported "7 Trillion Dollars in Wealth Destroyed." But if you had toured America, you would not have found any flooded homes, or any factories burned down. Nothing was destroyed except for our delusions. All that changed were some numbers on computer hard drives. But those numbers are absolutely critical. They tell us if we are adequately preparing for the future. As it turned out, we were not really as wealthy as we imagined, and the future is not what it used to be.

Thus do not forget: When we speak of investments, we do not mean your shares of a mutual fund. We mean the factories and equipment that are needed to produce the GDP of the future. Your mutual fund shares are only a shadow of those real assets, a shadow that is sometimes longer and sometimes shorter than the real thing.

17.1.2 Flows and Not Stocks

A second vocabulary lesson concerns the distinction between stocks and flows. When you speak of your savings and investments you are probably talking about the value of your assets. But we will need to use those words to refer to how much you add to those assets each year. One is a stock and the other a flow.

Better get very clear, the difference between a stock and a flow. It is the difference between how much water is in the reservoir and how much is flowing into the reservoir. The first is a "stock" measured in gallons, and the other is a flow measured in gallons per month. When you and I talk about our savings, we are usually discussing a stock: how much is in our accounts. But here and everywhere else in this book, we will do what economists do, and use the word "saving" to refer to a flow: dollars per year added to our accounts.

Stocks may be more accurately measured than flows. I have a pretty good idea how much is in my retirement accounts, and I have a vague idea of how much my home is worth. Those are stocks, and not flows. Savings as defined by economists and national income accountants is a flow, measured in dollars per year, not a stock measured in dollars.[1] I personally do not keep track of savings in that sense: I really do not have a good idea of how much extra I stash away each year to prepare for the future.

17.1.3 Savings Depends on What Consumption Is

Although I do not keep track of my savings and you probably do not keep track of yours, our federal government tries to do the job. Remember the national income accounting identity:

$$GDP = C + I + G + (X - M),$$

where C is consumption, I investment, G government, X exports, and M imports. We can use this definition to find an expression for national savings. Savings is what we earn minus what we spend on consumption. To estimate savings, we begin by finding out how much we earn. That would be GDP. The P in GDP stands for production, of course, and GDP is what we produce, but it is also what we earn, as every penny of the value of production is dispersed to workers or to lenders or to owners. Even goods produced but not sold are counted as earnings of shareholders. What we spend for current consumption is C plus G, C referring to the meals and clothing that we buy and G referring to government services.[2]

Thus our accountants define national savings as:

Gross National Savings = Earnings − Spending for Current Consumption
$$= GDP - C - G$$

If you try to compute your own savings by this definition be careful of what you subtract from earnings. Subtract from your earnings the money you spent on fast food, but do not subtract the money spent on remodeling your home. That is part of Investment. That is not current consumption. What about the car you bought? Isn't that an investment too? Well, yes, but that is not the way the government accountants

---

[1] Incidentally, GDP is a flow too, not a stock. That is production *per year.*

[2] A small portion of G is actually government investment.

do it. Spending on consumer durables is included in consumption C and subtracted
from GDP, to compute national savings. But then, if that vehicle is purchased by
a business, it is counted as part of Investment. Why is that? Well, life is full of
compromises. One has to draw the line between C and I somewhere. Investment
(I) is the acquisition of an asset that will yield a flow of services into the future,
like a new house. Consumption (C) is spending that yields pleasure only the day the
spending occurs. The borderline between these two is impossibly fuzzy. If we let you
include your automobile as an investment, someone else will want to include their
vitamins and their steroids, and someone else will want to include their vacation to
Mexico, the pleasant thoughts of which linger on and on.

Though we are not going to count your new vehicle as an investment, we will
count the new vehicles purchased by businesses. That is part of their "inventories."
If you want your automobile to count as investment, lease it. Then the asset remains on the balance sheets of business and our Bureau of Economic Analysis
will count it as an investment. (Compromises always involve inconsistencies, don't
they?)

For a University faculty member, the biggest error the BEA makes is that school-
ing is not considered as an investment. There may be some students who are earning
their MBAs strictly for the amusement value of the classes, but most are there to ac-
quire the skills and knowledge that will allow them to be more productive in the
future. But educational spending in our national accounts is counted as "consumption" and not "investment."

Granted, there may be some difficulties separating education spending into investment and childcare, but there is nothing gray about spending by businesses on
Research and Development. That is clearly investment. But the Bureau of Economic
Analysis treats research and development spending as a current business expense,
no different from the nightly cleaning of the buildings.[3]

Understand also that, capital gains are not part of savings, just as they are not part
of GDP. The retained earnings of the corporations in which you have invested are
part of earnings, but the capital gains on your mutual funds are not included. The
housing services of the home you own are included in earnings and called "owner-
equivalent rent" but the capital gain on your home is not included.[4]

OK, but what if you discover a pot of gold under the tree in your backyard?
That's earnings, isn't it? Is this part of GDP? Maybe and maybe not. If you have

---

[3] The BEA is undertaking studies to account for R&D as an investment, not as an expense. See
http://www.bea.gov/bea/an/1194od/maintext.htm.

[4] Actually, now that I think about this, the capital gains and losses on homes might be included
in GDP, they just net out to zero. You can book the increased value of your home as part of your
personal earnings, but exactly offsetting that gain is the loss suffered by the nice young couple who
will be buying your home in the future, and who will be paying that ridiculously high price. Thus,
when the price of your home elevates, that is not production, that is only a transfer out of their
pockets and into yours. Unless you have done some remodeling, the change in the value of your
home is only an accounting number and has no material manifestation. It is the same land and the
same structure that it was last year, and it will provide the same housing services in the future that
it did last year. No real savings there, and no real investment. Only a number on your computer
hard drive.

hired contractors to search your land for a pot of gold, the salaries you pay them are part of GDP, whether they discover gold or not, and if you are in the business of searching for gold, the value of the gold you discover is also part of GDP, but if your 5-year-old son stumbled onto that pot of gold at the end of the rainbow, that's not part of GDP.[5] Of course, if you insist, you can report your child's gold discovery to the IRS as taxable earnings. Then we will include it.

Remember the P-word in GDP: "production." To be included in GDP, there has to be someone working and there have to be recordable sales and recordable earnings. That means that the flashes of brilliance that got Google started are not included when they occur, and never included at their full values. What gets included in GDP are Google *earnings* when the earnings occur, if they occur. As the Google earnings flow through ad revenue, Google is treated as if it were a new way to distribute ads, and the value that you and I receive from its search engine is totally ignored, because we are not charged for it. By relying on "market values," we are missing a lot of Internet-related services that are distributed free to the users.

The bottom line is this: The measurement of GDP and savings can be done pretty well for a manufacturing society where the assets and the products are material and the work is physical: workers operating equipment in factories making shirts delivered in trucks. But we cannot measure GDP or savings very accurately in a knowledge economy in which the assets are ideas and skills, the work is thinking, and the product is advice delivered electronically.

Conclusion: this is pretty confusing. It contributes to poor collective planning for our aging America.

17.1.3.1 Do not Forget Depreciation

For deciding if savings is adequate, be sure to remove depreciation. The reason that the savings net of depreciation is the relevant concept is that you are only growing your nest egg if savings exceed depreciation.

Many of us, when we stop to think about our savings, ignore depreciation, but you do not if you lease the car. The monthly payment when you lease a car is partly a finance charge that depends on the rate of interest and partly a charge for depreciation, paying for the fact that when you turn the car back in at the end of the lease, it will be worth a lot less in the used market.[6] If you lease, each month you are forced to pull out of your earnings enough to offset that depreciation. If you buy the car with borrowed money, your monthly payment will be only the finance charge.[7] Then you may forget about the depreciation. If you buy it with cash, there is no monthly payment at all and you may ignore both the depreciation and the foregone earnings on that cash.

---

[5] The treatment of natural disasters such as hurricanes and floods raises similar issue. For the BEA treatment of these consult http://www.bea.gov/bea/faq/national/disasters_faq.pdf.

[6] There also is a fee for the "option" to buy/return the car in the future.

[7] Thanks to David Moskowitz, EMBA 2007, for helping me get this right.

Table 17.1 Accounting for US savings
Savings 2004 [Billions of dollars]

Bureau of Economic Analysis	
Gross saving	1,572.0
Net saving	136.8
Net private saving	549.1
Personal saving	151.8
Undistributed corporate profits with inventory valuation and capital consumption adjustments	397.3
Net government saving	−412.3
Consumption of fixed capital	1,435.3
Private	1,206.2
Domestic business	973.3
Households and institutions	232.8
Government	229.1

17.2 Do We Save Enough?

17.2.1 US Savings in 2004

Ignoring all the previous qualifications about the measurement issues, data on US savings in 2004 are reported in Table 17.1. Net savings of $136.8 billion consists of gross savings of $1,572 billion minus $1,435.3 of depreciation.

The pittance of net savings of the United States is composed of $549 billion of private savings offset by −$412.3 billion of dissaving done by our governments. More on this is in the next chapter. Net saving as a fraction of net domestic product is illustrated in Fig. 17.1. There has been a long decline in this savings rate from around 12% in the 1960s to only 1% today.

17.2.2 How Much Should We Save?

Is a 1% savings rate enough? To get us thinking about this, I propose we answer a different question: Should your savings depend on the interest rate? The bond market, which is now offering 10-year Treasuries paying only 4.5%, is telling us not to expect the rates of return to which we had become accustomed in the 1990s. So what should we do? Faced with lower rates of return, should we save less or save more? You are probably thinking less. Why save when the rate of return to saving is so low? If that is what you are thinking, better think again.[8]

---

[8] If jargon is what you like, the lowered interest rate creates an income and a substitution effect. The lower interest rate means that to get more current consumption you need to give up less future consumption – thus, there is a substitution effect in favor of current consumption. The lower interest rate also means your income can support a lower stream of consumption. The income effect dictates

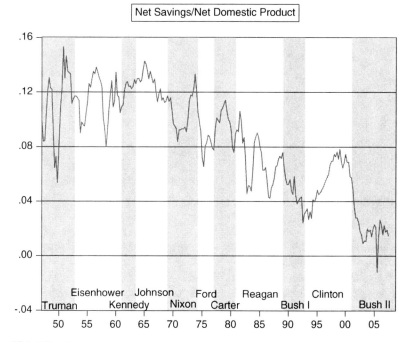

Fig. 17.1 US savings

The reason we need to save more and not less is that we are an aging society. When the baby boomers start to retire in 2010, the fraction of the population over the age of 65 is going to elevate from 13% to 21% in 20 years. (Fig. 17.2) We are going to need to accumulate the assets required to pay for the retirement benefits that will be demanded by that growing group of elderly and their powerful AARP lobby. To fund all those benefits, if the rate of return falls, we need to save more and not less, for then we cannot rely on the financial markets to create our nest egg through the magic of compound interest.

Figure 17.3 illustrates the kind of choices that we face. Here it is assumed that a working American at age 40 is expecting no increase in real earnings until retirement at age 65. This American is expecting to live until age 85 and therefore needs to accumulate assets to support 20 years of retirement. The savings plan is to keep consumption levels the same throughout the 25 working years and the 20 retirement years. What fraction of earnings needs to be saved to accomplish this plan? That is the question answered by Fig. 17.3. If the real rate of return is 12%, then saving 5% of income will do. But a 12% real rate of return is much higher than we can reasonably expect. If the real rate of return (adjusted for inflation) is 3%, which is about what it seems to be as I write this, then you would need to put away 30% of

---

lower consumption at every point in the life cycle. The question is which dominates: the income effect toward more savings or the consumption effect toward less.

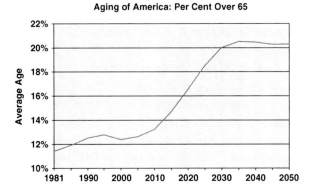

Fig. 17.2 Fraction of Americans over the age of 65

income to accomplish this plan. That is a whopping increase in savings; From 5% to 30% of current income.

This plan, of course, does not fit exactly. Many young Americans can expect increases in real earnings in the future, and they can grow their retirement nest egg when their earnings are greater. Many will need to spend less when they are retired. But whatever your situation may be, I think that you are startled by the numbers reported in Fig. 17.3. Faced with the unpleasant surprise that retirement planning might require such a high level of savings, most of you are going to want to put away more.

17.2.3 Do We Save Enough?

Compare Figs. 17.3 and 17.1, and answer the question: Is that tiny 2% savings rate enough? As we are an aging population and we need to accumulate some retirement

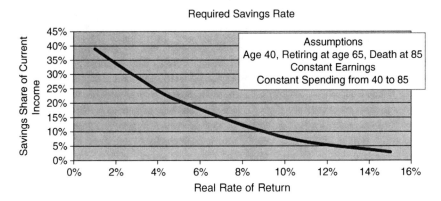

Fig. 17.3 Retirement planning and real interest rates

assets, we should be concerned by the decline in the net national savings rate in the early 1980s, from around 10% to around 6%, and we should be positively alarmed by the dip of the net savings rate to around 2% in the aftermath of the 2001 recession. How pathetic is that?

That low national savings rate promises a difficult future when there will be a lot of surprised and unhappy retirees, or a lot of angry working people who will be squeezed to pay taxes to support the retirement benefits of the "Consumption Generation" – the one that followed the "Greatest Generation." (Being firmly part of the consumption generation, I want in advance to thank all of you in the next generation, for taking care of me in my dotage.)

It seems pretty clear to me that we have a problem with low savings, but the iron rule of economics is that, for every strongly held opinion there is an equal and opposite strongly held opinion. Most notably, Larry Kotlikoff of Boston University is marketing a retirement planning tool that calls for much lower savings than the tools used by most financial planners. And using a complicated model not unlike the one embodied in Kotlikoff's planner, Scholz and coauthors find: "Fewer than 20 percent of households have less wealth than their optimal targets, and the wealth deficit of those who are undersaving is generally small."[9]

17.3 Another Important Accounting Identity: Savings = Investment

Now that we know what savings is, we can turn our attention to investment. Out of your current income, that which you do not spend will find its way into a bank deposit, or into a mutual fund or into your mattress. The bank deposit, the mutual fund, and your mattress are all investment options. Thus your savings = your investment. That must be true for each individual and for us collectively.

We can confirm that savings = investment for us collectively, using the national income accounting identity again: $GDP = C + I + G + X - M$. Subtract from both sides of this accounting identity $C + G$ to find

$$\text{Savings} = \text{Investment}$$
$$GDP - C - G = I + X - M$$

Oh, oh, this looks like savings equals investment plus the surplus of exports over imports. Something did not turn out right here. Actually, we are in good shape. That $X - M$ is a foreign investment. When exports exceed imports, we must create external balance by *importing* pieces of paper – promises by foreigners to pay for our exports later. When imports exceed exports, we are creating external balance by *exporting* pieces of paper – promises to pay for our imports later. Thus, the

---

[9] Scholz, John Karl, Ananth Seshadri and Surachai Khitatrakun "Are Americans Saving 'Optimally' for Retirement?", *Journal of Political Economy*, 2006, vol. 114, no. 4. 607–643.

equation above says that total national savings is used to fund domestic investment plus foreign investment.

There is one more accounting adjustment that can be made to allow us to distinguish private from government savings. Letting Tx represent taxes, and Tr represent transfers (Social Security and Medicare, especially), we can add and subtract Tx and Tr from savings to separate private from government savings:

$$\text{Savings} = \text{GDP} - \text{C} - \text{G} = (\text{GDP} + \text{Tr} - \text{Tx} - \text{C}) + (\text{Tx} - \text{G} - \text{Tr})$$
$$= \text{private savings} + \text{government savings}$$

Thus, total savings is private savings (total earnings including transfers net of taxes minus consumption spending) plus public savings[10] (Taxes minus government spending minus transfers).

Now we have what we the following very interesting accounting identity, which we can put into a box to help us find it again:

$$\text{Savings} = \text{Investment}$$
$$(\text{GDP} + \text{Tr} - \text{C} - \text{Tx}) + (\text{Tx} - \text{G} - \text{Tr}) = \text{I} + (\text{X} - \text{M})$$
$$\text{Private savings} + \text{Gov. Savings} = \text{Domestic Invest.} + \text{Foreign Invest.}$$

By the way, make sure you understand that the Foreign Investment term in this accounting identity is us investing in foreign countries, not foreign investors buying our assets.

17.3.1 US Savings and Investment

The next four figures depict aspects of this accounting identity. When you look at these figures, it may be useful to refer back to the accounting identity in the box above. Figure 17.4 separates total savings into private and federal government savings, the two components on the left in the accounting identity. Figure 17.5 illustrates the gap between domestic investment and total savings: it turns out that we do not save enough to fund our domestic investment. Confirm in the accounting identity that, if savings is less than domestic investment then "foreign investment" must be negative, meaning that we finance our investment by borrowing from abroad. Figure 17.5, therefore, expresses the gap between savings and investment in terms of the external imbalance, $\text{X} - \text{M}$, the current account. Figure 17.7 reveals the consequence of this dependence on foreign lending by illustrating the fraction of net domestic investment that is financed by foreigners and, in that sense, is owned by them, not us.

In Fig. 17.4, we see that declines in both private and public savings have contributed to a substantial decline in net national savings. Since 1985, private savings as a fraction of net domestic product has been declining ominously from

---

[10] The public savings is usually negative and usually called the public deficit.

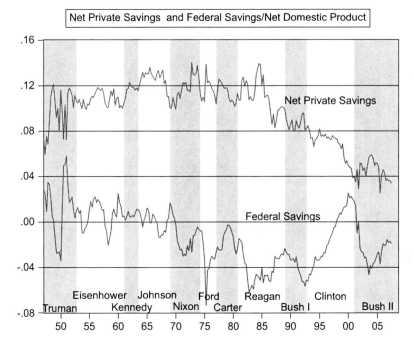

Fig. 17.4 Private and public savings

around 11 to 4%. Layered onto that decline, are the Federal government deficits (negative savings) that emerged in the Nixon presidency, and became persistently −4% of GDP during the Reagan presidency. The big recent news is that the Clinton administration reduced spending as a share of GDP and benefited from a surge in tax revenues during the Internet Rush, which turned the Federal deficit into a surplus. But the recession of 2001 and the Bush II tax cuts ended those surpluses abruptly.

Figure 17.5 reveals that domestic investment has had its ups and downs during the business cycle, and has a slight tendency to decline over time.[11] Also in Fig. 17.5, we can see that there was generally a slight excess of savings over investment from 1947 until the 1980s.

Three views of the inadequacy of domestic savings to finance domestic investment are offered. The gap is plotted directly in Fig. 17.5. Exactly the same gap is labeled "the current account" in Fig. 17.6. (The gap between domestic investment and domestic savings is, per the accounting identity, equal to foreign borrowing.) And, in Fig. 17.7, the foreign borrowing is expressed as a fraction of net domestic

---

[11] Can you think of reasons why net investment as a share of net domestic product, might decline. Here are some that I thought of: (1) The US has a mature economy with fewer investment opportunities. (2) Falling computer prices that allow a smaller amount of money to buy more computing power. (3) Rapid technological obsolescence of computers means more rapid depreciation. (4) The US has shifted from material investments to immaterial intellectual assets as a way to grow (That, incidentally, raises the important question: are our accounting systems up to the task of measuring our postindustrial economy?)

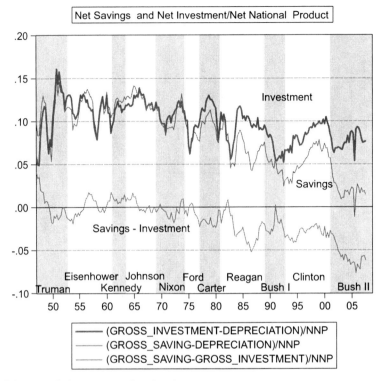

Fig. 17.5 Domestic investment and total savings

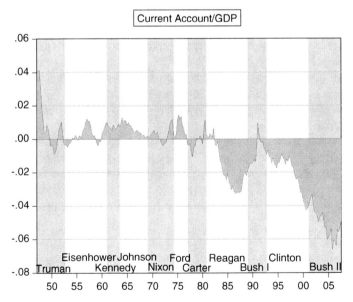

Fig. 17.6 Dependence on foreign borrowing: current account

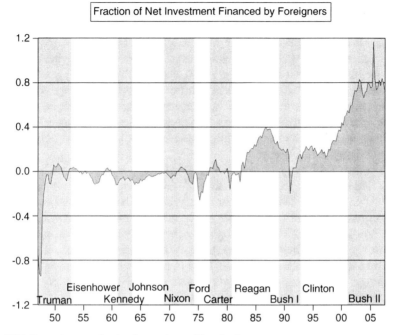

Fig. 17.7 Dependence on foreign borrowing: selling the future

investment to indicate what fraction of net investment is financed by foreigners. That's up to 80%, an alarmingly high number. This means a substantial fraction of US growth is starting to accrue to foreigners who are providing the financing.

17.3.2 What If There Is a Big Tax Cut and Public Savings Declines?

The accounting identity

Private savings + Public savings = Domestic Investment + Foreign Investment

can help us think about answers to an important "what if?" question: what if there is a big tax cut?. This accounting identity suggests three possible responses to a tax cut assuming that leads to a decline in public savings. Private savings can increase to make up for the decline in public savings, or one of the components on the investment side can decline: either domestic investment can decline or foreign investment can decline.

1. Crowding Out: The "*Crowding Out*" hypothesis is that the rise in public borrowing leaves less savings available to fund domestic investment. The route by which this would happen is through higher interest rates, with the government

out-competing the private sector for loanable funds. With a large and growing global market for loanable funds, this possibility seems pretty remote.

2. Ricardian Equivalence: Another possibility is that the private sector recognizes that the increase in public borrowing means that taxes will be higher in the future to pay the interest and to retire the debt. Faced with that future tax liability, the private sector increases its savings to offset the public dissaving. That is called *Ricardian Equivalence* after the classical economist, David Ricardo, who floated the idea in the nineteenth century. But taxpayers seem hardly capable of doing the hard work to estimate their future taxes and save accordingly. This possibility seems pretty unlikely too.

3. Twin Deficits: The third possibility is that foreign investment makes up for the decline in savings. Instead of calling $X - M$ "foreign investment," it might be better to call $M - X$ "foreign borrowing" as we seem mostly to be running an external deficit and to be growing our indebtedness to foreigners. If the pool of foreign savings is large enough, the increased public borrowing would not raise the interest rates, and domestic investment would stay the same. Then the increased public borrowing would have to mean that we borrow more from foreigners. That is the so-called "*Twin-Deficits*" hypothesis: our federal government is borrowing directly or indirectly from foreigners.

4. Laffer[12] Magic: Some suggest that there is a fourth possibility, *Laffer magic*. The tax cut will stimulate domestic investment and increase GDP. With higher GDP will come greater tax revenues, more than offsetting the effect of the lower tax rates. Thus a reduction in tax rates has such a favorable effect on the performance of the economy that all four items in the accounting identity grow: more domestic investment, more foreign investment, more private savings, and even more public savings. Do not count on this any time soon. In the longer run, increased investment and greater work effort help the economy grow and increase tax revenues even at lower tax rates. But in the short run, with GDP pretty much held fixed, we are faced with the reality of that accounting identity: more private savings, more reliance on foreign borrowing or less investment. And for the

---

[12] Economist Arthur Laffer drew a curve of tax revenues as a function of tax rates on a napkin over dinner with his Republican pals. He showed them zero revenue if rates are zero, and zero revenue if rates are 100%, with a peak of revenues somewhere between those poles. Who can question that? It reminds me of the story of the travelers lost in a balloon who hollered down for directions. The fellow below hollered back "You're up there." One of the travelers hollered back: "You're an economist, aren't you?" "Yes, but how did you know." "You answered very quickly, and what you said was absolutely true, but completely useless."

The same Arthur Laffer in a Wall Street Journal op-ed piece went for the Ricardian equivalence hypothesis for the latest Bush tax cuts because they went predominantly to people who do not work and cannot be expected to increase work effort:

"In this world of ours, those resources going to the rebate recipients, don't come from the Tooth Fairy. They have to come from workers and producers. If the resources come from workers and producers who thereby receive less for their work than they otherwise would have received, won't they in turn spend less? Of course they'll spend less, and the people who now supply them with less, will also spend less, and so on down the line."
http://online.wsj.com/article/SB120286935977964221.html?mod=Letters

pattern seekers among you, don't count on being able to detect this latter effect in the real data. Whatever effects might be there in the long run are masked by vast numbers of other events. It is not patterns that are driving this belief. The persistence and popularity of this idea rests on wishful thinking and the faith that repeated story-telling can provide.

17.4 Crowding Out, Ricardian Equivalence, or Twin Deficits in the 1990s?

So which is it: When taxes are cut and public savings declines, do we get crowding out of private investment, more foreign borrowing, or an increase in private savings? Looking at the data might help, but do not get your expectations too high.

Private and Public net savings as a share of Net National Product are displayed in Fig. 17.4. If the Ricardian equivalence view is right, private savings and public savings would be mirror images of each other. But there does not seem to be much relationship between these two until the 1990s. The improvement in public savings in the 1990s and the rapid turnaround after 2000 are potentially good settings to see what happens when public savings changes. Does private savings make up for inadequate public savings? Unfortunately, this experiment in the 1990s is not perfect, as the increase in public savings was a consequence of very favorable economic growth and large increases in tax revenue from capital gains and stock option income. It is true that private savings declined as public savings increased, but that decline in private savings was at least partly because the private sector was benefiting from the same run-up in equity values. Thus, it is impossible to tell from this experiment, if "Ricardian equivalence" came from awareness in the private sector that the public deficit creates private liabilities, or that both the private and public sectors were simply driven by the same tail winds from the equities markets that added tax revenue on the public side and a sense of wealth on the public side. In the absence of a perfect experiment, you have to make the call. As for me, I find Ricardian equivalence pretty far-fetched.

The post-2000 experiment produced by the Bush tax cut might be better but it is contaminated by the same force in the opposite direction: declining equity values driving lower savings and lower tax receipts, and then rising home prices driving the opposite direction. I had originally written a long paragraph here discussing each twist and turn in the data of the 2000s, but as it did not go anywhere, really, I decided not to subject you to it.

Bottom line, the tax cut "experiments" have all been contaminated by a swirl of other effects. It is like trying to measure the force of gravity in a hurricane. As for me, I am sticking with the "twin-deficits" view. I like that story best.

Chapter 18
Government

When we write GDP $= C + I + G + X - M$, G refers to federal, state, and local government *purchases of goods and services*, meaning purchases of laser-guided bombs and salaries of economists in the Commerce Department, and even salaries of UCLA professors, who are employees of the State of California. These are the goods and services that are extracted from the rest of the economy to operate the government. This is how much we are collectively paying for the services provided by our government.

Stop and think a minute about what you regard to be a reasonable fraction of your income that might be used to pay for the fire department, the police, the military, the teachers and the schools, and the roads and the legislative and administrative work done by our government. Is that 1%, 5%, 10%, 20% or what?

18.1 Government Purchases of Goods and Services Are Not as Great as You Think

Government *purchases* of goods and services as a fraction of GDP over the last 50 years are illustrated in Fig. 18.1. The total excluding defense is only about 15% of GDP. You might be surprised to learn from this figure that *Federal* purchases of goods and services have been withering away with cuts in defense spending, which is now a little over 4% of GDP, but on the rise, as a consequence of the War on Terrorism being waged in Afghanistan and Iraq and elsewhere. Federal government nondefense spending, which includes the salaries of all those bureaucrats you love to complain about, has been surprisingly constant for 50 years at a little more than 2% of GDP. It is hard to see the federal government "on the backs of the people" here. The growth in government purchases has been all at the state and local level, and all before 1975 when state and local spending peaked at 12.9% of GDP, though state and local spending seems on the rise again in the last several years. But when you start to complain about state spending, please keep in mind that I am an employee of the State of California, and I am working hard to earn the salary that you are paying

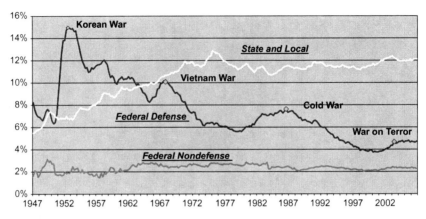

Fig. 18.1 Government purchases, per cent of GDP

me. And as you think kindly about me, think about the school teachers, nurses, the police, and firefighters who are also on your payroll. Maybe we should be hiring a few more of these.

18.2 It's Transfers

So where is the growth of government that we all complain about? The numbers we have looked at so far do not tell the whole story. Our Federal Government and our State and Local Government do *two* distinctly different things with the tax money that we send them. Some of the revenue is used to buy goods and services, and to pay for government employees. That is what we have just examined. But the rest of the revenue is passed back to us, to those receiving government assistance and to those who own the government bonds and earn the interest on it.

Tables prepared by the Bureau of Economic Analysis used to call government assistance "transfers" referring to the fact that the government is only transferring the money from taxpayers to recipients (with a processing fee of course!). The revised tables in 2004 give these "transfers," the more palatable name: "social benefits." Do you mind if I stick with the word "transfers" instead of "social benefits"? The word "transfers" correctly reminds us that with these social benefits come social costs – current and future taxes – needed to pay for the benefits.

Though it is hard to see the federal government "on the backs of the people" in Fig. 18.1, which depicts government purchases of goods and services as a share of GDP, something rather different emerges in Fig. 18.2 and 18.3. Figure 18.2 illustrates several types of Federal spending as a fraction of GDP including interest service and transfers, and Fig. 18.3 illustrates total receipts and total expenditures, the difference being the Federal surplus or deficit.

In Fig. 18.2, you can see the two culprits that have caused the rise in Federal Spending. *Transfers* increased dramatically from 5% to 11% of GDP beginning with

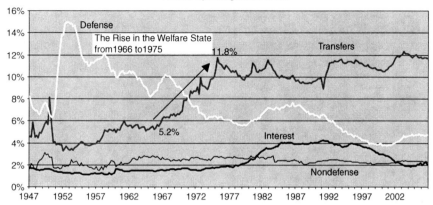

Fig. 18.2 Federal spending share of GDP

the Great Society programs of Lyndon Johnson in the 1960s. In Fig. 18.3, you can see that this rise in spending was matched by a rise in tax receipts until the mid-1970s, when taxes stabilized at around 18% of GDP. With ever-rising spending as a share of GDP not matched by receipts, we created the Reagan deficits of the 1980s, the consequence of which was the rising costs of debt service. *Interest payments* on the Federal debt rose from 1.6% of GDP in 1977 to 3.7% of GDP in 1991, with the Great Deficit programs of Ronald Reagan in the 1980s. Falling interest rates have recently lowered the interest charges on the Federal debt, but you can be sure of this forecast: those interest charges are going to rise in the decade ahead, both because of rising interest rates and also increased debt. President George W. Bush has had a Great Deficit program of his own which is evident in Fig. 18.3. Happily,

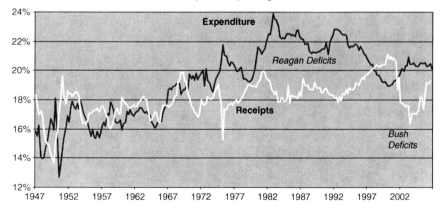

Fig. 18.3 Federal receipts and expenditures

the Bush deficits are disappearing more rapidly than anyone imagined, not because of the control of spending but rather because of a surge in taxes as a share of GDP. "Why is that?" you should be asking yourself. Coincident with the Bush tax cut was a sharp drop in revenue but then a very significant recovery. Why did receipts rise while the tax rates remained the same?

Source: New York Times, 8 June 2003

18.2.1 Transfers Are Done also by State Governments

State governments are also in the business of transferring income among our citizens. Figure 18.4 depicts the state and local transfers and Federal transfers as a percent of GDP. These transfers currently total little less than 12% of GDP, but that fraction has been rising slowly since 1975.

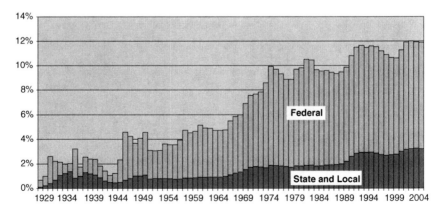

Fig. 18.4 Transfers by state and local, and by the federal government, share of GDP

18.2.2 Those Transfers Are Mostly Social Security, Medicare, and Medicaid

There are three programs that account for most of the transfers. Old-age, survivors, and disability insurance (Social Security), hospital and supplementary medical insurance for the elderly administered by the Federal Government (Medicare), and health care for the poor (Medicaid) administered by the States. There are, of course, also veteran's benefits, and food stamps and many other programs. For details see Table 18.1.

Spending as a share of GDP for the big three programs plus unemployment benefits are illustrated in Fig. 18.5. The first transfer program was unemployment insurance, initiated in 1938. Next came social security in 1941. The health programs of Medicaid (for the poor) and Medicare (for the elderly) came later, in 1959 and 1966, respectively.

Table 18.1 Government social benefits, 2005

Line		$ Billion	Share (%)	Share of GDP (%)
1	Government social benefits	1484.0	100.0	11.9
2	To persons	1480.9	99.8	11.9
3	Federal	1078.6	72.7	8.7
4	Benefits from social insurance funds	894.7	60.3	7.2
5	**Old-age, survivors, and disability insurance**	**512.3**	**34.5**	**4.1**
6	**Hospital and supplementary medical insurance**	332.7	22.4	2.7
7	**Unemployment insurance**	31.8	2.1	0.3
8	State	31	2.1	0.2
9	Railroad employees	0.1	0.0	0.0
10	Federal employees	0.7	0.0	0.0
11	Special unemployment benefits	0	0.0	0.0
12	Railroad retirement	9.2	0.6	0.1
13	Pension benefit guaranty	2.7	0.2	0.0
14	Veterans life insurance	1.6	0.1	0.0
15	Workers' compensation	2.4	0.2	0.0
16	Military medical insurance[a]	2.1	0.1	0.0
17	Veterans benefits	34.8	2.3	0.3
18	Pension and disability	32.4	2.2	0.3
19	Readjustment	2.4	0.2	0.0
20	Other[b]		0.0	0.0
21	Food stamp benefits	29.5	2.0	0.2
22	Black lung benefits	0.7	0.0	0.0
23	Supplemental security income	33.5	2.3	0.3
24	Direct relief		0.0	0.0
25	Earned income credit	49.2	3.3	0.4
26	Other[c]	36.2	2.4	0.3
27	State and local	402.3	27.1	3.2
28	Benefits from social insurance funds	17.2	1.2	0.1
29	Temporary disability insurance	4.6	0.3	0.0
30	Workers' compensation	12.6	0.8	0.1

cont.

Table 18.1 (*Continued*)

Line		$ Billion	Share (%)	Share of GDP (%)
31	Public assistance	364.2	24.5	2.9
32	Medical care	315	21.2	2.5
33	**Medicaid**	**303.9**	**20.5**	**2.4**
34	Other medical care[d]	11.1	0.7	0.1
35	Family assistance[e]	18.3	1.2	0.1
36	Supplemental security income[f]	5.2	0.4	0.0
37	General assistance	8.4	0.6	0.1
38	Energy assistance	2.4	0.2	0.0
39	Other[g]	14.8	1.0	0.1
40	Education	18.2	1.2	0.1
41	Employment and training	1.1	0.1	0.0
42	Other[h]	1.5	0.1	0.0
43	To the rest of the world[i]	3.1	0.2	0.0

Source: Bureau of Economic Analysis (Table 3.12)

The Big Three in Bold

[a]Consists of payments for medical services for dependents of active duty military personnel at nonmilitary facilities

[b]Consists of mustering out pay, terminal leave pay, and adjusted compensation benefits

[c]Consists largely of payments to nonprofit institutions, aid to students, and payments for medical services for retired military personnel and their dependents at nonmilitary facilities

[d]Consists of general medical assistance and state child health care programs

[e]Consists of aid to families with dependent children and, beginning with 1996, assistance programs operating under the Personal Responsibility and Work Opportunity Reconciliation Act of 1996

[f]Prior to 1974, consists of old-age assistance, aid to the blind, and aid to the permanently and totally disabled, when the programs were partly federally funded

[g]Consists of expenditures for food under the supplemental program for women, infants, and children; foster care; adoption assistance; and payments to nonprofit welfare institutions

[h]Consists largely of veterans benefits, Alaska dividends, and crime-victim payments

[i]Consists of Federal Government social benefits to the rest of the world. Prior to 1960, government social benefits to the rest of the world are included in other current transfer payments to the rest of the world (net) in Table 3.1

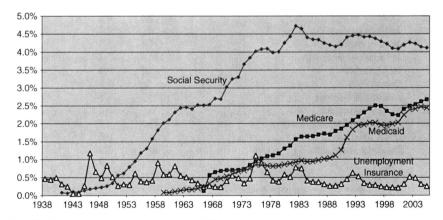

Fig. 18.5 Major transfer programs, share of GDP

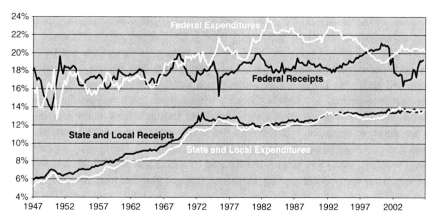

Fig. 18.6 Federal, and state and local government share of GDP

Unemployment benefits spike up in recessions, but as a fraction of GDP have been on a steady downward trend to only 0.26% of GDP in 2005. Social security payouts started to rise in the 1950s and reached a peak of 4.7% of GDP in 1982. It is the health care transfers that are reaching toward the sky, now over 5% of GDP.

18.2.3 The States Do Not Run Deficits

Figure 18.6 depicts receipts and spending by both the Federal Government and State and Local Government as a fraction of GDP. In contrast to the Federal government, state and local spending has been almost perfectly balanced by revenue. State and local governments are tightly constrained by their constitutions to operate on a pay-as-you-go basis.

18.3 An Accounting Scandal to Rival Enron: Phantom Assets Created by Government Borrowing

So what is wrong with the Federal government borrowing to get the money it wants to give it to someone else? The answer is in Fig. 18.2. Look at those rising interest payments in the 1980s, elevating from 1.6% of GDP to 3.7%. Those elevating interest payments will help you understand that: *There cannot be a tax cut without a spending cut. There can only be a tax postponement.* When the bills of the federal government are not paid for out of current tax receipts, those bills are still paid. The government pays its bills with borrowed money. But that borrowing does not come from some magic Sugar Daddy. It comes from you and me. And when we loan to the government, we expect to get paid back.

   Thus, we come to the $64 trillion question: who is going to pay back the Federal debt? Not me, I am thinking. Probably you, I am hoping.

The problems caused by government borrowing come from the fact that we do not do proper accounting. Suppose. I have a tax liability of $1,000 and I borrow from you, as I do not currently have the cash to pay my taxes. You put that $1,000 as an asset on your balance sheet, and I put it as a liability on mine, as I know you will break my knees if I do not pay you back. There is no net wealth creation by that transaction. My liability exactly offsets your asset. Suppose, on the other hand, President Bush, who is a close personal friend, comes to me and says "Ed, I am going to give you a $1,000 tax break this year. You worked hard to earn it and you deserve to keep that money." That's cool for me, but creates a problem for the President, as he has already committed to spend that $1,000. He has to get the money from somewhere and he, therefore, goes to you and asks for a $1,000 loan, which you graciously provide. Now we have an accounting problem. You put that $1,000 as an asset onto your balance sheet, but where is the offsetting liability? I do not put it on my balance sheet as I take the President at his word. He said he was giving me a tax reduction, not a tax postponement. The President puts the liability on the books of the fictitious entity called Uncle Sam, and you and I happily ignore the fact that Uncle Sam's liabilities are really our own. By moving the liability to an "off-shore" operation that we call Uncle Sam, the President has created $1,000 in phantom assets. It's an accounting gimmick worthy of Enron.

If the accounting were done correctly, in May of each year you would get a letter like :

1 May 2003
Dear Mr. Leamer:

I thank you for the timely payment of your taxes this year, but I regret to inform you that the money you sent was not enough to meet your share of federal government spending. You owe another $1,000. You can choose to pay this amount now, but you may prefer to add this to your share of the Federal Debt, which is currently $28,000. In making the choice between paying it now or adding it to your outstanding debt, you should keep in mind that we offer some of the best lending terms available, but, like any other debt, you will have to pay the interest charges and eventually have to repay the principal. Until the debt is discharged, this liability will affect your ability to get other loans, including home mortgages.

For the current terms that we can offer you, please visit our website at http://www.no_escape.gov.

Your faithful servant,

Uncle Sam

18.4 The Outstanding Federal Debt Is Great Enough to Be Worrisome

The phantom assets of the Federal Debt are now up to $6 trillion dollars. Figure 18.7 illustrates the per capita Federal debt, which has risen fivefold since the early 1980s, and is now equal to $28,000 per person. When you are computing your net worth, make sure you put that debt on your balance sheet. Actually, I am not going to put this debt on my personal balance sheet, as I am planning on retiring before "we" raise the income taxes to pay down that debt. What a cool way of avoiding my tax liability! It is the workers under the age 55, who can expect to have to service that debt and thus to pay my taxes. I thank you very much.

But it may not be this bad. We need to consider government assets as well as liabilities. If the federal borrowing is used to finance the acquisition of assets, such as roads or hospitals or even "human capital," then Uncle Sam's asset statement is in balance, with the liability to repay the debt offset by an asset of like value. Transferring both those assets and the corresponding liabilities properly to the taxpayer balance sheets would then have no effect on taxpayer net worth. But if that debt is used merely to finance transfers or current operations of government, then there is the phantom asset problem. We all act as if someone else is paying for those transfers and we spend as if we are wealthier than we really are. Then we let our saving rates fall to inappropriately low levels, making inadequate preparation for the inevitable rise in taxes needed to serve the debt.

According to the Bureau of Economic Analysis, government buildings in 2001 were worth $5 trillion, and there was another $1 trillion in government-owned equipment and residential buildings. Thus government assets more-or-less offset the government debt of $6 trillion, so maybe our personal accounting for the federal deficit is not as screwed up as I thought.

Think again. There are some other very hefty liabilities of the Federal government – promises to our future retirees. There is a big difference in the way our

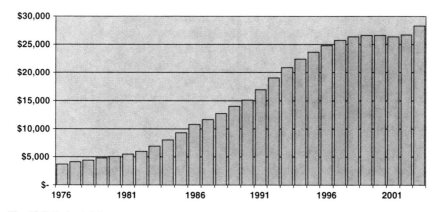

Fig. 18.7 Federal debt per person

Federal government keeps its books and the way private corporations keep their books. Corporations with defined benefit retirement plans are required to remove from the current earnings an amount that is projected to be enough to fund the accumulating retirement liabilities. The collapse in the stock market hit these corporate retirement assets very hard, but most corporations currently are using very optimistic assumptions about rates of return, and may be seriously under-funding their retirement plans. But at least corporations are making an effort. The Federal government has made hardly any effort adequately to support the Social Security trust fund. According to Peter G. Peterson in a New York Times article 8 June 2003 titled "Deficits and Dysfunction," the unfinanced liabilities for Social Security and Medicare currently are an astonishing $25 trillion. The highly readable and completely alarming book by Laurence Kotlikoff and Scott Burns, aptly titled "*The Coming Generational Storm,*" reports total debt of $51 trillion. That compares with the BEA estimates of the total assets (private and public) of the United States in 2001, equal to $31 trillion. If we were a corporation, we would be close to going under, with liabilities substantially exceeding assets. Of course, you and I know the bitter truth here: Those are not real liabilities. We are never going to pay those Social Security and Medicare benefits; we cannot afford them. As you must recognize that, why aren't you saving more?

18.5 The Real Effect of the Federal Deficit: Trickle-Down Social Responsibilities

We now have all the building blocks we need to figure out what are the real effects of the Great Deficits of Ronald Reagan and George W. Bush. It is the transfers. The cloud of a huge federal deficit puts a severe damper on the enthusiasm of Congress for more transfer programs. The sharp rise in the Federal deficit caused by the Reagan defense spending and the Reagan tax cuts ended the rise in the transfer programs supported by the Federal government. The Bush deficits will make it very difficult for Congress to extend medical coverage for the poor and the elderly, and may make it difficult even to honor the Social Security obligations. With the federal government out of the business of transferring money, that function is left to the States, who don't find the job an easy one. Matt Bai of the New York Times says it well:

Sunday, 8 June 2003

Drip, Drip, Drip   The New York Times

By MATT BAI

...

The tax cut will choke off revenue to the federal government, which is precisely what the conservatives want it to do. Their thinking is that the less money Washington has, the less it will waste. This means Congress cannot increase financing for the mandates its been heaping onto the states for 40 years. For instance, Congress shares with states, the cost of Medicaid, the health care program for the poor, which gobbles up huge chunks of state budgets. As Washington has not seen fit to provide elderly patients with a prescription drug plan, that, too, falls to the states. So does the overwhelming share of special education for disabled children, another federal program. And let us not forget more recent mandates – Bush's "No Child Left Behind" law and increased spending on homeland security – that the feds have passed on to governors with minimal assistance.

. . .

That said, you won't see Bush campaigning in 2004 on the notion that he shifted taxes to the local level and thus made government more accountable. There will never be a TV ad that says: "President Bush. He decentralized revenue." Instead, Bush will insist that he cut your taxes more than any president in history – and if some other moron raised them, you should throw him out of office. This is, at best, disingenuous. At worst, it helps create a cynical society where people believe that they shouldn't have to pay for anything and their elected officials are too afraid to tell them they should.

18.5.1 Being a "Grown-Up"

The last line in the Matt Bai quotation ("people believe they shouldn't have to pay for anything and their elected officials are too afraid to tell them they should.") refers to what is a very serious and fundamental conflict: The Politics of Abundance vs. the Reality of Scarcity. We let the market deal with scarcity issues for most of the goods and service that we consume. We might like to adorn ourselves with diamonds and treat our stomachs with lavish meals and repair our bodies with personal trainers, but we all can't do all of these. There is not enough to go around. So we put prices on each of these items, and let each of us decide what is really important. You go for the diamonds and I will go for the lavish meals. We will worry about the personal trainers later.

For items provided to us by governments, we have no effective mechanism for dealing with scarcity. We vote for candidates who have their pictures taken at the ribbon-cutting ceremonies, when new freeways are opened up. But when scarcity rears its ugly head, and the freeways turn into no-ways because of congestion, no politician wants to have his or her picture taken at the opening of a new toll booth. Instead of letting prices control the scarcity, we get hopelessly congested roads incongruously called "freeways." When the Western Grid states failed to create enough electric generating capacity to keep up with demand at the fixed residential rates, the Governor of the State of California, Gray Davis, announced correctly that he could cure the problem "in twenty minutes" by raising residential rates, but he was not about to do that to the (immature) voters of the State of California. Instead of higher residential rates, we had blackouts and brownouts. And we elected Gray Davis to a second term of office, though, quickly enough, we changed our minds when some better magic came along. We sent the Terminator to Sacramento to do what we all want our governments to do: Do not talk about taxes. Give us something good and have someone else pay for it.

Medicine is probably the most important problem on the desks of our elected officials. But state and local and federal governments are hopelessly incapable of making the extraordinarily difficult decisions regarding who gets access to which kind of medical care. Absent control over access, we get better but more expensive drugs, equipment, and procedures, and larger and larger bills. No problem, our elected officials respond, we do not have to raise taxes; can borrow.

18.5.2 *The Debate over the Privatization of Social Security Is Confusing All of Us*

The efficiency of our economic system comes mostly from the fact that the decisions about what we consume are made privately not publicly. Your clothes, residence, and food are for you to choose. I do not have to get involved in deciding if you should wear t-shirts and jeans instead of those Armani duds you are so proud of. That's what privatization of Social Security would do. It would create an important level of personal control and personal responsibility over retirement. But the debate over privatization is taking us in the wrong direction.

Politicians and even many economists in favor of privatization of Social Security are promising, if we privatize, a rosy future with a US GDP so large that taking care of our elderly will be a breeze. To get to this nirvana, we only need to divert retirement funds from bonds that have historically paid low returns to stocks that have paid much higher returns.

Sorry, this is flim-flam. Privatization will have virtually no effect on the future US GDP.

Logically, the argument in favor of privatization must rest on one of three ideas:

1. Better Investments: Privatization will improve the choice of investments, making the economy grow more rapidly, and creating a bigger "pie" in the future from which retirees can have their slice.
2. More Savings: Privatization will make the "pie" bigger not because of better investment choices but because we will save more.
3. Less acrimony: Privatization will transfer the responsibility for retirement from the Federal Government to private individuals, thus eliminating the agonizing discussion over just how big a piece of the national pie retirees deserve.

So which is it? Better investment, more savings or less acrimony?

Surprise: It is not better investments, or more savings. The real value of privatization is that it will take the determination of benefits out of the political arena, and halt the intergenerational political conflict that is already here, and sure to get worse.

Most commentators suggest that privatization will work because it will allow us to make better investments. The discussion usually begins with a comparison of rates of return on stocks (10%) vs. bonds (3%). It is argued that if we allow retirement savings to be invested in the stock market, then we can expect a huge increase in the return on our savings. This is faulty thinking that confuses the individual with the society. Looking backward, individuals who chose stocks have done better than individuals who chose bonds, but that does not mean that had everyone switched en masse into stocks, everyone would have done better. That could only occur if we collectively funded better investment projects that helped to grow the GDP. If we had funded better investments, then we would have a larger GDP today, and we could more easily afford all those retirement benefits. But that cannot be the reason for privatization of Social Security, can it? We have a very sophisticated financial system that does a superb job picking the best allocation of new savings to buildings and to equipment and to research and development. The choice of projects does not depend very much on whether firms finance new investments with debt or equity. Therefore with privatization, the economy will make about the same investments and have about the same amount of corporate earnings to split between bondholders and equity investors. The diversion of financial assets from bonds to stocks can only lower the return on stocks and raise the return on bonds, just enough of each to keep the total payout unchanged.

Although it is highly unlikely that privatization will have much effect on the rate of return to US savings, it is possible that total US savings will increase. This would be a good thing. After all, net private savings are now nearly zero. If we do not save, we do not grow our assets, and our future is starting to look pretty bleak, especially when the baby boomers are all retired and demanding benefits.

There is, however, a real and important benefit from privatization. It would take a very difficult income distribution question out of the hands of the government. We let the private market largely decide the distribution of income among members of the same generation, but we let the political arena decide how much you and I contribute to the welfare of our aged parents. This creates intergenerational conflict that seems relatively quiet now, only because the politics of aging are better understood by the old than by the young – there is an AARP but no AAWP, "W" standing for working.

When the baby boomers retire, their numbers will overwhelm, and the focus on the elderly is sure to increase. We have been there before. California, in the 1930s, had a large and politically active "elderly" population who put on the ballot the "Ham and Eggs" initiative that would have granted everyone over the age 50 "thirty dollars every Thursday." This generous transfer to the elderly was more than twice California's per capita income at the time, and it attracted 45% of the vote in 1938.

The reason for privatization of social security: Greater efficiency or less acrimony? It's less acrimony. Do not be misled by the promise of high returns in the stock market. Privatization will surely not mean better investments for the US overall. The core issue is a familiar one – personal vs. public responsibility. Privatization will take retirement planning out of the public arena and put the burden on those with the greatest personal stake – future retirees and their families.

18.5.2.1 Now Calls for Privatization of Medicare: a Familiar Refrain

Speaking of being misled, the same folks who have argued for privatization of Social Security are now pushing for privatization of Medicare for ostensibly the same
reason (greater efficiency):

New York Times, 9 June 2003

President Bush, most Republicans in Congress and some Democrats are determined that Medicare must not pay for prescription drugs the way it pays doctors,
hospitals, and other health care providers: with a rigid, complex statutory formula
that often bears little relation to the realities of local health care markets.

Republicans maintain, in the words of Newt Gingrich, the former speaker of the
House, that Medicare is obsolete and antiquated, because it does not cover drugs
and because it relies on "a command-and-control structure to control costs."

Testifying last week before a Senate committee, Mr. Gingrich said, "We are at
the dawn of an explosion of knowledge that will change everything we know about
science and the human body." Breakthroughs in biology and technology in the next
20 years, he said, will equal all those of the twentieth century, and the best way to
exploit the discoveries is to transform Medicare from a government monopoly into
a marketplace of competing insurance plans, so the elderly will have more options.

"*Choice creates competition, and competition drives down price*," Mr. Gingrich
said, in a pithy statement of the philosophy that inspires most of the Republican
proposals.

Maybe, but I do not think so, Mr. Gingrich. Of course, competition and efficiency
matter but the much bigger problem is uncontrolled access. I pay the Medicare bills
for your parents and grandparents, and you pay for mine. Since you are paying for
me, I am not about to say no to even the most expensive treatments. Likewise for
you. We are now devoting about 14% of GDP to health care, and 1% of GDP in the
last month of life. Those huge numbers do not come much from inefficiency in the
delivery of heath care. This amount of spending comes mostly from the way we (do
not) pay for health care.

Therefore, the primary benefit of privatization is that it turns over to the "market,"
the extremely difficult decision of who gets what treatment and which drugs. With
privatization, neither I nor my elected representatives would have to get involved
in the discussion over whether or not your elderly parents should receive the latest
life-extending drugs. That would be up to you and your family.

Relying on the market to decide who gets health care and who does not is a
tidy solution to a difficult decision, but not necessarily a fair or ethical decision,
as it allows the wealthy much better access than the poor. Whether this is fair or
not depends on how much the market rewards hard work and how much it rewards
dumb luck. As for myself, I have a hard time believing that Michael Jordan is a
more "worthy" human being than I am. But my opinions do not matter. The market
hath spoken: Michael Jordan is worth a 1000 of me, or more.

So which is it: greater efficiency, more fairness or less acrimony?

It's less acrimony.

Chapter 19
The External Deficit and the Value of the Dollar
Hu's in Charge?

Not long ago, one could safely ignore the value of the US dollar and the external deficit (imports exceeding exports) when studying the US business cycle. Back in the 1950s and 1960s, the US exposure to international markets was pretty minimal. The ratio of imports to GDP was only 4% compared with 15% today. The external deficit as a fraction of GDP was a small surplus of +1% compared with a deficit of −6% today. Many foreign exchange rates were held firmly in place by governments around the world. And the US government maintained the real value of the US dollar by fixing the price of gold firmly at $35 per ounce compared with a fluctuating rate around $900 per ounce today.

The subtitle quip "Hu's in charge?" is a reference to Chinese Paramount Leader Hu Jintao and to Chinese official purchases of US dollar-denominated assets that are partly responsible for the elevated value of the dollar, the flood of Chinese imports coming to the US, and, most importantly, to the growing dependence of the health of the US economy on decisions made by a small group of gentlemen in Beijing.

But this is a problem mostly made right here in the US. We have let our savings rates fall to miserably low numbers, and are increasingly dependent on foreigners to fund our domestic investment. With savings falling well short of the investment opportunities, what's the alternative? Should we find some way to kill off the investment opportunities? Wait a minute, you may be asking yourself: What does Paramount Leader Hu have to do with US savings and investment? To answer that one, we need to master an important accounting identity: The Current Account = The Capital Account.

This accounting identity really is not so mysterious. You are well aware of the fact that if you spend more than you earn, you have to make up the difference either by borrowing or by drawing down your savings accounts. Spending and earning are your Current Account. Borrowing and drawing down savings are your Capital Account.

If you are starting to get confused, it is only going to get worse. This is one of the most difficult areas of economics.

19.1 An Important Accounting Identity: The Current Account = The Capital Account

Let us begin with the accounting for external transactions. Here is the question we are trying to answer: How many dollars do we send abroad and how many come back? Keep in mind that we send the dollars abroad for two different reasons: to buy foreign goods and services and to buy foreign assets. The first is a "current account" transaction and the second a "capital account" transaction.

Table 19.1 reports the *Current Account* balance for the years 2000 and 2006 and the annualized rate of growth over that period. This "current" account records all the international transactions that involve the purchase or sale of goods, and the earnings from work abroad or from foreign investments.

The *Trade Balance*, which is the difference between exports and imports, is part of the current account. In 2006, we bought foreign goods and services worth $2,818 billion. This was partly offset by earnings on the sale of US goods and services worth $2096.2 leaving a trade imbalance of −$758.5 billion.

Just as you and I, when the US spends more on goods and services than it earns, somehow the gap must be closed. Earnings on investments abroad help out. Table 19.1 indicates that the US had a $36.6 billion surplus in this category. More than offsetting that surplus was a deficit of $89.6 billion of "unilateral transfers" including US. Government grants and also remittances that foreigners working here send home.

Add up the trade balance and the income receipts and the transfers to get to the *Current Account* Deficit of −$811.5 billion.

Current Account: −$811.5*b*
Trade Balance: Net Exports of Goods and Services: −$758.5
+
Net Receipts of Factor Income from Abroad
• Inflows and Outflows of Investment Income $36.6
• Grants, remittances and other transfers −$89.6

Ouch, $811.5 billion is a lot of money to be short. Just as you and I, when the US has a current account deficit, spending more than it earns, the gap must be closed either by drawing down foreign savings accounts or by borrowing from foreign lenders. Those are *Capital Account* transactions. Table 19.2 reports the Capital Account for the years 2000 and 2006. The confusingly labeled −$1,055.2 billion in Table 19.2 for the item "U.S.-owned assets abroad, net (increase/financial outflow (−))" means that we did not close the Current Account deficit by drawing down our foreign "savings accounts." We actually increased our foreign assets by $1,055.2 billion. What we did to close the Current Account gap was to greatly increase our foreign indebtedness in the amount of $1,859.6 billion. Out of that total, $440.3 billion was foreign official assets: think foreign central banks. And take a look at the last column to find the item that grew most rapidly from 2000 to 2006. There it is again: foreign official purchases of US assets grew at the annualized rate

Table 19.1 The trade balance and the current account, billions of dollars: BEA

	(Credits+; debits −)	2000	2006	Rate of Growth (%)
1	**Exports of goods and services and income receipts**	**1,421.5**	**2,096.2**	6.7
2	Exports of goods and services	1,070.6	1,445.7	5.1
3	Goods, balance of payments basis/2/	772.0	1,023.1	4.8
4	Services/3/	298.6	422.6	6.0
5	Transfers under U.S. military agency sales contracts/4/	13.8	17.1	3.7
6	Travel	82.4	85.7	0.7
7	Passenger fares	20.7	22.2	1.2
8	Other transportation	29.8	46.3	7.6
9	Royalties and license fees/5/	43.2	62.4	6.3
10	Other private services/5/	107.9	187.8	9.7
11	U.S. Government miscellaneous services	0.8	1.2	6.6
12	Income receipts	350.9	650.5	10.8
13	Income receipts on U.S.-owned assets abroad	348.1	647.6	10.9
14	Direct investment receipts	151.8	310.2	12.6
15	Other private receipts	192.4	335.0	9.7
16	U.S. Government receipts	3.8	2.4	−7.6
17	Compensation of employees	2.8	2.9	0.3
18	**Imports of goods and services and income payments**	**(1,780.3)**	**(2,818.0)**	8.0
19	Imports of goods and services	(1,450.4)	(2,204.2)	7.2
20	Goods, balance of payments basis/2/	(1,226.7)	(1,861.4)	7.2
21	Services/3/	(223.7)	(342.8)	7.4
22	Direct defense expenditures	(13.5)	(31.1)	14.9
23	Travel	(64.7)	(72.0)	1.8
24	Passenger fares	(24.3)	(27.5)	2.1
25	Other transportation	(41.4)	(65.3)	7.9
26	Royalties and license fees/5/	(16.5)	(26.4)	8.2
27	Other private services/5/	(60.5)	(116.5)	11.5
28	U.S. Government miscellaneous services	(2.9)	(4.0)	5.7
29	Income payments	(329.9)	(613.8)	10.9
30	Income payments on foreign-owned assets in the United States	(322.3)	(604.4)	11.0
31	Direct investment payments	(56.9)	(136.0)	15.6
32	Other private payments	(180.9)	(334.6)	10.8
33	U.S. Government payments	(84.5)	(133.8)	8.0
34	Compensation of employees	(7.5)	(9.4)	3.8
35	**Unilateral current transfers, net**	**(58.6)**	**(89.6)**	7.3
36	U.S. Government grants/4/	(16.7)	(27.1)	8.4
37	U.S. Government pensions and other transfers	(4.7)	(6.5)	5.6
38	Private remittances and other transfers/6/	(37.2)	(55.9)	7.0
39	**TRADE BALANCE: (2) + (19)**	**(379.8)**	**(758.5)**	12.2
40	**Net income payments (12) + (29)**	21.1	36.6	9.7
41	**CURRENT ACCOUNT (35) + (39) + (40)**	(417.4)	(811.5)	ct

Table 19.2 Capital account: billions of dollars, bureau of economic analysis

Capital account			
U.S. International Transactions Accounts Data Bureau of Economic Analysis [Billions of dollars]			
(Credits +; debits −)	2000	2006	Rate of growth
1 **Capital account transactions, net**	**(1.0)**	**(3.9)**	25%
2 **U.S.-owned assets abroad, net** **(increase/financial outflow (−))**	**(560.5)**	**(1,055.2)**	11%
3 U.S. official reserve assets, net	(0.3)	2.4	
4 Gold/7/	−	−	
5 Special drawing rights	(0.7)	(0.2)	−18%
6 Reserve position in the International Monetary Fund	2.3	3.3	6%
7 Foreign currencies	(1.9)	(0.7)	−14%
8 U.S. Government assets, other than official reserve assets, net	(0.9)	5.3	
9 U.S. credits and other long-term assets	(5.2)	(3.0)	−9%
10 Repayments on US credits and other long-term assets/8/	4.3	8.3	12%
11 US foreign currency holdings and US short-term assets, net	(0.0)	0.0	
12 US private assets, net	(559.3)	(1,062.9)	11%
13 Direct investment	(159.2)	(235.4)	7%
14 Foreign securities	(127.9)	(289.4)	15%
15 US claims on unaffiliated foreigners reported by US nonbanking concerns	(138.8)	(83.5)	−8%
16 US claims reported by US banks, not included elsewhere	(133.4)	(454.6)	23%
17 **Foreign-owned assets in the United States, net** **(increase/financial inflow (+))**	1,046 9	1,859.6	10%
18 Foreign official assets in the United States, net	42.8	440.3	47%
19 US Government securities	35.7	380.7	48%
20 US Treasury securities/9/	(5.2)	189.2	
21 Other/10/	40.9	191.6	29%
22 Other US Government liabilities/11/	(1.8)	3.1	
23 US liabilities reported by US banks, not included elsewhere	5.7	22.0	25%
24 Other foreign official assets/12/	3.1	34.4	49%
25 Other foreign assets in the United States, net	1,004.1	1,419.3	6%
26 Direct investment	321.3	180.6	−9%
27 US Treasury securities	(70.0)	(35.9)	−11%
28 US securities other than US Treasury securities	459.9	592.0	4%
29 US currency	5.3	12.6	15%
30 US liabilities to unaffiliated foreigners reported by US nonbanking concerns	170.7	235.8	6%
31 US liabilities reported by US banks, not included elsewhere	117.0	434.4	24%

(Continued)

Table 19.2 (*Continued*)

(Credits +; debits −)	2000	2006	Rate of growth
32 **Financial derivatives, net**	**n.a.**	**28.8**	
33 Statistical discrepancy (sum of above items with sign reversed)	(67.9)	(17.8)	−20%
CAPITAL ACCOUNT: (1) + (2) + (17) + (32) + (33)	417.4	811.5	12%
7 At the present time, all U.S.-Treasury-owned gold is held in the United States			
8 Includes sales of foreign obligations to foreigners			
9 Consists of bills, certificates, marketable bonds and notes, and nonmarketable convertible and nonconvertible bonds and notes			
10 Consists of U.S. Treasury and Export-Import Bank obligations, not included elsewhere, and of debt securities of US Government corporations and agencies			
11 Includes, primarily, US Government liabilities associated with military agency sales contracts and other transactions arranged with or through foreign official agencies; see table 5.			
12 Consists of investments in US corporate stocks and in debt securities of private corporations and State and local governments			

of 48% per year, increasing by a factor of 10 from 2000 to 2006! We will come back to this later but in the meantime keep in mind that over half of the current account deficit of $811.5 billion was offset by foreign official purchases of dollar-denominated assets. I wonder why those governments buy all those assets? Hu's in charge?

Capital Account: $811.5
Net Accumulation of Claims on Foreigners
Increase (−) in US-owned assets abroad −1,055.2
Increase (+) in foreign ownership of US assets 1,859.6
Financial derivatives, net 28.8
Statistical discrepancy −17.8

Confirm by looking at Tables 19.1 and 19.2 that the Current Account = the Capital Account. In 2006, US residents spent $811.5 more than they earned in foreign countries and they made up the difference by borrowing and/or selling assets. Better remember this fact. It is important but it is not widely understood. When our Treasury Secretary Snow complained to China about the US *current account* deficit with Asian countries, especially China and Japan, he was also complaining about lending by China and Japan to the US. Does he realize this? Does he realize that it is logically impossible to close the current account without also closing the capital account? Isn't Secretary Snow's China request like going to your lender and asking to pay higher interest rates? (Homework question for Secretary Snow: How can the US external deficit be closed without foreign demand for US assets declining? Answer later.)

> **Accounting Identity**
> Current Account = Capital Account

If this is completely confusing, an inscrutable Chinese fortune cookie might help: "You will borrow your way to happiness." That is ever so much more appealing than William Shakespeare's advice from "Hamlet", Act 1 scene 3:

Neither a borrower nor a lender be;
For loan oft loses both itself and friend,
And borrowing dulls the edge of husbandry.
This above all: to thine own self be true,
And it must follow, as the night the day,
Thou canst not then be false to any man.

19.2 What Determines the Value of the Dollar and the External Deficit?

The foreign exchange market is where the value of the dollar relative to other currencies is determined. When the demand for dollars increases, the dollar's value rises, meaning that the price of a dollar in Euros or Yen or Pesos increases.[1] The demand for dollars occurs when buyers bring their Euros or Yen or Pesos or Renminbi to the market to exchange for dollars. These foreigners buy dollars when they are coming to US for a visit, when they want to buy US products or US assets. The supply of dollars originates from the opposite transactions: from the US citizens traveling abroad, or buying foreign goods or foreign assets.

In the muddle of buying and selling of dollars and foreign currencies, the value of the dollar is determined, as are the amounts of trade in goods and services and the amount of exchange of assets. In other words, the values of currencies, the trade balance, the current account, and the capital account are all jointly determined. We need to understand this process. First let us take a look at some exchange rate data.

19.2.1 The Exchange Rate

The exchange rates of the US dollar vis-à-vis the German mark and the Canadian dollar are illustrated in Fig. 19.1. Discussing exchange rates is confusing since the rates are sometimes expressed, as in Fig. 19.1, in terms of the foreign currency paid

---

[1] Equivalently, and this gets really confusing, the price of the Euro or Yen or Peso in terms of dollars falls.

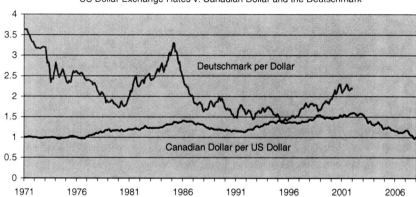

Fig. 19.1 US dollar exchange rates vs. German Mark and Canadian Dollar

per dollar and sometimes in terms of the dollar per unit of foreign currency. When commentators report that the exchange rate rose, can we buy more with our dollars or less? What rose: dollars per foreign currency or foreign currency per dollar? Is up, up, or is up, down? If we are discussing the US, I like to use foreign currency per US dollar, since then a higher exchange rate means a strengthening (or appreciation) of the US dollar (up is up). But be very careful. It is easy to make a mistake if you are not.

With the understanding that up is up in Fig. 19.1, we can see a long-term depreciation of the US dollar relative to the German mark, which means that your dollar will not buy as much in Germany. This long-term trend was offset by a short-lived appreciation of the dollar in the mid 1980s and another appreciation in the late 1990s. (That German data run out in 2001. Do you know why?)

The story of the Canadian dollar has been different. The US dollar in the 1970s traded at parity with the Canadian dollar, but since then has experienced a long-term appreciation, with most of the appreciation confined to the same two episodes in which the dollar rose relative to many currencies: the mid 1980s and the end of the 1990s. In 2002, the US dollar reached a peak of around 1.6 Canadian for 1 US dollar. But since 2002, that long appreciation has been completely undone, and we are back to parity: one US dollar for one loonie (a Canadian 1-dollar coin).

What about the other trading partners of the US? Figure 19.2 includes both the Canadian dollar for comparison purposes and the trade-weighted dollar which includes all the globe's currencies, weighted by the amount of trade each country does with US. Here you can see that the long-term appreciation of the dollar is more pronounced overall than against the Canadian dollar.

19.2.2 The Real Exchange Rate

Do you think that the big appreciation of the US dollar displayed in Fig. 19.2 means that you can buy more foreign stuff with each dollar. Have you ever done any shopping in Mexico or some other foreign country? You know it is a little hard to figure

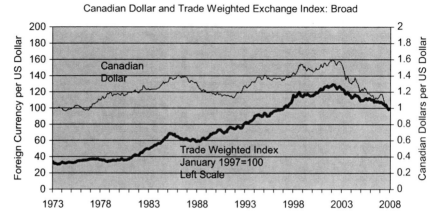

Fig. 19.2 US Dollar exchange rates

out what is a bargain and what is not. You know you can get that same shirt back in US for $40, but there it is in the window in Mexico City for 300 pesos. To buy, or not to buy, that is the question. If the exchange rate is 10 pesos to the dollar then the price of that Mexican shirt in dollars is 300/10 = $30 dollars. That's a good deal compared with the $40 you would pay back home. Better buy it.

This foreign shopper has used the three ingredients needed to define the "real exchange rate" – prices back home, prices in the foreign market, and the rate of exchange between the two currencies. The real exchange rate applies not just to shirts but to the broad basket of goods and assets that are internationally traded. The real exchange rate is the relative price of US tradable goods compared with foreign tradable goods.

*Real Value of the Dollar = **Real Exchange Rate** = (Exchange Rate: Foreign currency per $) times (US Price Level/Foreign Price Level) = **Relative Price of US Goods compared with Foreign Goods***

The message of this discussion of real exchange rates is that the (nominal) exchange rates displayed in Fig. 19.2 are not a good guide to the global shopping opportunities since the appreciation of the dollar evident in this figure could be undone if inflation is high in foreign countries. Figure 19.3 has both the nominal US dollar exchange rate and the "real exchange" rate, which adjusts for the inflation differences between the US and its trading partners. Sure enough, the real exchange rate has held pretty steady with significant appreciations in the mid 1980s and the late 1990s. You do understand why the real rate is flatter than the nominal rate, don't you? Inflation has been generally greater for trading partners of the US than for the US domestically. Mexico, for example, was racking up inflation rates sometimes exceeding 100% per year, compared with a maximum of only 15% in US.

Best to put into your memory banks the times the real value of the dollar peaked: March 1985 at 128 and February 2002 at 113. That was a good time to buy imported wines and visit foreign lands. With the real value of the dollar approaching

Fig. 19.3 Real and nominal exchange rates

its previous low value achieved in 1995, now is not the time to do any foreign shopping. We will need to understand those two peaks and the valleys too.

19.2.3 The Demand and Supply of US Dollars

What accounts for the strengthening of the US dollar in the mid 1980s and the late 1990s? It must be an increase in the demand for dollars or a reduction in supply. The demand for dollars by foreigners comes from their desire to buy our goods and our assets. The supply of dollars comes when US citizens buy foreign goods and foreign assets. Armed with a simple supply and demand model, we can do a little detective work to figure out why the value of the dollar rose in the 1980s and the 1990s. A clue is that the US was running a current account *deficit* in both periods. What increases in the demand for dollars by foreigners and what reductions in the supply of dollars by US citizens cause a current account deficit?

Explanations for the rise and fall in the real value of the dollar are summarized in Table 19.3, which identifies the direction of change in the dollar, the supply/demand changes that could have caused this shift in the dollar, the sources of that change and the consequent effect on the current account: deficit or surplus. On the left of this table are the conditions that give rise to an appreciating dollar: More demand or less supply. That might have come from the current account side: more demand for dollars to buy US goods or less supply of dollars to buy foreign goods. But those changes in the current account would create a current account surplus with the

Table 19.3 Conditions that occur when the value of the US dollar changes

	Dollar appreciates		Dollar depreciates	
Supply and demand for $	More demand/less supply		Less demand/more supply	
Source of the change	Goods and services	Assets	Good and services	Assets
Current account response	Surplus	Deficit	Deficit	Surplus

US exports rising and the US imports falling. What if the disturbance came from the capital account side: great new investment opportunities in the US, more demand by foreigners to buy US assets and less demand by Americans to buy foreign assets? This increased net demand for US assets would cause an appreciating dollar, which would make our exports more expensive and our imports less expensive, causing the US to export less and to import more. That's it! That's the deficit that we are looking for. A strong value of the dollar combined with a deficit on the current account is a symptom of the attractiveness of the US as a place to invest or the lack thereof for foreign investments. That's a good deficit. A **gold rush**, if you will.

Changes on the Capital Account side can also produce a surplus with a weak dollar because of weak demand for US assets by foreigners and strong demand for foreign assets by US investors – a capital flight, in other words. That **capital flight** causes a deteriorating value of the dollar, and, in response to the price changes, more exports and less imports. That's a bad surplus.

By a similar difficult logic, a deficit with a depreciating value of the dollar comes from the current account not the capital account, and is a symptom of weakness: deterioration of the quality of US goods compared with foreign goods, and the shift of consumers around the globe toward foreign made products. That shift in demand in favor of foreign goods increases the demand for foreign currency and reduces the demand for the dollar, which causes a depreciation of the real value of the dollar. That fall in the real value of the dollar makes US assets cheaper, and foreigners buy more, which reestablishes the balance of demand and supply for dollars.

A surplus can also be caused by a surge in receipts on the Current Account. If the US produces a new gadget that everyone is desperate to own, US citizens will cut down their spending on imports and spend more on the US gadgets, and foreigners will rush to purchase our exports. That creates an elevated value of the dollar and an external surplus.

19.2.4 US Deficits: Good or Bad?

Bottom line here: We should not prejudice the conversation by calling it a "deficit".

My Microsoft thesaurus offers four synonyms for a deficit: shortage, paucity, lack, and deficiency. Clearly we want none of these. To use this word "deficit" is thus to accept mercantilist attitudes that exports are good and imports are bad, as if the deficit had its roots in a failure of our exports. Better to call it a loan than a deficit. A loan is a good thing if the proceeds are wisely used.

The good deficits occur when the dollar is strong and the bad ones occur when the dollar is weak. The good deficits occur because foreigners want to invest in US and they can only do so if there is a current account deficit (don't forget: the current account = the capital account). A deficit with a strong dollar is a symptom of the interest of investors in US dollar denominated assets. The bad deficits occur when we cannot sell enough US made products to pay for the goods we buy, and the (temporary) current account deficit must be financed by borrowing from abroad. A deficit with a weak dollar then is a symptom of the price-cutting that we are forced into when we have trouble selling enough of our products.

It doesn't matter if there is a surplus or a deficit.
Strong Dollar Good; Weak Dollar Bad

So what about the US deficits? Good or bad? We can see some of each in Fig. 19.4, which depicts the US deficit and the value of the dollar. The dollar appreciated by about 40% between 1978 and 1985. During this period of a rising dollar value, the US went from external balance to substantial deficit – that's a good deficit, driven by the demand for US assets by foreign investors, which offered a safe haven in a turbulent world. Declining interest in US assets after 1985 drove the real exchange rate down and closed the external deficit by 1992. But from 1992 to 1995, an increasing deficit came with a declining value of the dollar – that's a bad deficit – a symptom of the erosion of US leadership in global manufacturing. The widening of the deficit after 1995 was accompanied by a rising value of the dollar, again symptomatic of the attractiveness of the US for foreign investors, in this case, the dot-com firms of the Internet Rush.

19.3 How Can the US External Deficit Close?

The size and persistence of the recent deficit have been a big puzzle for most economists. We all said that it could not last much longer in 2000, and we said the same thing again in 2001 and again in 2002, and again... But a sharp decline in the value of the dollar from its peak in 2002 has been signaling that the adjustment cannot be put off any longer. Finally, in 2007, we are getting stronger export growth, weaker import growth, and some reduction in the current account relative to GDP. This looks like another capital account adjustment, with the global investors getting disenchanted with US investments, causing a depreciation of the dollar, weaker import growth and a surge of US exports.

The adjustment could also come on the current account side with export promotion policies that create more exports and/or with tariffs or quantitative restrictions that limit the amount of imports. Or it could come from an increase in demand for US goods by foreigners, like the Chinese, for example.

Let us discuss the adjustment possibilities and try to formulate the best policy response to our lingering and substantial external deficit.

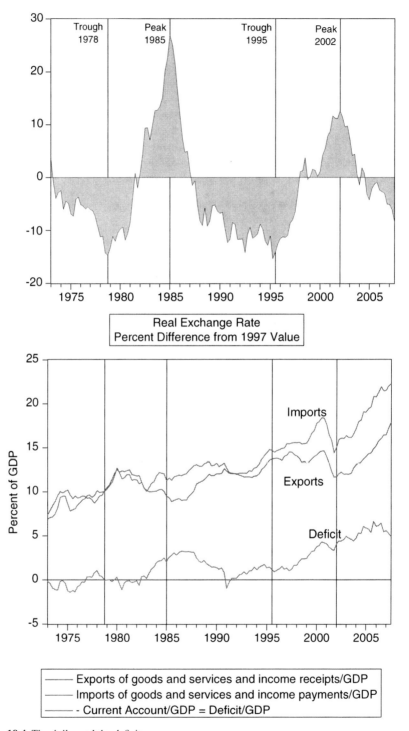

Fig. 19.4 The dollar and the deficit

19.3.1 Capital Account Adjustment: Foreign Investors Go Elsewhere

Sooner or later, global investors will force an adjustment, with or without any action by the US government. If the US growth and the equity appreciation weaken, and if things start to look better elsewhere, then global investors may return to the emerging markets or focus on Europe of all places, and abandon the US. If this happens, the US current account deficit will close – that's the accounting identity. What might else happen then? Think about that at a personal level. Suppose that you have been living beyond your means by building up credit card debt, but then your creditors say "no more." If your creditors give you enough time you can find an extra job so you can maintain your current lavish life style. If your creditors do not give you time to find that extra work, you are just going to have to cut back on that spending.

The big deficit of the 1980s closed over a six-year period of time from 1986 to 1992. That was a long enough period of time for the depreciated value of the dollar to slowly encourage more export growth. That extended period allowed an adjustment without any major damage to the economy. We ramped up exports slowly and kept import demand from growing any faster than GDP. But it takes time to develop and to expand markets for US exports, and rapid adjustment of the trade deficit can only be accomplished on the import side. Doing the correction rapidly on the import side is a painful process. If you are not willing voluntarily to spend a little less on imported goods for sale at Wal-Mart, and if global creditors insist, the global markets will have to find a way to compel you to change. The first step is to make all those imported products more expensive because of a depreciation of the value of the dollar.

A falling value of the dollar that makes imports more expensive can help to reduce US imports, but the price responsiveness of imports is too little to eliminate the US deficit rapidly. The initial response to a falling value of the dollar is actually to worsen the deficit, since with a weaker dollar we have to pay more for imported petroleum and other products. The current account can close only when the volume of imports falls more than the prices rise.

More likely, if global investors insist on a rapid elimination of the deficit, Mr. Bernanke and the Fed would be forced to lower US imports through an income effect – by tolerating a serious economic downturn by increasing interest rates to defend the value of the dollar. Those higher interest rates would keep inflationary forces of more expensive imports at bay, and they would make US bonds more attractive to foreign investors, but to create a $800 billion swing in the current account we will need interest rates high enough to cause a recession with incomes and jobs declining. Then we really will not be able to buy all those imported products. In other words, under the worst-case scenario, the US in 2009 or 2010 may look like Mexico in 1995 with high interest rates, slow or negative growth, and rising unemployment, but with the trade deficit closed. That is not a good solution.

Oddly enough our Treasury Secretaries on junkets to Asia seem to be asking for this outcome. What if Secretary Snow gets his wish and the Chinese stop supporting their exchange rate and stop buying US Treasury Bonds, allowing the yuan to float relative to the dollar? What happens if there is a sudden stop? A nasty US recession? A sudden collapse of Chinese growth? Is that what you want, Secretary Snow?

19.3.2 Capital Account Adjustment: More US Savings

We are now in a position to answer the homework question for Secretary Snow posed earlier: How can the US external deficit be closed without foreign demand for US assets declining? The answer is in the accounting identity: more US savings. If the savings side of the identity increases, then that savings will finance a larger part of US investment and reliance on foreign borrowing will decline. Thus, rather than pestering the Chinese, Secretary Snow should stay home and find ways to encourage US residents to be more frugal. That reminds me that in the 1970s the Ford administration fought inflation by passing out WIN buttons: Whip Inflation Now. What we need now are SAVE buttons: Stop Avarice, Vanity, and Envy. But don't do this all at once; that would cause a recession. Let us very slowly increase our savings, and start financing a larger share of our own domestic investment.

19.3.3 Current Account Adjustment: Barriers Against Imports

When our Congress reads about the deficit they never think of tax measures to encourage savings, like balancing the Federal budget deficit. They do not understand that the current account equals the capital account. To eliminate a deficit they focus on the current account and threaten barriers against imports, particularly imports from China. That is not a good idea. US commercial policies, except those that inappropriately discourage savings, should not be designed with reference to the trade deficit. I understand that the trade deficit has great power rhetorically in policy debates about trade and wages, but that is dangerous rhetoric since the income inequality issues will remain even if the deficit is closed.

19.3.3.1 Who Pays for Unfair Trade? (Trade Barriers Do Not Create Deficits)

US government officials usually assume that deficits are bad, and they often blame the deficits on foreign governments that adopt measures including transparent barriers like tariffs and nontransparent barriers such as health and safety regulations that make it difficult to sell US products in their markets. "We need a "level playing field" to get rid of the US deficit," is what our government officials argue.

Although we may need a level playing field, this has nothing to do with the external deficit. Here is a micro-economics homework problem, which I label UNFAIR

TRADE. Suppose that Japan is located at the top of a hill and the US is at the bottom. Suppose that Japanese goods can effortlessly be moved to the US market – they are just placed on a chute and gravity does the work. Suppose, that it is very difficult to lug US goods up the hill to Japan.

US Exports

Questions:

(a) Do these barriers cause a US trade deficit?
(b) Who pays for lugging US goods up to Japan?

ANSWER: The answer to part (a) is "not at all". Mountains of trade barriers do not create lasting trade deficits. Rational Japanese at the top of the hill are not going to give away their goods indefinitely with nothing in return. The US is going to have to pay for Japanese goods coming down the mountain with US goods lugged up to Japan.

The answer to part (b), the lugging question, is "It depends." It depends on how much Japanese want US goods vs. how much US consumers want Japanese goods. If the US consumers could care less, then it is the Japanese who will have to pay for the lugging. In micro-economics jargon, a disproportionate share of the transportation costs is borne by the economy with the least elastic supply and demand.

Thus trade barriers are not necessarily *unfair* to the sellers they are intended to exclude. For example, an ongoing and long-standing dispute regarding the exports of lumber from Canada to the US has led to duties being imposed by the US on Canadian lumber imports. Who pays these duties? Canadians think that they are paying the fees, but I suspect that it is mostly US homebuyers who are paying more for the lumber in their new homes. It is quite possible that the US duties have hardly any impact on the price received by Canadian lumber mills, and the US duties are entirely passed on to US consumers in the form of higher lumber prices. The winners would then be the US lumber mills and timber interests that get higher prices for their products. The losers would be US buyers of new homes. Adding insult to injury, the Byrd amendment directed the duties collected by the US to be handed over to the US lumber mills, making sure that they are getting the whole benefit of the higher prices charged to US consumers. (This Byrd amendment was ruled illegal by the WTO, but continues to be applied by the US government.)

But back to our central point. The persistent US barriers against Canadian lumber do not create or contribute to an external deficit with Canada. The trade barriers that make it difficult to sell US products in Japan and China and other Asian countries do not cause the bilateral deficits with those countries. Trade negotiations that open up the Asian markets to US goods would benefit both the US and Asia, but have no discernible effect on the US deficit. It lies mostly in the US mismatch between savings and investment: we have to borrow to finance our investments because we do not save enough.

Chapter 20
The Ups and Downs of Real Estate Values:
Can You Rely on Your Home To Pay For Your Retirement?

Do you own a home? That may be your most valuable asset (other than your diploma and your spouse, not necessarily in that order). If you have a home, you probably have a mortgage as well. That's a liability. The difference between the market value of your home and the mortgage debt that is still outstanding is your *home equity*, which is part of your "net worth."[1]

You need net worth to fund your retirement, as well as to provide for any rainy days or uncontrollable spending splurges that lie ahead. Do you have enough net worth? What about all of us together? Have we accumulated enough to take care of the aging baby boomers? What about that $10 trillion increase in real estate values from 2001 to 2006? Will that help take care of our elderly? (Foreshadowing: No)

20.1 Household Assets and Liabilities

Let us begin by getting a feel for how large the real estate assets and liabilities are. Is your house worth 4 times your income, or 8? Is your mortgage twice your income? What about the balance on your credit card? Is that 1% of the income? Your ratios are probably very different from other Americans.

Assets and liabilities of US households relative to the personal income from 1995 to 2005 are illustrated in Figs. 20.1 and 20.2, respectively. Both sides of the household balance sheets are greatly influenced by the real estate. On the asset side of the ledger, real estate is two times personal income. Offsetting that asset is mortgage debt equal to 80% of personal incomes. Assets, which are currently over six times personal income are dominated by equities[2] (three times personal income) and real estate. The other important assets are deposits in banks and other institutions, consumer durables, and bonds. Liabilities, currently 120% of personal income, are

---

[1] "Net" here means assets "net of" liabilities. Do you remember what it means in Net National Product? Not the same.

[2] Held personally and in pension fund reserves.

E. E. Leamer, *Macroeconomic Patterns and Stories: A Guide for MBAs.*
© Springer-Verlag Berlin Heidelberg 2009

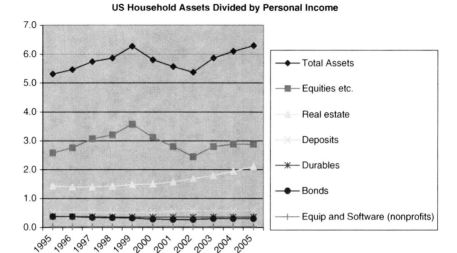

Fig. 20.1 Household assets

mostly home mortgage debt (80% of personal income) and consumer credit (20% of personal income).

Are you surprised by these numbers? If you own a home, its value is probably greater than two times your income and your mortgage likewise is probably much greater than 80% of income. The overall averages reflect the fact that 30% of

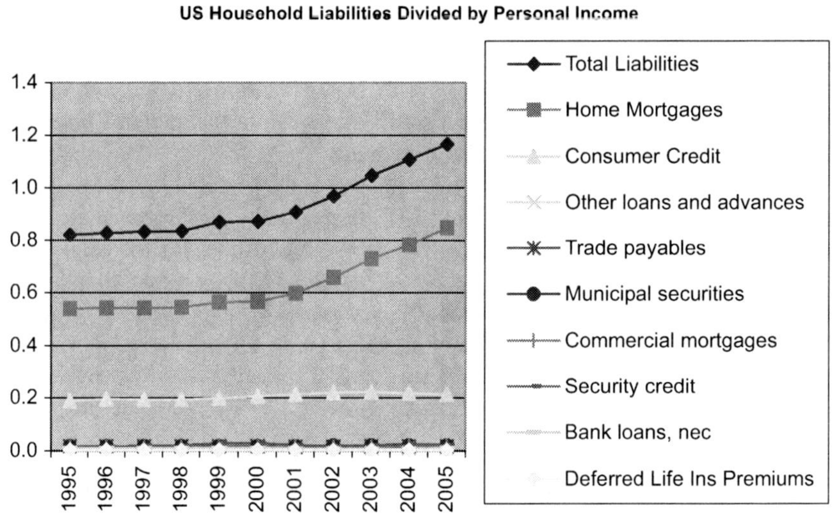

US Household Liabilities Divided by Personal Income

- Total Liabilities
- Home Mortgages
- Consumer Credit
- Other loans and advances
- Trade payables
- Municipal securities
- Commercial mortgages
- Security credit
- Bank loans, nec
- Deferred Life Ins Premiums

Fig. 20.2 Household liabilities

households do not own homes, and many owners financed their homes years ago when their incomes were lower.

Also what about your credit card debt and auto loans (consumer credit)? Are they 20% of your income like the overall average? I hope not. This average debt combines folks like you with low ratios of consumer debt to income with other folks with very high ratios. How high must be the consumer debt of some Americans to produce that overall ratio to income of 20%?

Best to keep in mind that you are not at all "average." For more information about the fractions of household who own home and have debt, see the Appendix.

It is evident in Figs. 20.1 and 20.2 that there has been a noticeable rise in real estate values on both sides of the balance sheet between 1995 and 2005. A hot housing market increased the ratio of real estate value to personal income from 1.5 to 2.1. At the same time, refinancing of the existing mortgages and new mortgages on purchases of existing and new homes increased the ratio of mortgage debt to income from 0.6 to 0.8.

The debt is real – except for defaults and foreclosures, the mortgage debt is going to be paid back. Whether or not the increase in real estate asset values is real is a matter of discussion to which we next turn. First, we can answer the question: so what, so what if it were not real? How much would it matter if the housing bubble inflated the measured value of the assets beyond what they could really sell for? Figure 20.3 illustrates the household net worth relative to income as measured by the Federal Reserve Board inclusive of the increase in the real estate assets, and also holding the real estate assets at their year 2000 valuations. Here we can see what the decline in the stock market from 2000 to 2002 did to the measured net worth, dropping it from almost 5.5 times the incomes to 4.5. But the increase in the measured value of real estate assets has by 2005 largely offset the dot-com bust, bringing the net worth to income ratios above 5 again in 2005. If those real estate assets had not increased, the household balance sheets would have remained

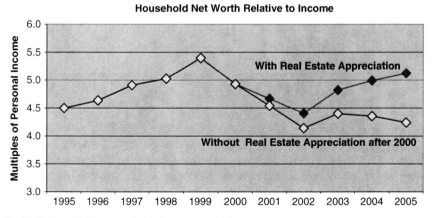

Fig. 20.3 Household net worth relative to personal income

troubled, holding the net worth to income ratio below 4.25. So it matters whether or not that real estate wealth is real.

With the benefit of hindsight, we now know that much of the improvement in household balance sheets from 1995 to 1999 was not real. We bought shares of those dot-com companies at values that could not have possibly been sustained because the business plans that lay behind them could never have generated the profits to support those valuations. The same is true for part of the increase in the real estate value from 2000 to 2005. We need to figure out how much. How much paper wealth is going to evaporate with the declining home prices?

20.2 It Is Not Real Until You Realize It

Are real estate values real?

In periods when home prices are elevating rapidly, homeowners dress in their finest outfits to attend cocktail parties where the conversation inevitably migrates to housing and where owners can bask in the glory of their superior intelligence. In 2005 and 2006, there were plenty of these parties around the United States and in many other countries around the globe, too.

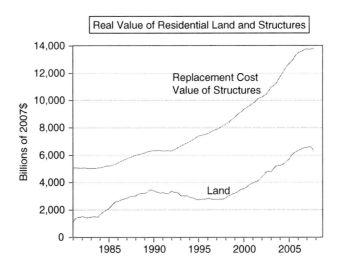

According to the Flow of Funds Accounts of the Federal Reserve Board,[3] the value of the residential real estate doubled between 1999 and 2006, rising from $10 trillion to $20 trillion. (That increase is about a full year's GDP.) According to the same source, about half of that increase was a rise in the replacement costs of the

---

[3] The access is not user-friendly, but you can find the information at http://www.federalreserve. gov/releases/z1/

residences and the other half was an increase in the value of the land on which these
buildings rest. The value of the land adjusted for inflation rose from $3.0 trillion in
1999 to $6.5 trillion in 2006.

But $3 trillion and $6.5 trillion are just numbers on computer hard-drives. Do
these numbers accurately reflect an increase in the *real* wealth? Was the residential
land of the United States "really" worth in 2005 more than twice what it was worth
in 1999? Walk around your lot and see if you can notice the difference. Can you feel
the improvement, or smell it or see it? Has the view improved? Is it closer to good
schools? That would be real. But if the land is exactly the same, why is the price so
much higher?

There is a good question that helps determine whether the appreciation is real, or
just a number on a hard drive: Does that increase in the price of land reflect some
increase in future GDP that flows from it? Real increases in wealth do increase
future GDP. That is exactly what being wealthier means: the future is better than
it used to be. Real increases in wealth include new equipment and new offices and
new homes and new improvements to land, all of which help create a larger GDP in
the future. But most of that residential land did not change at all from 2001 to 2006.
How could that possibly increase future GDP? (Hint: it would take a change in the
"technology" that transforms land into the services that land provides. This could
have happened, but it didn't. More on this below.)

To try to figure this out, it is helpful to consider three different cases. In each case,
the homeowner hears from her neighbor that: "Our lots are selling for $1 million
more than they did last year." So what? What is the operational significance of this
increase in the price of land?

Case 1. The homeowner will live forever and will stay in that same home for the
duration.

For a homeowner who is going to stay in the property forever, the "price" of the
home is completely irrelevant. The $1 million increase in the value of the land has
no impact on any cash flows and should not in the slightest change any decisions.
There is no real wealth corresponding to that $1 million.

Case 2. The home is going to be sold to the next generation.

For a family that will live forever and pass the home from generation to generation, the family overall has no increase in wealth from the news that the land is
worth $1 million more, but there is an intergenerational transfer. The homeowners
should put on their books the $1 million increase in the value of their land, but this
asset should be exactly offset by a $1 million liability on the balance sheets of the
young renters, since they are going to have to work harder to raise the cash to pay
the higher price.

When we book the asset but not the liability, we make an accounting error. We
are creating "phantom" wealth that encourages us to spend beyond our means. The
Flow of Funds accounting of the Federal Reserve makes this error by booking the
asset but not the liability. That is surely the case for private citizens. Homeowners
keep track of the increase in their wealth held as residential land, but the future-
buyers currently renting do not much notice their increasing liability. On the other

hand, if these renters are planning on avoiding that liability by never buying a home, then the error is on the asset side: homeowners are booking an increase in the value of their home that they will never realize.

This is a $3.5 trillion accounting error, which seems like a big number, but is actually small potatoes compared with the $50 trillion (or more) of unfunded Federal liabilities for Social Security and Medicare. We book these as assets when we imagine that the Federal Government is going to take care of us as we age, but we are not booking the future taxes to pay these benefits as a liability. (Ask again the question to determine whether these assets are real: Do the Federal Government promises to pay for Social Security and Medicare in the future increase future GDP in any way at all?)

By encouraging us to spend the income we will never have these phantom assets support our profligate spending, which is going to get us in trouble soon enough. The young people will never be able to pay all the taxes needed to keep Social Security and Medicare afloat, and they will not have enough left over to buy all those homes at the inflated prices. The consequences are obvious as we unwind all this bad debt. The elderly are not going to get as much Medicare and Social Security as they imagine, and homeowners are not going to find buyers for their homes at those sky-high prices. When that reality sets in, we are going to have a lot of elderly Americans living in their aging SUV's parked on the side of the road.

Case 3. The homeowner is planning to leave the area and will be selling the property to a new immigrant.

Remember that an increase in real wealth means that the future is brighter than it used to be. For land to contribute to a brightening future, we need a change in the technology by which GDP is created from that land. A good example is a gold rush. When gold was discovered in the hills above Sacramento, the land in the town increased in value as the prospectors rushed to California and needed places to stay. The value of the gold was, therefore, shared partly with the landowners in town. Do you understand how this is a change in the technology that transforms residential land into GDP? When gold was discovered the land became an input into the extraction of gold: miners, pans, shovels, and places to live are all required.

Incidentally, for those local homeowners who do not take advantage of the gold rush by either selling their property or renting it out to the prospectors, there is no increase in their wealth. It is not real until you realize it.

Now that we have a framework for thinking, which of these three cases applies to the appreciation of residential land from 2000 to 2006? Is the appreciation of real estate values: (1) an accounting fiction that should not have changed anyone's behavior, (2) a wealth transfer from renters to owners, or (3) a real increase in US wealth (greater future GDP) because of increased future demand for US residential land by foreigners?[4]

---

[4] Homework: what about lower interest rates? Don't lower interest rates imply a greater value for existing durable assets?

Answer: It's mostly (2), a big transfer of wealth from future owners to current owners, though not as much as the numbers suggest, because most of the current owners will never be able to make the sale at the current prices, corrected for inflation. More now on how prices are determined next, and what can make them wander from the real valuations.

20.3 What Determines the Price and What Determines the Value of Your Home?

20.3.1 The Rental Market and the Ownership Market

Before we plow into the relationship between the price and the value of your home, you need to grasp something that is confused by most journalists and some professional economists too. When it comes to homes, there are two distinctly different but interrelated markets:

- The Rental Market: There is a market for places to live that determines who resides in each existing dwelling.
- The Ownership Market: There is also a market for ownership of the places to live that determines who owns each existing dwelling.

When we hear the word "rent," most of us think of apartment buildings, and when we hear the word home-ownership, most of us think of single-family homes. But to understand the point I am making here you need to abandon this thinking. Keep in the forefront of your mind the fact that there are many multifamily buildings in which some or all of the units are owned by the occupants (condos), and there are many single-family homes that are rented by the occupants. Occupancy and ownership are thus distinct attributes.

In both the rental market and the ownership market, there is a price and quantity. The rental market determines a market clearing rental price of the housing units such that the demand for places to live equals the number of places available. The ownership market determines a market-clearing price of homes such that the demand for homes for ownership/investment purposes equals the number of homes available. When a new home is built, it adds a unit to both of these markets. When a family decides to buy the unit in which they reside, the rental market is completely unaffected but the demand for ownership goes up.

If there are too many people with high incomes competing for a few places to live, the rents will be high, and some people will be forced by those high prices to live in crowded dwellings. (Think of the gold rush, again.) Alternatively, if there has been a large number of new building and not much economic growth, rents will be low. That's the rental market that is determined by the *current* balance between people looking for places to live and available residences.

The ownership market should be driven more by the *expected future* conditions than by current conditions. If the area is encumbered with zoning restrictions and regulations that limit future building, and if the local economic growth is expected to be strong, there will be a scramble to own the homes to lock in the monthly payments before the rents rise. In these circumstances, home prices will be high relative to the current rents.

In principle, the rental market can clear first, with people bidding to live in the various available units. After that, the units can be sold to prospective owners, who will of course take the current rents into consideration when they decide how much to bid to own the properties, and who will be willing to pay more for the units that will command high rents in the future because of regional economic growth and/or lack of available building space and antigrowth zoning.

To help you understand the difference between the rental market and the owner-ship market, try answering the questions:

What are the units of the market-clearing price for places to live? Dollars or dollars per year?

Answer: Dollars per year. This is the rental market. If you live in a rental unit, you know how much it is costing you to rent, but if you own your own dwelling, there is still an "owner's equivalent rent," which is how much you could rent the unit for.

What are the units of the market-clearing price for ownership? Dollars or dollars per year?

Answer: Dollars, not dollars per year. You pay $500,000 to buy that house.

When you read in the newspaper that the supply of homes is at a record low, to which market does that refer?

Answer: the ownership market. This newspaper article only means that there are not many owners who have listed their homes for sale. It does not mean that some catastrophe has wiped out a sizable chunk of our housing stock.

When you read in the paper that California is not building enough homes to keep up with the increases in population, to which market does that refer?

Answer: the rental market. This is really saying that rents can be expected to be higher in the future.

20.3.2 Do not Confuse the Rental Market and the Ownership Market

I remember a realtor telling me some time ago that I should buy ocean front prop-erty because they are not making more of it and the price could only go up. The same kind of thinking has led many to conclude that, since California "needs" more housing, any run-up in the prices is justified by supply and demand, and no specu-lative bubble can ever occur. For example, the LA Times, Monday, 27 May 2002, reported:

"With limited inventory and tightly controlled lending for new projects, the in-dustry runs 'no risk of collapse' even if the economy stumbles, Economy.com ana-lyst Steven Cochrane wrote in a recent report on the state."

These thoughts reflect a lack of understanding of how asset values get deter-mined. They reveal the indifference to the behavior of rents, and/or they show a lack of understanding of the connection between the rents and the asset prices. This is the same error that Wall Street analysts made during the Internet Rush when they imagined that the New Economy changed the rules and created a fundamental disconnect between corporate earnings and stock prices. We know differently now. The stock markets in 2000 and 2001 rudely reminded us that when we buy a stock (an asset), we are buying an earnings stream. The price we pay for the stock should reflect current corporate earnings and reasonable expectations about what the future of earnings might be. An asset bubble is created when the valuation is way in excess of what the current and future earnings could reasonably justify. The same is true for homes; when the asset prices of homes float off into outer space, disconnected from the rental value, that's a bubble. But, as we will discover soon enough, housing price bubbles don't burst. Nominal prices hardly fall, though things have been different in the housing catastrophe we are experiencing in 2007–2009.

20.3.3 Survivor Investing Can Temporarily Disconnect Earnings and Valuations

It is easy to lose track of the connection between corporate earnings and valuations for corporate stocks. Indeed, many investors play Survivor Investing: Outwit, Outlast, Outplay. To them, the value of the stock is what someone else will pay for it. It's the greater fool and the last man in who loses this game. Survivor investing is a zero-sum game, which can transfer a massive amount of wealth from losers to winners.

20.3.4 Survivor Investing Requires a Good Story

When you are about to buy a piece of paper with no intrinsic value except that someone else will pay more for it, you definitely will not ask yourself what it is

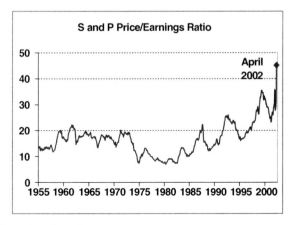

Fig. 20.4 S & P price/earning ratio

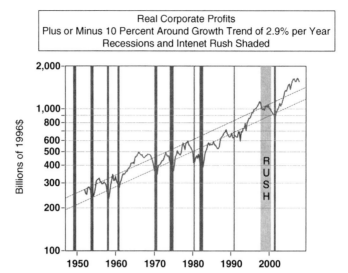

Fig. 20.5 Real corporate profits

"really" worth. You need a compelling story why someone else will pay more for the paper, a story that will divert you from such devastating thoughts. In my lifetime, there has never been as good a story as the New Economy. This story allowed the most cockamamie business plans to attract billions of dollars of new investment, and the story supported a whole new class of investments: all p and no e. Meanwhile, during the Internet Rush from 1996 to 2000, the price/earnings ratio of the venerable S and P 500 illustrated in Fig. 20.4 reached 40 times the earnings when 20 had seemed high by historical standards.

Exceptional growth in corporate earnings is a good reason for a high p/e ratio, if that growth can be expected to persist. Corporate earnings before tax are displayed in the Fig. 20.5 in constant 2007$ using a log scale, which means that straight lines represent constant rates of growth. Over the corporate earnings curve I have placed two straight lines representing the normal corridor in which earnings have grown: plus or minus 10% around a trend growth of 2.9% per year. The shaded regions are the US recessions and the Internet Rush. Generally speaking, earnings have grown smartly during the expansions, have collapsed in the recessions, and have maintained a long-term rate of growth of 2.8%, about the same as Real GDP.

In 1996, if your life as an investor did not begin until 1992, you would have seen a very different picture – Fig. 20.6 – which suggests "normal" corporate earnings growth of 10.4%, not the 2.9% from the longer view. A much higher p/e ratio is easily justified with this kind of growth and the elevation of the S and P p/e ratio from 7.5 in 1982 to 24 in 1993 is fully supported by this "new" 10.5% growth in earnings.

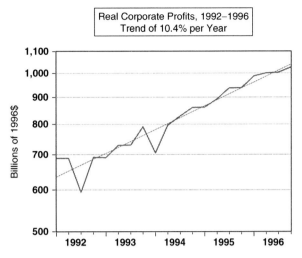

Fig. 20.6 Real corporate profits in the 1990s

But when the corporate earnings stalled out at $800 billion[5] in 1997, the momentum of the New Economy story, nonetheless, supported an additional 80% increase in the S and P 500 index from 824 in 1997 Q3 to 1475 in 2000 Q3. That's a bubble, unless these investors knew something about the future corporate earnings that was a complete mystery to me.

But look back at the Fig. 20.5 again. Since the 2001 recession, corporate profits have been on a tear, and profits are now well outside their normal range. Maybe those valuations back in 2000 were not so bad after all! Thanks in part to very strong growth in corporate earnings, the price/earnings ratio of the S and P is now back from the stratosphere, on the high side based on comparisons over the last 50 years (Fig. 20.7) but not totally out-of-whack with that historical experience.

20.3.5 Fundamental Valuation Depends on the Growth of Earnings and the Discount Rate

Now a brief primer on fundamental valuation: If we could see the future perfectly, how much should we pay for an asset that yields dividends this year and next and so on and so on? There are two variables to keep track of: the growth rate of earnings and the discount rate used to translate future earnings into today's dollars. The present value of a stream of future corporate earnings depends on the rate of growth of earnings and also on the risk adjusted discount rate that is used to translate uncertain future earnings into today's equivalent dollars. Fig.20.8 illustration p/e valuation ratios for two 100-year earnings streams with different rates of growth. The higher value applies to the stream that has 5% earnings growth. The lower curve

---

[5] In current $.

Fig. 20.7 S & P performance

is the valuation of a stream with a 2.5% rate of growth. A p/e ratio of 20, such as the S and P had in the 1960s applies to the 2.5% stream evaluated at an 8% rate of discount. At that same rate of discount, the 5% stream has a p/e ratio of 34, which is about what we had in the late 1990s. You can also get a 34 p/e ratio for the 2.5% stream if you use a lower rate of discount, about 5.5%.

Many academics are members of the "efficient markets" sect, which is premised on the idea that the equity values are completely determined by fundamentals, not by Survivor Investors. Those elevated p/e ratios for equities in the late 1990s produced a debate among these academics: More earnings or a lower discount rate? Were globalization and the New Economy increasing the long-term rate of growth of US corporate earnings, or were investors using a lower discount rate because earnings are less risky and/or investors more risk tolerant. For these efficient market zealots, those are the only two options. But I think it was neither. It was Internet day traders and asset managers playing Survivor Investing.

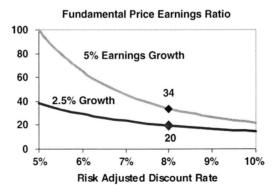

Fig. 20.8 Price earnings ratio

20.3.6 A House Has a p/e Ratio, Too

You may not think about it when you buy a house, but it's the same thing. The price you pay should reflect the present value of future rent. You should go through the same mental calculation in purchasing a home as in purchasing a stock. Ask yourself how much the house could currently be rented for on an annual basis. Subtract from that rent the maintenance costs and property taxes. Divide the seller's asking price by this adjusted rent number. That's the p/e ratio, the ratio of price to earnings. If a $500,000 house could generate $25,000 in annual rental earnings net of maintenance and management and property taxes, then the p/e ratio is 20.

A high p/e ratio for a house can be justified because of the considerable tax advantages that are afforded to housing. A high p/e ratio can be justified if other assets are similarly high priced, for example, if bond yields and mortgage rates are low. A high p/e ratio for homes can be justified in regions that can be expected to experience high growth and thus rapid appreciation in rental values, just like a tech stock can have a higher p/e than an automobile manufacturer. But you are completely deluding yourself if you think there can be a long-run disconnect between a house price and its potential rental stream. That's Survivor Investing.

I know it is hard to think this way. Unlike stocks, investments in homes do not come with quarterly earnings statements. Unlike stocks, the price of your home is not listed in the Wall Street Journal every day, which allows you to keep it on your books at whatever price suits your current mood.[6] You are not the only one having a hard time with the difference between the asset price and the rental value. Even the Federal Government did not do the right calculation when it computed the Consumer Price Index prior to 1983. (Think about it: for the CPI do we want the rental price or the asset price? See the discussion in an appendix to this chapter.)

Stock market p/e ratios can climb skyward for reasons that are hard to figure, and they can sit at painfully low levels for painfully long periods of time. The same thing is true for homes, even more so. As far as housing is concerned, we have a terrible bipolar disease, switching back and forth from periods of manic buying to periods of depressed waiting. In the manic phases, housing p/e's skyrocket, and in the depressed waiting phases, p/e's ever so slowly come back to earth, waiting and hoping for the next bout of mania.

20.3.7 The p/r Ratios in US Cities

I wonder what has been happening to p/e ratios of homes and apartments. Some data would help. To keep us all confused, apartment buildings do not have p/e ratios – they have "cap rates." A capitalization rate is the ratio of lease payments net of costs divided by the market value of the building. It's just an E/P ratio. Upside down or not, it is the same thing.

---

[6] http://www.zillow.com does allow some up-to-the minute estimate of the value of your house, but when things go bad, you do not really want to know, do you?

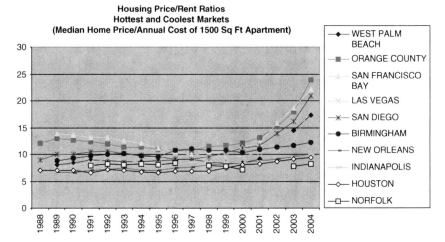

Fig. 20.9 P/r ratios

But homes do not have cap rates or p/e ratios because accountants do not routinely compute the rents net of expenses. So we have to content ourselves with price to gross rent ratios. That's not the only problem. No data of which I am aware track the p/r ratios of specific homes. The price data refer generally to the median *sales* price of homes, which causes problems as mix of homes sold varies over time. Even worse, the rental data are typically average rent per square foot of apartments not homes, which may bear little relationship to the rent of the home corresponding to the median sale price. But that's what we have to work with.

Figure 20.9 illustrates price-to-rent ratios in the five hottest markets and the five coolest markets in the period 2000–2004. The price is the median sale price, and the rent is the average price per square foot times 1,500 sq ft. These may not be perfect indicators of market excesses, but they seem to tell the story right. The five cool markets had the p/r ratios hover around 10. The hot markets started at around 10 and then double to 20. What justifies a doubling in p/r ratios in some markets and no change in others? How are West Palm Beach and Orange County different from Houston and Norfolk and Indianapolis?

I know you are bothered by the use of apartment rents to measure the rental value of the homes in an area, but try to keep in mind that rapidly elevating rents of apartments is a symptom of economic growth that is outstripping the available housing stock. That economic growth should have similar effects on the implicit rental values of owner-occupied homes. But the proof of this pudding is in the tasting.

The point of computing these p/r ratios is to try to figure out which markets are likely to fall the most in the coming correction. So check out Table 20.1 that is based on the OFHEO home price indexes[7] for these ten markets. The first column of numbers has the appreciation from 1999Q1 to the peak of the housing price, and the second has the subsequent decline through 2007Q4. The hottest markets

---

[7] http://www.ofheo.gov/

Table 20.1 Prices in the hottest and coolest markets

	Appreciation 1999Q1 to peak price (%)	2007 Q4 Fall from peak price (%)
Hottest Markets		
West Palm Beach-Boca Raton-Boynton Beach, FL	163	−10.9
Santa Ana-Anaheim-Irvine, CA (MSAD)	156	−6.2
San Francisco-San Mateo-Redwood City, CA	94	−2.2
Las Vegas-Paradise, NV	126	−6.0
San Diego-Carlsbad-San Marcos, CA	137	−8.1
Coolest Markets		
Birmingham-Hoover, AL	47	0.0
New Orleans-Metairie-Kenner, LA	66	−0.3
Indianapolis-Carmel, IN	25	0.0
Houston-Sugar Land-Baytown, TX	45	0.0
Virginia Beach-Norfolk-Newport News, VA-NC	126	0.0

have all had substantial declines, with more to come. The coolest markets have had no decline, or in one case, a very small decline. So there you go – p/r ratios have predictive value!

20.4 Some Realities of a Very Imperfect Ownership Market: The Very Persistent Gap Between Values and Prices

Fundamental analysis of the value of homes is a complicated business and few who name a selling price and few who negotiate a purchase price are even vaguely familiar with a p/e ratio.[8] So what determines home prices? The appraisal process is part of the story. Hormones of buyers and sellers matter too. But in the long run, the p/e takes hold as potential buyers think a little bit about what they could rent the same house for.

20.4.1 Home Appraisals: Bob's $1 Million Tie

Here is a story that helps us understand why market momentum is so important in housing. Appraisers, who decide whether or not you get the loan, ignore completely whether the current prices are sustainable or not. They ignore altogether the rental

---

[8] For a report on the hard work of fundamental valuations see Gary Smith and Margaret Hwang Smith "Bubble, Bubble, Where's the Housing Bubble," Brookings Panel on Economic Activity, 30–31 March 2006. These authors conclude: "These data indicate that the current housing bubble is not, in fact, a bubble in most of these cities in that, under a variety of plausible assumptions, buying a house at current market prices still appears to be an attractive long-term investment." (but a very bad short-term investment, as the collapse in prices has revealed)

value of the property, using instead "comparable" sales to value your home. Listen to this story.

Last week I came to work and found myself admiring Bob's tie. I offered him $5 for it, which seemed to offend him greatly. So I raised my offer to $10 and then $100 and finally to $1 million. At that price, Bob finally said yes, he would sell. Larry was listening to this conversation, and mentally comparing his tie with Bob's. Surely, Larry thought, his tie was worth a lot more than Bob's. Great, Larry thought, now I have a tie worth more $1 million. Needing money to pay for a trip to Las Vegas for himself and his friends, Larry went to his banker for $1 million loan. The banker looked at him quizzically. "Normally, we require some collateral for this kind of loan." "No problem," replied Larry, "I have this $1 million tie." The banker thought that was a pretty ridiculous statement, but decided to humor Larry: "OK, we'll have to get it appraised." To the banker's surprise, the appraiser found a "comparable sale" at $1 million and came in with a $1 million appraisal. Larry got his loan.

Of course, Larry will find himself soon enough in trouble unless he can find another lunatic like me who would pay $1 million for his ridiculous necktie.

20.4.2 Hormones and Housing: It's a Volume Cycle Not a Price Cycle

The appraisal process is part of the problem. Another is the close personal relationship we have with our homes.

Housing, like any other investment, has good times and bad. Unlike other investments, the price of homes is very resistant to downward adjustment. Sales go up and down, but prices go mostly up. The appraisal process, which of necessity looks backward, is part of the reason, but the biggest problem is LOVE and ENVY. Love for their homes and envy of their neighbor's sales price makes owners very reluctant to sell into a weak market, which sustains unsustainably high prices for very long periods, and causes large reductions in sales volumes.

Sales of new homes in four US regions from 1973 to March 2008 are illustrated in Fig. 20.10 with US recessions shaded. Each of the four panels here includes a trend line and a ±20% band around that trend line, which can be used to determine when sales are more than 20% above normal and more than 20% below normal. Notice that it is the South (638 thousand units in 2005) where much of the building is done, followed by the West (356) and the Midwest (203). Last is the Northeast (81) where buildable lots for single-family homes are scarce.

A hot housing market from 2000 to 2005 pushed sales rates of new homes well above that +20% line in all regions but the Northeast. The last time the market was so strong was in the 1970s when sales of new homes in all regions but the Northeast (again!) floated well above that +20% band. That housing market crashed in the double dip recession of the early 1980s, when sales volumes in all four regions dipped well below the −20% band.

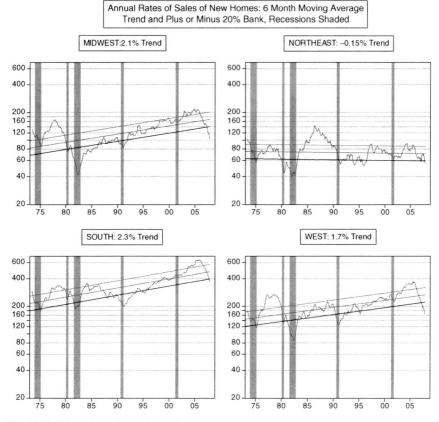

Fig. 20.10 Sales of new homes by region

A substantial dip in sales occurred in the other two recessions in this picture, the 1990/1991 and 1974/1975 events. The only recession of the ones illustrated in which sales did not dip below the normal band was the 2001 "business downturn."

From late 2005 through the end of the period displayed, March 2008, sales have plummeted and fallen below the −20% band in every region. As I write this, we do not have an official determination of recession, but housing is very clearly issuing a recession warning.

A somewhat different image of the housing cycle comes from an examination of the *housing units started*, Fig. 20.11, which is a longer time series and includes both single-family and multifamily dwellings. Here there are no evident trends in the building of housing units in three of the four regions, the exception being the downward trend in the Northeast. Take a good look at these pictures. The increase in building in the 1990s was very gradual, more like a 747 than a rocket, rather unlike the rockets of earlier expansions. But since 2005, our 747 has been dropping like a stone. Housing starts in early 2008 are well below the −20% band, except

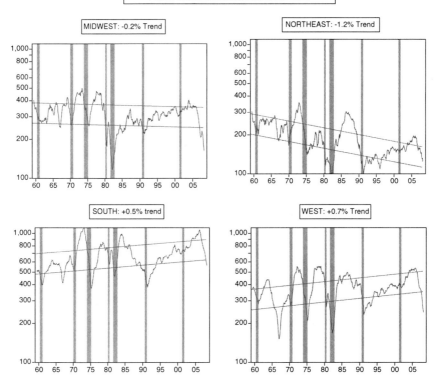

Fig. 20.11 Housing units started, single family and multifamily

for the Northeast, and threatening to go lower still. This is starting to look like the second dip in the 1980s. Ouch, that was really bad.

Never mind, you are thinking. It is not whether you can sell your home that matters. Sales volumes matter to your real estate broker and your title company, but not to you. That's their jobs and their incomes at risk. For you, it is the price. It is the well-being that comes from knowing that your home is "worth" twice as much as you paid for it. Might as well celebrate and buy another SUV. Sorry, better think again. The price of homes also varies, but in a way different from sales. The price trails the sales volume a bit. Remember that: "First comes volume, and then comes price." Something else to remember: the volume cycle is more extreme than the price cycle. It you want to simplify and exaggerate, just say "It's a volume cycle, not a price cycle."

Figure 20.12 illustrates the real prices of new homes sold in the same four regions, with trend lines and with ±10% bands. We needed the wider ±20% bands to capture most of the ups and down in sales volumes. Thus the cycle in volume is twice as amplified as the cycle in inflation-adjusted prices. Through 2007Q4, the

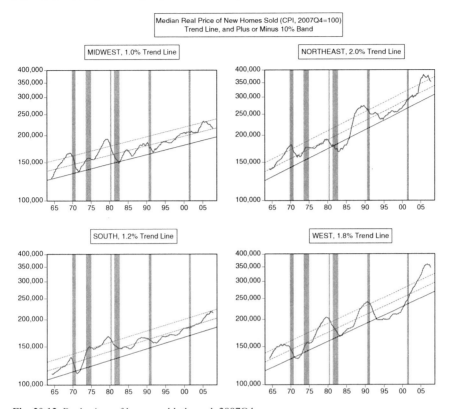

Fig. 20.12 Real prices of homes sold, through 2007Q4

price adjustment has been much milder than the volume adjustment. We are still well above the normal band in the West and at the higher end of the normal corridor everywhere else.

If the notion that your home can fall in value troubles you, skip this discussion and focus instead on Fig. 20.13, which illustrates nominal home prices, unadjusted for inflation. Here you can comfort yourself with the thought that home prices never go down; well almost never, and if they do, the decline is not very much.

There's a reason why home prices do not go down much. We love our homes. We do not love our investments in General Motors or IBM, and when the stock market sends us the daily message that share prices have plummeted, we reluctantly accept that unwelcome reality. Homes are different. We have a close personal relationship with our homes. When the market is hot, buyers stream by our front doors proclaiming that they love our homes even more than we do. Charmed by that flattery, many of us sell our loved ones, confidant that we have turned our home over to someone who will treat it well. Thus rising the prices and high sales volumes. When the market cools, however, only a few prospective buyers come to our front doors, and

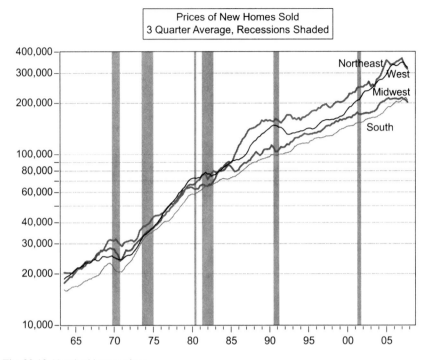

Fig. 20.13 Nominal home prices

those prospective buyers bring a most unsettling message: "We know you love your home, but it isn't worth nearly as much as you think." That can be a deal-breaker for female owners, but the clincher for males is the fact that their idiot neighbor sold his home for $1 million just last year, and the male owner is not going to take a penny less than that. It doesn't matter what the market thinks. This house is worth $1 million, period!

Housing hormones, both estrogen and testosterone, make owners very unwilling to sell into a weak market and that unwillingness tends to keep the prices of homes actually sold high while greatly reducing the volumes of homes sold. We get the sellers' prices not the market prices.

It's a volume cycle not a price cycle.[9]

The reluctance to sell into a weak market can keep nominal prices high, but real prices erode because of general inflation. The wiggles and waves in the real prices illustrated in Fig. 20.12 are caused to a large extent by the variation in the Consumer Price Index.

So now you have a choice: If what matters to you is that you have a $1 million dollar home, and it is completely inconsequential that your $1 million home can

_____

[9] To the surprise of both myself and Wall Streets home owners have been walking away from their homes in droven in 2007 and 2008, and banks, who do not love the homes they own, are auctioning off the properties, creation an unprecedented decline in nominal home prices in region where distressed sales are concentred.

only "buy" $1/2 million of "stuff", then go with the nominal prices illustrated in Fig. 20.13 and pretend that your home cannot fall in value. But if you want to do the accounting the way economists do, and value your home in terms of what you can buy with it, then go with the real prices in Fig. 20.12. If you do elect for the real prices, it is best to keep in mind that the way that real prices of homes decline is by holding the nominal price fixed for several years and letting the inflation of the CPI make the home less valuable. Using nominal prices, it really is a volume cycle, not a price cycle.

If your heart is up to it, take a look again at the real prices in Fig. 20.12. The south, where all that building is going on, has a lower real appreciation rate (1.1% per year) and the most stable prices. The northeast, where little building is occurring, has the highest real appreciation rate (2.0%) and rather volatile prices. That gives a hint about housing markets. It's not the structure that has a volatile price; it's the land. Where there is plenty of buildable land, the response to an increase in demand for homes is mostly to build more, not to increase prices. Where there is little buildable land, the response to an increase in demand for homes is mostly a price increase, sufficient to discourage buyers enough to reequilibrate the supply and demand.

Appendix: Homework re the LA Market

Figure 20.14 illustrates the median sales price and the volume of sales of existing homes in Los Angeles. Here you can see the sharp run-up in both prices and volumes from 1985 to 1989. Sales volume peaked in November 1988 and fell to half in a year

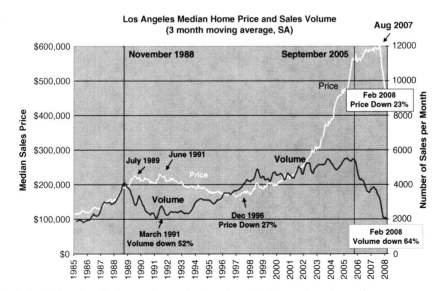

Fig. 20.14 Los Angeles home prices and sales volumes (exiting and new homes)\

and a half. Price appreciation continued for almost a year after the sale peak until July 1989, and then, even with the sales rates at half their previous amounts, prices simply leveled off. A year later in June 1991, prices began an ever so slow decline, reaching their low point four and a half years later in December 1996, down a total of 27%.

This was in the context of an economy that had lost a lot of high-paying defense-related jobs because of the "peace dividend."

It's a volume cycle not a price cycle.

And it's starting again. The February 2008 volume is off 64% from the peak in September 2005, and prices continued to rise even in the face of sharp reductions in volume. But after August 2007, prices started to plummet.

HOMEWORK PROBLEM: What is different this time? Why is there so much price reduction?

Appendix: Home Ownership Data from the Survey of Consumer Finances

Table 20.2 has data on home asset values and outstanding credit card debt by income and age from the 2004 Survey of Consumer Finances. Home ownership percentages naturally elevate with income but the value of homes reaches a maximum in the

Table 20.2 Home assets and credit card balances
2004 Survey of Consumer Finances

	Family holdings of primary residences		Credit card balances	
	Percentage of families	Median value if owner (thousands of $)	Percentage of families	Median value if debtor (thousands of $)
All families	69.1	160.0	46.2	2.2
Percentiles of income				
Less than 20	40.3	70.0	29.1	1.0
20–39.9	57.0	100.0	42.6	1.9
40–59.9	71.5	135.0	54.8	2.1
60–79.9	83.1	175.0	56.2	3.0
80–89.9	91.8	225.0	57.6	2.7
90–100	94.7	450.0	38.7	4.0
Age of head (years)				
Less than 35	41.6	135.0	47.5	1.5
35–44	68.3	160.0	58.8	2.5
45–54	77.3	170.0	54.0	2.9
55–64	79.1	200.0	42.1	2.2
65–74	81.3	150.0	31.9	2.2
75 or more	85.2	125.0	23.5	1.0

55–64 year old group. Credit card debt is a middle-income middle-age affair, though the outstanding balances seem surprisingly insensitive to both income and age.

Appendix: Rents or Asset Prices in the CPI?

This housing two-markets idea (a rental market and an ownership market) is confusing, but very important. It is important for your own decisions whether or not to buy a home, but it is also important for our Federal Government because the choice between asset prices vs. rental prices has a very large effect on how the Consumer Price Index is computed, and thus has a big impact on any contracts that are indexed to the CPI including Social Security and Treasury Inflation-Protected Bonds.

The Bureau of Labor Statistics in compiling the CPI waffled back and forth on this issue. From 1951 to 1983, the CPI measured the prices in the market for ownership, not the rental market. During that period, the CPI included components associated with: "(1) home purchase, (2) mortgage interest costs, (3) property taxes, (4) homeowner insurance charges, and (5) maintenance and repair costs. These are the costs associated with purchasing and maintaining a physical asset – namely a house."[10] In 1983, the BLS shifted to measuring the CPI in the rental market and substituted for home purchase prices and the other items in the list above a measure of "owner-equivalent rent." This is the right choice, since we want to measure inflation in terms of the increase in the prices of items consumed *this year.* When you buy a home, you are purchasing the service of the home this year, and next year and the year after and so on. The price of the home can go up because of the expected increases in the price of the services next year or the year after. We don't want to include that in the CPI. Wait until next year for that.

Owner-Equivalent Rent

How do you suppose the statisticians at BLS find the values of "owner-equivalent rents"? They could sample some owners and ask: "How much do you suppose your home would rent for?" This is not a very good idea, since most homeowners do not have a clue what their homes could rent for. The BLS instead finds comparable homes that are actually rented and uses these values for owner-equivalent rents. (Actually a regression is estimated that explains rents as a function of characteristics, and this estimated equation is used to estimate owner-equivalent rents as a function of their characteristics.) The BLS furthermore adjusts both the actual rent data and the owner-equivalent rents for improvements to the dwellings to remove from any increases in rents the part that comes from the improved quality of the units.

---

[10] "Treatment of Owner-Occupied Housing in the CPI", Robert Poole, Frank Ptacek, Randal Verbrugge, Bureau of Labor Statistics, Dec 2005.

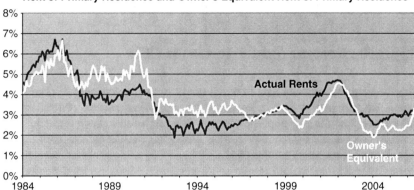

Fig. 20.15 Rent inflation

Figure 20.15 illustrates the rate of inflation of the rent of primary residences and the owner-equivalent rent of primary residences. These have great similarities but also important differences. For example in the low-inflation period from 2003 to 2005, the owner's equivalent rent was increasing at the rate of a little over 2% per year, while the actual rents were increasing at the rate of almost 3%. That difference is very important because the CPI has a weight of 6% on actual rents and 23% on owner-equivalent rents. Low inflation in owner-equivalent rents is a big reason why the overall CPI inflation rate was low.

Appendix: There Is no Such Thing as a Housing Shortage

Now let's get back to the idea that prices of homes can only go up because there is a housing shortage. This kind of statement is confusing the rental market and the ownership market, and misusing the word "shortage." There cannot be a shortage in a freely functioning market. A market system has high prices for some goods and services and low prices for others. A "shortage" is created when the price mechanism is not allowed to work. There can be a "shortage" of umbrellas in an LA rainstorm because sellers choose not to mark up the price to equilibrate supply and demand. Then the sellers run out of the goods, and you and I go without, even though we would have been willing to pay a handsome premium for an umbrella at just the right time.

But both the rental and the asset market for dwellings are highly evolved and do not suffer from the fixed price pathologies that cause shortages. We have high rents, or low rents, but no shortages. We have high home prices or low home prices, but no shortages. There is no "shortage" of dwellings any more than there is "shortage" of cars, or diamonds, or shirts.

Supply Restrictions Do not Guarantee that Prices Can Only Go Up

Just as with stocks, the housing p/e ratio can vary because of the changes in the fundamentals, but also can be greatly affected by "irrational exuberance" or "incapacitating ennui." These psychological factors can persist for very long periods of time in housing because most buyers and sellers are not connecting rental streams with asset prices. They are thinking like the realtor who told me that the prices of oceanfront property can never go down and like an economist at Economy.com who thinks that California prices overall cannot go down for the same reason: supply constraints. Let's think about these ideas like a fundamental investor would. Then it depends on what these growth limitations do to the path of rents, remembering that the price is the present value of future rents.

New limitations on building may cause rents to increase at an abnormally high rate for a period of time, but that higher rate of growth of rents should quickly be "capitalized" in the price of the asset, once the market realizes the impact of supply restrictions on future rents. That means a one-time jump in price, and, thereafter, price appreciation like every other asset – up sometimes, and down sometimes.

The supply limit on ocean front property was created in some earlier geologic age and should long ago have been capitalized in the price of ocean front realty. Thus expect high prices for oceanfront property, but no guarantee that the price can only go up. On the contrary, the rental price increase assumptions that determine the price premium for oceanfront property may be much more uncertain than the future rental assumptions that apply elsewhere, and revisions to these oceanfront fundamentals over time as more news arrives can cause large swings in the value of ocean front property, down as well as up.

Likewise, whatever effect the antigrowth forces may have had on California p/e ratios should have been absorbed by the market long ago, and is not a reason for continued appreciation of housing prices. Thus, when Steven Cochrane of Economy.com is reported by the LA Times to say "With limited inventory and tightly controlled lending for new projects, the industry runs 'no risk of collapse' even if the economy stumbles," he is completely wrong. Even with absolute supply constraints, like the oceanfront, asset prices can fall, and, if they do, that will surely be accompanied by a sharp drop in transactions and construction.

But remember Survivor investor requires a story. This story about ocean front property never falling in price is a good one, rivaling the New Economy story. The story that California antigrowth restrictions mean that housing cannot collapse is another good one. If enough buyers and sellers think this way, then the market can validate this thinking for a long time. But in the longer run, there has to be a comeuppance. In the meantime, there are two investments I would not be making: Pets.com.revival and overpriced California real estate. (Actually, after writing these words, median sales prices have started to decline throughout California.)

Index

Lightning Source UK Ltd.
Milton Keynes UK
25 January 2011

166348UK00002B/18/P